Grass Roots

Grass Roots

Heather Robertson

Photographs by
Myfanwy Phillips

James Lewis & Samuel
Toronto
1973

Cover design by Don Fernley
Design by Lynn Campbell

James Lewis & Samuel, Publishers
35 Britain Street
Toronto

Printed and bound in Canada

Contents

I gratefully acknowledge the assistance of the Canada Council, the Public Archives of Canada, the Saskatchewan Provincial Archives, and the many individuals who generously contributed personal information and opinions.

Two years, ten years, and passengers ask the conductor:

> *Where are we now?*
> *What place is this?*

> *I am the grass.*
> *Let me work.*

(Carl Sandburg, "Grass")

Chapter 1
Gordon Taylor

The knife makes a small cracking sound as it cuts through the vein and breaks the neck. The lamb grunts and makes frantic running motions with its trussed legs as the blood spurts out and runs down its side. Small, mangy black cats scuffle in from the dark corners of the barn and crouch in the straw in an expectant circle. Rolling its eye balefully upwards, breathing hard, the lamb raises and lowers its head. Close beside the lamb, the dog Ringo leans forward occasionally and tenderly licks the blood from the wound. "Sheep," says Gordon Taylor, "take forever to die."

We wait in silence. The barn is warm and cozy, the air heavy with manure. Old pieces of leather harness and rope and baler twine hang from the low beams; sweet straw piled high in the stalls is bright yellow where sunlight streaming in the door and through cracks in the weathered boards falls on it. The dozen sheep penned up outside bleat loudly.

The lamb begins to thrash convulsively. "Come on, boy," says Gordon anxiously, leaning over it in his big white paper apron, "come on." The lamb's eye is big with fear.

"You can't shoot a sheep. The brain is so far back it's hard to find. It's not very humane to do it this way, I suppose, but it's the only way. I can do a lamb in twenty minutes; this one will take longer because he's bigger."

When the lamb is dead, he hooks it to a block and tackle and strings it upside down to a rafter. With a quick stroke, he slits it down the belly and expertly skins it. He tosses the hide aside into the straw and dung.

"You know how much a sheepskin is worth? Ten cents. They sell for thirty dollars in The Bay in Saskatoon. I've got a pile of fifty of them going mouldy out in the yard; it doesn't pay us to skin them."

He ties up the esophagus and cuts off the penis. "A sheep

9

is the only animal you can do this with," he says; "usually the urine comes pouring out." Another stroke and the guts come spilling onto the ground; the cats fight over the liver and the dog sniffs experimentally around the stomach.

"You get sort of hardened to it after a while," says Gordon, hacking off the head. "Cold blooded. It's my livelihood. A lot of farmers won't do this, get their hands dirty butchering."

He takes a rag from a little plastic pail of water and wipes the carcass lightly with it. After the lamb has hung for an hour, Gordon lugs it to the station wagon. Later he will drive it to the butcher in town, who will cut it into chops.

"I killed the ram, the ugly one," he announces in the kitchen with a big smile.

A few hours later, he goes back to the barn, shovels the guts into a wheelbarrow, and dumps them out in the pasture. "The dogs and cats thrive on them," he says. "We even get coyotes coming in for them, magpies too. If there's anything left in the spring, I bring it back and bury it in the manure pile."

The ram will feed the Taylors for 25 meals.

Gordon and Norma Taylor farm 1,200 acres near Landis, Saskatchewan, about 75 miles west of Saskatoon, an average-sized farm for Saskatchewan. They own 800 acres and rent the rest from a neighbour who's moved to the city. The grow wheat, oats, and barley — the same as everybody else in the area — and Gordon keeps a breeding herd of 150 ewes. Their farm is worth $100,000, but the Taylors are poor. In 1971 net income from the farm was $2,900 and Gordon earned another $500 working part-time in a grain elevator. But after they paid $1,200 in taxes on their land, they were left with $2,200 to support themselves and their five children.

"As far as money is concerned," says Gordon, "it's non-existent."

Like all family farms on the prairies, the Taylors are slowly being squeezed into bankruptcy. They have dug their fingernails into the soil and hang on with fierce determination. The Taylors are fighting for their lives, and the struggle absorbs every ounce of their energy and intelligence. Behind their natural cheerfulness lies a strain of desperation which often brings them close to tears.

Thirty Canadian farmers leave the land every day. They have cut each other's throats. For 25 years prairie farmers have fought each other tooth and claw, have scrapped over more land, bigger machinery, and more bushels of wheat, with each man determined to be richer than his neighbour down the road, until the survivors find themselves impoverished. Over 150,000 farmers have been pushed off the land in western Canada in the interests of efficiency; the result is, in Manitoba Premier Ed Schreyer's words, "a rural slum."

The majority of prairie farmers are poor; even rich farmers are poor by urban standards. In 1971, which was considered a good year, the average Saskatchewan farmer made $4,616 — half what an urban construction worker makes every year. In 1970, the year of the most recent agricultural depression, the average farm income across the prairies was $2,500 — less than a farm family would make on welfare.

Saskatchewan farmers are relatively worse off than they were in the Thirties; for now, everyone is rich except them. Inflation is forcing them out. Gordon Taylor sells $9,000 worth of produce every year, but expenses eat up $6,000. Every year his margin of profit gets a little smaller. "You have one good year and two bad ones," he says. "You come up again, but you never come up quite so high." The squeeze is a deliberate policy of the Trudeau government, which hopes that within another generation only a quarter of Canada's 400,000 farmers will still be on the land. Farmers like the Taylors, who hang on, have been pushed back to a subsistence living close to that their grandfathers scratched off a homestead.

The Taylors live in the old stucco house where Gordon was born. The house has grown wrinkled and middle-aged along with him. The stucco is brown and stained, and there are patches of tarpaper where Gordon has replaced the windows. The house is on a little knoll; the land at the back slopes abruptly to a slough, where the sheep pasture in the summer. The unpainted farm buildings are grey with age.

There are big holes in the Taylors' living room walls
where the plaster has fallen away. The old-fashioned wallpaper is mottled brown and streaked with water stains.
Sunlight filters in through white plastic curtains with blue
flowers. On a black-and-white television in the corner stand
color photographs of all the children. Out in the porch, next
to two freezers, are cardboard boxes full of new wallboard
and ceiling tile for the living room. "The wallboard isn't
what I wanted," says Norma, "but we got it for half price."

A sign in Norma's kitchen says: "My kitchen is clean
enough to be healthy and dirty enough to be happy." The
floor heaves and sags, the pattern is worn off the linoleum,
and the walls have fingerprints on them. A big sign on the
freezing compartment of the ancient refrigerator says: "Do
Not Open!" It's a homemade, helter-skelter house with
rooms in unexpected places; walls have been put up and
knocked down to fit the needs of the people living in it.
Everybody uses the back door.

A little path leads from the back door of the house to the
biffy. It's a two-holer, with one hole directly facing the
door if you want to look out into the yard, and the other in
the corner for privacy. The wooden covers for the holes fit
loosely, because the boards of the seat have been worn
round and smooth. On hot days the biffy hums with flies,
and the stench is heavy.

The Taylors installed their first flush toilet in the spring
of 1972. They still use the outhouse after a heavy rain, when
mud seeps into the well and the indoor toilet fills up with
black water. Next winter, Gordon plans to put in the new
lavender bathtub and sink that are still crated up out in the
porch. Gordon does all the work himself, because he can't
afford to hire a carpenter. He borrowed the money to buy
the fixtures from the credit union in Landis.

"It's ridiculous," says Norma. "After twenty years, we're
still putting the *plumbing* in. You get a house in town that
doesn't have water and sewer and it's condemned."

The Taylors have been farming for 21 years, ever since
they were married. In only five of those years have they
earned enough to pay income tax. For seven years, Gordon
drove a school bus to earn enough money to buy groceries.

His bind is simple and universal. It costs him $17 to

grow an acre of wheat that he then sells for $11. The price of wheat in the summer of 1972 is less than it was in 1951, the year he started farming.

The Taylors live off the land. Their farm is a family commune; there is no distinction on it between life and work. Their relationship with the land is profound, primordial; the farm is a reflection of them, the fruit of their labor. Gordon goes about his primitive, menial tasks with joy, a sense of tenderness and responsibility. He would have been at home with Abraham and Isaac: he is a husbandman.

"I try to get the chores done before breakfast," says Gordon. In summer, he's up at 5 a.m., peering out the window to see if the wind is blowing. His round, open face is windburned red except for his forehead, which stays pale under his yellow plastic hard hat. He's worn the hard hat ever since he was caught out in the field in a hailstorm and had to huddle under the tractor for shelter. He tiptoes around the kitchen in thick socks and puts on several layers of old clothes that are stiff and black with grease and a khaki parka. By the back door, next to the old cream cans and the washing machine, be puts on high rubber boots and clomps out the door. Ringo, who sleeps in all weather on the concrete step outside, wakes up, puts his nose in Gordon's hand, and they're off towards the barn. The sun is just up.

The yard is sparse and barren. Trees in the windbreaks on either side of it are stunted and tattered by the wind; many are dead or half-dead where the weed spray has touched them. A few sheep clustered by the barn look up vacant and wide-eyed before tearing panicstricken out to the pasture.

Gordon climbs the low, rickety fence and makes his way through the round, dark balls of sheep shit towards the chicken house. A loud peeping starts up as he opens the door, sloshes water into a tiny trough, and tosses some feed from a bag into the small metal tray. The smell in the little stuffy house is musty, cloying. The chicks, just growing their long white feathers, dash for the tray. There are 50 of them — enough to feed the Taylors for a year — as well as 15 turkeys for holidays and friends. In the autumn, the roosters and turkeys will be killed, and the young hens promoted to the laying barn; the old hens will be killed and eaten. The following year, the cycle will repeat itself. He shuts the door.

In the barn, Gordon pitches hay for the three rams and the old ewes culled out for slaughter. He has two local customers for the mutton; an old ewe, alive, is worth ten cents.

If the black cow isn't dry, he milks her. "It takes about five minutes. Then I turn the calf on and he finishes up. It's a real good arrangement. I take what I need and he gets the rest." The cow is bred every year; the calf is raised for two years before being slaughtered and packed away with the lambs and chickens in the Taylors' freezer.

On his way back to the house, Gordon feeds and waters the 30 hens in the hen house on the far side of the yard and gathers the eggs from the communal nest. There are about 20 eggs a day, and the Taylors eat most of them. Those that are left over, Norma sells to neighbours down the road for 30 cents a dozen. "The Avon lady was asking forty cents for eggs this year," she says. "Maybe I'll raise my price." Norma, small and pretty with red-gold hair and green eyes, is up at six, furiously making sandwiches for the children's lunches.

The children are expected to be present — washed, brushed and dressed — for breakfast at 7:20 a.m. The shout goes up for them just after seven. The oldest, Judy, is away working in Edmonton. Cathy, 17, is already ironing her blue jeans; Jeff, 14, and Randy, 12, straggle up from the basement, their long hair hanging in their eyes; Glenna, nine, is the last. "Good morning," Gordon says formally to each in turn. The CBC is on somewhere in the background behind the din of eating and squabbling. At precisely 7:55 the yellow school bus arrives at the yard to take the children 15 miles to Biggar. The day begins.

The farm is a commune. Every child has a specific job according to his age and abilities; each shares equally in the returns. Cathy feeds the chickens at night, gathers the eggs, washes them, and sells them for the few cents she can get. She also does most of the baking and tends the garden. Most of her income comes from babysitting. When

Cathy leaves home, Glenna will take over the eggs. Her specialty now is helping Gordon when the lambs are born; she carries each frail, slimy lamb to its stall and holds it up to suck. All the children pitch in at lambing time — castrating, docking tails, sprinkling the lambs with louse powder.

Jeff, whom Gordon hopes will take over the farm some day, does an increasingly big share of the work. Jeff and Randy have both been driving trucks in the field since they were five. At twelve they learn to run the combine. When they were babies, Gordon used to hold them in his arms as he drove the tractor around the fields. As soon as they could walk, they were out in the yard following him around, helping, learning things. All of the children work in the fields during the summer holidays.

As payment, Gordon has set aside a quarter section for each of the three oldest children; the income from that land will go directly to them. Randy and Jeff also have a couple of ewes and get the money from the sale of the lambs. Gordon backs loans for them at the Landis credit union, which they pay off at ten per-cent interest when the lambs are marketed. They also collect beer bottles from the ditches along the highway and sell them for 20 cents a dozen in Saskatoon. Jeff has already bought one bike and is saving for a 10-speed; Randy has paid off a $125 set of drums.

"I want to be a famous drummer and live on a sheep farm," says Randy.

"We're trying to avoid slave labor," says Gordon. "That's what I was used as. My father said, 'When I die, you get the land.' I said, 'What about the meantime?' A lot of farmers get stuck in that bind. Past forty, they're hoping the old man dies."

By 5 p.m. the Taylors are all seated around the chrome kitchen table, their hands folded in prayer as Gordon says grace. Supper is boarding house style — big pots of stew and potatoes in the centre of the table, arms flailing out from all sides, a steady clatter of knives and forks on plastic plates, and talk.

"We try and kind of go over the events of the day at suppertime," says Gordon. "Get caught up on the news... we get some real goodies from the school bus. We talk about

everything — world events, news, the situation on the farm,
political parties. We can communicate with our kids; we
have some real good talks.

"We don't hide anything from the kids. OK, so they had
an animal and it died. We never ever tried to say it went
to heaven. The animal died. You might as well get to know
because it's a tough old grind, this world. So a cat died,
well that's too bad. We'll try harder next time.

"We try to teach them some of the realities of life. There's
no Santa Claus bit around here. Hasn't been for a good
many years. The kids know who Santa Claus is. The Easter
Bunny, he kind of went kaput too. He got shot. And the
Tooth Fairy lost her wings.

"Oh, we have a Christmas tree. Glenna likes to decorate
it. We haven't got a hundred dollars' worth of lights for the
house. There's no more than twenty lights on our string.

"We stopped a few years ago getting together with the
rest of the family at Christmas. We don't really get excited
about holidays like that.

"We haven't been to church or involved in church work
for six years. Easily six years. I don't think any of the
neighbours go to church any more. None at all.

The Taylors don't spend much time in town. They go to
Biggar once a week for groceries, and Gordon may go once
or twice more with a piece of broken machinery or a load
of grain. "I haven't been in the beer parlor in Landis for
two years," he says. "I guess we're kind of loners. The kids
like being alone. Just us. It's the tranquility out here. It's
quiet. Yet every day seems to be a little different. The kids
say they don't want to stay in town because they might miss
something." He smiles. "We have a very strong sense of
home."

The snow goes slowly and it leaves a mess. In the middle
of April, there are usually still dirty drifts in among the
trees, covered with a fine black silt that the wind has blown
in from the fields. The new lambs gambol about in the mud.
The sheep shearer comes in April. It takes him three days
to do the sheep. Wool sells for twelve cents a pound, and
the Taylors get six pounds from a sheep, or 72 cents.
However, it costs 60 cents to shear a sheep, and the freight
for a fleece is 15 cents. A few years ago, when the Taylors

went into sheep, wool sold for 40 cents a pound, but that included a government subsidy, which was removed in 1972.

Gordon heads out to the boneyard where the melting snow has uncovered his garden of avant-garde sculpture: iron tractor wheels, rusty augers and bits of old harrow teeth, the odd bedspring, a cookstove, ancient trucks in various stages of decomposition, a greasy yellow combine, and a mouldy, battered, 1951 Chev with 190,000 miles on it that still runs. The Chevy is a political statement. When Ross Thatcher got elected premier of Saskatchewan in 1964 by promising the farmers they could use cheap purple gas in their farm trucks, Gordon got out his torch, cut the back seat out of the Chevy and painted "Thatcher's Wagon" on the side in big red letters along with assorted other graffiti. The Taylors are NDP.

"Scrap iron," says Gordon reverently, "is liquid gold. Most of the stuff we've got here is made out of scrap iron. I go to the junk piles around, pick it up from other farms. Anybody that's thrown away an angle iron or a piece of flat iron, I'll trade him for some cast iron I can't use. I'm a scavenger.

"I'm always looking out for a bargain but I never have any money to buy it when I do see it. I've been looking for a truck for six years. Something with a good body I can fix up. Something I can more or less salvage from the junk yard and renovate it.

"That granary up on the hill is the first thing I've ever built with brand new lumber. I always tore something down and rebuilt it, made do with what I had. That big granary over there used to be the curling rink in Landis. It blew down. I paid a hundred dollars for it and hauled it home, piece by piece. Took me a whole winter. Did it all by myself. I suppose I'm one of the odd types that do this, not too many fellows would. I'm an individualist. If I can't do something by myself, I don't do it.

"I don't bother much with auctions. I got the car at an auction last year for four hundred dollars. Usually they fleece you. You pay new prices for crap. Gee, I missed some good buys at a sale I went to this spring. One guy was telling me he got twelve pairs of pants for a buck; eight fit him and four fit his wife."

Gordon surveys his piles of tangled scrap, the mouldy lamb hides, the hodgepodge of unpainted sheds. "I am not," he says reflectively, "a Master Farmer."

By May 10 the earth is dry enough for seeding; the temperature is in the low 50s, the wind cold and raw. Even under layers of parkas and sweaters, Gordon is still cold. "My ears," he says, "take a hell of a beating." He seeds the oldfashioned way, turning the soil over with a cultivator and lopping the seed in underneath. He seeds the soft wheat first, then the oats and barley and flax in the order they come off in the fall. The tractor covers 60 acres on a good day. This year, he's seeding 630 acres. He starts at 6 a.m. and quits when it's dark.

"I enjoy being out rubbing cheeks with Mother Nature. Sure, we need money, but this isn't the thing I farm for. I farm because I like farming. I don't find it boring. It's sort of a feeling of satisfaction. I go over that ground and I think of all the things I'm going to do. I have so many plans, things I'd like to make, how I'd like to remodel a piece of equipment. I dream a lot, especially if the weather's nice. Time just flies. In four hours it's dinnertime and in five hours you have supper.

"You watch your neighbours. This is part of farming; I look out and I can see my neighbours going. I don't want to see a vast expanse with nobody on it.

"I'm usually the last one on the land in the spring. So OK, fine. By the time everyone else is pulling their sprayer out, I get out to seed. I kind of work my way into it. Sure you try to get the crop in as fast as possible. But it depends on the weather. Everything depends on the weather. You get it all planned out; I'm going to have it done by next Tuesday, say. Then a wheel falls off. So you fix it and get going great guns and on Thursday night it rains cats and dogs and that throws you back. I don't get uptight about it. The Lord gives you time enough to seed and time enough to take it off. We just live from day to day. A thunderstorm comes, we unplug the TV set. If it hails, it hails. So it's windy today and it rains tomorrow. We enjoy the rain because as farmers you have to enjoy the rain.

"But we raise just as many bushels per acre as the guys who are out first. They get all riled up and want to be the

first one on. I do the best I can, maybe it takes us three
days longer than anyone else. Our machinery is old but we
own it. I haven't got a cab on the tractor and the truck
isn't new. Prestige doesn't bother me."

The land here is sensual, female, a great pregnant belly
rolling away to a horizon of breasts and buttocks and thighs,
and lips, round and smooth but full of surprising creases
and crevasses, thatched here and there with dark clusters of
willow trees. The farm runs on Old Testament time, not
Christian and capitalist time, which ticks off the hours to
salvation, but rather an eternal linking of the sun and earth
in a sacred cycle of procreation, of which Gordon Taylor,
farmer, going round and round the field on his old green
tractor, is the centre.

In the summer, Gordon goes down to the slough for water
along an old rutted trail almost overgrown with wild roses.
He points to a stamping ground near the water where, every
fall, prairie chickens come to dance. On autumn mornings,
the slough is black with ducks.

"Sometimes when I'm summerfallowing," he says, "I'll
turn up a mouse in the subble. In thirty seconds, a hawk
will be on the mouse. They fold their wings and drop like
a stone. All of a sudden. Wham!

"You get a cab on your tractor and you miss a lot. Like
the smell of the soil being turned over. The days in spring
when we've just had a rain and the ground is moist and the
air is fresh and still, it's heaven to be out there. I guess it's
just the peasant in me coming out when I look back and
there's that beautiful black soil just turned over so nicely.
And the trees. You can look around and see all the trees
budding.

"Sometimes I have a little sleep out in the field. I'll lie
down beside the tractor in the sun when it's cold and in the
shade when it's hot and drift off for ten or twelve minutes.
You get real tired after dinner, about two o'clock. A little
sleep keeps me going till eleven p.m. or midnight; otherwise
I'm done in.

"I sing a lot on the tractor. It passes the time of day. On
a calm night you can hear me for miles. I sing those old
songs, the ones Bing Crosby made popular. 'Up the Lazy

River,' I really like that, and 'Mississippi Mud' by the
McGuire Sisters."

Gordon goes patiently over his land four or five times a
summer, harrowing, spraying, turning the summerfallow. He
works a twelve-hour day, coming in for dinner and supper,
his face and hands black as a miner's from the fine dust.
Haying starts July 1, as soon as the kids are out of school.
It's the hardest job, out by the slough under the blistering
sun. Glenna runs the tractor; Gordon and the boys pitch
bales.

Harvest starts in late August. The dew is heavy in the
morning then, but if the wind is up, they can be in the fields
at 8 a.m. Jeff is on the clattering combine; Randy follows
alongside in the ancient red truck catching the grain as it
cascades out of the funnel. "Combining," says Gordon, "is
a real dirty business. When the wind blows from your back,
that chaff comes right at you. That dust just drives you.
You get that fine coating all over you and down around
your shirt collar and it just itches and then you sweat a
little bit, oh boy."

They eat in the fields. Norma and Cathy pack the
lunches, usually just sandwiches and fruit but sometimes a
hot stew, and drive out to the field.

"The kids think it's so exciting, they just love it. We sit
in the car or squat down on the ground amongst the grasshoppers and the dust. If the grasshoppers are bad, I tell
them to put a little butter on them and swallow them
down."

They work steadily, spelling each other off, until midnight
or 1 a.m., when the grain is wet and heavy with dew. At
twilight, when the sky turns red, the combine lights go on.
The wind is down, the air still. The combine roars and
lunges along, a gigantic one-eyed dragon, its breath hot and
reeking of gas fumes, belching out great clouds of filthy
chaff behind it. In the harshness of the truck's headlights,
the Taylors' faces are black with dust and streaked with
sweat; their eyes, rimmed with white, are bloodshot from
fatigue.

"It's beautiful, really beautiful," says Norma. Beyond the
circle of heat and dust, the autumn night is luminous silver-
green. From high on the combine you can see, on every

rise and knoll, a tiny cluster of moving lights. Trucks, like fireflies, trace out the roads in the darkness with pinpricks of light. A whole city of combines is out there, their lights, like beacons, a signal of shared labor.

A fierce tension and worry surrounds harvest, especially if it rains and the grain lies sodden and sprouting for weeks on end. Sometimes it snows in September, and ducks on their way south squat in the grain and gobble it down. Sometimes there's no crop to harvest; in 1971, they were 75 per-cent hailed out.

"This is your wages," says Norma. "This is your income. All depends on getting this crop in. In that one week or ten days, you get your whole source of revenue. You sell the grain right away, as soon as it's in the bin. You haul it to the elevator as quick as you can. With the money, you pay the overdrawn cheques you've written."

The Taylors live entirely on credit. They have long-term loans and short-term loans. "Sometimes," says Gordon, "our loans are quite a lot past due. In fact, most of the time they're past due. We're only in debt about $10,000, maybe $12,000. Most people I know are up to $150,000 and more. They get in so deep the bank can't afford to lose them. Bad as it seems to be, it's when your debt equals your assets that you're really in trouble."

Every year Gordon gets a little quota book from the Canadian Wheat Board telling him the number of bushels of grain he can sell from an acre of land. Gordon's quota is usually eight or nine bushels. His average crop is 20 to 30 bushels an acre. So he sells about half of what he produces every year; the rest goes into granaries. When it rots, the sheep eat it.

The price of wheat in the summer of 1972 is $1.23 a bushel for No. 1 hard. Gordon's return is about $11 an acre. His cost of production is $17. He uses no fertilizer, because fertilizer is $113 a ton and it takes twelve tons to cover 630 acres. "I can't see where I should be putting money out to produce something I can't sell," he says.

"Sure I could buy more land. Heck, I could go into Landis tomorrow and come home with many thousands of dollars without batting an eye. I could have our yard *full* of machinery, brand new machinery from a wheelbarrow to a $15,000 self-propelled combine. All I have to do is go in and sign my name. But we don't want to end up working for the machine companies and the banks. We're trying to stay off the wheel."

After Thanksgiving, Gordon fires his shotgun over the sheep's heads and sends them all tearing up the hill to the barn. He culls out the lambs and begins to slaughter them. He gets $18 for an average spring lamb; when he went into sheep six years ago, lambs sold for $40. He doesn't know how much it costs him to raise a lamb.

"I'm not sure I want to know. I'd see how much money I was losing and this would really dishearten us. What we don't know doesn't hurt us."

Gordon gives a couple of lamb hides to local farmers to cover their tractor seats. The dealer from Saskatoon wouldn't even pay ten cents a hide last year; the year before that Gordon sheared the wool off and sold it. The Taylors have tried unsuccessfully to tan the hides themselves. "I'll burn them," Gordon says.

The Taylors eat a lot of lamb. "We like lamb," says Norma. "Thank God."

In 1970, which was an average year for the Taylors, Gordon made a little over $9,000 from the farm. His grain brought in $3,500 and he made $5,000 on the sheep and wool. The government paid him $600 under the L.I.F.T. program not to grow wheat.

His expenses were $6,000. Aside from $800 in interest payments, he spent $900 on the car, $275 on the truck, and $235 for gas and oil for the tractor. Building and fence repairs cost $223. (Fencing is $1,000 a mile.) Machinery repairs and hardware came to $333. He spent $340 to hire help. Power and phone, which are deductible, came to $275. Depreciation on machinery and buildings was $2,500; fire insurance cost $150. (The Rural Municipality of Biggar, to which Gordon pays $1,200 in taxes every year, has no fire engine.)

The actual cost of the crop was only $103; his cattle, sheep, and poultry cost $150.

One thing is missing from Gordon Taylor's expenses — labor. He pays himself no wages.

In the half a lifetime they have been farming, the Taylors

have made no headway. "Gordon has nothing and neither do I," says Norma. "We're pretty close to the wire."

Norma manages the house. "I'm not that good a house-keeper. I used to run around after Gordon with the vacuum cleaner until he complained that I stuck it up his ass. I *don't* bake bread. I used to sew a lot, but now the girls wear jeans. It's the greatest thing that ever happened.

"I pick strawberries first thing in the morning after the kids have gone to school. You have to get them before the bugs eat them. They start to ripen about the middle of June. I pick them until the snow comes; sometimes we pick them out of the snow. I get about seven, eight quarts a day. Sometimes I wish they weren't there. It's a chore. Then there's the raspberries. They take me three and a half hours every day. I weed the garden in the afternoon. There's too many mosquitoes at night; they're really vicious. I lose a lot to cutworms. And every year the sheep get into the garden. One finds a hole in the fence and they all go through — they're quite dumb. Cathy and I were on Weight Watchers last year; we had turnips and broccoli and cauli-flower. The sheep ate every one.

"I do the chickens in the fall. I have a hard time eating them right after we've killed them. Ugh. I don't mind drawing them but I can't take them with the legs still on."

The family survives all winter on her labor. Norma used to get the wool money. Now that's gone, she manages on what's left over. "You set up a budget and bam! a tire blows on the tractor. Well, that's three hundred dollars. It doesn't matter if we planned to spend the money buying the kids clothes for school or not. If it has to go for a tire for the tractor, that's where it goes.

"Some of the wives have tried to work. You run the wheels off the car. The wages are terrible and what money you do make is eaten up in gas and food. The men can only babysit in winter, so you have to pay a babysitter for six months.

"A lot of men won't let their wives out of the kitchen. Oh, it's OK for another man's wife to get a job or work for the Farmer's Union, but jeez, you want your wife right at home. You want that meal on the table at twelve noon.

"There's no way to pay women anything. The farm wife is the hired man."

Saturday morning. The hard white snow is piled up around the old wooden Landis arena. A dozen cars and pickup trucks are drawn up to it like piglets at a sow. Inside the chill gloom, parents stand around the canteen drinking coffee out of white plastic cups or huddle in parkas and big fleece-lined boots on scarred and splintered wooden benches. Their faces are pale and bleary with sleep; they tuck their hands up their sleeves for warmth.

The Landis Pee Wees, in blue and white sweaters like the Maple Leafs' with a big "Landis" in scroll across the front, clatter in from the dressing room and skate out onto the ice. A loud "Yay!" goes up from a bunch of small boys on the Landis bench. The Landis parents, all sitting on the Landis side of the arena, clap and shout encouraging things.

The Landis players skate coolly around the rink, their faces expressionless, ignoring the applause. Wilkie, the opposition, is in red and white, with big crests on the backs of their sweaters that say "Victory Motors," "Wilkie Co-op," and "Smith Bros. ESSO." Wilkie skates around near their own bench, eyes down, glancing sideways. Their skates make a crisp, sharp sound on the fresh ice; their voices drift hollow up to the rafters.

The biggest player is four feet tall, including skates; the smallest is so small his sweater hangs down past his knees, the shoulders sagging off to his elbows. Dwarf astronauts, they are strapped into plastic helmets, shoulder pads, knee pads, elbow pads, mouth guards, and jockstraps. "They really don't need jockstraps," says Gordon; "they don't raise the puck that high." Hockey pants bagging down near their ankles, they glide around like fat snowmen. The oldest is ten, the youngest eight.

The puck is dropped in a flurry of flailing sticks, arms, and legs. A Wilkie player, peering out through hornrimmed glasses from under a vast red helmet, slaps the puck down the ice, trips on his stick, and falls down. Four other players trip over him. While they try frantically to untangle themselves and stand up, the rest of the players herd down to the other end of the rink and swarm in the corner.

A Landis player gets the puck tangled in his skates. As the other boys stand and watch, he digs for it with his stick, going around backwards, hacking and jabbing, until he falls over. Another Landis player grabs it with his stick and streaks down the ice for the big breakaway; a desperate Wilkie defenseman runs at him, knocks him down, and falls on him. The goalies stand nonchalantly in their nets, leaning on their sticks.

When time out is called or a goal is scored, the players do slow, gliding turns on the ice, heads bowed, sticks trailing, like pros on TV. They skate fast and strong and fight often. The smallest boys play fanatically; their intense, red-cheeked little faces glow with excitement. Each player has his own style, his own sophisticated moves. One very small boy who goofs up every play he is in makes up for it by skating furiously around in a circle yelling loudly and pounding his stick on the ice. The parents bellow from the sidelines; one mother moos "Come on, Chuck" through the whole game.

Wilkie wins 2-0. The Wilkie players hug each other and jump up and down. Faces crumpled and close to tears, Landis throws down their gloves and sticks and lines up at centre ice. The teams skate slowly past each other, shaking hands, and tromp off to have a Coke and an Oh Henry!, being careful not to talk to the enemy.

Jeff and Randy Taylor were on skates at three, ankling around the small rink Gordon flooded for them in the yard. At four they were playing organized hockey for the Landis Pee Wees in the age-four-to-six league. At six, they were going to practices three nights a week and playing games on weekends.

The Taylors drive them the 14 miles to Landis for practices; they drive them 60 miles to North Battleford for games. Different age groups practice on different nights and farms around Landis are so scattered it's almost impossible to set up a car pool. There have been winters when the Taylors have been in Landis every night of the week.

"We're working it to death," says Gordon. "If you have two sons under fourteen, you meet yourself coming back. It makes Imperial Oil just clap their hands, I tell you, all that gas being burned. And Goodyear, all the tires being burned.

"We watch. I have helped coach. What I usually do is campaign while I'm there. Flag-wave for the National Farmers' Union. I discuss farming, you know, with the other people there and talk NFU. Not directly. You've got a captive audience. There's no way they can leave. I can discuss farm problems with a lot of people I never get to otherwise."

"We like to go along," says Norma. "For women it's a social thing. I have a real good friend in Landis that I see at hockey games. We get together and we hash over the *whole* thing. We just love to talk and to laugh. We laugh until the whole building just flutters. We really enjoy getting together and going over what's been happening in the community. Generally it's not gossip. We have some good discussions. It's about the only time that I see her in the wintertime because our children don't go the same direction."

Randy is a rock star. He plays drums for a local group called Grand Maw. The Taylors spend a lot of time at teen dances. They load Randy's drums and amplifiers into the green station wagon, drive him to the dance, and wait patiently in the noise to drive him home. Cool, good-looking, meticulous about his shoulder-length hair and the holes in his jeans, Randy is four feet nine and in grade seven. He is mobbed at dances by girls who say, "Gee, are you only *twelve*?" A fan club of grade nine girls sends him cards and small presents. Winnipeg is the centre of Randy's world, because Winnipeg is the home of the Guess Who. Grand Maw started playing for Cokes and chips; then they got $5 each for a dance, then $10, and finally $30 before school closed for the summer. Grand Maw will probably break up because the two guitar players are going to university.

When the White Shore Rural Telephone System, named after the local salt slough, went out of business on July 12, 1972, the big wooden telephone by the Taylors' back door was taken away and the Taylors got a new plastic telephone with a dial. Telephoning at the Taylors had been a guerrilla campaign, a war of nerves with the operator, a fat man who lived behind the switchboard in a little house in Landis.

There was no escaping him. To place a call on the White Shore Rural Telephone System, you pushed a button on the phone and cranked. The cranking lit up the switchboard in Landis; the operator asked for the number and put in the appropriate plug. The number was really a code: the Taylors' number, for instance, was 10 ring 5 — line ten, five rings. They were on a party line with six other farms.

The fat man was paid $900 a month by White Shore Rural to maintain the 20 party lines and provide 24-hour service. He employed his wife and twelve-year-old daughter on the switchboard. "She was," says Norma, "real snippy."

The operators did not approve of children using the phone, and would pull the plug on them in the middle of a call. They also offered gratuitous insults if they thought someone was making excessive demands and gave a running commentary on the calls. "Oh, you can't phone Harry," they'd say; "he's across the street." Anyone making an early morning call was greeted with: "You up already?" And if anyone swore at the fat man, he swore back.

White Shore Rural was a farmers' company, a descendent of the days when farmers rigged up their own telephone lines along the fences. Everybody on the exchange paid $26 a year plus long distance charges. An attempt to get rid of the operator failed because he went from farm to farm with a petition supporting his service. "There he is on the doorstep," says Norma; "what do you do? You have to sign it." This year, government telephones put him out of work.

White Shore Rural is going to be missed. It was a fire alarm and a newspaper. If any farmer had a fire, he called the operator. The operator put out a fire ring — ten consecutive rings — on all the phones close to the site of the fire. People rushed to the phone, the operator gave the message, and neighbours were in the farmer's yard within five minutes.

For three dollars you could buy a general ring — one long ring on five lines at once. When people picked up the receiver, the operator might announce a dance on Saturday night, a funeral that afternoon, a meeting, a bonspiel, or a lost cow.

Hot news you picked up from listening to other people's phone calls.

White Shore Rural is the latest loss in a long process of community disintegration. As a boy, Gordon rode his horse two miles down the road to Bushville School, a small, white country school. Twenty years ago, Bushville School was moved into Biggar to be part of the consolidated school unit; now Glenna goes there for grade four, 15 miles each way by bus. Three years ago, the Taylors pulled their children out of Landis school because they felt the standard of education there was inferior. As the farm community around Landis shrinks, the social rituals which held it together decay.

Pinwherry United Church stands on a little knoll on the bald prairie about a mile and a half north of Gordon Taylor's farm. It's a dark brown wooden building, boarded up and listing to one side.

"We used to go to church down here, and then they closed it," says Gordon. "We used to go diligently, very conscientiously. All the children have been baptized. It wasn't possible to keep the church open. There wasn't the money. The building was starting to fall apart. But we went. Everybody went. You saw everybody on Sunday. You'd dress up in a suit and tie and the kids were all knickered down. We took turns having the minister and his family in for dinner. It was a traditional thing — you made the rounds. It wasn't spontaneous at all. It was set up. It was your *turn*. It was a responsibility. Generally the day you were having the minister in, the wife stayed home and cooked. Ministers used to make them mad!

"I guess we lost some of the responsibility we used to have. We felt we *had* to keep this little church open; when it closed, well. . . . We felt, 'There's enough people around, they won't miss us.' So we dropped out.

"What precipitated it was what's happening in the rural community. We feel the church has failed; it's socially crippled. The church chose to be a place to go to worship God rather than have a look at what's happening around and take a stand on it. It's not doing the job it should be doing; it's not coming to grips with the problems that are confronting us. We feel that it's just sitting around on its hands.

"It's just another useless gathering to go to, apart from seeing neighbours you haven't seen in a while.

"I used to be a Mason but I dropped out of that. Just a waste of time. I had things to do that would reward society a lot better than me going through that ritual of absolutely nothing. What really angered me was in 1962 when the Grand Somethingorother came up from the States and talked to a meeting in Toronto about those Communists out in Saskatchewan who were trying to put medicare through. And I thought to myself, you.... If he can't mind his business and stay in the States where be belongs.... That was the last straw. I just couldn't mix with the people that were in there. We weren't of the same thinking. And you can only talk about weather so long. That's all you were allowed to talk about.

"Oh, I went through all the chairs. I went through the whole thing. I'm a past Master. I did a good job. They were quite sorry I quit, I could memorize real well. I used to deliver work flawlessly. But it was. . .ech. . .a waste of time."

Gordon was on the board of the White Shore Rural Telephone System. He is on the board of the Landis Co-op and the Biggar community clinic. He used to be on the rink board, the church board, the credit union board, and the Wheat Pool board. Norma was a member of the Co-op guild, the Landis home and school, and the community club. Between them they belonged to more than a dozen organizations; many times, they'd have five meetings in a week.

"Women's groups," says Norma, "mostly exist to eat and collect old clothes.

"It can be fun. We have what we call galloping teas to raise money for the community club. One woman will start driving around picking up the women; you have to drop everything and come as you are. You all land in on some poor woman for tea. She hasn't a clue that you're coming and she has to feed you; you pay twenty-five cents to the kitty. Sometimes you hit the same woman three times in a day; sometimes you land in at eleven thirty p.m. It's usually done on birthdays. The community club still has money they can't get rid of.

"We also make arrangements to meet the women who

used to live here and are now in Saskatoon. A couple of carloads of us go in; we tour some place in Saskatoon, have lunch, and go to a good restaurant for dinner. You pay part, the club pays part. We keep in contact. The trouble is, we're running out of places to tour.

"The home and school repaired books for the Landis school. We soon heard comments from the teachers about parents interfering, so we quit. We had a course in sex education for adults and young people. From the reaction, you'd have thought we were teaching intercourse on the stage. Some parents tried to throw the kids out; the kids were bored stiff."

In January, it's dark when the Taylors' television set goes on at 4:30 p.m. for *Get Smart*. The TV stays on all evening. The kids do their homework on the living room floor or at the kitchen table, one eye on their book, one eye on the TV. Once a week, they all gather around to watch *All in the Family*; on Saturday nights, Gordon and the boys watch *Hockey Night in Canada*.

"Oh, I'm a hockey fan," says Gordon, his face lighting up with pleasure. "Toronto I guess is my favorite team. I started out listening to the radio. Foster Hewitt was the best player Toronto ever had. Oh, when I was a kid, hockey was it. Listening to the broadcast, well, I would sooner have lost my right arm than missed that!

"We don't curl. That's the big social function in the wintertime. If you curl, you have to drink. You have to be able to afford the liquor that goes with curling; we don't feel we can. Most people curl three times a week; there's a bonspiel about every third week. The bonspiels go day and night. Farmers pick rocks in the summer and throw them in the winter. Some people drink while they curl and after. It depends how conscientious you are about either; some drink through the whole thing, some party it up after."

"I curled a few winters with the women," says Norma. "I remember one bonspiel. It was about nine a.m. and I could see seven brooms at the other end, because we'd had 7-Up mixed with vodka to keep warm. We lost about 14-1 but I never enjoyed a game so much in all my life.

"It got so that unless you took your own car you didn't get home until three or four or sometimes five in the morning. I can remember coming home when we stopped at just about every farmer's place on the road and got someone out of bed. Our neighbours aren't that bad; they thought it was quite funny. It can become a way of life. It has, too."

Norma reads 50 or 60 books a winter. She likes Pierre Berton. The Taylors subscribe to the *Union Farmer, The Western Producer*, and the local weekly. The reading matter beside the lavender toilet is a women's liberation publication and *Dimension*, a Canadian political magazine. Every mail brings a bundle of co-op, NDP, and Waffle literature. "We don't go to town on Saturday night," says Norma. "The kids go in for the occasional movie. I can't remember the last movie we saw. I guess it was *Carnal Knowledge* in Saskatoon. We laughed the whole way through. And Gordon took the kids to *The Million Dollar Duck.*"

Every four or five years, it's Gordon's turn to run the snowplow. The snowplow is just a big blade you fasten to the front of your tractor; four farmers own it jointly and take turns at the plowing. He's out right away after a blizzard, clearing the road for the school bus. "I plow three miles and clear four farmyards. I get paid seven fifty an hour. It's not all that much. The wear on the tractor is heavy. And the wear on you. I put on all the clothes I own. When you're out there at thirty below, wow! It's colder 'n hell.

"It's a lot warmer when it's dark. It's eight o'clock in the morning when it hits you. Generally our winters aren't windy; when they're windy, they're damn bad. I have my own weather forecast system. When I was driving the school bus I used to do the chores every morning beforehand, and when I got up on that bale stack about fourteen bales high, I could pretty well tell what the weather was like. Because man, when you got up there, you had a real bird's-eye vision of it. If my nose froze before I could get my hand up to it, I knew it was too cold. And I'd phone in and say I'm not going today."

"Sometimes I wish for a good storm so we don't have to go *anywhere*," says Norma. "The kids stayed home about three days last year. It was nice. There's no place to go.

The kids are happy, we're happy. I wouldn't mind being snowed in for a week."

Usually they're out cranking up the Falcon to go to a farm union meeting and scraping the frost off the windshield as they clunk clunk down the road on square tires. The Taylors are dedicated and militant union members; they drive as far as Rosetown, Saskatoon, or Regina for as many as ten or 15 NFU meetings a month.

"Oh, we don't get *bored*," says Norma cheerfully. "There's no way we get bored. We get tired of going to meetings."

Gordon potters in the winter. He hauls a load or two of wheat to Springwater; maybe he trucks some wool to Saskatoon. He loves to look at new machinery, and hovers like a bee around the dealerships in Biggar and Rosetown. He cleans the barns and builds new pens or stalls for the sheep. This year he'll put up the wallboard and lay the new linoleum on the kitchen floor; last year, he converted the basement cistern into a bathroom. Out in the little granary he's converted into a shop, he makes useful gadgets out of his scrap iron. He pops in and out of the kitchen regularly for coffee and tarts.

In February the lambs start to come, and Gordon moves out to the barn for six weeks. He sleeps on a cot next to an oil stove. Every half hour he wakes up to check the sheep, to haul newborn lambs in from snowdrifts, to hold them up to suck. Suddenly the barn is bursting with lambs, the sun is warm, and big patches of wet earth are showing through the snow. The air is rich with the stench of rotting manure. The sparrows begin to sing again.

"If somebody came along and offered us two hundred dollars an acre spot cash, I don't think I could take it," says Gordon. "What do we do at forty? What would we do for the rest of our lives? What on earth would we do?"

Chapter 2
The West

I can remember how my father went — from our Lake Simcoe farm — to the first Manitoba boom of over fifty years ago — before the railway. He had an idea that what the West needed was British energy and pluck. He came back broke in six months... Going West to a Canadian is like going after the Holy Grail to a knight of King Arthur. All Canadian families have had, like mine, their Western Odyssey.

(Stephen Leacock, *My Discovery of the West*)

The history of the West is a chronicle of voyages, a ceaseless ebb and flow from east to west and west to east of human beings in search of fur, buffalo, land, wealth, salvation. The quest never ends. Waves of people wash across the prairies and disappear, cast up on the island promontories of the inland cities or wrecked at last on the beaches of Vancouver where they spend the last days of their lives gazing wistfully out to sea.

The tide is ebbing now, sucking people off the land, eroding the prairie towns and villages until they collapse like sand castles. Between 1966 and 1971, Saskatchewan lost 30,000 people, and its rural population decreased by more than 50,000. Alberta is losing 5,000 rural people a year, Manitoba 3,000. Most of them move to cities: the young go east, the old go west. Almost all of them are farmers. Agriculture is no longer the economic backbone of the prairies. In Manitoba and Alberta, farming accounts for less than 20 per cent of gross productivity; in Saskatchewan, it's less than half: urban people outnumber rural in all three provinces. The retreat from the land has been in progress for 30 years; between 1940 and 1970, the number

33

of prairie farms dropped from 350,000 to 150,000, with a loss of more than 300,000 farm people. Most of those who are left are old, and within the next generation they will die.

The West is young. Many of the original settlers are still alive; their own lives have spanned the birth and death of an agricultural civilization. For all Westerners, even city people, the farmer is the touchstone, our fertility symbol, the core of our mythology. He is the grass roots, the salt of the earth, the moral fibre of the nation: he is The People. His gradual disappearance shakes our sense of identity and makes us question the validity of our history. Those of us who remain in the West feel a small chill, as if the farmer's flight from the land has blighted our own hopes and brought on us a sense of attenuation and decay. The history of western Canada is almost obscenely brief. Is that all there is? The farmer is the guardian of the western dream; without him, the West is just the East.

I was born in the city. Going to the country was always an event, a major expedition into foreign territory associated with family festivals, funerals, and disaster. The only time I lived in the country was during the great Winnipeg flood of 1950, when I was evacuated to a small town in western Manitoba. The town was full of churches and soughing pine trees; everything in it seemed very old. The brick school was dark with sticky brown varnish and stifling from the smell of oiled wooden floors. My uncle's house was tall and narrow and full of tiny wallpapered rooms. I had a chamber pot under my bed. In the daytime we used the chemical toilet next to the shelves of preserves in the spidery basement and washed our hands at the little pump attached to the side of the kitchen sink. Every day I went to the farm at the end of the street to get milk and contemplate the legendary bad-tempered bull. The milk was yellowish, thick and warm; I carried it home in a quart bottle along streets that were two ruts in the mud. Only Main Street, which was one block long, was paved. I had never before experienced a house that did not have plumbing and a paved street in front of it, but my uncle's house didn't strike me as odd. This was the country, and in the country that's the way things were. I went home with a grateful sense of superiority.

Western Canada has never produced a frontier myth, a
body of lore and legend which defines its traditions and
gives it style and coherence. An American version is found
in the cowboy country of southern Alberta, where the local
shoe salesmen waddle around in levis and stetsons, their
soft bellies hanging over engraved silver belt buckles, and
even the undertakers wear cowboy boots. But this is just
because there's no Canadian myth to imitate. The Canadian
West has been considered of no account: either we never
had a frontier or it was boring. No attention is paid to it.
The West has no validity except as an appendage of the
East. Ambitious young people grow up in the West with one
obsession — to get out — and at the first opportunity, they
hotfoot it off to Toronto or Ottawa where, cleverly disguised
with a pinstripe suit and a prep school accent, they spend
the rest of their lives in mortal fear that someone will find
out they're from Elbow, Saskatchewan. Plied with cocktails,
they'll confess in a confidential whisper that they're from
Saskatchewan, but never will they admit they were born
on a farm. The West is the boondocks, the sticks, a place
inhabited by ignorant peasants with cowpies stuck to their
shoes. "It's a prejudice a lot of people have," shrugs Conservative MP Jack Horner, a Saskatchewan farm boy who
now owns a 33-section ranch in southern Alberta. "I've been
in groups of people and if I'm introduced as a rancher, then
I'm OK, they look on me as the Hollywood bit, but if I'm
introduced as a *farmer*, oh gosh. I wear western-cut suits in
Ottawa now. I didn't used to. People have often said to me,
'Why don't you wear the boots and hat in Ottawa?'; but
you're really handicapping yourself. Everybody would then
say, 'Do you think we're going to take advice from this
farmer, this stupid cowboy?' That's the last level of society
people will take advice from. Society will take advice from
anybody rather than a farmer."

People *come* from small prairie towns; they don't go
back. Occasionally a famous old man, on his retirement as
president of the Bank of Montreal or the CPR, will remi-
nisce about his prairie youth, using the memories of his
barefoot boyhood to illustrate the depths of poverty and
deprivation from which, by pulling hard on his own boot-
straps, he miraculously rose. The West has produced a

whole literature of nostalgia written by people who left,
books about childhood and coming-of-age which end as soon
as the writer grows up and goes east. It has given the
prairies a peculiarly abbreviated self-image and, for those
of us who have remained behind, a guilty sense of failure.
"You're writing about *Biggar*!" exclaimed a woman I met
on the street in Biggar, Saskatchewan. "What on earth could
you possibly find to say about this place?"

I didn't go east; I went west, an accidental city slicker
looking for roots, a third-generation Canadian in need of a
history and a sense of place. The West is still unknown
territory. We have almost no information about ourselves —
a smidgen of history, a handful of political and sociological
studies, some novels and autobiographies; the newspapers
and TV are full of eastern news. News travels only one way
in Canada. Nobody in Manitoba knows what's happening
in Saskatchewan or Alberta. Who's out there? Why are they
there? What are they doing? I steer by rumors and a few
cartoon stereotypes — the happy farmer, the Socialist
hordes, the Bible belt — and when those begin to crumble,
there's nothing to do but go see for myself. Going west is
still a journey into a strange and empty land. My own
odyssey began in the summer of 1971.

I am driving west into the afternoon sun along a highway
littered with disemboweled rabbits. Bloated ravens flap up
lazily from their feast. PREPARE FOR ETERNITY, says a
billboard, YOU'LL SOON BE THERE FOREVER. The
small towns loom out of the horizon like sailing ships as
the car wafts along on waves of sweet clover and pig shit
rolling in from the fields, propelled by the endless motion
of the land. The road is the central fact of life on the
prairies. As one farmer puts it: "In the city time is measured
in minutes, in the country it's measured in miles." The
importance of a prairie community is derived from its
relationship to somewhere else: a farmer takes his identity
from the town where he goes for mail, a village defines
itself in terms of the town down the road, and a town by its
distance from the city. Status in the relationship is reflected
in the quality of the roads, which, as you go farther away
from the city, deteriorate from concrete to asphalt to gravel
to mud, until they finally peter out in a farmer's yard. The

roads indicate not only economic and social status but also political distance, since highway construction has been a traditional form of political patronage in the West.

Coming around a bend in the road, I see dozens of cars drawn up in a field around a white farmhouse. The house has been gutted, its furnishings dragged out onto the lawn and arranged in neat rows under the trees. Varnished dressers and tables stand knee-deep in the tall grass, their shabbiness indecently exposed to the rummaging eyes of the young women in hair curlers who are sifting ruthlessly through mounds of battered kitchen utensils and old bedding. The mirrors multiply the swarm of people rooting through the junk in the yard. A few have come to buy, most to look. Fat old women sun themselves on the stuffed sofas and sagging iron beds and stare appraisingly at the furniture and the people. Behind the steady gabble of the crowd, the auctioneer's singsong rises and falls.

The auctioneer is standing on the back of a pickup truck near the machine shed and leisurely disposing of bits of old wire and scraps of machinery to a mob of elderly farmers in baggy pants and wide suspenders. Things go for a few cents, a couple of dollars. I approach a group of village geezers, three aged scarecrows with stubbly chins and no teeth who are gossiping in a corner. Why arc these people leaving? Oh, they're retiring, pipes one. Going to the old folks home in Winkler. "They're Mennonite people, you know," he adds, lowering his voice on the word "Mennonite" until he's just shaping the word with his lips. "They want to be near their own people, I guess." He points. In the shade beside the house, an old lady in a babushka sits in the midst of her lifetime's possessions complacently serving lemon pie to her guests.

The West is a country of old people. They set the style and determine its politics.

Halloween, 1971: the occasion of John Diefenbaker's official Seventy-fifth Birthday Party in Minnedosa, Manitoba. Or is it his seventy-sixth? Who cares? The Chief is here, resplendent in immaculate blue overcoat and black homburg, bubbling over with good humor and pleasantries as he is borne around town on a wave of adulation followed, at a respectful distance, by a whole retinue of worshipping politicians. In the afternoon he arrives at the Golden Age Club in the basement of the United Church. The oldsters, many of them younger and more chipper than Mr. Diefenbaker, are seated expectantly at card tables around Chinese checker and crokinole boards, their gnarled hands folded primly on the table, like small children. Two blue-haired ladies in drag are performing a musical farce on the stage. Mr. Diefenbaker arrives as they stand to take the applause. All eyes immediately turn to the door, and the old people rise spontaneously to their feet. At a gesture from the recreation director, they break into a loud, quavery chorus of "Happy Birthday." Mr. Diefenbaker acknowledges the tribute with an anecdote about Moses, and reminisces a little about his homestead years. He shakes a few hands, but most of the old people hang back, smiling shyly. As Mr. Diefenbaker turns to leave, an old man comes up and silently touches his coat.

Going to the country is a journey back in time. Rural culture on the prairies is Victorian, a quaint puritan ethic of hard work, clean living, and penny pinching, patriarchal, authoritarian, and chauvinist. Children are to be seen and not heard, and women are kept in the kitchen. The West has only one generation. The young people who settled it are now helping to sustain it in their old age by being fed and cared for by the young. The personality of the prairies is determined by the querulous stubbornness and deliberate conservative passivity of the old.

From the main road, the little town looks charming; its sparkling white elevators stick out of a clump of trees. But when I drive in along a road choked with weeds, I find the town silent and empty. The old false-front stores on Main Street are ragged and blank-eyed; a door bangs in the wind. Tattered green blinds flap in the broken windows of the big general store on the corner. Inside, the store is cold and smells of rot; sunlight streams in through holes where the wooden siding has been stripped away. The dead merchant's name is spelled out in faded black letters across the front. Down the street a rusty tin sign creaks above two shattered ESSO gasoline pumps. The brick school is a heap of rubble, its pink and green plaster walls exposed to the sky. The grass grows tall in the schoolyard and around the piles of junk in vacant lots; grasshoppers saw in the dust.

The faint sound of hammering breaks the stillness. A man in overalls is banging on the roof of his house. The house has a sign in the window: GROCERIES; there's a gas pump by the door and a glass telephone booth in the ditch. The whole commercial life of the town has been compressed into this yard. The town's narrow, weather-beaten houses all have new aluminium doors and a geranium in the window, but I see no people.

Autumn 1971: Saskatchewan is desolated; sightless farmhouses keen in the wind like ghosts from the Thirties. The countryside looks as if it has been overrun by an army or swept by the plague. The small towns lie stranded out on the prairie like the bleached skeletons of buffalo. They say that the last business to leave town is the Chinese restaurant. That's not true. The last business to quit is the bank.

The bank is the grandest building in almost every prairie town, and its imposing presence lends an aura of permanence and stability to the shabbiest village. The Bank of Commerce is everywhere in the West, and all the Banks of Commerce look the same, varying only according to the era of financial elegance in which they were built. They make it hard to remember which town is which. Prairie towns all look alike: identical grain elevators, identical banks, identical railway stations, a main street that is called Main Street and a road along the tracks called Railway Avenue — when you've seen one, as they say, you've seen 'em all. The images of dusty streets and cheap cafes blur together to create the misleading impression that the prairie is both flat and boring. The towns are, in fact, very different, with different personalities and histories; they look alike because they were all laid out according to one plan drawn up by the Canadian Pacific Railway. Civilization in the West was imposed from without, according to a standardized corporate blueprint; the people came later and fitted in as best they could. The towns do not reflect the people who live in them but rather the repetition of technology; prairie towns were one of the first products of Canadian industry to be mass-produced.

I choose five: Miami, an agricultural village of 350 people, WASP and Conservative; Bienfait, a coal-mining town of 800, famous for whiskey smuggling and the murder of three miners by the RCMP; Biggar, a railway town of 2,600, heartland of the Saskatchewan NDP; Winkler, a Mennonite, Bible belt boom town devoted to free enterprise; and Moose Jaw, a boom town grown old, a city which symbolizes everything corrupt and absurd about the prairies. My trip lasts a year. I spend about a month, off and on, in each community, asking questions. Is the town living or dying? Why? Who lives here? Why are they here? Though I deliberately select communities with different economic, ethnic, and political traditions I am startled by the similarities in them. There is a uniform rural culture in western Canada which cuts across provincial boundaries and goes deeper than political labels, a common structure, a code of values which enforces a single standard of behavior and represses deviance. This code is Anglo-Saxon, Protestant, middle-class, and materialist. All prairie towns are cut to English cloth — even Ukrainian communities have English names — and the code to which everyone conforms is based on British justice, fair play, and greed. It is an imperialist code brought to the West with the railway and enforced through the schools, military conscription, and the RCMP; its strength and universality are exemplified by John Diefenbaker, a grass-roots populist who devoted his political energies to the Queen, the Red Ensign, and the veterans.

The West is colonial; it was developed not as a frontier but as a corporation, a business enterprise whose sole purpose was to turn a profit for the investors, all of whom lived in the East. Money is the West's justification and its obsession. Its history is a perpetual cycle of boom and bust, as capital has been injected and raw material taken out; its tradition is one of debt, manipulation, and impoverishment. The prairies are the hinterland of eastern Canada, as Canada itself has become the hinterland of the United States. Small towns have been the agents of exploitation, the flacks, the advance men, the tollgate keepers, the hundred thousand scratching fingers of free enterprise; and they have made their money, but it is a drop compared to the tide of commerce which has flowed through. This commercial preoccupation has given small towns their peculiar, backward style; small town culture has been determined not by isolation but by an ethic of salesmanship:

"The dominant note of this life is circumspection. (It might also be called salesmanlike pusillanimity.) One must avoid giving offence, cultivate good will at any reasonable cost and continue unfailingly to take advantage of it; and as a corollary to this axiom, one should be ready to recognize and recount the possible shortcomings of one's neighbours, for neighbours are (or may be) rivals in the trade... One must be circumspect, acquire merit and avoid offence. So one must eschew opinions, or information, which are not acceptable to the common run of those whose good will has or may conceivably come to have, any commercial value. The country-town system of knowledge and belief can admit nothing that would annoy the prejudices of any appreciable number of the respectable townsfolk. So it becomes a system of intellectual, institutional and religious holdovers." (Thorstein Veblen, *Absentee Ownership and Business Enterprise in Recent Times,* 151.) Conservative and static, prairie towns grew old before they grew up; now obsolete, they, like the farmers, are being phased out.

Farmers, who form the overwhelming majority of the rural prairie population, don't have much use for the town. Sometimes they move in and destroy it by ignoring the businesses and lowering the taxes; usually they bypass it for the city. The farmer is the laborer in the prairie corporation; he is needed, as one early historian put it, "not as a citizen or as a patriot, but as a tiller of the land, a builder of railroads, a digger of sewers, a hewer of wood and a drawer of water." (N. F. Black, *History of Saskatchewan and the North-West Territories,* 740.) The countryside is the hinterland of the town; farmers are at the end of the road. The farm, however, has its own life and tradition; agriculture is an older, more universal economy than industrial capitalism. Although prairie farmers as well as townspeople are immigrants, many have retained an almost mystical relationship to the land, a profound respect which treats the possession of earth as a sacred trust and responsibility. They have been swallowed by the prairie; they are inside the universe looking out. With its roots in the Bible and a democratic concept of property, this relationship has provided the moral and spiritual strength for the family farm and the justification for farming as a way of life. Agrarian society is not just a watered-down version of the city; it has its own structure and legitimacy and is deeply hostile to the commercial system. Agrarian rebellion began simultaneously with the opening of the West; waves of political movements propelled by populist rage and indignation have rolled across the prairies. Resistance has been the classic stance of the West; repression has been the consequence.

The tradition of the West is one not of peace but of pacification; its violence is not the flamboyant, romantic violence of the American West, but a petty, Canadian bureaucratic violence consisting of threats and payoffs and bribes, the petty violence of people desperately scrabbling for survival, who resort to the greed and lust and cruelty of a jungle economy. We tend to forget that western Canada was born in rebellion; the grass-roots history of the West begins with Riel.

Chapter 3
Breaking

The morning opened bright and clear; frost had fallen. At 8 o'clock the execution party went up the rickety ladder upstairs and proceeded along the left to the far end, where was found Louis Riel kneeling near the door leading to the scaffold, with Pere Andre and Father McWilliam reciting prayers for the dying. The noose was visible dangling beyond. Around stood a guard of police.

At 8:05 Pere Andre administered the last sacrament to Riel. Riel gave the responses firmly. Although pale he was firm. He was dressed in black coat, brown tweed pants and moccasins. The figure of the hangman now appeared out of the gloom of the loft holding straps to bind Riel. He wore a mask over his face.

At 8:15 Riel rose to his feet and was pinioned by the hangman. Deputy Sheriff Gibson superintended the operation. Riel, standing with eyes open praying in French, the priests standing up front. He then walked firmly to the scaffold repeating "In God do I put my trust." His head was erect and his step firm, never showing the least tremor; as he repeated the prayerful exclamation half a smile lit up his face. Descending down a few steps of the scaffold he stood on the drop with his face turned northward. Pere Andre and Father McWilliam continued to pray, and Riel said in English "I do ask the forgiveness of all men, and forgive all my enemies." He then prayed a short time in French. The executioner now took his place. The white cap was drawn over Riel's head, both priests holding lighted candles, continuing to repeat prayers for the dying. Father McWilliam repeated the Lord's Prayer. At the words "Lead us not into temptation" Deputy Sheriff Gibson gave the signal to the hangman to pull the lever and as Father McWilliam said "and deliver us from evil" the bolt was drawn.

Riel fell a distance of nine feet. The rope had been placed with the knot under the left ear, but with the jerk the knot moved up to the base of the skull. For a moment the body was quiescent, when the legs were drawn up rapidly three times, very slowly the last time, a quiver ran through it, and Riel was dead.

(The Daily Manitoban, Nov. 16, 1885.)

The execution of Louis Riel on November 16, 1885, removed the last obstacle preventing the transformation of western Canada from a colony of the Hudson's Bay Company into a colony of eastern Canada in which wheat would replace fur as the principal export and the farmer would oust the Indian as the indentured serf of monopolistic capitalism. Riel was the most powerful western leader to defy the territorial ambitions of the rapacious Ontario businessmen who, under the guise of pious nationalism and a blanket of government protection, swarmed into the West to plunder the land from which they had driven the native people. Twice Riel led popular rebellions in an attempt to achieve self-government and equal provincial status for the West; both rebellions were put down by military force. "I hope sincerely that he will be hanged," said Edgar Dewdney, the new lieutenant-governor of the North-West Territories, when Riel was captured after his defeat at Batoche in the spring of 1885; "he is too dangerous a man to have a chance of being loose on society."

Riel had emerged as a populist leader and champion of the Métis of the Red River settlement in 1869, when the Hudson's Bay Company sold all of what is now western Canada to the Canadian government for 300,000 pounds sterling. Primarily an imperial strategem to prevent American expansion to the northwest, the acquisition became virtually inevitable after one of the fathers of Confederation, leafing through his Bible, selected the name "Dominion of Canada" from the grandiloquent phrase "and he shall have

dominion from sea unto sea." Canada was a reluctant pur-
chaser. Mystified about what to do with several million
square miles of what was considered to be uninhabitable
desert and concerned with the cost of military defence, the
government attempted to pass the North-West off on Great
Britain as a Crown colony, but Great Britain promptly
handed it back. These hot-potato dealings over the imminent
withdrawal of the Hudson's Bay Company monopoly
attracted hundreds of scavengers, speculators, and squatters
to Red River, where they cleaned out the furs, mopped up
the last of the buffalo, and staked out prime pieces of land
in anticipation of annexation. An accidental by-product of
the fur trade with no assurances of protection from the
federal government, no legal rights to the land they occupied, and no voice in the colonial administration, the half-
breed Métis became convinced that they would simply be
shoved aside by a massive immigration of Canadian settlers.
Their fears, heightened by the crowing arrogance of the
obnoxious Ontario Orangemen who had populated Red
River, were confirmed in the autumn of 1869, when
Canadian surveyors staked out the prairie south of Red
River before Indian title had been relinquished, before the
local inhabitants had been consulted, and before the colony
had received an official government. Riel tore up the
stakes. On November 2, the Métis seized Fort Garry and
set up a provisional government to negotiate the terms of
union with Canada: Riel demanded full provincial status
for the North-West including self-government, protection of
Indian and Métis land rights, and equality with the other
members of Confederation. An organized and disciplined
society structured around the buffalo bunt, the Métis outnumbered the "Canadas," as they called the white immigrants, by more than six to one. (A Manitoba census in
1870 showed that of a population of just under 12,000, 82
per cent were Métis, five per cent Indian, and 13 per cent
white.) Representative government would give the Métis
control over the province. Their considerable wealth, overwhelming numbers, and obvious military strength raised the
possibility that western Canada could become completely
independent; already the Métis proudly referred to themselves as "the new nation." Not only was this possibility

completely unacceptable to the Canadian government, but
the prospect of admitting a Métis nation into Confederation
was equally unsavory. Canada was appalled at the thought
of having white people governed by half-Indian nomadic
hunters; it offended their sense of British propriety, and
since most of the Métis were French-speaking Roman
Catholics, it suggested that Quebec could establish a cultural beachhead in the West from which French Canada
would eventually dominate the nation. Determined that if
the West was going to be Canadian it was going to be white,
British, and Protestant, Sir John A. Macdonald planned to
stall self-government long enough for Ontario to establish
a firm commercial grip on the North-West. He sent troops
against the Métis government in Red River; Riel fled to the
United States and western Canada's nine months of independence came to an end. Canada granted provincial status
to a postage stamp version of Manitoba, but the federal
government retained control of all public lands both in
Manitoba and the North-West Territories, which, during the
next ten years, Macdonald proceeded to give away to his
cronies in Ontario. According to historian W. L. Morton,
"One of the greatest transfers of territory and sovereignty
in history was conducted as a mere transaction in real
estate."

Purchase of this valuable property transformed the two-
year-old Canadian government into an imperial power,
which treated the West not as an integral part of the nation
but as an appendage, a source of raw materials the buying
and selling of which would enrich the merchants along the
St. Lawrence. The government essentially adopted the
attitude of the Hudson's Bay Company. Their direct connection with The Bay existed in the person of Donald A.
Smith, the tough little Scotchman who had risen from lowly
factor at a desolate trading post in Labrador to Sir Donald
A. Smith, chief officer of the Hudson's Bay Company in
Canada. In 1869 Macdonald sent Smith to Red River as his
secret agent in an attempt to quell the Riel Rebellion; Smith
failed, but he remained in Red River, where he became
chief factor of The Bay, a major investor in land, railways
and steamship lines, Conservative Member of Parliament,

and, in 1880, a principal shareholder in the Canadian Pacific Railway.

The building of the railway was the key to the Conservative government's colonial ambitions, which Macdonald enunciated in the election of 1878 as the "National Policy." Couched in the romantic rhetoric of nation building, the "national dream" of a united Canada from sea to sea was little more than a brilliant commercial scheme to pull eastern Canada out of a serious economic depression. Unable to compete with the burgeoning American economy to the south, Canadian manufacturers were losing markets to American companies. The best land in eastern Canada was already in private hands; new settlers ignored the Ontario bush for more attractive prospects in the American West. Investment fell off, immigration slowed to a trickle; Canada was poor and stagnant. The Americans, elated by the railway revolution and the opening of the western frontier, were loudly advertising their manifest destiny; it seemed only a matter of time until Canada would be economically and geographically absorbed into the United States. To prevent this, Macdonald's national policy proposed to protect by means of high tariffs Canadian industry against American products and to open a new frontier of investment in the Canadian West. The construction of a transcontinental railway would precipitate a massive real estate boom; Macdonald would pay for the railway with land, and the railway would make a profit by selling the land to settlers. Immigration was essential to the success of the national dream; settlers would be needed to create a demand for land, to supply the labor to mine the raw resources, and to provide a market for the manufactured goods of eastern Canada. The function of the immigrant was concisely summed up by the editor of an Ontario newspaper: "We have for some time past enjoyed a valuable influx of Emigrants, or as it might be termed, a valuable import trade of the nerves and sinews of prosperity, of the true wealth of the country, an industrious peasantry."

The National Policy won Macdonald a resounding victory in an election in which the interests of western Canada were chiefly represented by Sir Donald A. Smith. (Louis Riel was elected MP for Provencher in 1873, but was forbidden to

take his seat in the House of Commons.) Little more than
a year later, the government awarded the contract for the
construction of the CPR to a consortium of eastern finan-
ciers headed by George Stephen of the Bank of Montreal.
In addition to subsidies of $62 million, the government gave
the CPR 25 million acres of tax-free land in the most fertile
areas of the prairies — a belt of property extending 24 miles
on either side of the main line — and a monopoly over all
railway construction between the CPR track and the
American border. The control that the Hudson's Bay
Company had exercised over the North-West was transferred almost intact to the CPR, which preserved in its east-
west rail line the traditional fur trade route and continued
to channel the wealth of the West into the pockets of
Montreal traders.

The settlement of the West was to be accomplished by the
sale of huge tracts of land to private "colonization" companies. The government originally planned to sell 10 million
acres at $2 an acre; if the company succeeded in locating
two settlers on every section of its property within five
years, it would be reimbursed $1 an acre. The scheme would
locate 100,000 immigrants on the prairies, the government
would make $10 million to offset the cost of the CPR, and
Macdonald would be able to pay off some old political debts
with cheap land. Although several of the colonization companies, such as the Barr Temperance Colony established at
Saskatoon, were formed by religious or philanthropic organizations, most were real estate companies put together by a
small group of prominent bankers and politicians eager to
make a killing by floating stock on the eastern exchanges.
Six million acres were allotted to 106 companies in 1882;
only 27 paid the first installment on the purchase price. A
down payment of one-fifth the total value of the land gave
these companies complete possession of tracts of land
ranging from 10,000 to 213,000 acres, which they could sell
for whatever price they could get; they were also entitled
to build roads, railways, bridges, telegraph lines, flour mills,
town halls, general stores and hotels and to lend money to
prospective buyers in return for a mortgage on the property.
Colonies were particularly attractive to British landlords
anxious to get rid of their excess population: the model of

munificence was Lady Gordon-Cathcart, who established each of her impoverished Scottish crofters on a farm in the North-West with a $480 loan repayable at five per-cent interest over three years.

This medieval system did not encourage settlement. Many of the colonization companies held on to their land waiting for the price to rise. So did the CPR. Land prospectors travelling the CPR across the prairies were so depressed by the desolation of the CPR-owned land along the track that they decided the West was, in fact, uninhabitable. Jealous of its monopoly, the CPR discouraged investment and competition. The West sank into the same stagnant family compact cartel which had already made Ontario an economic backwater.

When the North-West Rebellion broke out in 1885, fewer than 1,000 settlers had been located on colonization company property; the West was still virgin. The rebellion brought immigration to a standstill, threatened the CPR with bankruptcy, and destroyed the colonization companies. Riel was a much greater threat now than he had been in 1869. Once more Canadian troops were sent to quash the uprising, which this time had the support of Indians and disgruntled white farmers. Riel was defeated and brought to Regina for trial, where he was found guilty of treason and hanged. As compensation the government paid the colonization companies, none of which had fullfilled its obligations, $1.1 million, or approximately $365 for each immigrant settler. Unintentionally, Riel had provoked a crisis which broke the back of the family compact in the West; the CPR monopoly was removed in 1888, and the West was thrown open to an orgy of speculation and one of the greatest mass migrations in the history of mankind.

Agricultural settlement on the prairies began in the spring of 1812, when a group of destitute Scottish crofters were located on riverfront farms near the Hudson's Bay Company post of Fort Garry. Evicted from their highland farms, the crofters had been brought to Red River by the Earl of Selkirk, who had acquired a controlling interest in the Hudson's Bay Company and had purchased from it, for the nominal sum of ten shillings and an annual payment to the Indians of 100 pounds of tobacco, 116,000 square miles of land in the North-West. On this grant, which was only slightly smaller than the United Kingdom of Great Britain and Ireland, Selkirk undertook to establish 1,000 families within ten years. Selkirk liked to fancy himself a philanthropist, but the real purpose of the colony was to supply cheap food for the fur trade.

Involved in a bitter fur trade war with the North-West Company of Montreal, The Bay was forced to seek out furs in remote parts of the West and to establish dozens of forts to protect its monopoly against the depredations of the *voyageurs*. The spiraling costs of this competition resulted in the introduction of the whiskey trade as a means of making money in the West and in the increased demand for cheap manpower and supplies. In the West fur brigades were fueled with pemmican, and since the Métis enjoyed a monopoly on the buffalo trade, they were able to play off one company against the other for the best price. The settlers were intended to produce a local supply of flour, butter, and meat, which would break the Métis monopoly and relieve The Bay of the high cost of importing food from England. The amenities of civilization would, in addition, persuade retired traders to remain in the community and spend their life's earnings in the company store. The presence of several thousand people would act as a ready pool of manpower (Selkirk contracted to supply The Bay with 200 servants a year) and a bulwark against possible attack by the North-West Company. (When such an attack occurred in 1816, 20 settlers along with the governor of the colony were massacred by Nor'westers.)

Selkirk sold each farmer a 100-acre plot for five shillings an acre, payable in produce, a requirement which was waived after the settlers had suffered years of crop failures and were saved from starvation only by the generosity of the Indians and Métis. Certainly the company gave them no consideration. The attitude of the Hudson's Bay Company was made clear in the autumn of 1813, when a boatload of crofters arrived at Fort Churchill after a voyage during which many had died in an epidemic of scarlet fever. "On our reaching Fort Churchill," says one of the settlers, "we were so emaciated and reduced from the fatal effects of the plague, which proved the death of so many of us before our arrival, that we had scarcely strength to stand, and some were dying almost daily. For the sake of those who were recovering, however, some of our people tried to hunt, to get a fresh partridge or something of the kind; but this being observed by Mr. Auld, who was then master at the post, he decoyed our guns away from us, under pretence of putting them in better order; the moment he got them into his possession, so uncharitable and unfeeling was he, that he ordered all the locks to be taken off, and then, with a sarcastic leer, returned them back to us lockless; adding 'You shall eat nothing but what can be charged against the colony' for he could not well charge a pheasant or a rabbit of our own killing."

During the decade that passed before the settlers were able to become self-sufficient, they were required to buy all their provisions, implements, and clothing from a store provided by Lord Selkirk. All of the goods were sold on credit at exorbitant prices. "Is it any wonder," asks contemporary historian Alexander Ross, "if the settlers, after so long a period of difficulties and disappointments, should be deeply involved in debt? Many of them, however, during this unfortunate period, had been at various times employed in what was then called 'colony work' such as housebuilding, road-making or tripping; and at such jobs had earned considerable sums of money, which were to have been placed to their credits as so much reduction of their debts; but such was the iniquity of those entrusted with power in the colony, that the money in some instances was never credited and the colonist sought redress in vain. False entries, erroneous statements and over-charges were afterwards proved in nearly every instance; but most of the officials had then left the country and their correction was next to impossible: neither contracts nor vouchers could be found. To crown all, the settlers at the end of each year had been compelled to sign their accounts as correct; for until they did so their credit was stopped by the offended Governor and necessity soon forced them to submit. On debts thus contracted a further charge of five per cent was levied as interest."

As long as the colonists produced only a small amount of
food for sale, the company paid high prices for it; as soon
as they were able to meet all the company's needs, prices
fell. If the settlers grumbled, the company claimed that their
butter was rancid, their cheese mouldy, and their flour fit
only to poison pigs, and once more imported its supplies
from England. "The settlers," says Ross, "were left, after
all their improvements, in a worse predicament than if they
had never extended their farms; since they were now
deprived of that market which their additional labour and
additional expense had led them to expect." The farmers
had no recourse from corruption in the government of the
colony, since it was composed almost exclusively of company employees.

Immigration into the North-West ended with the merger
of The Bay and the North-West Company in 1821. No
longer needed as pawns in a corporate price war, the handful of Scots, French Canadians, and retired Swiss soldiers
were allowed to establish a form of subsistance agriculture
which brought them comfort and even prosperity under the
benevolent thumb of The Bay. When Sir John A. Macdonald
purchased the North-West from the company in 1869, it was
to Lord Selkirk that he looked for a pattern of western
settlement.

Like Selkirk, the Canadian government believed that the
poor should be encouraged to settle the prairies, since only
they would be desperate enough to farm the wilderness
with tools and provisions they were forced to purchase from
Canadian stores, on credit. To facilitate this kind of immigration, the government passed the Homestead Act in 1872,
offering 160 acres of prairie land to any head of a family
or any person over the age of 21 for a fee of $10. Before he
could receive full title, the homesteader had to live on the
land for six months of every year for a period of three years
and to bring at least some of the land under cultivation. In
1879 the act was enlarged to enable a homesteader to
acquire an additional 160 acres adjoining his farm for $1 an
acre. This "pre-emption" clause was cancelled ten years
later, not only because it interfered with the sale of private
property but also because many homesteaders were so

anxious to acquire more land that they mortgaged the original homestead and lost both.

Disregarding the advice of planners who advocated village-style settlement in the West, Ontario surveyors laid out the prairies according to the American checkerboard plan; they ignored topography and vegetation and divided the whole prairie into one monotonous grid of sections exactly a mile square. The sections they grouped into identical townships six miles square; a homestead comprised one-quarter of a section. Of the 36 sections in each township, fewer than half were available for homesteading: two were set aside as "school lands" to be sold to pay for the construction of a school; one and three-quarters belonged to the Hudson's Bay Company, which had been given one-twentieth (6.6 million acres) of all the best land in the North-West as part of the sale of 1869; and all of the odd-numbered sections belonged to the CPR. In a typical township, therefore, only sixteen and one-quarter sections were "free"; these allowed for a maximum of 65 families. Farmers wishing to expand their homesteads through pre-emption were usually forced to buy from the CPR; although the CPR often sold cheap ($2 to $5 an acre) to encourage settlement, in areas where it chose not to sell a severe tax burden was placed on the remaining families. The grid system was cheap and easy to lay out, but expensive to maintain; each township had between 40 and 54 miles of roads and a school to keep up. Since CPR land was tax-free, the railway paid nothing towards the maintenance of the community. In winter the roads were allowed to drift in; in summer many of them just blew away. As farms expanded and the number of people in each township decreased, the grid system not only was uneconomical, but also it intensified the loneliness and isolation which contributed to emotional breakdowns commonly known in the West as "prairie madness."

Since the survey gave no indication of the nature or quality of the land, prospective homesteaders were advised to go and look for themselves before filing a claim. For a $10 fee, professional "land locators" would do the looking for them and frequently come up with a patch of miserable scrub. Most homesteaders simply purchased a copy of *The*

Land Prospector's Manual and Field-Book , and in groups of
three or four set out in Red River carts loaded with
surveying equipment and enough bannock, bacon, and tea
to see them through two or three weeks of camping out on
the prairie. Warning explorers to travel light because of
swamps and sloughs, the manual listed the supplies each
homesteader would need on the trip: a red-and-blue pencil,
a black lead pencil; knife, fork, and spoon; tin plate and
pint drinking cup; change of shirt, drawers, and socks; a
towel and a pair of blankets; mosquito netting; a long water-
proof coat, poncho, or sheet; long boots, a buffalo robe, and
a gun. Armed with a map and a compass, the little groups
of immigrants ventured west along the old trails worn like
wrinkles in the land's face by the annual migrations of the
Indians and Métis, who now, in the face of the alien tide,
sold the government scrip entitling them to land and
retreated north. The Indians offered no resistance to the
newcomers, except to accost them occasionally for a little
tea or tobacco. Apart from the flash fires which roared
through the tall grass in the summer heat, the greatest
danger on the prairies was not Indians but insects: "Manly
Prospectors will not feel discouraged if they should be
bitten by a mosquito, or teased by a fly, during sultry
weather," chirped the   *Prospector's Manual.*. "Experience
shows that a 'tender-foot' as the new arrival in the North-
West is called, invariably attracts the largest share of the
attention of these pests, which, it is comforting to know,
always disappear as the settlement and cultivation of the
country progress."
  Since the greenhorns heading west in black serge suits,
pinstripe shirts, and bowler hats were entirely ignorant of
the prairie, most of them chose the kind of land they were
familiar with back home: Ontario people headed like
lemmings for the bush, the Icelanders starved on a wooded
muskeg swamp at the edge of Lake Winnipeg, Scotch
crofters plunked down on the nearest available pile of
stones, and the Ukrainians, who came last, got whatever
was left, which was often very good land. In passing up
acres of prime land for some desolate, nostalgic outcrop,
thousands of western pioneers were doomed from the
beginning to repeat the cycle of poverty from which they

had fled. Sometimes the most naive and gullible won the biggest prize in the land lottery, for example, those trusting members of the Barr Temperance Colony who chose their land in the middle of the Atlantic. "When we were about half way across," says a colonist, "some of the men said that they had filed for their land. I heard them telling that Barr had a large map on which the sections of his colony were marked, and that he had it arranged so that people from the same area could live together. My father said he was not going to file for his land while still in the middle of the ocean; he wanted to see the land first. This sounded very farsighted of him, but actually he did not know a thing about soil, and would not have known good land if he saw it. As it was, dad ended up with a quarter section that had about 50 acres of alkali slough on it while some of those who had filed on ship for their land ended up with very good farms."

Thousands of homesteaders came west before the railway, but their farms were so isolated and produced so little that they were simply absorbed into the landscape. Even after the CPR went through and the first grain elevator was built in southern Manitoba in 1881, the West was caught in a post-boom slump. Wheat fell from $1.33 a bushel in 1881 to 80 cents in 1883, the same year the Canadian government raised the tariff on farm machinery from 25 to 33 per cent. The loosening of homestead regulations in 1884 permitted people to claim land they had no intention of farming. "Portable shacks were built," says one pioneer, "which the homesteader could load on his wagon and move from place to place, thus helping him to qualify for several patents." People who had paid exorbitant prices for worthless farmland in the railway speculations of 1881-82 hung on to it hoping the price would rise once more; townspeople convinced that their little hamlet was going to be the Chicago of the North discouraged settlement by buying up all the land for miles around. Most of southern Alberta was leased out to giant ranching conglomerates at one cent an acre; owned by Canadian financial tycoons and friends of Sir John A. Macdonald, the ranches supplied cattle to feed the crews building the CPR through the Rockies and also specialized in raising polo ponies for the English aristocrats

who were prominent among the shareholders. By 1884, 41
companies had been granted leases covering more than 1.7
million acres; six leases covered 100,000 acres and ten were
for 50,000. Not only did the owners make a handsome profit
from the CPR (one ranch paid an average dividend of 19
per cent), but also they could sell their culled and worthless
cattle to the Department of Indian Affairs to feed the
starving Blackfoot on the nearby reserves. (Controlling
interest in the largest of these ranches, the North-West Cattle
Company, was held by Sir Hugh Allan of Allan Steamship
Lines, a Montreal capitalist of vast wealth who had been
awarded a contract to build the CPR in 1873, but who had
been forced out after it was revealed that he obtained the
contract by bribing Conservative cabinet ministers and
Macdonald himself.)

Precipitated by the depression and the government's
apparent intention of turning the West into the fiefdom of
a new landed gentry, the North-West Rebellion unintentionally provoked a technological revolution which transformed
agriculture from a peasant ritual into a capitalist industry:
the rebellion brought money into the North-West. Reduced
by poverty and brought to gathering buffalo bones and
selling them to the CPR for $7 a ton, homesteaders
welcomed the chance to earn 50 cents a day marching with
the government troops against Riel: small fortunes were
made by farmers who rented their teams and wagons at
$8 a day to haul supplies to the north. Homesteads prepared
for seeding lay fallow all that summer; when farmers sowed
their crops the following year and found the yield was much
higher, summerfallowing became common practice in the
West. With their army pay, homesteaders were able to
purchase the new John Deere steel plows and high-quality
Red Fife wheat; their investment triggered a trade boom and
enabled the farmers to grow enough grain for sale to acquire
more cash. Geared up to a semblance of efficiency by
ferrying troops and provisions back and forth from Ontario,
the CPR began to perceive the economic advantages of
running trains full of people as well as trains full of wheat;
their perception of the consumer economy was matched by
the government's new desire to populate the West as quickly
as possible to prevent another uprising. Like the trade war

between the Hudson's Bay Company and the North-West Company, the rebellion stimulated a wave of aggressive investment and economic development which, like The Bay, depended for its success on cheap food and cheap labor:

ALLAN STEAMSHIP LINES
CONSISTING OF 22 FIRST CLASS STEAMERS
Having unsurpassed accommodation for
cabin travellers and tourists.
STEERAGE AND EMIGRANT TRAFFIC A SPECIALTY!
Arrangements complete!
Accommodation to satisfy all reasonable
demands and at *rates exceedingly low.*
Thousands of immigrants will testify to the exceedingly
good treatment received on its steamers.

Almost everybody who came to Canada came on an Allan boat. For $60 or $80 (gold) one could purchase a cabin; the ads did not state the price of a steerage ticket, which entitled the emigrant to a wooden berth in the hold. Among the many advantages offered by the Allan Line was the promise that steerage passengers would be "boarded and lodged while in England waiting for the departure of the steamer, receive a free supply of cooked provisions served up three times a day during the ocean trip and medical treatment in case of sickness." Each steerage passenger was allowed ten cubic feet of luggage and was required to provide himself with "a plate, mug, spoon, water can and bedding, all of which can be bought for 10 shillings or less at Point of Embarkation."

The Canadian government blanketed the towns and cities of Europe with posters showing golden wheat fields and two words:
FREE LAND.
GO IN THE SPRING
of 1898
And take a home in the
CANADIAN WEST!
No taxes except for school purposes
Farm produce paid for *IN CASH!*
You will live longer and have better health.

You can make a living easier and get rich faster.
There are more chances for profitable
investment of capital than anywhere else on
the continent!

Pamphlets extolling the fertility of the soil and the bracing
climate of the prairie were churned out by western journa-
lists, and the newspapers were full of testimonials from
early settlers attesting to their marvellous success in the new
country. The government sent a cautionary letter to land
agents telling them to instruct new immigrants to lay in
plenty of food and fuel for the winter: "It is very important
that none of them suffer from cold or hunger so that the
reports may be favorable."

Although the government aimed its campaign primarily
at Caucasians, it was extraordinarily undiscriminating;
anyone with a strong back and the price of passage was
welcome regardless of race, language, religion, nationality,
literacy, or financial resources. The resulting mass migration
into the North-West represented the first substantial immigration into Canada of people who were neither English
nor French; since they settled virgin land in a territory
which did not enter Confederation until 1905, they considered themselves to be "founding races" on an equal footing
with the British and the French. Their presence guaranteed
the West not only a personality different from the rest of
the nation, but also a tradition of race and class hatred and
resistance to political oppression resulting from subsequent
attempts to anglicize the ethnics. Their presence also
guaranteed that the West would be poor.

With their ID cards in their pockets and, in the case of
those who didn't speak English, a tag printed with the name
of their destination around their necks, the immigrants were
loaded into wooden colonist cars where, on a hard plank
bench, they lived, ate, and slept for the five to ten days it
took the train to rumble across the country. At station
stops, the children got out and gathered sticks to fuel the
stoves on which the settlers cooked their meals. Between
1885 and 1930, almost 3,000,000 people emigrated to the
prairies; 675,000 homestead entries were filed, two-thirds
of them between 1900 and 1915. Between 1907 and 1912,

40,000 homesteads were claimed every year. The population of the prairies increased 500 per cent in 30 years until, by 1931, prairie residents made up 25 per cent of the Canadian population. The response to the ads had exceeded the wildest expectations of the government and the railway; even the worst land was optimistically grabbed. Although the West was far from crowded, many areas were fairly densely populated; a township where all the land was occupied could have as many as 144 families in an area six miles square.

While some settlers received an annual "remittance" from home and more than one black sheep son of the English aristocracy furnished his sod shanty with oriental rugs and Limoges china, most homesteaders bought their farming "outfit" on credit. It wasn't cheap; the bare minimum for one family in 1889 came to over $450: one wagon, $67.50; one ox, $70; five cows and calves, $175; harness, $4.25; lumber, $42; stove and pipes, $25; axe, 94 cents; saw, 65 cents; hayfork, 39 cents; spade, 79 cents, plus 20 lbs. nails, wagon grease, a hoe, and a pick. In addition the family needed enough food to sustain them until they harvested their first crop: one bag oatmeal, $2.70; 100 lbs. flour, $5.80; 100 lbs. pork, $11; 25 lbs sugar, $1.78; five lbs. tea, $1.65, plus salt, pepper, matches, soap, a gallon of syrup, 20 pounds of rice, baking powder, and potatoes. Everybody bought exactly the same things, mostly on the advice of the storekeeper, who usually knew as little about farming as they did. "I vividly recall watching the inexperienced colonists buying horses, oxen, machinery and wagons," says the sharp-eyed son of a Barr colonist. "They had no idea how to take care of horses or how to harness them. When they bought harness the storekeeper would have to put it on the horses for them. There they would leave it for days afraid that if the harness came off they would never be able to put it on again. I was fascinated watching them try to get a bit into a horse's mouth, a job that often took a long time. They did not know how to grease the wagons and some of the wagon wheels were squeaking in loud protest before they even started on their trip. Some colonists even bought binders to cut their crops, a very optimistic purchase as it would be two years before they would need one."

As soon as he reached his property, the homesteader ploughed four or five rows around the site he had chosen for a home as a guard against the prairie fires which, ignited by sparks from the locomotives, destroyed his crops and left his cattle with charred hoofs and burned-out eyes. Impeded by clouds of flies and the tendency of the oxen to bolt for the nearest slough, breaking was slow and painful: "We harnessed the oxen and took the whiffletrees from the wagon, but since dad did not know how to fasten them to the plow, he simply tied them on with rope. We had no idea how to adjust the plow, but started out bravely enough, with me leading the oxen and dad trying to keep the plow in the ground. Because of the awkward way he had tied the plow, dad had to wrestle with the handles pointing straight up into the air. The sod was hacked out in kinks and I had to come along afterwards and turn them over." Vegetables were planted in the fire guard, and the sod was used to build a house. A sod shanty indicated a man of substance and responsibility; the bachelors usually made do with shacks thrown together out of packing cases, poplar poles, and bits of tin.

"It was a handy place to live, that little tar-paper shanty around which the prairie wind whooed and whiffed with such disdain," reflects one homesteader. "So small was it that it was possible to wash oneself, dress oneself and get breakfast without getting out of bed. On the wall was a shelf which did duty as a table. There was also a little box stove and some odds and ends. When the roof leaked, which was every time it rained, it was necessary to put pans on the bed to catch the drip." It was useful to have a strong wife who could churn butter, shoot gophers, and earn a little money by taking in the laundry of the neighbourhood bachelors. Newspaper articles extolling the West as fertile ground for prospective wives and domestic servants made it perfectly clear what kind of woman was required: "The women wanted in western Canada," stated the *Canadian Gazette* of 1902, "are those healthy, country-bred women who love and understand animal life and who prefer the freedom of the country to the conventionalities of the town. They must be women of some culture, but who have had training in domestic arts by practicing them and who will keep up the tone of the men with whom they mix by music and book lore when the day's work is over."

To pay off his debt, the farmer grew wheat to sell in the town, which the railroad had thoughtfully located no more than a day's team haul from his farm.

Chapter 4
Moose Jaw, 1882

The location of a given town has commonly been determined by collusion between interested parties with a view to speculation in real estate, and it continues through its life history to be managed as a real estate proposition. Its municipal affairs, its civic pride, its community interest converge upon its real estate values, which are invariably of a speculative character and which all its loyal citizens are intent on "booming" or "boosting."

(Thorstein Veblen)

Towns sprang up around the railway stations set out every seven to ten miles across the prairie, and the intimacy of their relationship was reflected in the fact that all the biggest and most important buildings — grain elevators, banks, and hotels — were built as closely as possible to the station. The towns grew or shrank according to the size and prosperity of the railway establishment. Moose Jaw grew into the biggest railway town west of Winnipeg; its story is that of almost every prairie town.

Moose Jaw is a grudge town. Prior to 1882 it was a stopping place on the road to somewhere else, a bend in the creek which the Indians called *Monsochapiskanis*, or Moose Jaw Bone Creek. A pleasant wooded gully, it marked the boundary between the territory of the Assiniboines and that of the Blackfoot confederacy, a demilitarized zone beyond which either tribe ventured at its peril. Sitting Bull camped there when the Sioux fled north after the Custer massacre. A few miles to the south at Wood Mountain were a Hudson's Bay trading post, a North West Mounted Police station, and a log shack with a couple of buffalo robes known to travellers as the Denomie Bros. Hotel.

When the CPR reached Brandon, Manitoba, in 1881, it appeared certain that the railway's next divisional point would be at Pile o' Bones on Wascana Creek, 230 miles to the west. The rumor unleashed a stampede of speculators, who squatted on every available piece of property along both sides of the creek. The principal squatter was Edgar Dewdney, lieutenant-governor of the North-West Territories; acting on information he acquired by virtue of his position, he secretly purchased 480 acres of the best land from the Hudson's Bay Company and claimed the rest on behalf of the government as the site for a new territorial capital. (Dewdney was acting on behalf of a syndicate which included five politicians, a Hudson's Bay official, and the comptroller of the North West Mounted Police who located the future RCMP headquarters in Regina.) Not only did this move guarantee Dewdney a slice of the profits from the growth of his new capital city, but also it deprived the CPR of its customary profits from the sale of land in the townsite; offended, the CPR moved its divisional head-quarters 40 miles west to Moose Jaw when a fortuitous fire destroyed its Regina roundhouse in 1883.

In Moose Jaw, the CPR had a freer hand. Its only compe-tition came from James H. Ross, an enterprising young man from Ontario; acting on a tip, he and three companions had streaked across the frozen prairie in January 1882 and taken up "homesteads" on the bluff overlooking Moose Jaw Creek. They were squatting there when the track approach-ed in the spring of 1882. Ross's companions seem to have sold out immediately, but Ross hung on to become the principal citizen and leading landlord of the city of Moose Jaw. Considerable as the value of Ross's property was, it was miniscule compared to that owned by the CPR, the Canadian government, and their mutual agent, the Canada North-West Land Company.

In the summer of 1882, the CPR sold five million acres of land in 47 western townsites, including Moose Jaw, to the Canada North-West Land Company for $13.5 million, or a modest $2.70 an acre. The bargain is understandable in view of the fact that controlling interest in the Canada North-West Land Company was held by CPR director Sir Donald A. Smith, in conjunction with a group of British

aristocrats and a consortium of eastern Canadian businessmen headed by E. B. Osler, a millionaire lawyer and member of one of the country's largest real estate families. In
return for selling the land, the Canada North-West Land
Company was to retain half the profits; the other half was
to go to the railway. Since the Canadian government still
retained half the land in every townsite, it authorized the
Canada North-West Land Company to act as its agent as
well, and so gave the consortium complete control over all
the land in 47 prairie communities. It paid the company a
three per-cent commission on sales and, of course, gave
company directors and agents first crack at buying unlimited
quantities of prime government land at prices they set
themselves. Thus the most valuable property in prairie
towns and cities fell into the hands of eastern Canadian
investors, who made fabulous fortunes selling and renting it
to immigrants.

Having acquired a virtual monopoly of land in Moose
Jaw as well as the surrounding farm land (which it sold at
$5 an acre payable over six years at six per cent a year),
the Canada North-West Land Company boosted the price
of townsites to $30 an acre; settlers and speculators pro-
tested by camping out in the streets. The end of steel until
the railway pushed on in 1883, Moose Jaw was little more
than a large construction camp with a floating population of
2,000 to 3,000, a jumping-off place for the Barr colonists
headed for Saskatoon.

"In the year 1883, on the first day of May, I first saw
Moose Jaw, when coming in on the second CPR passenger
train into the station," writes Grandma Bellamy, one of the
first women to settle in the North-West. "Looking up the
street I wondered whether or not this was the front street,
as there were no sidewalks. We walked up the middle of
the street looking for the tent which we had made up and
sent to Moose Jaw two weeks earlier. It was a long tent
with doors, windows, three rooms and a wooden floor. We'd
had an inside roof made to protect us from the extreme heat
of July. It was fairly comfortable, so we lived in it until we
put up a cottage. The next morning I looked around for the
post office and found only a packing case in the corner,
near the station, into which the railway men threw the mail.

Before the end of the week Mr. Hunter who had the general store took pity on it and made a few pigeon holes and looked after it.

"I went to church in Moose Jaw on the second Sunday in May. There were fifty men present and only one woman. The first church was very crude; the wind blew through the cracks in the walls and the small collection coins disappeared through the cracks in the floor. On Sunday mornings the minister would go through the rows of tents calling 'Wake up and go to church!' but the people did not always respond co-operatively. On that Sunday a building was moved. The movers said that Sunday had not passed by Regina yet."

"The town consisted of a few frame buildings and a number of tents," says Archie Brown. "Frame buildings were rapidly being erected and the population increasing. Hundreds of railway contractors' horses were wintered here and the death rate had been heavy. Coyotes and buzzards were plentiful and acted as scavengers, but they were unable to keep up with the carcasses. When the warm weather came and the wind blew in the direction of town from the camps, the stench was awful. Buffalo had been practically exterminated; a few herds were brought in from the south of the town near the boundary during the summer for shipment to Winnipeg, there to be mounted by the taxidermist."

Although Moose Jaw was full of tent hotels, they were little more than billiard parlors and bars; travellers slept on stretchers on the floor. Everybody threw his garbage out the door or into the same creek the community drew its drinking water from. "We could cut good hay on Main Street in 1883," reflects J. J. McLean, who purchased a store on his first day in town. "Buildings were being erected on both sides, but they were very largely one-storey in height. But it seemed all right to me, for there were plenty of stores and 'Push Moose Jaw' was the cry among real estaters."

To encourage speculation the Canada North-West Land Company awarded free corner lots to the first newspaper publisher, the first baby born in town, and all the winners of horse races held on Main Street. The *Moosejaw News* reciprocated by hailing Moose Jaw as "The Prettiest Town-site on the Canadian Pacific Railway" and "The Future Great Central City of the North-West." "Two months ago," it stated in May 1883, "the city of Moosejaw was distinguishable from the boundless prairie only by its natural beauty and two buildings. Today it contains upwards of one hundred buildings, many of which are handsome and substantial structures." The lies and exaggerations of the local press were echoed in accounts placed in eastern and foreign newspapers; thus began a deliberate campaign of flimflam and puffery which, while it made personal fortunes for the landowners, eventually bankrupted the city.

The CPR did its best for Moose Jaw; it invested more than $5 million in rail yards and roundhouses, and it imported Scottish machinists, including a whole squad of soccer players, so Moose Jaw could boast that it had more WASPs than any other town on the prairies. Everyone worked for the railway. "The pinnacle of Moose Jaw society was to be an engineer or a conductor," says a man who grew up there. "They always lived in the big houses. The superintendent lived in a *mansion*." The CPR built a beautiful brick station with a clock tower, smaller than Winnipeg's but more elegant, which was renowned for the excellence of its restaurant and the comfort of its hotel accommodation upstairs (both achieved by a system of hidden pipes, through which excrement from the hotel toilets was funnelled down to the hotel garden to fertilize vegetables fed to passengers in the station restaurant). Otherwise, however, the Moose Jaw station was a model of gentility. "It is commodious, clean and well-appointed both inside and outside which cannot be said of every station in Canada," wrote a British journalist shortly after the turn of the century. "What is the earthly use of putting up half-a-dozen notices in waiting-rooms to the effect that 'smoking is strictly prohibited' and spitting on the floors is punishable with a fine of $50 when absolutely no notice is, apparently, ever taken of any breach of these laws? I have from time to time encountered men by the dozen smoking in places where smoking was 'strictly prohibited' and spitting here, there and everywhere goes on incessantly. At the Moose Jaw station a small room is provided for smokers, consequently it is possible for the attendant to keep the general waiting-room a picture of cleanliness, orderliness and comfort."

With its high, vaulted ceiling and echoing stone floors, the Moose Jaw station was mystical, like a cathedral. "People used to go and stand in the station," says a Moose Jaw man. "There were big boards with all the trains listed, where they were going and where they were from. People would just stand and stare at these boards. Every time a train left the conductor in a sonorous voice would reel off the names of all the stations it was going to 'and alllll poooints weeessst.' People thought that was beautiful."

The agent for the CPR and Canada North-West Land Company in Moose Jaw was William Grayson, a young lawyer who also specialized in mortgages and loans. Through a system of foreclosures and judicious purchases from the company he represented, Grayson quickly acquired most of the land in and around Moose Jaw; he used the money he made from interest on his loans to build large business blocks in the downtown area, which he rented out to merchants. By 1900, Grayson had virtually bought out the CPR and the government and was the most powerful man in Moose Jaw.

To protect their investment, both Grayson and Ross ran for public office. Ross, described as "an exceedingly handsome and pleasant young man" who sat on the edge of the wooden sidewalk and smoked with the men in the evenings, was elected to the council of the North-West Territories in 1883. Free with money and booze, especially at election time, Ross was re-elected continuously until he was appointed Commissioner for the Yukon in 1902 and, in 1904, named to the Senate. William Grayson was elected mayor of Moose Jaw for one term in 1893 and served on the school board for 30 years; he was appointed crown prosecutor in 1903 and served almost continuously as city solicitor, a position from which he found it convenient to arrange tax concessions for the Canada North-West Land Company and himself. (CPR and government lands were tax-exempt; Grayson paid no taxes on the one-quarter share owned by the Canada North-West Land Company until 1890, when the town settled for a cash payment of $5,000 and a promise that the company in future would pay its share of the assessment.) The town of Moose Jaw was, in effect, a subsidiary of the Canada North-West Land Company.

Egged on by fierce rivalry with Regina and the fever of inflated expectations which gripped every frontier town in the wake of the CPR, the motley crew of horse traders and moneylenders who formed Moose Jaw's business community engaged in a flurry of investment and construction. Their enthusiasm was kindled by the enormous influx of immigrants who poured into the North-West as a result of the aggressive immigration policy pursued by the Liberal government which had broken the power of the Conservatives in 1896; Moose Jaw's population zoomed from 1,000 in 1901 to 15,000 in 1910. After a fire conveniently destroyed most of Main Street, the downtown core was rebuilt of brick and steel into a miniature version of Winnipeg on the theory that if Moose Jaw looked like a city, it would become one. In their eagerness to keep up-to-date, the coterie of businessmen who formed the Moose Jaw city council were more willing to spend public money than their own; Moose Jaw's urban sophistication was based largely on a massive program of public works.

"Moose Jaw is building up very rapidly now," observes Moose Jaw homesteader George Tuxford in 1904, "and there is quite a gang of men engaged in laying water mains and pipes. It is amusing to see the water cart on the city streets in this hot weather. It goes up one street sprinkling and by the time it returns the street is quite dry again. The council, I see, are beginning to lay Granolithic sidewalk now on Main St. and Moose Jaw proudly boasts one automobile.

"With the installation of waterworks and electric lights this summer, city lots may still be a source of profitable investment. For instance, a lot on Main St. in the main business part that in 1889 could have been purchased for $400 is now asking $4000. Jim Thomson bought five lots to build his livery stable at $200 apiece. He told me these are now assessed at $500. The city is spreading east and west and south on the hill over the creek at a terrific rate."

The taste of the Moose Jaw city fathers ran to the flashy.

In 1911, an electric street railway tootled around an eight-block section of the city to impress parties of real estate prospectors with the glories of downtown Moose Jaw; yet the only street that was paved was Main Street, and it was inlaid with a cobblestone effect of wooden blocks which, in a heavy rain, floated out and drifted away into the creek, where they were used as firewood by the hobos who camped on the bank. So dazzling was the effect of electric lights on Main Street, however, that it was dubbed "the Golden Mile." In addition to these civilized amenities, the civic construction boom included an astonishing number of vast government edifices obtained through the efforts of the prominent Liberal, Senator James Ross.

Instead of paying for these improvements with taxes, the city sold debentures in eastern Canada and Great Britain; in 1912 alone, Moose Jaw floated $1 million in debentures at five per-cent interest. Many of these debentures were purchased by the investors and corporations behind the Canada North-West Land Company. By using money obtained in this manner, Moose Jaw was able to provide modern civic facilities while boasting that the city's tax rate — 12 mills — was the lowest in western Canada. By 1920, Moose Jaw had over $5 million in debenture debt; the annual interest alone was $200,000, or one-fifth of the city's total budget.

To boost the city's sale of debentures, the Moose Jaw Board of Trade launched an intensive campaign of inflated and misleading rhetoric which proclaimed Moose Jaw as "the Wheat City, the Commercial City, the Industrial City of Saskatchewan, the Mecca of Investors, Professional men and laborers of all kinds, the Buckle of the Greatest Wheat Belt in the World, destined to remain for all time one of the greatest cities on the plains...Moose Jaw — proud, rich and prosperous — mighty today but still mightier tomorrow — for the world lies at the door of Moose Jaw and the smile of confidence is on her face." Stated R. A. Krikwood of the Moose Jaw Board of Trade: "A good city is a small city that's certain to grow into a big city; that is where all the easiest fortunes are made." In 1912, ads extolling Moose Jaw's investment opportunities were placed in more than two dozen Canadian and British publications,

and a weekly press release was sent to 70 Canadian newspapers; an article praising Moose Jaw appeared in the
London Illustrated News, and the *Winnipeg Saturday Evening
Post* ran a 14-page supplement; 20,000 copies of an illustrated booklet were printed, 25,000 Moose Jaw postcards
were distributed to citizens to be mailed around the world,
and 10,000 "I Have Faith in Moose Jaw" buttons were
pinned to the lapels of local residents.

Civic enthusiasm triggered a boom in private development.
Robin Hood built a big flour mill in Moose Jaw, and Swifts
opened a meat-packing plant. By 1913, Moose Jaw, which
until 1911 had only a brewery, had a flock of new
industries, including a binder twine company, the Moose
Jaw Tent and Mattress Company, the Western Canada Brush
and Broom Manufacturing Company, the Canadian Incan-
descent Light and Stove Company, the Chemical Soap Company, and the Governor Controlled Metallic Wind Mill Company. The new industries attracted immigrants to Moose
Jaw; swelled by a big influx of American settlers after the
Soo Line to Minneapolis was opened, the population of
Moose Jaw soared to 25,000 in 1912. The demand for housing created a construction boom and wild speculation in
land; building permits topped $5.2 million in 1912, and
downtown property was selling for as high as $2,000 a foot.
The city had 13 banks, which did an average monthly business of $7 million, and 110 real estate companies, many of
which represented outside interests. "Winnipeg firms have
invested heavily in Moose Jaw property," reported *Canada
Magazine.* "One buyer obtained a piece of property in
January for $5000 and sold it in April for $11,200. A Liver-
pool syndicate has secured business property amounting to
$250,000 as well as 800 acres of farm lands close to the city.
The Rex agencies recently sold 320 acres for $100,000 or
approximately $300 per acre. This land, which adjoins the
city, will be placed on the market in England and Eastern
Canada by a Winnipeg syndicate." Since most of the downtown land was taken, the real estate companies speculated
primarily in land on the fringes of Moose Jaw; the biggest
speculator was the city itself.

Anxious to keep up with its advertising, the city of Moose
Jaw embarked on a spree of public investment; over $1

million was spent on water works and beautification, and $750,000 was invested in the construction of a hotel. Eagerly anticipating future growth, the city purchased 320 acres on the south side of the CPR tracks for $225 an acre in 1911. Streets were surveyed and graded and a bridge was built over the tracks to link the new subdivision to the city. A cement gateway was erected at the entrance bearing the name "University Heights." This public investment gave everybody confidence in Moose Jaw. Speculation was solidified in stone: the Presbyterians and Methodists outdid one another building churches, rows of gingerbread Victorian mansions sprouted on the crest of North Hill, and downtown Moose Jaw blossomed into a modest concrete jungle. With its streetcar, electric lights, and 33¼ miles of sidewalks, Moose Jaw was, as the ad said, "The Finest City in Saskatchewan."

Moose Jaw's boom was paid for by the farmers. Once the CPR was in operation, virtually all of its revenue was derived from the business of shipping wheat east and bringing manufactured goods west: the farmers paid the freight both ways. "Everyone knows," said the *Grain Grower's Guide* of 1911, "that the Government has always allowed the CPR to charge the people of the West from 66 to 100 per cent higher rates for the carriage of freight and express parcels than it charges in the East for the same service." High freight rates to eastern markets successfully stifled western industry, and tariffs of 15 to 30 per cent on American goods gave eastern manufacturers a monopoly of the lucrative western trade at inflated prices. "Every shoe that has to be worn on those prairies will be a Canadian shoe," vowed Prime Minister Sir Wilfrid Laurier. Moose Jaw owed its entire existence to the profits made from this trade monopoly. Not only were all Moose Jaw's industries dependent on agricultural production, but the rush of settlers into the West created a captive market of eager consumers. In 1910, more than 10,000 homestead entries were filed in the Moose Jaw land titles office, representing a new rural population of 25,000; an average initial expenditure of $1,000 per family meant a boost of $10 million for the Moose Jaw merchants. Many of these immigrants were Americans who had sold their farms in the United

States and were re-investing their money in Canada; the 133,000 Americans who came to Saskatchewan at the peak of the land rush were worth an estimated $200 million.

Not content with the normal profits from the lucrative immigrant trade, Moose Jaw merchants practiced ruthless extortion. Goods bought on credit were marked up 30 per cent; the money to purchase them was often borrowed from the storekeeper at an interest rate of 12 to 20 per cent. All the storekeepers traded grain for groceries and took a rake-off at both ends. The streets were full of peddlars and horse traders offering deals on second-rate homestead outfits that indigent settlers couldn't refuse; when the homesteader couldn't pay his bill, the goods were reclaimed to be sold again and again. To increase credit purchases, money was monopolized by the lawyers, loan sharks, and privately owned banks. "Money is so scarce," stated George Tuxford during the boom, "that it reminds me of the old days when people here used to declare that there was only one five dollar bill in the city and someone would add 'It's my turn to get it tomorrow.'" With land, livestock, and machinery mortgaged to the hilt and his small patch of broken ground able to yield only a few bushels of wheat, a homesteader was hard pressed to meet even the interest payments on his multifarious debts.

"I have threshed all my crop," Tuxford wrote to his father in the fall of 1893. "After deducting next year's seed and feed it will leave me 800 bushels to sell. At the present price I will net $368. Out of this I am obligated to meet a debt of $1405. This excludes the cost of living. How will I pay the bills? The worry is enough to drive one insane!" Tuxford's father sent him some money, and he proceeded, through a series of complicated financial manoeuvres, to buy off the host of creditors who hounded him on the streets of Moose Jaw.

"I have protection now until February 1895," he wrote jubilantly. "I paid (groceries) Baker $250 and have given him a note for the remainder with his written guarantee not to recover until then. He agrees. Acting on Gordon's advice (he is my lawyer, the agent for the Loan Company and the CPR Land Company) I have paid the mortgage company $100, likewise guaranteeing immunity until February 1895.

I had my payment to the CPR postponed for a year. The
Bank I have reduced to their original amount of $350 also
with a guarantee to run me to February 1895. And I have
paid the note on the rig and harness purchased last spring,
which was repossessed being two months past due. The
Massey-Harris Implement Company agreed to accept $50
until fall. Then I have cleared many smaller bills besides
the wages of my hired hand during threshing. The note on
the horses at the bank has to be renewed every three months
and backed by someone. Tom Francks who sold me the
horses so far has done this. The Bank offers a mortgage on
my horses for the balance of the $350 at 15 per cent
interest."

Bankrupted by this spiderweb of debt, thousands of
settlers were forced to give up their homesteads; during the
ten years of drought that plagued southern Saskatchewan
after the North-West Rebellion, one-third of all the homesteads in the Moose Jaw area were cancelled. Much of the
land fell into the hands of the Canada North-West Land
Company and William Grayson, who subsequently sold it
to new immigrants. Some farmers preferred to stay on the
land as tenant farmers, hoping eventually to pay off the
mortgage; they were encouraged to do so by corporations
like the Colonization Finance Company, a conglomerate of
nine loan companies, and the CPR, which saw the obvious
advantages of a steady rental income. Having acquired a lot
of cheap land through foreclosures, the Moose Jaw merchants attempted to "boom" their property by a flurry of
investment and speculation financed by the usurious profits
they had made by fleecing the settlers; the boom attracted
another flock of immigrants, and the shakedown cycle
repeated itself. "The merchants in Moose Jaw are not
content with profit," stated Tuxford bitterly, "they want
everything!"

The territorial government provided a small amount of
relief in the form of municipal labor — digging wells,
ploughing fireguards, scraping dugouts — but since such
work was awarded on a patronage basis, it enriched party
hacks more than it assisted homesteaders. Many farmers
went to work for the CPR in the winter or migrated to
northern logging camps; some put up hay for the North

West Mounted Police or worked on the telegraph line linking the NWMP post at Wood Mountain with Moose Jaw. A few were reduced to trapping foxes and rabbits for furs and, before the prairie was fenced, small fortunes in bounty money were collected by "wolfers," who ran the wolves down with hounds or poisoned them with carcasses loaded with strychnine. The major quarry was gophers:

W. W. BOLE — DRUGGIST
Drugs, Patent Medicines and Cigars
GOPHER POISON!
Buy Your Strychnine from Bole and Get a Few Good
Hints For Using It.

A box of gopher tails brought a modest bounty. The Moose Jaw Agricultural Fair of 1889 offered $10 for the largest number; the winner brought in 2,446. (May 1 was declared Gopher Day; in 1916, 880 Saskatchewan schools competing for a shield, a medal, and a gold watch produced 500,000 gopher tails.)

Having paid for the civilized comforts of Moose Jaw, where Chinese houseboys served fresh oysters to the horse traders in the big houses on the hill, the homesteaders enjoyed a life of spartan poverty. A family of six could live comfortably on $1 a day. "They used to say that when people came to the West with any capital they had to lose it all before they ever began to succeed," reflects a farm woman who was the second white girl born in Moose Jaw. "There were long periods of drought, bad hail and wind storms and frost and many knew bitterly hard times and there was no kind of relief available, government, city or anything else. I can remember when our principal article of food was what mother called 'thickened milk' made by thickening milk with flour, adding salt and a little sugar and eaten with milk or cream. Our appetites were good and we rather liked this. We seemed to thrive on it although at times it would be a little monotonous. My father always raised some hogs and we had milk and eggs and vegetables when anything at all would grow.

"We knew nothing of other children and when once a year we attended a Sunday School picnic in Moose Jaw it was an occasion long to be remembered. In fact one of these picnics was a liberal education and gave us matters to talk and romance about until the next year. We thought the Moose Jaw children were superior beings living in an enchanted environment and we would pretend that we were different ones that we had met. I remember seeing my first popcorn package at a picnic and getting a ring for a prize and I thought as much of that ring as if it were pure gold. I can remember the first fresh apples we ever saw as up to then our acquaintance had been with the dried variety as a special luxury. Oranges and bananas came later and were a wonderful treat. I can remember the first ripe tomatoes I had ever seen, and each of these discoveries produced an impression that is strong to this day."

When the outbreak of war in 1914 staunched the flow of European immigrants to Moose Jaw, the boom collapsed under its own weight. Whatever money remained in the city was largely in the hands of William Grayson, a sparse, dry man with a clipped beard and cold eyes who was known as a Methodist, a Liberal, and a "gentleman of culture and refinement" who had acquired a valuable art collection. Mr. Grayson was the only Moose Jaw citizen to be written up in *Saskatchewan and its People,* a provincial Who's Who which paid him this accurate tribute: "As Mr. Grayson has accumulated a fortune by his own unaided efforts, having made his way in the world without financial assistance since he was a very young man, he has proven himself to be a barrister and businessman of superior abilities." Yet Grayson's personal fortune represented only a tiny part of the wealth which had passed through Moose Jaw, the flotsam and jetsam of the land rush; the rest had all gone out of the city and out of Saskatchewan. Moose Jaw remained a backwater, a small provincial city which was little more than an overgrown railway town. To makes ends meet, the merchants turned to vice.

Prairie towns have always taken a lenient attitude to crime, especially to the kind that made money. Street brawls and drunkenness were taken for granted, accepted as part of the entertainment which made Saturday night in town a keenly anticipated event in the lives of the neighbourhood farmers. Liquor was forbidden in the North-West until 1905, but Lieutenant-Governor Edgar Dewdney was generous with permits and booze flowed freely in Moose Jaw. "It is quite a common occurrence to see men battered, bruised and bleeding on our streets, while the noise of their drunken revels is heard until long past the hour of midnight," complained the Moose Jaw *Times* in 1892. "I doubt if you can find a town or a village in the whole of Assiniboia where the Liquor Licence Ordinance is being so frequently and grossly violated. There seems to be no limit to the number of offences these licenced rumsellers can commit, and not have a single effort made to have the law enforced." Only 15 liquor offences were brought to court in the ten years between 1888 and 1898; those convicted were fined $5 to $10. The town's attitude was made clear by Mayor Charles Unwin, who said that "any officer should be allowed to use his discretion and not enforce the provisions of the by-laws too stringently where no injury or harm was done to anyone." As far as the Moose Jaw town council was concerned, the police were there to protect property: the most serious crimes were theft, stealing rides on the CPR, and trespassing on CPR property, for which the offenders were sentenced to from ten days' to six months' hard labor.

"The police force is admitted to be the finest in western Canada," stated a 1913 pamphlet. "The Force averages 6 ft. one and ½ inches in height and one hundred and eighty-two pounds in weight. The merchants of Moose Jaw obtain burglary insurance at a reduced rate on account of the efficiency of its police force."

In view of this high reputation, respectable citizens of Moose Jaw became mystified when, after prohibition was put into effect in 1917, several private "clubs" opened up in the back rooms of hotels on River Street, where, it was commonly known, men were able to drink and gamble and cavort with loose women. River Street quickly developed into a roistering slum, two long blocks of sleazy hotels, blind pigs, gambling joints, opium dens, and whorehouses conveniently located one block north of the CPR station. Moose Jaw's reputation spread throughout the West, attracting crowds of winos, hoods, pimps, drifters, and thieves, as well as trainloads of Regina businessmen who regularly came down to Moose Jaw for a night on the town. Moose

Jaw in fact became the sin suburb of Regina, a repository of the capital city's vice and corruption, which enabled Regina to have its fun and keep its reputation clean. A popular oasis in the liquor drought, Moose Jaw soon enjoyed a profitable monopoly on vice, which enabled the city to achieve a stature it had failed to acquire through real estate. After Al Capone was rumored to have holed up on River Street for a week, Moose Jaw was dubbed "the Chicago of the North."

Crime was organized by the Chinese who worked out of little ground-floor cafes in the River Street hotels and boarding houses and rented out upstairs rooms to prostitutes, for whom they procured customers in the cafes. One of the most notorious dives was the Yip Foo block, which had a grocery store in front, an opium den next door, a poker game in the basement and a dozen whores upstairs who solicited customers by waving at them out the windows. "They were normal looking girls," recalls a Moose Jaw newspaperman. "They weren't garish or anything, a little more dashing maybe. They walked up and down River Street. The prostitutes never went on Main Street. There was a deal. As long as they stayed on River Street they didn't get busted. It was a definite district. The townspeople never walked down River Street, respectable citizens stayed on Main Street." River Street was always full of rowdies and drunks; opium was sold openly across the counter in the cafes, and no effort was made to conceal the gambling clubs, but Main Street was safe as a church under the watchful eye of the Moose Jaw police department.

After the false advertisement of real beer provoked a near riot in front of the River Street hotels in 1921, an investigation of the Moose Jaw police department was undertaken. It failed to show any evidence of bribery or payoffs, mainly because the police didn't bother keeping any books; traffic fines and bail money were simply pocketed by the officer on duty or thrown in the desk drawer. At the yearly audit, Chief W. P. Johnson made up the deficit by writing a personal cheque for $1,500 or $2,000. Nobody asked how the chief had acquired a fortune. The police were, in fact, efficient at confiscating illegal booze. "Some was sent to the hospitals," testified the deputy chief, "some was kept at the station, some was given away. Some of the leading citizens had some. They had said they were sick." The mayor decided which of his friends were to receive the free booze, and it was personally delivered to their homes, and to the mayor's own, by members of the police force.

In spite of a couple of spectacular bank robberies, the murder of a CPR constable who was shot dead while checking boxcars, and a continual hullabaloo over the flagrant revelry on River Street, no action was taken against the Moose Jaw police until February 1924, when the chief arrested his entire force for shop-breaking, theft, and possession of stolen goods. Three members of the night patrol had been seen entering a downtown clothing store; a search of their homes turned up a truckload of stolen merchandise ranging from household appliances to automobile tires. All of the policemen had been in the habit of jimmying the locks on the city's stores to pick up shoes or hats or whatever their families needed and when the thefts were reported to the police, they were written off as shoplifting. When the case came to trial, most of the policemen were acquitted; the one constable who confessed was sentenced to two years in the penitentiary.

None of the investigations into River Street vice revealed that most of the brothels and poker dives were owned by Moose Jaw's most prominent citizens, including the leading banker, Arthur Hitchcock, and the widow of a former mayor. William Grayson held two mortgages on the Yip Foo block, one in his own name for $5,000 at nine per cent issued in 1911 and another in the name of the Executors and Administrators Trust Company for $4,000 at ten per cent issued in 1921. Yip Foo was also into the Toronto General Trust Company for $9,000 at eight per cent. Grayson had mortgages on other slum property, including the Bamboo Cafe on River Street, a name which turns up frequently in press crime reports. The financial relationships between the wealthy landlords and their dubious tenants were never explored; they were all, however, very good friends of the chief of police.

The money which circulated around Moose Jaw as a result of the River Street vice boom attracted a large number of fast-buck artists, among them two American organizers for the Ku Klux Klan, who set up the first Klan cell in Moose Jaw in the spring of 1927 and started selling memberships at $13 a head. Racist propaganda was directed against the European and Oriental immigrants, who now formed one-fifth of Saskatchewan's population; Klan spokesman J. H. Hawkins called them "the slag and the scum, the men who eat spaghetti and hotdog and rye bread for lunch or suck on a limburger cheese, the men who came to Canada with tags on them telling their destination," and Dr. G. E. Lloyd, Anglican Bishop of Saskatchewan, referred to them as "these dirty, ignorant, garlic-smelling, non-preferred continentals." A monster Klan rally on the outskirts of Moose Jaw in June 1927 attracted 8,000 people; after an address by the Rev. T. J. Hind, Moose Jaw's leading Baptist minister, a huge cross was burned while Klan members flapped about in white bedsheets. Within six months, the Klan claimed to have 40,000 member in southern Saskatchewan. A form of fundamentalist Protestantism based on a WASP theory of white supremacy, the Klan took a high moral tone that was particularly attractive to civic-minded Moose Jaw reformers. Said the creed: "The Klan believes in Protestantism, racial purity, Gentile economic freedom, just laws and liberty, separatism of church and state, pure patriotism, restrictive and selective immigration, freedom of speech and press, law and order, higher moral standards, freedom from mob violence and one public school." Latching on to the connection between Orientals and vice on River Street, the Klan soon spread the cry through Moose Jaw: "Clean Up River Street!" Seeing a chance to break the hold of the Moose Jaw establishment, or the "River Street gang" as they were called, and to feather their own political nests, Moose Jaw politicians took up the cry, and a wave of reform was unleashed on the city. In spite of the fact that the Klan organizers disappeared with the funds in the fall of 1927, three Klan members were elected to the Moose Jaw city council and in 1929, Klan member James Pascoe was elected mayor of Moose Jaw, a position he held until his death in 1931. By then the Klan was broke and so was Moose Jaw.

The Depression abruptly and completely destroyed Moose

Jaw's prosperity in 1930. Drought and grasshoppers devastated the crops for hundreds of miles around the city, industries closed, 60 per cent of the CPR employees were laid off. The whores and high-rollers of River Street disappeared overnight, replaced by crowds of hungry men seeking relief. Moose Jaw's relief bill in 1932 came to $105,800, half the total revenue collected from taxes; 5,000 people, one-quarter of Moose Jaw's population, were on the dole. Between 1930 and 1936 Moose Jaw gave out $3.1 million in relief; the city paid 40 per cent, or $1.25 million. Ironically, Moose Jaw's reputation for wealth attracted hundreds of unemployed, who formed an Unemployed Union to negotiate with the city council for relief. Dues of ten cents a month entitled a member to play whist in the Unemployed Hall, where transients were allowed to wash up and sleep over one night. "People used to go to the Sally Ann, to the churches and get charity if they could," says Tom Bailey, an organizer for the Communist Party. "You'd bum the bread for a sandwich, a piece of stale cake, a cup of coffee from the merchants. We had a 'bumming squad' who used to go around to the different places, Eaton's, Safeway, to get scraps of food. The best talkers were always on the bumming squad." The most desperate were sent to a big relief camp north of Moose Jaw; the others camped out on the streets and in the CPR station, or hunkered up against the stone walls of the city's public buildings.

Moose Jaw's most urgent problem was not relief but debt. The crash caught Moose Jaw with a crushing public debt of $5 million, most of it in the form of 40- and 50-year city debentures which had been sold in the boom between 1904 and 1914. The bonds had been sold on the basis of a grossly exaggerated civic assessment of $52 million, which had resulted from inflated real estate prices; by the Thirties, Moose Jaw's assessment had shrunk to $14 million and tax revenues diminished accordingly. The city was hard pressed to pay even the $250,000 annual interest on the bonds. By 1932, when half the city's taxes were in arrears, the annual interest on the bonds equalled the total tax income. Moose Jaw's tax base was not strengthened by the CPR exemptions or by the lavish tax concessions which had been used to lure new industries. Since the money from the bonds had been spent to provide deluxe public services for a population which had never materialized, Moose Jaw was stuck with a lot of white elephants; in 1930, the city was still paying for a bridge which had long since been demolished and for an incinerator abandoned in 1917. None of the money invested in University Heights was ever recovered, since the subdivision was never inhabited. Because the city was unable to afford repairs, Moose Jaw's streets and public utilities gradually deteriorated. The city began to look shabby and down-at-heel.

In 1930, Moose Jaw sold its only money-making asset, the Electric Light and Power Plant, to a subsidiary of an American company for approximately $3 million. The street railway was scrapped. In the next six years, all but $735,000 of the money from the sale was used to pay for the debt and to meet the cost of relief. City employees took pay cuts, and operating costs were cut to the bone. When the money was gone, Moose Jaw was bankrupt. The city declared itself in default on its bonds in December 1936 and handed over its civic government to the Local Government Board administrator. It was one of the last Saskatchewan municipalities to give up. "Continuence of the present burden is impossible," stated the council. "Our once busy wholesale district has become a street of almost empty warehouses. There will be no real ability to pay taxes unless there is a general increase in business. We feel that it would be both injudicious and unfair to ask our citizens and our employees to make further sacrifices by way of services and salaries. It would be economic and social folly to allow our public utilities to deteriorate any more. Essential services cannot be reduced below a certain minimum consistent with the economic and social health and the political stability of the community."

Moose Jaw did not get off the hook. The city's major creditors immediately banded together to form the Moose Jaw Debenture Holders' Association and hired a lawyer to wring whatever blood he could out of the turnip. Claiming to represent hundreds of "widows and orphans" in Canada and Great Britain, the Debenture Holders refused to accept any compromise which would force them to take a loss; most prominent among the widows and orphans were the

Great West Life Assurance Company, which owned $108,498 worth of Moose Jaw; Toronto General Trust ($102,511); Canada Life ($100,500); Mutual Life ($69,277); the Brotherhood of Railway Trainmen ($43,500); and the United Church of Canada ($30,500). Moose Jaw remained in receivership for eight years, while the Debenture Holders and the provincial government haggled over the price of settlement. In 1939, it was described by a London newspaperman travelling across Canada with the King and Queen of England as "the unluckiest town in the Dominion."

"Ten years ago," he wrote, "Moose Jaw was a prosperous prairies city. Today it is ruined. Seven years of drought and pestilence have destroyed its wheat crops, its only source of living. For months the people who live on the prairies around Moose Jaw have been collecting pennies for the visit of the King and Queen. They have held jumble sales and whist drives and house-to-house collections. And so Moose Jaw came through. They had only simple little chairs for the King and Queen to sit on instead of thrones and they had only a cheap Oriental rug instead of red plush carpeting; but what they lacked in magnificence they made up in spirit."

In 1945, when it looked as if Moose Jaw's economy was picking up, the city finally agreed to pay its entire debt plus 40 per cent of the interest incurred during the eight years of bankruptcy. The Local Government Board remained in control of Moose Jaw until the entire sum was paid in 1957. Penniless, Moose Jaw was unable to profit from its buoyant postwar industrial boom; it remained as frumpy and bedraggled as it had been before the war began. Flaunting its exhausted charms like an aging River Street whore, Moose Jaw began to tout itself as "The Friendly City," capitalizing on the only asset it had left. Its fate is simply described by George Tuxford:

"How many of the men who made real money during the good years helped to build up the town? Not many. They made their money and took it elsewhere to invest."

Chapter 5
Coalsamao

When the feudal monopoly favored by the CPR and the colonization land companies collapsed in the West, it was replaced by a more efficient commercial cartel, which knew how to take advantage of debt. To encourage the wheat economy, the CPR gave free land to grain companies to build elevators along the tracks; three-quarters of the elevators were owned by five companies, all of them based in the Winnipeg Grain Exchange. In 1897 these companies formed a combine, the North-West Grain Dealers Association, which set the price for grain at every elevator across the West. The farmer's only recourse was either to sell his grain to one of a myriad of street buyers, who usually offered less money, or to barter it with the local merchant for groceries. A farmer could load his grain directly into a boxcar only if he had a full carload and the CPR squeezed out farmers' warehouses by denying them boxcars in the autumn rush. The grain companies cheated the farmers by giving them short weight and downgrading the quality of their grain; the price was always lowest at harvest, when farmers were forced to sell to meet their debts, and highest in the winter, when there was no grain left.

Farmers coped with low prices by increasing production; wheat acreage zoomed from four million acres in 1901 to eleven million in 1911 to 23 million in 1921. In 1918 wheat was Canada's largest dollar value export. Expansion required more land, more livestock, more machinery, all of which was bought on credit against the next year's crop. The investment boom drove the cost of production up, and the resulting glut of grain dragged the price of wheat down. Farmers had no control over either. They were on the wheel; they went into debt in hard times to pull themselves through, they went into debt in good times to expand. By 1932, 81 per cent of Saskatchewan farms were mortgaged on the average of $4,000 per farm. The banks were there for a reason. "I knew everybody in the goddam country and what they made and their dogs and horses and when they drove into town," says Alex McAvoy, who worked for the Royal Bank in Saskatchewan in the Twenties. "I knew his wife and whether she shopped at the co-op. I knew if their land was well worked and if their machinery was well maintained. I loaned millions and only lost eighty dollars. Who the hell do you think made the Royal Bank? It was the customer, the debt customer." The severe Depression of the Thirties has obscured the fact that the prairies have lived in a state of almost chronic depression. Even before 1930, the provincial debt on the prairies was over $300 million, the municipal debt $200 million. Wrote one farmer in the Twenties: "Each dirty little schoolhouse, with its pitiable equipment for the work of literary and vocational instruction, character-building and training in citizenship, is roofed with debentures and plastered with a current loan." The economy of the West is not wheat but usury. The money piled up in magnificent office buildings and stately homes in the East, which the farmers went to gawk at whenever they could scrape up the price of a train ticket.

The most remarkable thing about the western cartel was the farmers' failure to break it. They had overwhelming strength in numbers and a sharp perception of their own menial position in the economic scheme. The flagrant abuses of the CPR and the grain companies roused them to violent anger. "There was incipient rebellion when we organized," wrote W. R. Motherwell, the founder of the Territorial Grain Growers' Association, in 1901. " 'It's too late for organization; it's bullets we want,' the men were saying. But we really didn't know what we wanted; we were in despair." Farm leaders like Motherwell, articulate Englishmen schooled in the rhetoric of Ruskin and Carlyle, flayed the eastern landlords with their tongues, exposing the exorbitant profits of the "pushful pirates" (the CPR paid out $220 million in dividends to shareholders between 1910 and 1920) and bitterly protesting the institutionalized rip-off of the farmers. Grass-roots organizations — the Patrons of Industry, the Grain Growers, later farm unions and the Progressive Party — sprang up across the prairies, demanding free trade, equal freight rates, and an end to monopoly. In 1902, the Grain Growers successfully prosecuted the CPR at Sintaluta, Saskatchewan, for failing to provide boxcars for the farmers' elevator; the railway was fined $50 and costs. In 1905, Sintaluta farmer E. A. Partridge was sent to spy out the Winnipeg Grain Exchange. A feisty radical with a muckraker's eye for corruption and a wicked tongue, Partridge, in a brilliant stroke of one-upmanship, organized a farmers' co-op, the Grain Growers' Grain Company, and bought a seat on the exchange for $2,500. The Grain Growers were immediately expelled from the exchange, accused of having offended its "honor and dignity" by distributing patronage dividends. The Grain Growers reorganized as a joint stock company, but the exchange still refused to admit them; to avoid the law, it reformed as a voluntary club without a charter. But the cartel was broken; the Grain Growers' Grain Company was an enormous success and rapidly acquired the lion's share of the farmers' business. It was, however, just another company. It ended the worst abuses, but it did not change the system. Its failure forced the farmers to establish the wheat pools in another attempt to gain control over prices and markets; the pools in turn have been absorbed into the free enterprise ethic of the grain trade.

One after the other, farmers' populist movements have collapsed on the verge of success, mysteriously ruptured by scandal or destroyed by internal disputes, and their eloquent leaders suddenly turn up as tame cabinet ministers or senators in the camp of the Liberal enemy. Prairie politics has always been dirty. The old parties were machines well oiled with patronage and greased with bribes, serving primarily to promote and defend corporate investment, with the government acting, said E. A. Partridge, as "partial Umpire in the game of Grab." In a debt-ridden prairie constituency, political support was easily purchased with money or jobs, which were always plentiful, since pork-barrelling extended down to the level of game warden, heavy horse judge, and superintendent of neglected children. (The Patrons of Industry collapsed in 1896, when one of its leaders was found to be travelling on a CPR pass, and the president was pensioned off as a provincial inspector of

noxious weeds.) A new cabinet minister was swamped with
thousands of pitiful begging letters from his constituents:
"I would like to ask you not to forget the members (especially myself) of the old guard when distributing the spoils,"
wrote a Manitoba farmer to the minister of agriculture,
Valentine Winkler, in 1915. "I spent a good many years in
the active service of the party and would like to get a
position. I am qualified to fill almost any position." Distributed as a form of welfare and pension plan, patronage
built up an efficient and authoritarian system of government
in which public office could be purchased by the rich, who
then consolidated their position by payoffs; dynasties were
established in which political office was handed down from
father to son as a right of birth. Prairie governments lasted
a very long time, until they eventually collapsed under the
weight of their own corruption. (The most sensational
smash was the rout of the United Farmers of Alberta by
Social Credit in 1935, after the premier was put on trial for
seducing his teen-age secretary.) Institutionalized wealth
and power made it easy for the old line parties to intimidate
people who were financially dependent — party bagmen
were usually the local merchants and horse traders — and
to undermine agrarian movements; an offer to instigate
popular reforms through the vehicle of the party machine
was one which most farm leaders were unable to refuse, so
that between 1900 and 1930, the Liberals swallowed almost
all the prairie radicals and the entire Progressive Party.
Reforms were forgotten.

Betrayal by the traditional parties pushed grass-roots
politics to the left and right, and disgust with political graft
and deceit gave the new movements a moralistic, apocalyptic
passion: "Bible Bill" Aberhart preached Social Credit into
power in Alberta not because the people had suddenly
turned into religious fanatics but because, in a time of
poverty and disillusionment, he restored their political faith.
Whether anarchist or Communist, the extreme, revolutionary
nature of prairie politics is a universal response to an
economic system people feel is unjust. The logical outcome
is a movement of national liberation.

The West has been threatening to secede from Confederation ever since it joined, although talk of separatism has,

until recently, been suppressed as subversive. The separatist manifesto was written in 1925 by E. A. Partridge as part of his book *A War on Poverty*, an extraordinary diatribe, part impenetrable verbiage, part brilliant analysis, which became an underground classic of western Canadian literature and made Partridge, dismissed by the establishment as a madman, a prairie hero in the tradition of Riel.

Rejecting Confederation as a "cold-blooded business proposition, a confidence game," Partridge predicted that Canada would shortly break into three parts, with both the West and the Maritimes splitting away from central Canada. "Confederated Canada," he chortled, "will pass away, unwept, unhonored and unsung." Partridge loathed the jingoistic "God Bless the Royal Family" kind of corporate nationalism which justified poverty and repression in the name of loyalty. "Patriotism," he said, "is surely the last and best refuge of the scoundrel manufacturer." In the West, Partridge proposed to set up a kind of Platonic Republic, a "co-operative commonwealth" called Coalsamao, which would have no taxes, no rent, no debt, no profits, no interest, no banks, no politicians, no lawyers. (The name is a combination of the first two letters of each province plus a slice of northern Ontario. It is pronounced Co-al-sa-*ma*-o.) All property, including land, would be held communally and wealth would be shared. People would live in camps, or communes, of 3,500 to 7,000 residents; each camp would be economically self-sufficient and self-governing. The state would be governed by a "high court of control" of 25 members elected annually. Everyone would wear a simple uniform; houses, cars, and other consumer goods would be standardized and the state would provide medicare and an old age pension. Puritan, agrarian, and militaristic, Partridge's ideal state bears a remarkable resemblance to the Maoist communal system which was to emerge in China 25 years later; in western Canada, Coalsamao provided the ideological foundation and the name for a revolutionary attempt at democratic socialism, the Saskatchewan CCF.

Yet in spite of almost 23 years of socialist government since 1944, Saskatchewan has become one of the poorest provinces in Canada, the West remains in Confederation, and the provincial premiers, three of them NDP, continue

to complain to Ottawa about freight rates, tariffs, and the
arrogance of the CPR. The West has no history, because
everything has remained the same. In spite of overwhelming
popular support, both Social Credit and the CCF proved
unable or unwilling to make basic changes in the corporate
system. They have been betrayed by the farmers themselves.

The homestead survey, by isolating farmers psycholo-
gically and economically, made it virtually impossible for
them to establish a collective identity. Each man on his own
little plot of land was locked in combat with his neighbours
in a struggle which only the ruthless survived. To a peasant
people emigrating from essentially feudal countries, the gift
of free land was in itself revolutionary. To them land
ownership meant not only great wealth but also social
prestige and autocratic political power. Every immigrant
envisaged himself as a landlord, a man of property who
would, in turn, control other men, the founding father of a
political dynasty, an aristocrat whose children or grandchildren would, through his toil, be freed from labor. The
trick was to acquire as much land and as much money as
possible as quickly as possible. This was the Western Dream.
It was irresistible. Although people of similar racial and
national backgrounds settled in ethnic pockets on the
prairies, the individual homestead destroyed the ancient
European village pattern and eroded the social structure on
which their cultural traditions had been built. Farmers
became Victorian free enterprisers. Political action on the
prairies grew out of resistance not to big business but to
monopoly. The farmers' anger was directed not against the
companies but against government regulations which gave
eastern business an unfair advantage and hindered their
own ability to make a dollar. Farmers took their stand
firmly in favor of free trade. Their position was entrenched
by the Liberal rhetoric of the *Winnipeg Free Press*, which
was owned by Sir Clifford Sifton who, as minister of the
interior, was responsible for initiating the mass immigration
to the West. The *Free Press*, which, oddly, enjoyed a virtual
monopoly of rural circulation, attacked any attempt at
collective action as evidence of "Bolshevism" and to the
best of its ability attempted to keep the farmers if not within
the fold of the Liberal Party, at least firm believers in the

capitalist ethic. Through the extraordinary influence of its editor, John Dafoe, who dominated the paper from 1901 to 1944, the *Free Press* promoted a romantic, bucolic image of the Independent Farmer, a man with windburned face and brawny arms who, although simple and without much education, fed the world and provided the moral sinew of the nation. Poor but proud, the Independent Farmer said little, worked hard and thankfully accepted whatever material reward chanced to come his way. It was an image universally accepted by farmers across the prairies. The ethic was put to me by a Saskatchewan farmer in 1971: "A man's obligation to society isn't that much. He's gotta raise his family and hold his end up."

Farmers' acceptance of the economic status quo as a way of life was reinforced through the school system; as part of its abbreviated and haphazard education, it taught rural children to recite the Country Boy's Creed:

"I believe that the Country which God made is more beautiful than the City which man made; that life out-of-doors in touch with the earth is the natural life of man.

"I believe that work is work wherever we find it but that work with Nature is more inspiring than work with the most intricate machinery.

"I believe that the dignity of labor depends not on what you do but on how you do it; that opportunity comes to a boy on the farm as often as it does to a boy in the city, that life is larger and freer and happier on the farm than in the town, that my success depends not upon my location but upon myself — not upon my dreams but upon what I actually do, not upon luck, but upon pluck.

"I believe in working when you work and playing when you play and in giving and demanding a square deal in every act of life."

Farmers' faith in free enterprise was justified by the booms which periodically hit the West when high wheat prices coincided with a bumper crop. These fabulous years — 1915, 1940-45, 1951 — are etched on the prairie, because that's when all the new farmhouses were built. Since the most spectacular booms have been caused by war, farmers tend to be patriotic. "The war has been the salvation of Saskatchewan," declared Premier C. A. Dunning in 1917.

"At its outbreak men viewed the situation with alarm but the Province and its people are more prosperous than ever before. The war has brought ruin and desolation to all the countries engaged in the war; it has brought money to you and me." Influenced by wartime propaganda, farmers tend to view the production of wheat not only as a sacred duty but as a moral obligation in the interests of freedom.

The boom and bust cycle of prairie agriculture has turned farmers into gamblers, eternal optimists willing to endure years of privation in the expectation that, next year, they will hit it big and live happily ever after. Rural society runs like a poker game. The farmers hoard and bluff and play their lives close to the chest, suspicious, selfish, isolated. As one farmer expressed it: "Our whole system makes people tightfisted. The good boy is the boy who saves his pennies in the hope that some day he'll make the other fellow do the work and ride on his back." Farmers don't fight the system, because they believe in it.

Chapter 6

The Industrial Revolution

The western dream dies hard. Everywhere I went in the summer and winter of 1971, I heard the story of the rich farmer. "Poor? Whaddya mean, poor?" it would go. "Those farmers have got so much money they don't know what to do with it! Oh, sure they whine, farmers are always bitching about something, but look, they're driving new cars every year. And they don't talk about the $50,000 they got stashed away in the bank. Why I know this fellow...." And there follows an account of some local Midas. If this man can be found, it usually turns out that he sold his land in the big boom eight years ago, or he's $100,000 in debt, or he owns a brewery on the side.

The average prairie farmer earned $4,500 in 1971. That was a good year. In 1970, a Manitoba farmer cleared $2,300; *Crap* in Alberta, the land of legendary wealth, he made $4,200.

A Manitoba family of four trying to live on $2,300 was making 60 per cent of what they would get if they sold the farm and went on welfare. In that same year, an urban industrial worker in Canada was making $6,595 and a construction worker earned $8,692. The Manitoba farmer has an average of $55,000 invested in his farm; with an income of $2,300 he is making only about four per-cent return on his money; he would be better off selling the farm and putting his money in a savings account.

Two-thirds of farmers on the prairies are poor; the number is steadily growing. There is a very small elite — about seven per cent — who own more than $100,000 worth of land and equipment and are, in farming terms, considered rich. These are usually corporate, agribusiness farmers. They produce most of the food and make most of the money.

Not only are farmers' incomes inadequate, but their financial position in relation to the rest of the economy has slipped drastically. In 1971 prairie farmers made less money than they did in 1961, yet the cost of living had climbed 40 per cent. The cost of goods farmers buy (machinery, fertilizer, weed spray) increased 23 per cent between 1965 and 1971; during the same period the price of wheat dropped 30 per cent. Farmers actually earned about half what they made in 1961.

crop

The cost of food in Canada has gone up more than 34 per cent since 1962, but the profit has not been passed on to the farmers. Farmers, in fact, are getting a dwindling portion of the food dollar. Of the $386 each Canadian spent on food in 1971, farmers got $129; processors and retailers took $257. A farmer got 23 per cent of the price of a loaf of bread in 1949; now he gets nine per cent. Canadians are also importing more food. Agriculture now accounts for only eight per cent of Canada's export trade.

Although a farmer may sell $40,000 or $50,000 worth of produce, expenses eat up 75 per cent of his earnings; 20 years ago the cost of production was only 40 per cent of his gross income. No matter how much a farmer sells or how much he is paid for it, his income is dwindling steadily. In 1971 prairie farmers earned a gross income of $2.5 billion; their net return after expenses was $985 million. In 1972, with the same volume of sales, their income dropped to $918 million. Profits made in periods of boom are mostly cancelled out by rising costs: though the price of grain, beef, and pork was rising in the spring of 1973, the cost of production zoomed up by ten per cent in three months.

Most farmers are "land poor," with enough machinery for three farms and $60,000 tied up in assets which produce an inadequate income. Farmers do not make up for it by living off the land. It is not cheaper to live on a farm. Prices in rural stores are higher than in the city; home-grown produce which the family eats costs money to raise as well as the profit they could make by selling it. When the value of home consumption is added in, farm families spend more on meat than city families do. Farmers can raise their own vegetables, but they need a freezer to store them in; they can deduct two-thirds of their car expenses from income tax, but they drive 15 miles to the store. Farmers pay no taxes on their house and yard, but they pay between $1,000 and $2,500 a year on the rest of their land. Farmers smoke and drink and pay as much for luxuries as anyone else. Rural people live at city prices.

Farmers are, however, richer than people who live in the smaller towns and villages. In Manitoba, the average wage in 1961 was $4,816. Winnipeg people earned $5,874, farmers made $3,538, and villagers (in centres with less than 1,000 population) earned $3,378. The smaller the town, the poorer it is. Rural people in Manitoba make up 43 per cent of the population, but they earn only 30 per cent of the income and pay just 20 per cent of the income tax. In even the wealthiest areas, income is well below the provincial average. Because farmers measure themselves against the standards of the local village, they consider themselves to be well-off, yet even a well-to-do farmer earns less than the average urban worker. Rural people are unaware of how prosperous city people have become. To a small town garage owner who clears $3,000 a year, a farmer who makes $5,000 is rich; $10,000 is still regarded as a spectacular income in the country, yet to the urban middle class it's the borderline of poverty.

Rural poverty is taken for granted. Nobody thought it odd that Gordon Taylor didn't get electricity until 1955, although agriculture accounted for 80 per cent of Saskatchewan's wealth. Sixty-five per cent of rural Manitoba homes were still without running water in 1961; half were without central heat. Bowsman, Manitoba, burned its biffies in 1967 as a Centennial celebration; some towns don't have running water yet. Although agriculture has provided the bulk of prairie prosperity, rural people have not profited from it, in spite of the fact that until recently all three provincial governments were dominated by rural politicians. Rural poverty is, as the politicians are fond of saying, a way of life. Farmers, says Wheat Board Minister Otto Lang, are receiving noneconomic benefits to make up for their lack of money, such as "independence, fresh air, quiet and privacy and the intimacy of neighbourliness."

How do farmers survive? They eat plain food and shop in the bargain basement. The wife gets a job. Then they take out a loan at the bank. Canadian farmers are $4.5 billion in debt — an average of $12,000 per farm. The debt has tripled in ten years. Seventy per cent of the money loaned to farmers is short-term credit at 10.8 per-cent interest; only 11 per cent of the loans are farm improvement capital. Farmers are borrowing to stay alive. By mortgaging their land, they have almost unlimited access to credit; if the bank turns them down, finance companies are glad to see them. Credit enables farmers to drive big cars and to keep up a respectable front in the middle of a depression; many of them are, in fact, working for the bank. Their debts exceed their assets, and their monthly payments consume the bulk of their income. As long as the farmer keeps working, the banks are satisfied. Foreclosures are few.

Farmers were brought to the West to grow cheap food for eastern industry and to provide a market for manufactured goods. They were simply industrial laborers whose menial work and investment in machinery enabled industry to thrive and expand. Rendered increasingly obsolete by the gradual automation of agriculture, farmers are now being pushed off the land by a deliberate federal government policy of depopulation which, if carried through, will place all Canadian agriculture in the hands of a corporate cartel. The West is in the grip of an industrial revolution which is replacing people with machines. The revolution is being accomplished by encouraging farmers to eliminate themselves.

Rural depopulation began in 1945, when the arrival of the rubber-tired tractor marked the end of the farm as a place to live and the beginning of the farm as a place to make money. People began to speak of agriculture as an industry: the watchword was efficiency. Farmers were persuaded that a large, highly mechanized operation would lower their costs and yield greater profits. Smaller, older farmers were urged to sell out. Expansion triggered a boom which drove up the price of land and machinery; the subsequent glut of wheat knocked the bottom out of the grain market. Farmers' costs went up while prices went down. Thousands of farmers left the land; those who remained were poorer than before.

To pull the prairies out of periodic slumps caused by

overproduction, the federal government has instigated artificial booms by making cheap credit available for further expansion. Between 1964 and 1969, the federal Farm Credit Corporation loaned $309 million to Saskatchewan farmers to expand their farms; the price of land shot up from $40 to $83 an acre. Many farmers sell out to take advantage of the good prices; in the ensuing slump, others are forced out through bankruptcy. The FCC has denied loans to marginal farmers in order to ease them out of business. It has also manipulated credit to force farmers into products such as hogs, chickens, and eggs, thereby glutting each market in turn and pushing farmers into a cycle of investment far beyond their needs or resources: a Saskatchewan farmer's acreage has increased 60 per cent since 1941, but his capital investment has gone up 900 per cent.

Having sunk all their money into land and machinery, farmers come to depend on periodic expansion booms as a guaranteed pension. When a farmer wants to retire, he has to sell out, and it's in his interest to sell in a period of inflation, when land prices are high. If his son wishes to inherit the family farm, he has to buy it (except in Saskatchewan, where he can rent it back from the government). He borrows the money, and so goes deeply into debt to support his parents in respectable old age. Prairie farmland is refinanced every generation, and at every turn of the wheel the price goes up; what the homestead grandfather paid $10 for will cost his grandson $100 an acre. The winners are the people who put up the money.

Agriculture is not an industry. Industry controls its production and sets its prices; farmers do not. Western agriculture remains colonial and Victorian; farmers sell on an unpredictable world market governed by natural disasters and international politics, but they buy from a small, tightly-controlled cartel of multinational corporations. The techniques of mass production and automation, which are profitable for industry, are ruinous for agriculture; ruthless competition has impoverished farmers and given corporations the capital to impose an even tighter grip on the western economy.

Between 1945 and 1965, Canada's farm population was cut in half; it continues to shrink by 10,000 farms a year.

The federal government expects that by the end of the century, two-thirds of Canada's farms will have vanished and those that are left will be corporations. Agribusiness companies, which have traditionally lived off the institutionalized poverty of the prairies, are now finding it more profitable to move directly into production; in the process, they reduce the farmer from middleman to hired hand. Corporate expansion is being encouraged by the federal Liberal government, which continues to promote the myth of efficiency. (In 1971, the Liberals came up with the Farm Adjustment and Resource Mobility Plan, which proposed to push three-quarters of Canadian farmers off their land and sell their property to private corporations.) Although provincial governments have through legislation stopped corporate take-over, they have failed to break the cycle of debt and depopulation. As farmland falls into fewer and fewer hands, it becomes increasingly susceptible to conglomerate control. If the present trend continues, the economy of the prairies will revert eventually to the kind of corporate monopoly Sir John A. Macdonald and the colonization companies originally envisioned in the West.

This book is about the people who have stayed. They are the hard core — tough, reactionary, archetypal people whose lives have been determined by the scramble to survive in an alien land and a cruel society. "We were isolated from the rest of the world," recalls a farmer. *"The Free Press Weekly Farmer* was our only means of communication. There were no daily papers. I can remember listening to Lorne Greene read the ten p.m. news on the CBC. That was a big thing. The old man really laid down the law. There was no fuckin' noise in the house when he was listening to the ten o'clock news!" This tenuous connection with the outside world has made most prairie communities intellectually arid, deserts of ancient clichés sticking through the sand of conventional wisdom. "I envy my parents," says the farm boy. "They ran a closed shop. They didn't have to deal with all these alien thoughts coming into their kid's head." Intellectual isolation in rural areas has become more extreme as the exodus has sucked all the young people out for the last 25 years and no new people have entered the community to replace them. Most rural people now draw their impressions of the outside from television, a shadowy contact which gives them a flamboyant and romantic conception of the world. Rural people are suspicious of outsiders, especially city people, self-conscious, on guard against a snub or an insult. Experience has taught them to be defensive, to mistrust politics, and to dislike government.

The style of contemporary rural society has been set by diminution — of people, money, power, youth — and its rules are the rigid routines of energetic people hoarding a diminishing stock of political and cultural currency. Rural people have lost caste. Like the Taylors, who are gradually withdrawing from conventional community activities, many prairie people no longer see themselves as a prosperous petite bourgeoisie, men of property and civic responsibility, but as working-class people without land or independence. This new perception makes the old landed gentry routines seem obsolete and irrelevant, trivial, sometimes absurd. The people themselves often appear exaggerated, eccentric. Small towns are full of the mad and the lonely, idiots, saints, cripples, hermits, the unwanted and the antisocial, the too young and the too old. It's a society of nickels and dimes, where money is important because of its absence and the personality of each community is determined by the people's extraordinary attempts to make a living out of scraps of financial leftovers. Rural communities are oldfashioned, almost mythical, governed by ancient customs of class, charity, and parsimony; the vitality of each community can be dated from the last big event that remains in the collective memory. Some communities are living, some dying, but all are nostalgic, with a remembrance not so much of things past as of things which might have been.

Chapter 7

Miami

Biff! Bang! Balligator! Chick-a-wa-duck!
Miami! Miami! Keep it up! Keep it up!

(Miami, Manitoba, school yell)

The RCMP were furious. Their investigation of the explosion was getting nowhere. Corporal McClare was shocked. "Our investigation is being met with constant humor," he told the press stiffly. "It's very obvious that nobody wants to help us."

Someone had blown up the hill west of Miami, Manitoba, that the Manitoba Motorcycle Club used for its annual hill climb. The hill was not exactly demolished, but dynamite had made a hole five feet wide and three feet deep in the side of it. Sixteen additional, undetonated sticks of dynamite had been found planted in the hillside. The Miami police inspected the hole and turned the case over to the Mounties, who called in their demolitions squad. The hill climb was cancelled. Miami was pleased. The local people answered all the Mounties' questions with wisecracks and loud guffaws. The mystery of the hole remained unsolved. "This is ridiculous!" snapped Cpl. McClare, who took the hole very seriously. "Most of the people we've questioned so far say they're disappointed the person who set the blast didn't do a better job!"

The motorcycle club was offended. It had used the Miami hill for 40 years. The bikers were polite young mechanics from Winnipeg, who transported their motorcycles tenderly on trucks and cared for them like precious relics. For one weekend every September, they bunked in at the Grandview Hotel in Miami and patronized the beer parlor and poolroom. The town appreciated their business, and the local farmers brought their children to watch the big bikes gun up the steep incline full throttle. But last year there had been an incident. A bunch of greasers in boots and black jackets had come up from the States and set the town on its ear, roaring around the streets throwing beer bottles and making rude remarks to the widows. On Saturday night they had taken over the poolroom. They shoved the local kids out of the way and shouted obscenities at the crippled proprietor. Then they moved over to the beer parlor, where one of the hoods transfixed the Saturday night crowd by pouring gunpowder out of a bullet and fiddling with his matches. The evening culminated in an orgy up on the hill with, according to subsequent rumors, gunshots, knifings, and murders. On Sunday morning the greasers had breakfast at May's Diner on the highway, threw the food in May's face, and stomped out without paying. May and Miami were goggle-eyed. It is, as local residents like to say, a quiet little town.

The following June, the RCMP published a warning in the local paper advising that the Hell's Angels of California were coming to Manitoba to attend rock festivals and hill climbs. "They are known to terrorize small towns and to leave before police can arrive," said the bulletin. "They travel in from different directions, converging on a town and making liquor outlets and young girls their prey." The Hell's Angels did not arrive in Miami, but many businessmen quietly made arrangements to close early or leave town the night before the hill climb. Nobody heard the explosion, although somebody reported a sonic boom. The hole was found the next morning by a hired man. The person who set the dynamite considerately left a little placard beside the hole saying: "Caution — Undetonated Explosives May Be In This Area." It was signed "Cit. Comm."

A $200 reward posted by the motorcycle club failed to turn up the culprit. Dynamite, after all, can be bought for $25 a case at many rural hardware stores, and most farmers have a few sticks lying around. "These people don't have too much to do with the police," Cpl. McClare hinted darkly. "They like to handle things themselves." The CBC did a television documentary about the hole, but everyone interviewed flatly denied knowing anything about a citizens' committee. "If it had been me," cackled one farmer, "I'd

have filled that hole up with liquid pig manure and let 'em
ride through that!"

Miami was embarrassed. It's not that the village is down on
law and order. They just don't like hippies, greasers, bums,
or delinquents. They also enjoy a practical joke, especially
at somebody else's expense. They laughed at the hole, but
they were not amused by the publicity, which depicted the
town as a roistering den of vigilantes. There was, of course,
a citizens' committee, but it was a local sore spot and
nobody wanted to go into that. Scandal, in Miami, is
something that happens somewhere else.

Miami is a respectable town, a tiny cluster of white
gingerbread houses 70 miles southwest of Winnipeg on a
minor highway that comes to a dead end 100 miles farther
west. A big billboard that says "EAT — at Bird's ESSO"
and, farther down the road, a red Coca Cola sign that
indicates May's Lunch and Texaco station are the only
spots of color, thrown out like fishhooks to catch the odd
traveller. Bird's is just the local garage, a white shed rising
out of the mud with a heap of ancient cars and wagons
piled up behind and, off to one side, a grubby hamburger
stand owned by a former Miami policeman who was fired
for driking in the pub in his uniform. Bird has gone into
Renault cars on the side; three shiny red and yellow bugs
are lined up along the highway. He's done a good business
among the retired farmers in town, who still like to drive
downtown even though the village is only five blocks long
and three blocks wide. Everybody drives to work in Miami.
A car is a flag signalling where you are. Without a car in a
small town, you're invisible.

May's Lunch is up for sale. No sign is posted, but May's
husband Roy hands out illustrated brochures to all the
customers. May and Roy Dave have had the coffee shop
and gas pumps for 15 years and they're ready to retire.
"Yes! Business is growing and becoming too much for us!"
says the brochure. It's not very convincing. You can sit in
May's cozy plywood diner for an hour before a car will
turn in. The business is mostly local men stopping in for a
Coke or coffee or a plate of french fries. Along with the

food, May and Roy provide a running commentary on every event, great or small, that has happened in Miami in the last 50 years, complete with analysis, opinion, and brief character sketches of all the people involved. May's is one of the key gossip centres in Miami, because they get the news from the outside first. Truckers roost in for lunch like carrier pigeons, bringing the latest tidbits from Swan Lake or Brandon, and the grapevine of telephone linemen and construction crews carries news up and down the highway all day. In their smiling, polite way May and Roy discreetly pump all strangers as to where they're from, where they're going, and what they're doing in Miami. In a small village where very little ever happens, people are news and a stranger is an event. The diner is a tiny, homemade building with half a dozen stools at the counter and little arborite tables. A sign on the wall says: "No Cheques Please!" Roy and May live 20 feet away in a small white cottage with a hand pump over the well outside. They're asking $35,000 for the diner, the house, a garage, an empty machine shed, two antique gas pumps, and two acres of land.

South of the highway, the land rolls away in lush folds and ripples, a quilt of coal-black earth with patches of acid green that change slowly to yellow in August. Every year the pattern is a little different. Wild grass by the road waves like hair in the wind; the ditches are full of dandelions and thistles as big as bushes. In the glare of noon, the light is so pure that the leaves on every tree two miles away are as clear and sharp as the blade of grass at my feet. It's the light of Italian painters in those tiny crystal landscapes that stretch away to infinity in perfect miniaturized clarity. Five miles away the fields dissolve to water, an undulating mirage in which the farmsteads with their windbreaks float like islands in a stream. In spring the blue flax blooms like patches of fallen sky, and the air is full of the sweet smell of lilacs and freshly cut grass. At night the highway reeks with the perfume of squashed skunks, and fat bugs plop against the windshield. The darkness is thick with the sound and smell of growing. Summer is a miracle. The bare frozen earth turns green overnight as the crops pop out of the ground with an almost audible "sproing," like bed-springs; they grow and ripen, ready for harvest, in ten weeks. Summer on the prairie is passionate and selfish, a desperate grab for warmth and life.

Miami's two white grain elevators stick out against the green backdrop of trees along Tobacco Creek, which borders the town to the north. There used to be more elevators, people say, but they were torn down long ago, leaving vacant patches of tall grass by the CNR tracks. Miami's population is a little less than 400. People have come and gone, but the town has remained the same since it was built in 1889, when the CNR came through. Miami still has only one main street, a long gravel road running parallel to the railway with all the shops facing the tracks like soldiers standing at attention. Like all prairie towns, Miami was designed for the convenience of the railway. Main Street is exactly as long as the average freight train. Goods were unloaded from the train into vacant lots or sheds next to the tracks and then lugged across the street to the stores. Ideally, the position of the boxcar carrying a storekeeper's merchandise would perfectly match the location of his store on the street. Too cheap to pay the drayman, most merchants carried their own stuff or hired the local barflies for the price of a glass of whiskey or a plug of chewing tobacco. It was in the merchants' interest to snuggle up as close to the tracks as they could. They could not, however, build on the side of the street the tracks were on because that land was owned by the railway.

Miami's tallest building is the two-storey Grandview Hotel at the west end of town near the CNR station. The Grandview used to be three stories, but it has shrunk with the commercial traffic. The tiny old rooms are neat and clean; most of them have been closed off and turned into a residence for the owner, who makes his living from tending bar in the beer parlor downstairs. The rest of Miami's single row of shops are small frame buildings, some with false fronts, some little more than sheds. It's hard to tell them apart because, except for the Bank of Commerce, which is dull yellow, they're all painted white with maroon trim and some don't bother with signs. There's no need to, because there's only one of everything in Miami — one bakery, one meat market, one hardware store, one church — and everybody knows where they are. Most of the signs are hand-painted wooden boards, worn and weathered, but all the proprietors are known by name anyway — Vern's Cafe, Moorey's store, Westaway's drugstore — and most of them have been there forever. The street, which for a reason everyone has forgotten is called Norton Avenue, has seen one or two coats of asphalt, but the mud has quickly taken over again, pitching and heaving against the frail buildings in great waves. At night, only the cheap neon sign over the Grandview Hotel is illuminated, and half the letters are burnt out. Three or four dim streetlights are spotted along the entire length of the street. The wind hums through the wires and through the tinsel Christmas decorations left up from last year. Even the new buildings look old. The stores do not share common walls; a tiny gap of two or three feet is left between stores and screened from the street by a white picket fence. Intended as protection against fire, the gaps fill up with weeds and scrap paper and give the main street a snaggle-toothed look. Because few of the stores have basements, they quickly lean and sag, each little box tilting at a slightly different angle. Every store has venetian blinds. In the afternoons, when the blinds are drawn against the sun, they look closed, gone out of business. It's a shock to open a door and find a man, snug as a snail in the gloom, ready to sell you a roast or a cheese or a pair of Stanfield's jockey shorts.

Miami is a neat, clean town. Everybody says that. They've been saying it since 1909, when the school yearbook stated, "Nowhere would one find a neater or a cleaner town." The people are very proud of the town. The streets are wide and level, covered with fine gravel and shaded by large, stately trees. The boulevards, like the lawns, are neatly mowed. There are no weeds in Miami. The old brick houses with their verandas and carved cornices and weather vanes are well-kept, trim, and shiny with white paint; their tidy lawns are enclosed by little iron or picket fences. Almost every house has a nameplate by the front door — A. C. Orchard, A. Moreton, J. Murray — which is odd for such a tiny village, where everybody knows everybody else and the houses don't bother with numbers. "The hardware dealer

got in a big stock of nameplates about 1955," says J.
Murray, scratching his head. "I guess they were all the thing
then." The names are different, but all the plates are the
same. Some shabbier houses are hidden discreetly behind a
screen of trees or sleep beneath a tangle of ancient hawthorn
hedge. The houses are decaying like old wedding cakes, but
they still look elegant, picturesque. There are no shacks in
Miami. People here have good taste. Pink plastic flamingos,
which are very big in Plum Coulee, do not walk Miami
gardens.

Miami is proud of the countless awards it has won from
the Manitoba Good Roads Association for being the best-
kept village in the province. Its crowning triumph is the
Miami Citizens' Park, a sliver of land near the tracks where
the CNR section house used to be. The park was built by
the retired municipal reeve, Lorne Kennedy, who lives
across the street. Mr. Kennedy's own yard is clipped and
trimmed and weeded and filled with a whole population of
painted wooden gnomes and a stone wishing well. When he
ran out of space in his own yard, Mr. Kennedy moved across
the road to the vacant lot. With money provided by the
village, he installed a cookhouse and a picnic table, built a
shuffleboard court and a horseshoe pitch, and ran up a
Canadian flag. He collected and painted a lot of litter barrels, put in a Men and Ladies, and erected an ornamental
steel windmill he'd found on a farm. There's a wooden box
in the park provided with a guest book, and there's another
wooden box with a padlock for donations. Everything is
shiny with paint and neat as a pin. The name of the park is
spelled out in round whitewashed stones set in a bed of red
and white petunias.

Every day Mr. Kennedy can be found in his park, a thin,
stooped, woodland deity, clipping, watering, weeding, digging, picking up scraps of paper, and keeping a hopeful eye
out for tourists. The park has caused a terrible feud between
Mr. Kennedy and his neighbour, Mr. Dundas. Mr. Dundas's
yard is also spic and span, but unadorned. Fearful that the
evermultiplying horde of gnomes would spread across the
road to the park, he accused Mr. Kennedy of "junking it
up." Mr. Kennedy keeps close count of the number of
campers and trailers that stop in the park, and greets each

new catch with the glee of a fisherman who has just reeled
in a whopper.

"It's a nice quiet town," says Mr. Kennedy. "Our little
village might not have any future but that's what's at a
premium now, a quiet place to live. I'm not in favor of
getting industry in. They pay the lowest wages and when
the time comes, they lay all the people off and then they're
on relief."

Mr. Kennedy, a farmer, was elected reeve in 1956 by two
votes over the incumbent; he was considered a radical and
a screwball because he wanted concrete bridges. "We were
still in the horse and buggy days. One councillor had been
on for twenty-one years. He was a nice fellow and needed
the money; we couldn't get him out. He got in every time
through the sympathy vote." Mr. Kennedy was defeated in
turn in 1962 by a group of younger men who thought he
was holding back progress. "Retired people pay their bills
and there's no problems," says Mr. Kennedy. "You got to
have a place to live your lives out."

Miami streets are free of litter, thanks mainly to the
unpaid efforts of a tall, dignified gentleman in a gold-
braided cap who wanders about relentlessly pursuing gum
wrappers and odd bottles. "He thinks," snorts the druggist's
wife, "that he's the FBI." There are no junkyards piled high
with rusty tractors, no gutted cars in the high grass along
the ditches, no stray dogs. No dogs. The silence makes itself
felt first in Miami. The silence and the stillness. The sidewalks are deserted, winter and summer. No one sits on his
front porch or rakes his lawn, no children zip around on
tricycles, no teen-agers bomb down the main streets in
souped-up cars. No one shouts or cries or laughs except in
the schoolyard at recess. If you look at the houses, you see
there are curtains in the windows and plants on the sills.
They are occupied. But where are all the people? Inside.
Knock on any door, and it will yield a woman doing the
wash, an old man watching television, a covey of matrons
printing nametags for a convention. Life in Miami is intense,
but it all takes place inside. There is something indecent, un-
respectable, almost dangerous about sitting outside exposing
oneself to the sharp eyes behind the flickering lace curtains.

The evening of June 27, 1972, is soft and warm. The sun is slipping slowly into the southwest. All the buildings on Miami's main street have their eyes closed against the glare. The brightness makes their faded white faces luminous, translucent, like marble tombstones. The I.O.O.F. hall, a thin, two-storey building squished between Moorey's grocery and Westaway's drugstore, is peeling, shabby, sinking. The Odd Fellows would like to sell the hall to the village, but it's owned by the Grand Lodge in Winnipeg and they won't permit it. The Odd Fellows worked hard last year fixing up the inside; they laid tile on the floor, panelled the walls with varnished plywood, and installed flush toilets in the Men and Ladies. "Before that," sighs one old member, "we carried it in from the well and carried it out again the next day." There are only five Odd Fellows left around Miami; they're all over 70.

Tonight they are all standing in front of the hall looking pained and uncomfortable in their Sunday suits, huge gnarled wrists hanging out of their sleeves, heavy with the weight of hands as rough and twisted as the roots of wind-fallen trees. The suits are brown and olive drab, too tight across the shoulders and too baggy in the legs, suits bought on sale at Eaton's five or ten years ago and worn, reluctantly, for weddings and funerals ever since. Their red necks bulge out of shirt collars choked tight with narrow silk or string ties. Their long, rawboned faces are burned red too, except for their foreheads, which are fishbelly white like the skin over their ears where Mac Nast, the barber, has given them a close trim with the electric clippers in honor of the occasion. Shoulders heavy and sloped with labor, heads bent to contemplate the ground, they stamp and shuffle at the door like a small herd of lost and aged buffalo.

The hall inside is full of elderly ladies in white dresses. Mayflower Rebekah Lodge No. 12. Normally lodge meetings are secret, but every year the Rebekahs and the Odd Fellows hold a memorial service in honor of their departed members which is open to the general public. Tonight's service has been well advertised in the Dufferin *Leader* and the Morden *Times* (both correspondents are Rebekahs), but there are only one or two strangers. Everyone takes a seat on the chairs ranged in a single row around the walls. The Rebekahs bustle around making last-minute arrangements. One woman lays out identical pink peonies on a table covered with a white tablecloth. Their dresses, short and fashionable, are cut to an almost identical pattern; like the peonies their faces are pink and white, rather overblown and chalky with heavy powder. They have bright china teeth and glasses with swirly frames set with rhinestones. They've all had their hair done by Fern, the hairdresser, in an identical style — a short cap of tight, lacquered curls. Plump and matronly, they clack around the room in tiny high-heeled shoes, a flock of white leghorn hens pecking up juicy tidbits and seeking a comfortable roost for the evening.

"We bury the dead and look after the sick and the widows in distress," says the grandmother sitting next to me. "We used to have a special graveside ceremony every time a member died but, well. . .it's getting kind of hard on the Noble Grands. We help sponsor the eye bank and we do our floor work and drills." She looks apologetic.

"Our youngest member is over fifty. We can't get any new members." She looks at me hopefully. No. "It used to be that you have to be 'of pure white blood' but that's gone now. The younger women just don't want to join. If you ask me the lodge is going to have to get over this ritual business if it's going to succeed. People are too busy now. We have sixty members but twenty are non-resident and a lot are inactive." She sighs and looks down at her hands. Her fingernails are bright scarlet. "Sometimes you're so embarrassed at the turnout.

"Years ago the thing to do was to belong to the church and the lodge. I can remember when the memorial service was just jammed and the room was filled with banks and banks of peonies. Well last year everybody was so busy in June that we just let it slip by. We finally had it at the end of September. Oh, we used plastic flowers."

The Odd Fellows clump in and take their seats in a row by the door. The service begins unannounced, as if by some unspoken natural understanding. We stand and sing "Rock of Ages," thin and quavery, to the acompaniment of a tinny upright piano at the front of the hall. Three ladies in floral prints grouped by the piano sing the Twenty-third Psalm. The reading of the names of the dead begins. The list goes on and on: Campbell, Kestirke, Smith, Graham, Kerr, Lawson, Umphrey, Stubbs, men and women, each with his appropriate title in the lodge. The list is endless. The population of the dead far outnumbers those present. Invoked, their shadows rise and fill the room.

The lights are turned out. Four grey-haired women in flowing white satin dresses enter from the back of the hall, each carrying a lighted candle of a different color. Hesitant and teetery, they make their way to the centre of the room and take up positions at the four points of the compass. They look self-conscious, like little girls in nightgowns on their way to bed. A woman at a lectern reads the memorial service from a large looseleaf book. Couched in vague and flowery rhetoric, it is about the seasons of man and the seasons of the earth, life and death and eternity. As each season is mentioned, the woman symbolizing it performs a few drill steps and holds her candle high. The woman reads with sincerity and conviction. The rise and fall of her voice, the warm twilight, the peonies, the crowd of friends make death seem promising, pleasant. There is a touching, clumsy honesty in the tribute, a sense of peace and solace. God is seldom mentioned; the theology is simple and optimistic. "Good night down here, good morning up there," sing the three ladies by the piano. The ceremony is a celebration of the earth and an annual placation of the gods. As a prayer for fruitfulness, it comes not accidentally at the summer solstice.

We all stand and sing "Abide With Me." The lights come up. The service dwindles away as inconclusively as it began. The Odd Fellows clump out and stand once more in a herd by the door, while the Rebekahs have their regular business meeting. Then, once all the outsiders have left, a few will go to the cemetery to place a pink peony on the grave of each dead friend.

The cemetery is the first thing you notice about Miami. It's on a little rise off the highway just as you come into town. Cemeteries are guidebooks to prairie towns. A glance tells whether the residents are Catholic or Protestant; Catholics prefer marble angels and flowery inscriptions, Protestants

plain black granite. Names are a clue to race and ethnic
prestige; older Anglo-Saxon tombstones frequently state the
birthplace in Britain or Ontario, others do not. There are
no Jews or Orientals; they have their own burying grounds.
The cemetery indicates a community's wealth, social structure, taste, and its respect for death and tradition. Miami's
respect for its ancestors is elaborate enough to be Egyptian.

The graveyard is not, as in most rural communities, a
patch of ragged prairie sod or even mowed city grass: it's
a garden. The grass has been carefully exterminated. Each
grave is a rectangle of black soil sprinkled with sand inside
a neat concrete curb, planted with peonies, caragana,
juniper, ornamental cedars, geraniums, and petunias. The
graves are connected by dirt and gravel paths and shaded
by large spruce trees, which sough in the wind. In June,
when the peonies are in bloom, the cemetery is filled with
their odor of sweet putrefaction. The cemetery has the
symmetry and restraint of formal gardens at Versailles; the
dead, in Miami, are cultivated.

The largest tombstone, a carved pile of pink granite,
belongs to Miami's patriarch, William Thompson. The
inscriptions indicate that the Thompson family has, through
tragedy and spinsterhood, virtually died out, a fate which
overtakes an astonishing number of pioneer families who
achieve instant and extraordinary success on the frontier.
There is a whiff of witchcraft about it, as if they had been
silently and sullenly hated to death. All the other grave-
stones decrease in size and cost according to the social
prominence of the people lying underneath. Most are plain
black granite cut to an identical pattern. There is, as everywhere, a special corner for orphaned men, veterans of the
two wars, who are buried by the Legion with simple grey
markers. There is one grave, a Mennonite's, outside the
fence in the grass. Miami has a lot of widows; dozens of
graves have only a man's name on the stone, which indicates
that these widows have money, since in poorer areas it is
now fashionable to engrave the stone with both names at
once, a sort of two-for-the-price-of-one arrangement, and
to leave only the date blank for the survivor.

The remarkable thing about Miami is the astonishing old
age to which many of the residents manage to survive.

According to the markers, some of the first children born in
Miami lived to celebrate Manitoba's centennial in 1970.
Obviously if they could endure the frontier they were
indestructable. Miami is still full of old people; longevity
is now the norm. These old people are not vegetables locked
up in geriatric centres; they're tough, strong-willed, and
independent. The Struldbrugs have formed Miami's personality and determined its destiny. Their influence in the
community is decisive.

Billy Thompson, an English harnessmaker from Uxbridge,
Ontario, homesteaded the piece of land which became
Miami in 1874, 15 years before the railway created the
town. He brought his wife and eight children by ox cart
southwest from Red River along the trail which had led the
Métis buffalo hunters to the headwaters of the Missouri
River. Almost the entire population of Uxbridge followed
him and took up land on adjacent parcels, transplanting
vast family networks almost intact to the new world and re-
establishing the old Scottish clan system of mutual help and
self-defence. By 1880, a year before the CPR reached
Winnipeg, 400 homesteads had been taken up in the Miami
area, and settlement was virtually complete by 1900. (Only
234 of the 700 quarter-section lots around Miami were
occupied under homestead regulations. Sixty were military
bounty grants, payment for Wolseley's soldiers and the
veterans of the North-West Rebellion, five were retirement
gifts to members of the North West Mounted Police, and
the rest were sold by speculators, the railways, and the
government.)
    The settlers crossed the Red River valley, a large slough
which flash spring floods turned into an inland sea of mud
and ice, and took refuge in the low hills which had formed
the western shore of Lake Agassiz, where they found wood
for houses and fuel. They built their first homes of oak logs,
chinked them with mud and straw, and whitewashed them
inside and out. The cabins were roofed with lumber or
thatched, depending on the financial resources of the homesteader. Since lumber had to be hauled by wagon from
Winnipeg, it was expensive and the extent of its use indi-

cated a farmer's social status; a homesteader with a wooden floor was a man of means. Most made do with mud. The cabins were divided into rooms by sheets of cotton stiffened with whitewash; the family slept on straw mattresses covered with feather ticks.

Land was cleared slowly, acre by acre, the dense stands of oak and poplar cut by hand and the stumps hauled out by a yoke of oxen harnessed to a chain. The poplar was stripped and used for fences, the scrub was burned. The land was broken with a single-furrow steel plow; the farmer, strapped into a harness and bracing his feet against the sod, yelled a constant stream of oaths at the oxen as the blade dragged him along. The oxen were stupid and slow, but they were also strong and, if worst came to the worst, edible. Their manure was spread on the fresh ground, harrowed in, and the seed was sown by hand. The ripe grain was cut with a scythe and laid out to dry in long neat windrows before being stooked and threshed in the farmyard, where the waste straw provided a winter bed for the cattle.

Every farm had a cow or two. Cattle provided meat, milk, and fertilizer, which was cleaned out of the barn and spread on the fields every spring; and their only fuel was oats and hay, which grew luxuriantly in the marshes, free for the taking. Milk, kept suspended in sealed cans in the well or stored in an earthen cellar, was the staple diet, along with bannock, biscuits, and porridge laced with brown sugar. Butter, churned by hand crank in a little wooden barrel, could be bartered off at the nearest store for sugar, salt, and kerosene, the only staples, apart from the big tin boxes of tea which travelling salesmen brought around twice a year, which the settlers could not raise themselves. A motley flock of chickens, ducks, and geese lived off the land, laid eggs daily, and offered themselves for festive occasions. Every year a few bags of grain were put aside as seed for the next spring's crop, a few more were reserved to be ground into flour, and the rest were sold. Most farmers got enough cash to buy a horse, a few more acres, a bolt of cloth, and shoes for the kids — enough to keep them going. In a frontier community money was virtually useless, since there was nowhere to spend it. Almost everything was bartered and nothing, absolutely nothing, was wasted. You could always tell which girls were sisters, because they wore identical dresses cut from the same bolt of cloth; it was cheaper to buy in bolts than in pieces. Younger children inherited the older ones' clothes like cast-off skins, and worked their way through three or four transmogrifications until they finally emerged, with considerable resentment, as identifiable individuals. When grain was ground into flour, the bran was saved for baking and the screenings for chicken feed. A pig was slaughtered every fall just before freeze-up: the guts and blood were made into sausage and the head and feet were boiled for soup.

A homestead farm was self-sufficient and functional. Clothes were washed in snow melted on the kitchen stove in copper boilers or in rainwater caught off the roof; women made their own soap, vinegar, and even yeast out of hops the children gathered in the fields. Rags were colored with dye made from native plants and woven into rugs to cover the straw matting on the floor. Roasted barley made good coffee. The produce of the vegetable garden was supplemented by the natural bounty of the prairie, which every spring yielded wild strawberries so plentiful that the wheels of the ox carts ran red with their blood. The prairie was Paradise, a garden teeming with birds and fish and wild beasts in which man with his soft domestic animals was an intruder. Cinnamon bears raided the pigpens; wolves fattened on the chickens and made off with the sheep. Flocks of wild ducks and geese blackened the marshes every spring and fall and filled the valley with their honking. The woods were full of hazelnuts and high-bush cranberries, and the long grass was a rippling carpet of wild flowers alive with rabbits and deer; prairie chickens flew up at every step and wild pigeons were so plentiful that, in the fall, branches of trees would break off under the weight of large flocks coming in to roost. The settlers lived off the land during the five or ten years it took them to establish their farms. The bears they shot, the government paid a bounty on wolves, and the pigeons had completely disappeared by 1900. As the cultivated land extended farther and farther across the valley, the marshes were drained, the woods stripped of trees, and the birds and animals slowly vanished.

Farming was done by hand. The tools were cheap and simple, and the labor was provided by the farmer's family. Women milked the cows, churned the butter, baked the bread, plucked and eviscerated the chickens, cooked the meals, made the clothes, and raised the children who chopped the wood, hoed the garden, gathered the eggs, and went to work in the fields as soon as they were strong enough. A farm was a piece of land a man could walk around, and its wealth was what he could raise with his hands. A farmer's future was in his back, strong and sinewy with muscles that soon stood out like ropes on his neck. As he walked over his land behind the oxen, he could feel the grain of it under his boots and could test its texture when he crumbled a clod in the palm of his hand. He knew where it was wet and where it was sandy; he recognized every stone, every stump that had beaten him, every bush and bird's nest; he knew he could see the next farm house from a particular rise. He knew the land in the sound of the grasshoppers and in the sting of the mosquitoes at twilight. He felt it in the sweat that ran down his back in the afternoon sun and in the way the muscles in the backs of his legs ached. He knew the land the way he knew the oxen, as a person, a living thing. It was his. He had created it.

The solitary homestead farm formed the core of a simple agricultural society, a community of survival centred on the seasonal ritual of harvest. Since the community had only one threshing machine, an incredible steam contraption that ran on straw and water and made the rounds of the farms one by one, everybody pitched in to help, feeding sheaves in one end and bagging the grain that came out the other. The day's hard labor was topped off with an enormous feast — roast pork, beef, and chicken, garden vegetables, hot biscuits served with fresh butter and jam, homemade pickles, fruit preserves, rich cream and five different kinds of pie. The harvesters ate until they were stuffed. A pioneer woman was judged on her ability to cook, and her whole reputation rested on the one or two days of harvest. Word was passed quickly from farm to farm. Quantity counted as much as quality, and the most devastating humiliation was to run out of food and be considered, as the Scots put it, "a bit careful." If the sun was shining and the crops were good, harvest was a time of comradeship, a joyful relief from the long, solitary hours behind the plow, which brought a sense of profound satisfaction and the knowledge of triumph. Harvest was a moveable feast, an Indian potlatch in which each farmer in turn celebrated his wealth by inviting his friends to devour the fruits of his labor.

The centre of the little community was Billy Thompson's farm. He built a Presbyterian church on a corner of his property and donated land for a cemetery beside it. The first school was in his log house. The children were delivered to school every Monday morning in a buckboard owned and driven by the schoolteacher, the Reverend J. B. Borthwick, who was also school inspector, Methodist minister, and Sunday school teacher. On Sundays, the kitchen chairs were lined up in the Thompsons' living room, and Rev. Borthwick conducted the service. Sunday school was held in the kitchen, where the children recited Bible verses and sang hymns. Rev. Borthwick was a missionary, a bald, kindly man with rimless glasses and a Santa Claus beard who travelled from house to house preaching in front of homemade altars contrived out of sewing machines and ironing boards. His moral power was absolute.

Community life was intensely Protestant. The church was essential; its importance was assumed without question or criticism. The familiar rituals and dogmas brought culture, tradition, and continuity to the isolated frontier settlement; the church meant home, security, hope. It was a rock to which people could cling to prevent themselves from going native like the local bush rat, who wore animal skins, lived on wild game, and drove around in a buggy pulled by two tame deer. The church knit the community together on Sundays and provided a certain spare dignity to weddings and funerals. God mattered. The God of the Scotch Protestants — that fierce old man with the long grey beard who floated around the sky zapping sinners with bolts of lightning — was strangely appropriate to the prairie, where farmers were frequently struck and killed by lightning and families huddled under wet blankets in the turnip patch while prairie fires destroyed their life's possessions. He had been created by other nomadic, agricultural people in another harsh and beautiful land where death and disaster were swift, capricious, and inexplicable. God made sense out of typhoid and blizzards and plagues of locusts; he gave people who worked hard for very meager results a promise that their labor would be rewarded after death. He was a defence against the silence of the snow and the emptiness of the summer sky. The church's spartan morality, symbolized by the pale clergymen like dead branches in their black suits and round white collars, was protection against chaos and a bulwark against the violent, seductive fecundity of the land.

In feasts and celebrations, the settlers found a comfortable refuge from the terror and loneliness of the prairie, where often the only sound to break the silence was the yap-yap of coyotes and the distant chorus of wolves. Bands of Indians came by and camped in the bush, begging old clothes and tea at the cabin door, occasionally carrying a corpse to be buried up in the hills. Many were Sioux, armed with guns, bowie knives, and tomahawks. Some wore scalps dangling from their belts, blond ones and red ones with curly hair. When Billy Thompson opened his post office in 1878, General Custer was only two years dead.

Thompsonville, as the post office came to be called, was completely overshadowed by the rival community of Nelsonville, twelve miles south on the Missouri Trail. In 1878, Adam Nelson slid a sawmill 60 miles across the frozen prairie on a stoneboat pulled by 14 yoke of oxen and set it up where the Missouri Trail crossed Dead Horse Creek. He was soon providing everyone for miles around with lumber, shingles, and flour. Half a dozen homesteaders built houses nearby and began dealing in groceries which came in from Winnipeg by Red River cart. Within a year, a church and a school were built, and Nelsonville was a thriving village. By 1879 it had a newspaper, the Nelsonville *Mountaineer*, and a temperance lodge headed by the Rev. Mr. Borthwick. The commercial activity at Nelsonville quickly attracted a flock of lawyers, doctors, bankers, and would-be politicians. A verbal promise was extracted from the Manitoba Colonization Railroad to build a branch line to Nelsonville, and the village began to agitate for recognition as the most important community in southwestern Manitoba. When the town was incorporated in 1882, it was the fourth largest settlement in Manitoba with a population of more than 1,000. As a result of intense lobbying by the newspaper and politicians, rumors began to circulate that Nelsonville would become a city. A frenzied land boom broke out. Nelsonville lots were auctioned off every night at the Queen's Hotel in Winnipeg. Corner lots were selling for $1,000. Homesteaders divided up their property and grew rich. The town floated $20,000 in debentures and built a substantial brick town hall with a registry office, council chambers, a courtroom, and a meeting hall. The federal government opened a Land Titles office. Only five years after the first house was built, Nelsonville boasted three general stores, two private banks, a liquor store, three doctors, three lawyers, a jeweller, a real estate office, and rows of houses neatly laid out with lawns and gardens. It did not, however, have a railway.

Member of parliament for the Nelsonville area between 1871 and 1880 was CPR tycoon Donald A. Smith. Smith was casting his eye about southern Manitoba, plotting the location of branch lines. Late in 1882, the CPR bought up the Manitoba Colonization Railroad and laid its new track across the bald prairie three miles south of Nelsonville. The town was aghast. Its protests were loud and shrill, but in vain. "If the railway will not come to us, then we will go to it!" announced the *Mountaineer* in 1883. In the winter, Nelsonville's wooden buildings were loaded on skids and pulled by horses across the fields towards the new railway station. The town hall and the brick church were sold to Mennonites, who carted the bricks off to build stoves and bake ovens. The hotel burned to the ground. By 1886, after less than ten years of existence, Nelsonville had vanished. Abandoned sheds were used as granaries, and its lawns were ploughed back into fields. For generations the old people, remembering that thin black line of houses inching slowly across the snow, called it "the town that walked away."

The railway completely transformed the primitive pastoral life of the wilderness homesteads. Civilization came chugging in dressed in workmen's boots with a packsack on its back and a sharp eye out for the main chance. Survival was no longer sufficient. The railway told homesteaders why they had come west. It gave them a job. A farmer's identity was his name stamped on a sack of wheat; the more sacks, the bigger the man. Wheat was cash and cash was everything.

The village of Miami began to grow in 1889 after the railway had decreed that a station would be built across the dirt road from Billy Thompson's farm. By the time the first steam engine thundered into town, more than a dozen buildings had risen out of the ground and the platform was crowded with cheering businessmen. The train brought loads of lumber; soon the prairie was echoing to the tack tack of hammers as the town was thrown up — first a grain elevator, then the Grandview Hotel, a blacksmith, a butcher, Angers' livery barn, Collins and Munroe general store, and a harness shop.

The Methodists and the Presbyterians engaged in a frantic race to see who would have the first church in Miami. They finished in a dead heat. The Methodists, however, were embarrassed by being unable to afford a permanent minister and were forced to rely on the services of the itinerant preacher; a permanent minister, who required a manse and a salary of $525 a year, was a tremendous achievement and a prize coveted by every rural congregation.

Everything was up-to-date in Miami. The buildings smelled of fresh lumber and varnish; they were trim and bright with white paint and big plate glass windows shaded by awnings on summer afternoons. Ambitious merchants built their shops two stories high, and the family lived upstairs over the store. Lesser men, unable to afford so large a structure, put up false fronts on their humble shacks to make a single storey look as if it were two, and lived in back. The shops were all built to an identical plan — long, narrow, rectangular boxes stretching back from the street, dark except for two windows in front the size of which indicated the affluence of the proprietor. They were all built jam up against the road, and opened directly onto the wooden sidewalk. No money was wasted on lawns, fences, or steps. The design was a deliberate strategem to save taxes, since a store could be assessed only on its narrow frontage. Wooden signs as wide as the shop announced the name of the owner and the type of business in plain block letters; the only other decoration was a little carving over the windows and a fancy cornice across the top like a fringe of hair. The stores had an attractive, humanoid look — the door in the middle like a mouth and the two windows across the top like eyes whose expression changed daily depending on the hang of the lace curtains and the degree that the sash, like an eyelid, was open. The grandest building of all was the Grandview Hotel, three stories high with a view of the Pembina Hills from the top floor and a splendid, carved oak bar.

By 1901 Miami had a newspaper, an offshoot of a little printing company that specialized in printing names on grain bags. The carpenter, T. W. Stubbs, also ran a furniture and undertaking business and upstairs he operated a photo studio. In 1912 he sold out to the harness maker, who added shoe and harness repair to the list. His wife, who had a sewing machine, did the work on binder canvasses, awnings, fur coats, gloves, and shrouds. It was common, and not considered greedy, for businessmen to maximize their income by picking up three or four jobs. The baker baked bread in a big brick oven behind his confectionery store, which specialized in fruit, soft drinks, and ice cream; he was also a painter and decorator and an occasional butcher. The Massey Harris agent, Sandy Kerr, sold real estate and insurance, he also bought grain, owned a creamery, and looked after the affairs of the municipality from a little office in the agency. In addition, he repaired all the Massey Harris machinery that he sold and apparently financed many sales out of his own pocket, since a 1908 advertisement declared that Mr. Kerr had "money to loan." Sandy rented out a cubbyhole in the Massey Harris building to the lawyer and the doctor worked out of the drugstore, where he had an office upstairs. The doctor didn't miss a trick either; he advertised himself in gothic script as:

A. L. Shanks
M.D. C.M.
Physician
Surgeon and Coroner
issuer of Marriage Licences.

The drugstore had the telephone exchange.

The doctor, however, had competition from the midwife, a Mrs. Cole, who had trained at the Leicester Borough Asylum in England. Mrs. Cole took in sewing and pregnant women. The women boarded in her house for a few days before and after the baby was born; Mrs. Cole delivered the baby and called in the doctor if there was any emergency. The service was designed primarily for women living on isolated farms, who were cut off from medical assistance. Mrs. Cole was in such great demand that a small stone hospital was built beside her house in 1921, built and equipped entirely by public subscription. More than 1,000 babies were born in the Miami Cottage Hospital before it was closed in 1956 for lack of patients.

Although the village had only about 300 people, it was busy and hustling. Farm wagons pulled by big Clydesdales stamping their hairy feet at the hitching posts lined the main street in front of the bank and the elevators, smart buggies zipped between the livery barn at one end of town and the drugstore at the other, and gay blades rode bicycles when it didn't rain. The first car arrived in 1904; there were seven by 1911, the year the wooden sidewalks were replaced with concrete. Miami had a policeman (the owner of the livery barn) and a little red two-cell jail with bars on the windows to contain the Saturday night rowdies. Crime was so minimal in Miami that the jail was soon moved to the fairgrounds, where it was used as an office for the caretaker.

Money was made quickly and spent even more quickly. The farmers enriched the businessmen who in turn spent the money on turning Miami into a miniature version of rural Ontario. They built houses of brick, three stories high with gabled roofs and leaded stained-glass windows and neat lawns out front surrounded by iron fences. Stone was scarce, so the most elegant houses were built of concrete blocks manufactured in the cement plant up in the hills, each block carefully shaped to look like cut stone. They were decorated with shutters, ornately carved white wooden verandas, and little wrought-iron railings around the captain's walk on the roof. Maple, ash, and elm trees were dug from the creeks and ditches and planted in the yards; corseted ladies in silk and taffeta gowns served afternoon tea on the grass. The train brought mysterious treasures from eastern factories and wealth and social status were measured in luxuries: Miami soon acquired a jeweller, who specialized in watches and eyeglasses, a dressmaker, a tailor, and a Chinese laundry, and the general store featured "twenty-century suits" ready-made from Toronto. Banquets of seven and eight courses featured venison, oysters, and half a dozen different kinds of wine. Several meat markets offered fresh sausages every day and fish in season, but the gastronomic sensation was Ferris' Ice Cream Parlor, where homemade ice cream was served at dainty wrought-iron tables. Mr. Ferris also advertised 30 different kinds of chocolates and cut hair on the side. Beautiful picture post-cards of Miami were available at Westaway's drugstore, and the printer did a brisk business in calling cards and engraved invitations, which the dozen members of the social elite exchanged with solemn civility.

The culture of Ontario was imported along with its trappings. Dozens of clubs, lodges, and fraternal societies sprang up as barricades against anarchy. The most formidable was the Royal Templars of Temperance, mobilized in 1895 by the doctor, the druggist, and the undertaker's wife, who rounded up all the children into a Band of Hope, which sang temperance songs in the Odd Fellows' Hall but had no noticeable effect on the amount of liquor consumed in the Grandview Hotel bar, where the men drank standing up, apparently on the theory that when they'd had enough, they'd fall down. Everybody, of course, belonged to all the organizations. Shut up in their concrete houses with their heavy oak panelling and flowered wallpaper, served on linen and silver by farm girls disguised as cooks and house-maids, they tried to forget that they were stuck out on the bald prairie in a shack town engaged in a desperate and sometimes ludicrous struggle to make ends meet. Civilization, lovingly dismantled and imported on the train, was a truculent and feeble transplant. Cement houses were cold as death, dust blackened the lace curtains, and tea parties were spoiled by black flies and grasshoppers. Savings vanished in swindles and bad gambles, businesses dissolved into bankruptcy. The vulgarity of the prairie was irrepressible.

Only three of Billy Thompson's eight children lived to see the end of the century. Men maimed themselves with axes and were mangled in farm machinery. Children died of diphtheria and women of tuberculosis. People aged quickly; the men went bald and their deep, sunken eyes peered sternly out of craggy faces burned mahogany by the sun and wind. Their wives weathered, their jaws set square and determined and their hair pulled severely back into a bun. Nobody smiled in the early photographs, because their teeth had usually rotted and fallen out. Billy Thompson's little cemetery filled up quickly. It was a great achievement to be old.

As the centre of social gravity shifted to the town and the pastoral values of husbandry and hard work fell into disrepute, Uncle Billy leased his farm and moved about from daughter to daughter, an old man with a long white beard carrying all his belongings in a grain sack on which was printed in large letters: WILLIAM THOMPSON — MAYOR OF MIAMI. He had wanted the village to be named after him, but it was named instead for a tribe of American Indians by a party of disgruntled surveyors who complained that there were already too many towns in the North-West with the same English name. Local residents pronounce it with a drawl — Mahamuh. It's a trick, a code which identifies strangers and sets them apart.

A stranger is behind the worn wooden counter among the old-fashioned pill bottles at the back of Westaway's drugstore. A retired druggist from Winnipeg, he is tending the store while Jack Westaway is on vacation. "I have written a song in honor of Manitoba," he says. He rummages in back and produces a child's scribbler, the kind with a sheaf of wheat on the cover. He opens it and begins to sing in a tuneless singsong tenor as he conducts with his right arm:
Fresh bread, fresh bread!
Manitoba, Manitoba!
Love, love, love
Fresh bread, fresh bread, etc.

The song was rejected in the competition for the official
Manitoba centennial song.

"What do you think?" he asks.

Fresh bread?

"Of course!" he says. "That's what prairie towns are all
about, the smell of fresh bread coming from the bakery
early in the morning as you walk to work. It means everything — life, food, home. You don't smell it in the city.

"This is a great little town," he says, leaning close, "a
fabulous town. Think of the potential of that name! Miami!
Why you could develop it into a real resort, just like the
other Miami. Somebody with a few bucks could build big
hotels with swimming pools, campsites, trailer parks. . . ."
He waves his arm around. "Build ski runs in the winter,
snowmobile trails through the hills. Boy, with a little
imagination you could really cash in on the name of this
place! It's a natural!"

Miami never made it to being a real town or even a real
village. It's an unincorporated village, governed by a three-
man committee with an annual budget of $9,000. They're
really caretakers, who dole out money for street lights,
sidewalk repairs, gravel, and culverts. Miami is a farmers'
town; it has never achieved an existence or identity separate
from the agricultural community. The town is a convenience
for the farmers, a place to shop, a place to retire; when
they're through with it, Miami will vanish as quickly as it
came. Most townspeople understand that.

The population of the entire Municipality of Thompson
of which Miami is a part is only a little more than 1,000 and
shrinking steadily. Miami reached its peak in population and
prosperity shortly after the turn of the century; once all the
land was taken up, the tide turned. The exodus began to run
the other way in 1914, as trains gathered up all the young
men they had brought west only five or ten years earlier
and carried them back to boats headed for Europe. Hardest
hit by the war exodus were the patriotic Anglo-Saxon areas
like Miami.

It was funny how the economic booms, which had
brought young people to the West, took only the young

people away. Young men returning from World War II found themselves displaced by the combine, so they went to the cities to work in factories that built combines. Generation after generation, the young people grew up and left. As the farms increased in size, the town shrank. It lost its newspaper, photographer, undertaker, ice-cream parlor, Chinese laundry, lawyer, and movie theatre. The doctor now comes only three afternoons a week from a nearby town. Roy Compton closed his John Deere farm machinery agency in 1951. "If we'd have kept on," he says, "we would have been the same as the rest — a big 'For Sale' sign outside saying we're broke."

The people are mystified by Miami's decay. It is seen as a conspiracy and it is blamed on an undefined, amorphous "They," a powerful bogeyman who reveals himself, under pressure, to be anything from the prime minister to kids with long hair. Survival is not a necessity for Miami, it's a matter of pride. Criticism of the town is taken personally. Any suggestion that Miami may be slipping or stagnant is interpreted as a slur, a deliberate insult to everyone who lives there. The residents react with fierce, defensive rage, a torrent of vituperation against socialism, abortion, pollution, and all the other urban vices that are killing small towns. "Discipline!" shouts a bleary farmer, holding forth in the Grandview Hotel pub about the difficulties of finding kids to work for $1.50 an hour. "We need to bring back discipline! Those kids need to know who's boss. Those lazy bums can make more on welfare than they can working!" He stares defiantly at his cronies, who nod in agreement. "This welfare is such a racket, why, it's just Communism! We're goin' right over the top, it's Russia all the way!" The farmer lowers his voice and looks around conspiratorially. "Honest John," he whispers, "he would help us. If we could bring back Honest John." The other farmers all nod again, and taking a big swig of beer in memory of Honest John, savor their political exile.

The spiral of extinction begins slowly, imperceptibly, and ends quickly. A few businesses close down, the tax base shrinks, and a greater financial burden is borne by the residential property. When people begin to complain about high taxes, services are curtailed; then the town begins to look crummy, and people move away. Miami is hanging on the edge of the final precipice. "We have fifty homes with one widow in each of them," sighs Jim Murray, the municipal secretary. The village has no bicycle licences, no animal licences, no business licences, or no building permits. "We're so pleased if anyone wants to build here that we don't restrict them," says Mr. Murray. There is one new building in town, the credit union, and one new house, the credit union manager's. Miami has sewers but no waterworks; each house has a well and a cistern. The abundance of water that made Miami such a good place to settle in in 1889 has probably destroyed it. "Towns without water installed waterworks years ago, because they had to," says Mr. Murray. "Water attracts industry. They've got development now and we don't." Without industry, Miami can't afford waterworks. Like a princess in a fairy tale, Miami makes herself beautiful in the hope that someday a prince will gallop by and bless her with wealth and eternal life.

The only thing that's galloped by so far is a garment factory, Miami Fashions Ltd., a subsidiary of a Winnipeg company specializing in nylon parkas which has established branch plants in several Manitoba towns and Indian reserves where labor is cheap and captive. The company was invited to Miami in 1966 by the Miami Industrial Development Corporation, a group of local farmers and merchants who raised $8,000 to renovate the old movie theatre. The garment factory rents the building for $90 a month and employs about 20 local women. "These things don't make a profit for the town," says Mr. Murray. "It just puts money on the main street on payday."

The garment factory was the achievement of the reeve, Rudy Hink, a gentle, sensitive man who farms just south of town; he negotiated the deal in the face of much taunting and razzing from the local sceptics. Hink has a farmer's awkward shyness, almost an embarrassment, about his lack of education, which stopped abruptly at the beginning of the Depression, when he was 16, but his self-effacement conceals intelligence and strong convictions. Hink has suffered a series of nervous breakdowns, which everyone

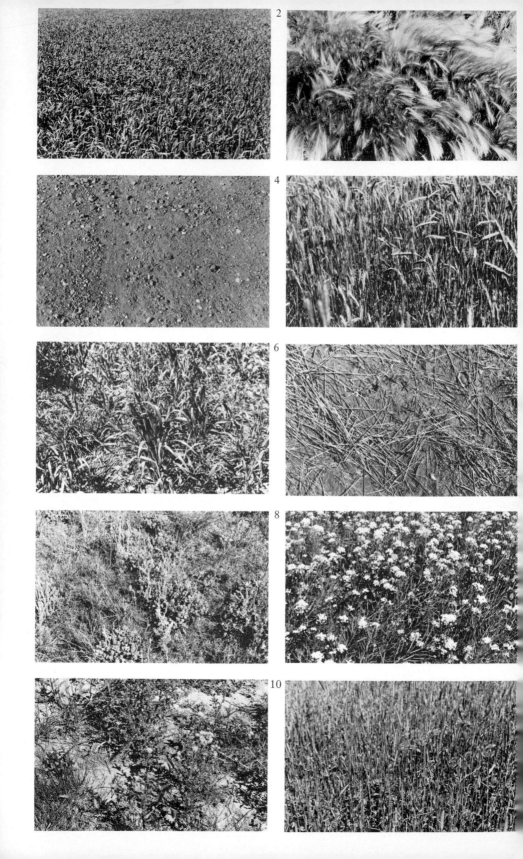

2

4

6

8

10

12

13

14

15

16

17

18

19

20

21

22

23

24

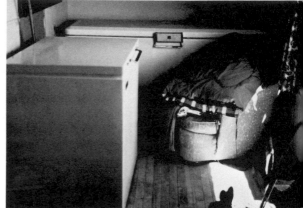

44

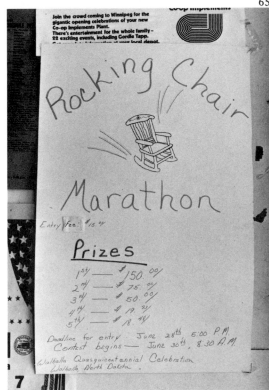

97

98

99

100

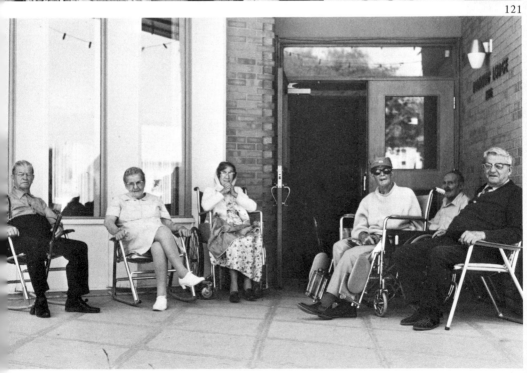

discusses openly. They have enhanced, not hindered, his political influence, since people are convinced he worries a lot about the community. He does. Rudy Hink is an anomaly in Miami, an Austrian Roman Catholic who votes NDP — a combination of eccentricity so extreme that it makes him a figure of mystery and respect. His unorthodoxies exclude him from the social circle in Miami, but at the same time they protect him from the infighting and clan warfare which is always rending the community. As an outsider he is safe.

Rudy Hink's hands are scarred and horny, his fingers swollen and knobby like a fistful of potatoes. Black grease is ground into the rough skin on his palms and wedged under his cracked fingernails. He looks at his hands as he talks.

"We had a guy last year who wanted to establish a hockey stick factory," he says wistfully. "But it didn't work out. We tried out some of his sticks with the kids. They broke and bent and they were too heavy. So we told him we weren't interested. However we have a guy now who wants to start a trap factory." His eyes light up as he reaches for a thick file of letters.

"He's a former prison guard from the U.S. who's invented this humane trap for animals, a kind of a big metal cage." He shoves a diagram across the table. The file is full of testimonials from wildlife organizations endorsing the excellence of the trap. "He can build them himself, with his three sons, but he's got no money to start up. He wants us to put up $20,000 to get him going for the first year. Most of it's just wages for him and his boys; we figured it was a lot of money so we persuaded them to cut their wages in half, seeing that they were all sharing a house and everything.

"I dunno," he says, riffling through the documents, "we'll have to do some more investigating on this."

Miami had an aluminium window factory that operated for a couple of winters in the abandoned egg grading station, but then the fellow left and never came back. A lot of houses in Miami have aluminium windows and doors.

"The bakery started up again," says Rudy, "and the TV shop is open again. Three or four families have left this year but there's four moving in — we're hanging in there."

Community business in Miami is measured by the meetings
— the less business, the longer the meeting. The Thompson
municipal council meets all day. There's always lots of
correspondence and delegations but no spectators. It's
considered in bad taste in small towns to attend meetings.
The councillors are embarrassed by having to speak in
public and they resent the implication that they are not
doing their job. The minutes of the meeting are given to the
local newspaper correspondents, who write up a short summary for the weekly papers. This way the public knows
only what the council wants them to know. Incompetence
and corruption are allowed to persist for decades before
anyone finds out enough to do something about it. Few
people even know that council meetings are open to the
public, and the length of the meetings is enough to dis-
courage all but the most stubborn spectators. Of course, if
the public attended, the meetings would be much shorter.

The six farmers arrive all clean-shaven and dressed up,
their hair slicked down and their red faces scrubbed shiny.
The older ones wear suits and ties; only their earth-stained
fingers and the heavy black boots below their pantlegs give
them away. Sometimes a strip of longjohn appears between
the cuff and boot-top. One of them carries a shiny black
attache case, which he snaps open and shut with great
authority. The younger men wear their newest and cleanest
jeans and windbreakers. They roar up in their pickup trucks
in a cloud of dust, beaming, pregnant with civic responsibility. The meeting begins with a jovial exchange of dirty
stories and the choicest gossip. Everyone has heard it
already, but they enjoy telling it again.

The handyman appears to report that the fire engine
leaks and his new low-bed truck is too long to turn the
corner onto Main Street. A debate follows on whether to
widen Main Street or shorten the truck. It's decided to
shorten the truck.

A culvert salesman is next. "How are we fixed for
culverts?" asks Rudy, looking solemnly around the big oak
table. No culverts today, thanks.

The postmaster appears to complain about the broken
sidewalk in front of the post office. The widows are giving
him hell. Council promises an official inspection. Another

man stomps in to complain that the boulevard in front of his house has not been mowed. This precipitates a heated discussion on the handyman's laziness, complete with councillors' eyewitness accounts of precise times and places they have seen him sitting around. One of the councillors says he'll mow the lawn himself for only a nominal fee.

The handyman reappears to complain that he is being paid only $1.75 an hour while a new man has been hired at $1.90 an hour. The councillors purse their lips and go all steely-eyed, muttering to themselves about greed and extravagance. The council believes in getting the most for its money. The town foreman is paid $5,000 a year; his titles include caretaker of cemeteries, sewage engineer, water tank caretaker, fire chief, fire hall caretaker, and caretaker of Miami and Rosebank disposal grounds.

A letter is read from a lawyer on behalf of a Mr. Warsaba, who is going to sue the municipality because a bridge was washed out somewhere in the hills in a flash flood, and Mr. Warsaba sailed over the edge of the bank in his car and landed in the mud on the creek bottom. Several hours later his wife found him and dug him out, but before he could pull his car out, a second car sailed over and landed on top of it. Mr. Warsaba is claiming $450 damages for the total destruction of his car. Council has a big laugh.

The delicate question of the Miami police force is raised. Two policemen were hired in the summer of 1970, after the school principal complained that some boys had thrown beer bottles at his house and squealed their tires on the boulevard in front of his property.

"We just took a couple of the worst hellraisers and made them the town police," smiles Sid Cox, a member of the village committee. "It sure stopped the trouble."

The Miami police had only been on the job a month at the time of the great hole mystery. "What do you do?" I asked one of them, whose ears stuck straight out on either side of his big blue hat. He grinned and blushed. "Try to look busy," he said. At first the police took themselves very seriously. They patrolled the empty highway in front of town and caught farmers speeding down Main Street in their pickup trucks; they nabbed a few housewives making illegal U-turns and lay in wait for drunken teen-agers outside the school dances. Looking snappy in their brand new blue uniforms, which were just a little too large, they swaggered into Vern's Cafe every morning for coffee, stamping their feet hard on the floor to make their shoes sound like RCMP boots and fingering the revolvers in their belts as they cast a suspicious eye over the crowd of cheerful farmers. They were paid $200 a month each and worked out of an office in the basement of the municipal building behind the men's washroom. It was, in fact, part of the men's washroom.

A year later, one of them was caught drinking on duty. He was fired and got a job bartending in Morden, a town 15 miles south. His buddy quit in sympathy and joined the Morden police force. His loss was a severe economic blow to Miami, because he owned the Miami police car, a blue station wagon with a detachable red light on top and a cot in the back which was also the Miami ambulance. This policeman was also the television repairman and agent for Admiral appliances; his shop closed down when he left. He took his mother with him to Morden; she was the baker, so the bakery closed. His wife worked in the bank; that job fell vacant. The volunteer fire brigade was decimated, because the two policemen were its backbone. They held fire drills twice a month in the men's washroom, and finished them off with a case of beer and a poker game. The loss of the local police suddenly exposed the Miami people to the financial ruthlessness of the RCMP traffic patrols, since previously the town constables had widely publicized the location of hidden radar traps and had alerted everyone as to which nights the RCMP detachment would be away attending a wedding or a stag.

A year has passed and Miami remains without police. "We've been real lucky," grins Rudy Hink. "It's been quiet. It saves us $5,000 a year."

By noon the little council chamber is rank with sweat. Yet all these issues are essentially trivial. The council has only one overriding concern — roads. Roads are an obsession. Most of the municipal budget of $76,000 goes for road maintenance and snow removal. The topic of roads brings the councillors to life; hands waving and nostrils flaring, they can happily discuss gravel, culverts, and machinery for hours and days. They are connoisseurs of gravel, authorities on its cost and quality, experts on the precise day of the year on which it must be applied. The purchase of a new road grader can consume months of weighty deliberation. Like all farmers, municipal councillors are machinery freaks; each purchase is entered into only after the utmost investigation and the most subtle negotations. All of the councillors go along to Winnipeg to inspect the road grader. They can charge $1.50 an hour and 10 cents a mile for inspection tours, which usually include a rollicking afternoon in a Winnipeg pub featuring topless go-go dancers. The councillors do a lot of inspecting, but they are paid only $600 a year. (The reeve gets $1,200). Local farmers conscientiously bring every rut, pothole, and blocked culvert to their attention. The better the roads, of course, the easier it is for farmers to bypass Miami and drive to other towns.

Although they will quickly plunk down $50,000 for a new piece of machinery, council will not approve even a tiny amount of welfare without a howl of protest. Excluding an annual grant of $3,400 to the nearby hospital, the municipality's health and welfare budget is $5,600 a year. Every cent of it is begrudged. Although the administration of welfare is handled by the provincial government, which pays the total cost of transients and 40 per cent for residents, welfare is regarded by each councillor as a personal affront and an appalling drain on the community resources. Discussion of welfare consumes about as much time as roads. The municipality has two families receiving assistance — a musician in town who plays with a rock band and a colony of hippies in a shack in the hills.

"We're not burdened too hard," chuckles Delbert Snider, who has the hippies in his ward. "We make it quite rough for them. Cut off their cigarettes. Hold back on payments. If the welfare bums were shot and the funeral expenses were on the municipality, we'd be dollars ahead."

Most of the welfare money goes to pay the medicare premiums of farmers who are too poor or too crafty to pay their own. These are usually the farmers who let their taxes fall into arrears, a growing problem which is fast becoming a bugbear for the municipality. In extreme cases, a list of recalcitrant taxpayers is published in the weekly paper, but this is considered a harsh humiliation for those who are genuinely poor. "It's hard to dun your neighbours for money," sighs Rudy Hink. "You're liable to get thrown off the yard."

The meeting resolves itself into a leisurely gabfest, a communal chewing of the fat which is conducted with decorum and politeness. Everyone is allowed to talk as long and as often as he likes while the rest listen in respectful silence. Great weight is placed on personal observation and anecdote. Every picayune detail is raised, every matter examined from all possible angles; there's no rush, no urgency, no railroading. No grievance, no expenditure is too small for consideration. The delicate matter of the silver tray is raised last. Ralph "Mac" Nast, the town barber, who has served on the village committee for 15 years has been forced to retire because of failing health. Council has purchased a silver tray for him in Westaway's drugstore. Jim Murray produces the bill. "He quoted us twenty-four dollars plus six dollars for the engraving," says Rudy Hink, clearing his throat. "The bill comes to fifty-two dollars." There is an angry silence around the table. "Jeez," says one councillor, "I said we should have got it in Winnipeg." Rudy Hink pulls the tray out of its box of tissue paper. It's elaborately engraved with Mr. Nast's name and his years on the council. He looks at it. "Well," he shrugs, "I guess we can't take it back."

Mr. Nast and his wife, who have been waiting outside, are ushered in. The councillors stand up and look very red and shy. Rudy Hink makes a short speech and thrusts the tray at Mr. Nast. The councillors applaud. Mr. Nast, trying to look cool and nonchalant, blushes and gazes down at the ground.

"We're like a wheel with spokes in it and everybody does his share and I done mine," he blurts out. Jim Murray takes flash pictures of Rudy Hink handing the tray to Mr. Nast. There is an awkward silence; people shuffle their feet. No one can think of anything to say.

"Mac," one of the councillors suddenly booms out, "whenever I think of sewage in this town I think of you. You know more about every pipe in Miami than anyone else I can think of."

Mr. Nast shakes hands all around. Then he puts the tray under his arm, and as he limps out, he is wiping the tears from his eyes.

Mac Nast's barbershop is spotlessly clean and empty except for the old barber chair, a Coke cooler, and a small table littered with Superman comics. The little building looks 100 years old. "I built it myself," says Mac, "in 1948."

Miami's downtown has been swept by fire and many of the first buildings destroyed, but their style has been carefully reproduced. Rural prairie architecture is not a holdover but a unique, deliberate, and distinct tradition. It's homemade and unprofessional, a plain, functional style which, like the log cabin, evolved out of the strictures of land and weather and the aesthetic sensibilities of the community. Prairie cities try to look like Toronto, but small towns try to look like the Old West. They are conservative; their repudiation of the progress symbolized by steel and glass indicates not only respect for the past but the pride of people who like to make things themselves, with their own hands. They also suggest decent poverty. It takes money to buy culture, and Miami hasn't had that kind of money since the turn of the century. The buildings are plainer than they used to be. The fancy cornices have been stripped away, the hardwood floors have been covered with tile, the fronts are faced with stucco and cheap fiberglass. All the Victorian gewgaws imported from Ontario have been gradually jettisoned like so much excess baggage. The buildings look pasted together, transitory. Although Miami has been in existence for almost 85 years, it looks as helter-skelter and impermanent as it did in its first decade of life.

"It used to be that you cut people's hair as to what suited them best," mutters Mac. "Now you get nothing but complaints. Parents complain about long hair on the kids. They make you feel you don't know nothing about cutting hair. Everyone's dissatisfied." Mac used to have a poolroom in back but he closed it down a few years ago, sold his house, and moved into the back of the barbershop. He's lucky to make $75 a week cutting hair and selling pop and tobacco.

"If I was to start today I wouldn't go into a small town," he says. "But I'm too old to take training. I'll just hang on."

Hanging on is what most merchants are doing. The younger ones scramble. The young man who runs the new pool hall has gone into lawn chairs, fishing rods, and suede handbags, and his window is plastered with signs advertising sunglasses, air freshener, cigarette lighters, watch straps, and pocket knives. Carr's Hardware around the corner is an odds and sods place, a small store that specializes in galvanized pails, baseball bats, teapots, barn spray, warble powder, potato dust, and fishing licences, a place you go to pick up a new rake or a couple of nails when you run out. Carr's prices are high but profits are small, so in 1970 he went into snowmobiles. In one year Mr. Carr sold 120 snowmobiles, more than any other Moto-Ski dealer in Manitoba. He didn't actually sell them; he traded them for wheat, barley, and cattle, giving the farmer a price just below market value. "Carr's got a whole herd of cattle," says a farmer, pointing down the highway to the pasture behind Carr's house. Carr made enough money to expand into campers and trailers, which he displays in his front yard. His hardware store is up for sale.

The meat market next door gets a steady trade from the widows and schoolteachers in town. The butcher offers a small selection of roasts and chops in a glass case. Buying is an intensely personal experience, a contest of will and ideology with the beefy butcher who has very strong and vocal opinions on every topic. Once in the door you are obliged to buy something. To walk out without a purchase is an insult.

Shopping in Miami is a stately procession, a royal progress down the street, an adventure fraught with dangers and discoveries. You say hello to overyone and everyone says hello to you. Each encounter comes freighted with information about weddings, pregnancies, and sickness, and offers the opportunity, through a chance remark or observation, to change the social course of the community. Notices of meetings are posted in the entrances to the grocery stores and cafes, and a welter of little handprinted signs pasted to windows advertise everything from baseball bats to the next meeting of the Slim and Trim Club. A trip down Main

Street makes you au courant of all the latest events. Miniscule changes are noted and commented upon — an empty beer bottle on the step of the Grandview Hotel, a strange car, Elsie Hink's new hairdo. The excitement comes from chance. Although the people are always the same, the kaleidoscope changes slightly every day. As Sid Cox says, "There's always something doin'." Shocking and traumatic events are so rare that even the tiniest interruption in the smooth flow of time is treated as an occurrence of immense magnitude. Small towns are anthropocentric. People revolve in fixed orbits like stars and planets, each one convinced that he is the sun of the universe. The immediate galaxy is the local community; distant cities and foreign countries take on the quality of mysterious and hostile outer space, reachable only after several million light years of travel. What happens out there is interesting, but beyond control. This pleasurable sensation of personal significance is reinforced by all the rituals of the community and by the decorum of trade.

The centre of trade in Miami is Leathers' General Store, which is in the very middle of the main street. "I have fed five generations," beams Mr. Leathers. The store is a work of art. With the exception of electric lights and venetian blinds, it is preserved exactly as it must have been the day Mr. Leathers started work in 1916. Stanfield's are stacked high on old wooden counters next to tidy piles of stiff blue jeans and striped overalls; shoe boxes are piled up to the ceiling, so that Mr. Leathers has to scramble up a ladder if anyone wants an odd size. The only concession to fashion is a shelf of red and purple polka dot caps, which are all the rage among farmers this summer. Racks of bright jelly beans and striped humbugs are placed tantalizingly on the oak counter worn hollow by thousands of hands. Behind the counter, shelves and shelves of neatly stacked tins rise up to the ceiling; bananas, oranges, cake mixes, and cookies are arranged on the countertop and onions are in cardboard boxes on the floor. The store is dark with old wood and jammed full with goods, but everything, including round, bald Mr. Leathers, is clean and neat as a pin. The clock is stopped at ten to four.

Mr. Leathers does all the shopping himself. The store is

too crowded to roam around in, and only Mr. Leathers knows where everything is. He waits on each customer personally, patiently, with courtly politeness, going off to find each item individually, one at a time. He walked back and forth behind the counter so much that he eventually wore right through the oiled hardwood floor and had to have it replaced. One by one he stacks the items on the counter and adds the cost on the adding machine.

Shopping at Leathers' can take hours. It's a social occasion, a meeting of minds and a reaffirmation of existence. The vulgar and impatient can always shop down the street at the Co-op, a bright and shiny supermarket which is teetering on the verge of bankruptcy. Mr. Leathers does a comfortable business. The store and his house were paid off long ago, he spends nothing on improvements or advertising, taxes are almost nil. When he dies, his store will vanish.

Business in Miami is family business, handed down from father to son. The name of the store is the name of the owner; only in a small town is it still possible to open the door of Leathers' store or Moorey's grocery or Westaway's drugstore and be waited on by Mr. Leathers, Mrs. Moorey and Mr. Westaway in person. Jack Westaway was a successful druggist in Kapuskasing, Ontario; he came home to Miami to take over the family business when his father died in 1942. It was the natural thing to do. Westaway's is a child's garden of delights, a wild chaotic confusion of hair spray, oven mitts, rat poison, and *True Confessions* magazines. You can get anything you want in Westaway's drugstore including famous Westaway's Stomach Powder, a home remedy with fans as far away as Vancouver. Being the only drugstore in a small town full of old people is profitable, but Mr. Westaway carries on a sideline. The Miami liquor store is located in a dark corner of Westaway's drugstore between the hair color and the pills. A sign in the window announces that it is open from 11 a.m. to 12 noon and from 1 p.m. to 6 p.m. and CLOSED ALL DAY MONDAY. Everything in Miami is closed all day Monday to give the merchants a rest after Saturday night shopping until 10 p.m. Most of the merchants spend Monday in Winnipeg, shopping.

"It cost me $4,000 to buy the liquor to set up," beams Mr. Westaway. The bottles are hidden away in a little cupboard; a few dusty specimens are displayed along the top, and you make your selection from a list posted on the wall. The selection is quite broad. "Rye mostly," says Mr. Westaway. "I don't sell much wine. It's big for wine around Swan Lake — Indian reserve you know." He speaks enviously of the druggist in Swan Lake. Mr. Westaway buys his liquor directly from the provincial government in $1,500 lots; he makes a profit of ten per cent on every sale. The rural liquor trade is not restricted to druggists; down the road the furniture dealer has the booze.

Progress is catching up to Mr. Westaway, "They told me I have to tear down the wall to *show* the liquor," he says in a shocked voice. "And the next licence holder will have to put it in the *window*!"

He scampers in to get the bottle and wraps it up quickly in white paper with a big "Rexall" stamped across it in blue ink.

Most winter mornings, Miami is full of farmers. They all arrive about ten o'clock, just in time for coffee at Vern's Place, nosing their pickups and cars up to the sidewalk the way they used to tether their horses. They swarm in like an army in their khaki coveralls, quilted khaki parkas, and black work boots heavy with mud. In their greasy clothes with the stuffing coming out through the rents they look enormously fat, like teddy bears, and they walk with a rolling waddle. Once they're inside and unzip their parkas, it's obvious that the quilting is only the outer layer of an onion that begins with white longjohns and works its way up through a cotton shirt, a wool plaid shirt, trousers, one or two sweaters, and overalls. The man at the centre of this mobile chesterfield is often quite frail. Their caps are the only mark of identity; most wear khaki to match their uniform, but some have blue ones with white polka dots or red baseball caps or rescue orange hunter's caps. A farmer's affection for his cap is as enduring as a cowboy's love for his horse; he likes it to be flashy, stylish, but not bizarre. He goes nowhere without it except on Sunday, when he

reluctantly exchanges it for a fedora with a little feather
sticking out of the band.

Vern's is a man's cafe, a dingy, homely, bachelor's kitchen
where nobody gives a damn if there's mud on the floor or
spots on the knives. Seven old-fashioned arborite tables,
relics of World War II, are surrounded by red plastic
kitchen chairs; the floor is worn, multi-colored linoleum,
which hides the crumbs and spots. A lunch counter with
stools runs down one side opposite the Coke cooler and ice-
cream freezer, but nobody sits there. The drab walls are
splattered with blackboards and menu cards courtesy of
7-Up, Canada Dry, and Pepsi-Cola; the special of the day is
scribbled on one, another carries the old standbys: fish
and chips $1.25, fried chicken $1.50, pie 20¢. A black-and-
white TV up in one corner is tuned into an American
station. The coffee is set out on a hot plate on an old brown
kitchen table in the middle of the room; everyone helps
himself. A sign on a post over the coffee pot says:

T-bone — 25¢
with
meat — $2.25

Women feel awkward in Vern's. It's not a family cafe.
There are no plastic plants or fancy wood panelling or
indoor-outdoor carpet. Nobody around Miami would dream
of going out to Vern's for supper. In fact, the only times
that Vern's is totally deserted are noon and suppertime,
when the town shuts up tight and everyone scurries home
for dinner. The only people who seem to eat at Vern's are
strangers and newcomers.

Vern does all the cooking himself on a grill in the back
and waits on tables when things are slow and his waitresses
have gone home. His hamburgers are limp and grey, but
they come with plenty of ketchup and Worcestershire sauce
to wash them down. An aging, beefy man in rolled-up
shirtsleeves with a stiff grey brushcut and a stubbly chin,
Vern looks like an army cook or a caricature in a Greasy
Spoon cartoon. A man of few words, he presides like a
morose Buddha behind his counter stacked with potato
chips, razor blades, and sunflower seeds. Small boys clutch-

ing dimes and quarters in their fists bang in the door to contemplate Vern's selection of chocolate bars, jawbreakers and bubble gum. High school kids don't hang around, because there's no jukebox or padded booths, but the farmers like the kitchen chairs.

Vern's Place is the village square, the switchboard on the community grapevine. Its relaxed camaraderie is seductive, and farmers become addicted to Vern's — not to the coffee, which is terrible, but to the companionship. The community recognizes this dependency, and farmers who hang out too much in the cafe are subject to the same social opprobrium that afflicts those who sit too long in the beer parlor. Fleeing the isolation of their land and the loneliness of their work, farmers seek out social gatherings that will reassure them of friendship and sympathy. Farmers love to talk; their conversation is that peculiarly rambling, pointless, comfortable, masculine drone commonly known as bullshit. They tell stories and state opinions that everyone has heard a hundred million times before but that everyone enjoys hearing again. Time and repetition do not take the edge off a complaint or dull the emphasis with which opinions are voiced. Talk isn't so much a source of information as it is a reassurance, a coming together of familiar ideas and familiar faces. It also fills up time. Every topic raised is gone into exhaustively — the weather, a television show, the price of rapeseed — and the talk goes around and around until the idea is ground into a fine powder. A good blizzard or an accident can keep the kaffeeklatsch going for months and years. Farmers have an infinite capacity to endure boredom. They learn it in the fields in summer and during the long months of winter when they labor to fill the empty hours with tedious chores or television or sleep. They wait; they wait for the snow to melt, the sun to shine, the crops to grow. They learn patience. They adapt to earth time. They walk slowly, deliberately, and they speak slowly, with long pauses for rumination; they have adjusted to the steady plod of the horse and the rhythmic chugchug of the tractor. Farmers move along at a relentless four miles per hour.

The leisurely pace of rural life is exasperating, almost unendurable, for an urban person. A farmer explained the rural attitude to me. When I met him on Main Street, he

was driving his friend's pickup truck to the garage for repairs. Four days later I met him on the same spot on Main
Street in the same truck. He blushed. "I'm still taking this
truck in for repairs," he confessed. "Got a little sidetracked
last time." He nods at the pub, grins, and shrugs. "What
does it matter? There's always tomorrow. Mañana."

Miami is a safe, secure place. Everyone in the community
has grown up together, as their parents did before them.
Land is passed on proudly from father to son; some farmers
are the fifth generation. There is great antagonism to selling
out to outsiders, especially Hutterites. "The old man would
spin in his grave," people clucked about a farmer who
allowed his land to be posted for taxes. Miami is an island,
a separate, self-enclosed social universe from which people
venture out only with great fear and trepidation. Familiar
faces and traditions bring a profound sense of peace and
comfort. Miami exists only to perpetuate itself. Business is
carried on more out of habit than out of necessity or greed.
Trade is considered vulgar. No one would consider advertising, and competition is almost nil. Personal relationships
are so constant and so well-defined that people tend to lose
their individuality and become archetypes — The Banker,
The Village Idiot, The Postmaster. Once thrust into a role,
the person adopts it; he becomes exaggerated, like a character in a play, and ceases to perceive any difference
between himself and the community's perception of him. As
long as he remembers his lines and behaves in a predictable
way, his acceptance is assured. The community gives him an
identity and relieves him of the responsibility of working
one out for himself.
    "People accept eccentricity in a small town," says a
teacher. "In that way they're more tolerant. There's not
enough people to be able to shut people out. Everyone is
accepted for what he is; he has an identity, he's not ignored.
Even the town bum. In the city he would be alienated, but
poverty isn't that embarrassing in a small community.
Everyone knows who the real poor families are. People give
them odd jobs to do and sort of look after them. There's
the bootlegger and the town whore and the local drunk;

they're not run out of town. They're expected to behave in a
certain way. If you step outside your image people are less
tolerant. Country people are not willing to accept anybody
who can't be pigeonholed. They label everyone, like anyone
with long hair is immediately labelled a 'hippie.' It's very
hard to break out of that. It's difficult to grow up in a small
community. There's a crucial point where if you don't get
out now, you never will. It's too comfortable, an incubator.
You know exactly where you stand. If you don't show up
at the poolhall for a couple of days somebody's bound to
say, 'Hey, where the hell is Herb?' What you are is determined not by your job but by your relationship with people.
Anyone who stays in town long enough becomes a folk
hero. It's just a matter of time."

Miami's biggest folk hero is the school principal, a local
boy who went away to university and then came back, a
remarkable decision which won him the love and gratitude
of the community. A silent, easy-going young man, he farms
in the summer and belongs to all the organizations in town.
His advice is sought on every question and his opinion is
taken as truth. He is the local wise man, a traditional role
in an agricultural community where, in the absence of doctors, lawyers, and bankers, the male teacher was the entire
professional class, the equivalent in secular matters of the
preacher.

The Miami Collegiate, a single-storey brick and glass box,
is the newest and most impressive building in town and it's
treated with great respect. The village sets its watch by the
school buses, which bring the 190 farm kids in every
morning at precisely 8:40 and trundle them off again at
3:30 p.m. "It's the school vans that are keeping the town
going now," muses a Rebekah. "You get a dozen vans in
town every day. The drivers go uptown, do a little shopping
for their families, sit in the cafe. They bring a lot of business into town. Any day there's no school, it's a pretty dead
looking place."

"The school is the *big thing* in the community," says a
farm woman who came to Miami as a teacher. "The
teacher is idolized. If you ask why, people say 'They're
clever people.' The parents use their children as status sym-
bols. As soon as the report cards go out the phone relay

begins: 'And how did *your* boy do? Johnny got a B,' and
they go down the whole card comparing marks. A lot of
parents take it so seriously they want the report card sent
home in secrecy! I've had parents come to the school to pick
up the report card themselves. The competition is terribly
important. The parents coach their kids so they'll do better.
You're expected to help your child do well in school; if he
doesn't, you're a poor mother. I've had a child burst into
tears because he got a B. The parents are terribly upset.
They phone you up and ask you to give their child a better
mark."

Miami kids are almost always in school, even at night.
Miami is very strong on "school spirit," and the principal
believes that education is mainly character building; the
school year is a staggering round of spelling bees, oratorical
contests, art fairs, teas, concerts, plays, bonspiels, and
basketball tournaments, so that just about everyone receives
some kind of prize at graduation. Miami Collegiate has more
scholarships and bronze medals than students; even the
grade ones win awards for perfect attendance, courtesy, and
having only A's and B's on their report cards.

Teachers are Miami's biggest industry, and the town milks
them for all they're worth. "Every teacher usually has a
talent," says a student. "They can sing or play the piano.
Well, the community just pounces on them. The teachers
wind up not only teaching but looking after Scouts and
Guides and up to their necks in church activities. They're
really exploited, the local people just squeeze them dry."
The school board refuses to provide them with housing, so
the married ones rent draughty old mausoleums and the
unmarried board out in various spare rooms and basements.
Not only do Miami people depend on this supplementary
income but they also like to have the teachers under their
eye and in their financial grasp. "There was no way I could
spend an evening sitting in the pub," says a man who
boarded with the town carpenter. "It just wasn't done. I
went for a while, but many people felt that something
strange was going on, so I quit going. The kids at school
always razz you about picking up a case of beer. It was an
unpleasant situation. All of a sudden I was community
property."

Miami's emphasis on education reflects the enormous importance and responsibility of the schoolteacher in a frontier community where the majority of the people could barely read and write. Children were entrusted to the teacher, whose moral character as well as her scholarship had to be above reproach and her discipline severe. School was an extension of Sunday school; the Bible was the principal textbook and hymn singing the main form of recreation.

"I knew that people didn't like me," recalls a woman teacher who came from the city, "but I didn't know why. I found out later. They thought I was conceited because I didn't say hello to everybody on the street. I drove my boyfriend's car to school; I was considered wild. One day I walked home from school barefoot. It was hot and I just slipped my sandals off. Jack Westaway came out of his house and said, 'I think you should put your shoes on.' 'Why?' I said; 'there's nothing wrong with my feet.' I apparently caused a great uproar. You're always being watched. What you appear, you are."

"The only fresh blood that's ever come into this community," reflects Sid Cox, "was the schoolma'am. There weren't many of them that ever left the district. Even the ugly ones. Ugliness was no deterrent. An awful lot of mothers are former schoolteachers." He shakes his head. "It's caused a lot of ructions in the school. The mothers' ideas didn't jibe with what the teacher thought."

The teacher has usually been an outsider with values and assumptions antagonistic to a peasant, pastoral society. Of the thousands of schoolma'ams who came west in the hopes of finding a husband (a good bet, since men outnumbered women ten to one, and a teacher, because of her education, was considered a good catch) most were poor women of good breeding and refined manners who had failed to find an appropriate husband in England or Ontario because they lacked a dowry. Their attitudes were bourgeois and urban. Later their ranks were swelled by the daughters of the rural elite, farmers and businessmen wealthy enough to send their children to teachers' college at a time when education was an extravagance for rural people and almost unheard of for farm women. Teachers were the instruments of civilization.

They taught a rigid curriculum which had no relevance to and no respect for rural children; they inculcated firm faith in patriotism, progress, and wealth.

Farm children were not to be educated so much as transformed, washed and polished, divested of their crudities of speech and manner, mass produced as members of an industrial culture with no room for agricultural rituals or folk history. Teachers not only taught a curriculum which substituted myth and propaganda for knowledge but also they radiated middle-class snobbery, a firm conviction based on their own position in life that the fragmentary and adulterated scraps of learning they offered measured intelligence and equalled success.

"The teachers usually have a better opinion of themselves than the rest of the town is prepared to accept," admits one. "We have more education, more money. We feel we are the elite. Other people don't."

The influx of schoolma'ams had a profound impact on rural ambitions. Farming was no longer respectable. "Parents worked their hearts out to get their kids off the farm," says Sid Cox. " 'Get that mud off your boots,' they'd say. It was *menial*. The kids were taught to look on the farm as the last place on earth to be. Parents still don't encourage their children to stay on the farm. The kids wanted out. They wanted to get away from the lousy drudgery. When I was a boy, I walked to school. I saw other kids riding in a van. I knew they had a better way of life. The only reason a lot of us stayed was because we were hamstrung. There was no way out."

"Mothers used to tell their children, 'Do your homework so you won't have to be a farmer like your dad,' " says a farmer's wife. "If you were a failure, you farmed."

The old agricultural values of land, fertility, and hard work fell into disrepute. When children became an economic liability during the Thirties, school was a handy way of easing them out of the community. During the Second World War it was patriotic to send the young people away, and after that technology made it necessary. In Miami, the ultimate goal of the educational sweepstakes was university and a professional career. Having children in the city became an achievement which made up for the farmer's own

sense of failure and humiliation. Taxes rose swiftly to pay
for the big new schools, and as the farm population declined, each farmer's share of the financial burden became
larger. But they paid cheerfully, ashamed of their own lack
of learning. (Seventy per cent of prairie farmers have less
than grade nine education; until the Forties, most rural
schools stopped at grade eight, when children quit to work
on the farm.) Older farmers apologize continually for their
bad grammar and clumsy language and writhe with embarrassment at the prospect of having to make a speech.
Although they read avidly and soak up television, they
harbor a lingering suspicion that this kind of learning is
illegitimate. Farmers have just enough education to perceive
how little they know, and their insecurity gives them an
exaggerated respect for school. They treat education with
awe, as a sacred ritual from which they, the humble, are
forever excluded.

The children so hopefully invested in Agriculture and
Home Ec. courses at university did not return, and the rural
standard of living did not improve. Farm income shrank in
the Sixties, until by 1969 farmers were earning four per cent
of the Manitoba income and paying 21 per cent of the
education taxes. The enrolment in the Miami schools began
to drop. Alarmed, the farmers looked around the empty
countryside and asked, "What happens when all the children
are gone?"

The Miami Citizens' Committee was organized in the
summer of 1970 to save Miami's schools. A policy of rural
school consolidation had been railroaded through by the
provincial government in 1967. Miami people reluctantly
voted for it, probably assuming that like most new things in
the country, it would die from inertia. However, a huge new
collegiate was built in Carman, a town north of Miami, and
the school board announced a policy of closing down the
smaller village schools and bussing the children to the
collegiate. The news came as a shock. Nothing had appeared
in the local paper (the school board news was reported by
one of the trustees), and nobody ever bothered going to
board meetings. The Miami trustee, an old man who had
been in for ages, had not told anyone. The citizens' committee was formed for the express purpose of defeating him

and electing a trustee who would stand up for the interests of Miami; they found an articulate young farmer, Alan Kennedy, to run. The confrontation threw the area into an uproar. It's not polite to run against an incumbent official who is heavy with years. Many people dismissed the citizens' committee — mostly made up of young farmers and their wives — as rabble-rousers and troublemakers. "They're just a bunch of bitches," scoffed Jim Murray. The election campaign was bitter. Rural politics is strictly personal: policies are irrelevant; what counts in a campaign is the candidate's drinking habits, his sex life, his wife's cooking, and his children's grades at school. It's important for a successful candidate to have a few glaring faults so the voters are convinced he's no better than they are. No effort is spared to find these faults; the candidate's past is dredged up and sifted through with a fine-tooth comb. The campaign is conducted in a haze of whispered slander and innuendo as the candidates and their friends cheerfully throw mud at each other's reputations and spread all kinds of vicious rumors about hanky-panky and rip-offs. To the winner goes the privilege of publicly assassinating his opponent's character until, eventually, he is defeated himself and suffers the same fate. Defeated politicians vanish quickly from sight, neither remembered nor revered.

The Miami hill was blown up in the middle of the election campaign to embarrass Alan Kennedy and the citizens' committee. Everybody laughed because the RCMP were too obtuse to appreciate the more imaginative and exotic forms of rural politickin'. Alan Kennedy won handily.

"It's dirty," says Kennedy. "Grass-roots politics is a dirty mess. People will cut and knife you. It's not done in the open. That's not polite. It doesn't make one dime's worth of difference to me. But I wouldn't be as big with my mouth if I were a businessman. You cross a few people and your business will go way down. In a small town business is shaky at the best of times. One board member refused to run again last year. 'I make my living in business,' he said. 'They'll ruin my business.' It's done easily, through whisper, innuendo."

Miami's schools are still open and the big collegiate in Carman sits partly empty, "a frilly dilly white elephant," snorts Kennedy. At school board meetings, which are now faithfully attended by a group of Miami parents, Alan Kennedy is locked in primeval combat with the old bulls of the community. The struggle is silent but fierce and bloody, a war not of words but of insinuation and allegation waged over incredibly petty grievances. (When Kennedy fixed the furnace at the Miami collegiate, one of the trustees suggested he had broken the furnace deliberately to profiteer on the transaction. Kennedy retaliated by proving the trustee had illegally commandeered a school bus to pull his car out of a snowdrift.)

"There's always one or two big men on the board," says Kennedy. "What they say, goes. They threaten to get mad and other board members back away. They intimidate everybody. If they notice you, OK, if not, you're squelched. It works on the seniority system. If someone challenges the old guys, everyone else just sits back to see what happens. The new person either drops out or takes over.

"The trick is to hit these old decrepits when they get past their bedtime. You have to start the meeting in a couth sort of way, very civil and parliamentary. Then they get ruder and ruder as you go along. Along about ten, ten-thirty, these old guys start to tire out and you can really put the blocks to them. It's kind of like a comic opera in a way; it would be funny if there wasn't so much at stake.

"The boredom is terrible. That's their tactic, to bore people to death. It's hard to sit them out. I've had a hell of a fight just to stay awake."

Why does Kennedy care so much about keeping the school alive?

"If you take the school out," he says, "the community dies, because everything's centred around the kids."

The ice of the Miami arena is bathed in soft blue light. The lobby is crowded with parents peering through the big windows screened with heavy wire mesh. The bolder mothers and fathers make their way to the wooden benches on both sides of the darkened arena, where they huddle together with woollen blankets over their knees. It's March. The ice is getting soft. The Miami Figure Skating Club's ice carnival is the last event of the winter.

One after the other, sometimes alone, sometimes in groups of three or six, the girls trot out onto the ice to perform to music played over the loudspeaker. Even the littlest girls, who fall down a lot, go through elaborate routines dressed up as pigs and bears and mice, ankling along lickety-split to "Talk to the Animals." There's just enough time for them to rush off and change costumes before they're back in the "Wizard of Oz." Every number requires a whole new set of matching outfits — witches, dwarfs, flappers, showgirls, senoritas — plus specialty jobs like the Tin Man. The costumes are dazzling, not just skating dresses with a few ribbons tacked on or stuff rummaged up around the house but brand new satin and chiffon outfits complete with hats and bows and stage makeup. The carnival goes on and on. There are 26 numbers on the program, and every girl appears in two or three. The skating deteriorates as the girls get older and fatter. Miami's little girls are very well fed, with big behinds and thick legs, but they make up in perseverance what they lack in grace. Five of the soloists, each more elaborately dressed and clumsier than the last, have the same last name. Miami has its share of skating mothers.

Mothers are what the Miami carnival is really all about. The mothers plan the program, drive the girls to practice, and design and sew all the costumes. The carnival is spectacular, a triumph of organization for the mothers. The mothers, of course, say they're doing it for their daughters, but there is an overtone of competition, fierce, vicarious satisfaction in their daughters' success as a measure of their own social prestige.

Miami kids are always in uniform. There aren't any kids on the street playing kick the can or making mud pies in the ditches. Kids are hard to find, because they're all in the same place somewhere playing baseball or hockey in green-and-white Miami sweaters or going to a Scout or CGIT or 4-H calf club meeting. Miami is jock country. The village claims to be the sports centre of southern Manitoba, and great victories are recalled dating back to 1933 or 1906 in leagues which most people have never heard about. The town's reputation rests, however, on sports that were played by men. (Old photographs of hockey and lacrosse teams show bankers, carpenters, and morticians with handlebar moustaches, bulging biceps, and chests puffed out proudly beneath their striped jerseys grouped stiffly around a silver cup.) When the West was young, sports were a good excuse for a party and a general booze-up. Now the kids provide all the entertainment in the community, conscripting their parents as audience. There is nothing left for the adults to do except drink. Even dances have faded away. There are only one or two a year in the Miami area, and they all have cabaret licences. Because of the liquor, people can't bring their kids. "It used to be that everyone went," says a farmer who used to play sax in the community orchestra, "and you'd dance with everybody. Now people go with a little group and dance with them. You don't get to see anybody else. A lot of people won't dance until they've had three or four beers. That's what people like, they like to drink."

The dictatorship of the pee wees is accepted without question. Miami believes in discipline. The strategy is to keep the children too busy to get into mischief. "The kids," comments one grandmother, "are played out. They come back to school on Monday dead beat. Some of them fall asleep on the desk." The routine exhausts the parents as well, but many of them welcome the busyness and boredom. They escape into childhood. The children only appear to be in control. It's the adults who impose and enforce the routine. The children are enslaved by their parents' nostalgia.

"The kids are still in the Fifties," says a teacher. "There's a big emphasis on drinking, roaring around in cars, good times, you know, yuk it up. The pool hall culture. Hanging around."

Miami kids are clean, tidy, and well-behaved. "There's no peace kids around here," grunts a Legion member with satisfaction. A few kids hang out in the pool hall, but the pool hall is clean and tidy too. I feel a little sorry for the knot of boys lounging around the door. Their hair is short, their clothes are pressed, and their faces are clean-shaven; they have a puzzled, rather pathetic, James Dean look. Life is frozen in 1956. The feeling is oppressive.

"We were a dead bunch," admits a man who grew up near Miami in the Fifties. "I didn't even start drinking beer until I was in grade twelve, and I was considered wild."

"There's a real in-group of girls who run things, who consider themselves 'queens,'" says the teacher. "They're socially active, always the leaders. They feel they're a little more attractive, better dressed; they have a greater sense of their own competence. They're in the minority, but there's more of them in Miami than in other communities. You could call them the nicey-nice girls.

"A strange thing about Miami is the lack of high school girls who get pregnant. There seems to be less screwing around going on. If a girl was willing to get laid, she could really pick and choose. . . . There's no population of grubby girls. No gang. The guys don't have a ladies' auxiliary to their gangs. Gangs have to hang around the chocolate shop and you can't do that in Miami."

The kids' only escape from parental surveillance is on the highway. A car is a necessity for rural kids. A car is liberty and love, a dark secret place where they can be alone with each other. They live in cars because it's the only private place they have. Equipped with a radio, a heater, and booze, a car is a little home on wheels, an instant escape. The kids' conventional dress and manner is a disguise; conformity protects them from scrutiny and allows them, in the privacy of their cars, an intense, sexy, and joyous personal liberation. Clustered in hidden ravines by the creek, the car radio on for entertainment, they can say fuck all they like, drink warm beer from the trunk, and enjoy the exquisite pleasure of necking in the tall grass. If somebody has a little dope, they'll smoke it in the dark, but a better high is to bomb down a gravel road drunk as a skunk at 90 miles an hour with the soft sweet-clover night rushing in the windows. Every now and then a kid rolls the car and breaks his neck. "It's sort of like the Viet Nam war," says the teacher. "You get to expect a daily number of napalmings, you learn to expect a certain number of deaths. Parents don't attach the blame anywhere. It's an act of God." Parents establish scholarships in their dead sons' names. They exert no pressure on the RCMP to police reckless driving more vigorously. In fact, parents are angry and humiliated when their children are arrested for speeding and drunk driving, especially if the trial is written up in the local paper. Death is accepted as a natural part of being young.

"Saturday night is the big time," says a young man. "When you're younger you go to a movie. All the kids sit in the back row in the theatre. There's always lots of mooching and smooching in the back. When you get older, you drink. Kids start to drink about sixteen. Drinking just takes over. If you're a big strapping farm boy, you gotta prove that you can be a big drinker. The big fellows, they gotta drink like crazy! It's the real thing on the weekend. You go to the next town and you drink like a son-of-a-bitch.

"Parents look down on drinking. The kids have to hide it. I remember one mother saying, 'My Margaret is a good girl.' Christ, she drank like a fish. Everybody drinks like crazy at dances. Cops set up roadblocks to every goddamned dance. You send a scout car through. He'll go without beer and he'll phone if he hits a roadblock: 'Look out for those cocksucking cops!' You always go in bunches. The car is always crowded. If there's any screwing it's on the grass or in the back seat of the car. If a girl gets pregnant she'll vanish. Suddenly. On there's lots of accidents. I've been in an accident. Most kids wind up in court by the time they're twenty-one.

"There's two kinds of kids, the sissies and the bad boys. The bad boys drink and smoke. I started smoking at eleven. Everybody does. And you swear like a bastard. Parents don't really object. Swearing is a part of life. The church doesn't have any hold on us. Fuck the church. There's a lot of driving around just for something to do. If I've gone over a road once I've gone over it a hundred times. You get bored. Sure you get bored. That's why most younger kids play hockey. What the hell else is there to do?

"Quite a few kids drop out of school, go to work on construction, driving a truck. Everybody wants to get a job. It doesn't matter that much what kind of job. Once you're out of school you're a man. You can do everything a man does, screw and drink and everything. Your friends can be seventeen or thirty-seven. You're accepted in the workaday world. You're not young anymore."

The station agent is out hoeing his garden next to the tracks. He spends a lot of time in his garden. "We get about one train a week," he says. "It usually comes through in the middle of the night. It doesn't stop unless it's got some grain cars to drop off."

The station is due to close in a couple of months. The agent, a young man in his thirties, is just putting in time until he is transferred.

"I started as a telegrapher," he says. "I do none of it now. They've taken telegraphy out of the small stations. I billed the boxcars until six months ago; now that's done out of Winnipeg. There used to be a signal board out front for train control; I don't have train control any more. The freight goes by truck. Our freight rates are too high for small stuff." He shrugs. "You can't fight progress."

The agent's only job is to sell tickets on the main line passenger trains; the passengers have to drive to Winnipeg to catch the train. "I've sold forty-seven tickets so far this year," he says proudly.

The station was built in 1893, remodelled in 1922, and painted CNR white and green sometime in the Forties. It has not been painted since. Although the silent waiting room has been modernized with chintz curtains, house plants, and varnished plywood, the agent's office is a living museum, a comfortable nook crammed with dark oak furniture, a rolltop desk, an antique safe, and a shredded green window blind that looks as if it has been hanging in the bay window since 1893. He and his family live in back in a dark, sagging room painted institutional green. They have no running water; the primitive oil heater was installed in 1967. The agent doesn't mind because it's free.

The railway tracks, which used to be kept meticulously clean, are choked with weeds and grass. The railway has phased out its section gangs. Five years ago, there were 20 men caring for this stretch of track; now there are five to look after 60 miles. They travel around in a truck. "It's funny," says the agent; "people have already paid a high price to build the railroads and now we are paying again to build highways."

A lot of people are leaving Miami. Terry Atkinson, the manager of the Bank of Commerce, has been transferred to another bank, and Emil Desjarlais, the popular Métis owner of the Grandview Hotel, has made enough money to buy a bigger hotel in another town. "He's done real good for an Indian," says Roy Compton. Miami is suffering from potluck fatigue. Every time someone leaves town, an enormous farewell banquet is held in the curling rink or the basement of the United Church, and a collection is taken up around the community to buy a cigarette lighter or an engraved ashtray for presentation during the awkward period of corny jokes and testimonial speeches that follows supper. The banquets are always the same and everybody goes; squashed in at long trestle tables, they gobble down chicken and pie as they shout at each other over the din. As more and more people leave, the banquet circuit provides a dizzy whirl of gluttony. Almost anything is a good excuse for a piss-up and a feed. Emil Desjarlais threw a big going-away party for himself in the pub, where he treated the whole community to free beer and cheese and crackers. Miami lives to eat. Food is the cornerstone of the village economy, and eating is its principal social activity. The banquets make money for the United Church Women, who do the catering, and provide work for the minister, the Rev. Edward Bennett, who is grateful for the opportunity to say grace since almost everyone has quit going to church. The Miami United Church has 180 members and is still, next to the school, the most important organization in the community, yet poor Rev. Bennett has a hard time getting 40 people out to a Sunday service. He tries. During the Stanley Cup playoffs in 1972, he rounded up all the local hockey players and their parents for a Sunday morning "hockey service." Two star forwards read the Bible and Rev. Bennett preached on "Playing in the Major League." But the church has not been so much ignored as transformed. As Miami's commercial activity has dwindled, the old agricultural rituals have re-emerged through the veneer of imported civilization. Protestantism has been routed by a kind of Dionysiac revelry led by the local trio, the Three Musty Steers. The real action in the church takes place not at the altar, but in the basement, which is the scene of a hilarious round of bridal showers, club socials, initiations, feasts, wakes, parties, and games, all of which are, in a peripheral way, connected with religion but which have acquired a life and decorum of their own and their own rigidly formalized and unvarying codes of decoration, costume, and behavior. The series of feasts is sensual and materialistic: Rev. Bennett has been completely eclipsed by Terry Atkinson, one of the Musty Steers, who is famous for his corny jokes and skill on the ukulele, and is no longer needed around the church because the activities are now completely dominated by the women.

Miami is full of lodges, clubs, and secret sisterhoods, to which everyone belongs. Life is a series of initiations, elaborate inductions into a complex social hierarchy which begins with baptism and ends with burial. The rites of passage are celebrated with pomp and ceremony; the women talk of nothing else for days, and Fern the hairdresser is swamped. All celebrations are exactly alike; only minor variations in the color of the streamers or the manner of serving food are permitted. Sameness is essential to the tradition. The stages of initiation are clearly marked and certain set tasks must be performed. Men move through hockey to cars to jobs and community office; women go through CGIT, a wedding shower, marriage, children, and Rebekahs. Breach of the rules is met with severe reprimand. Various levels in the social hierarchy are easily recognizable, because they require different codes of conduct and appearance; as men and women move from one to the other, their appearance changes sharply. Eligible young people are stylish and sexy; as soon as they marry they dress plainly. Most women cut off their hair (Fern charges less for short hair), slop around the kitchen in bare feet and soup-stained sweatshirts, and saunter uptown with the baby carriage in old moccasins with their hair up in rollers as if they almost deliberately made themselves unattractive. A woman's sense of fashion remains frozen from the day she is married; generations of social history are visible in Miami gatherings like layers in rock.

"You do what everyone else does," sighs a middle-aged woman. "You dress a certain way, say certain things, go certain places. You almost know what everybody is going to say before they say it. First you discuss the weather. Then they say 'How are you? How is your mother-in-law?'

Then you discuss your baking and it's 'Well, I have to go now.' You have no conversations with people."

The most important level in the social cycle is reached about the age of 50, when the children are grown and the adults have the time to devote to community activities. Middle-age is the peak of power; the middle-aged no longer obey the rules, they make them. Now that they are wrinkled and withered, the women once more spend a great deal of time and money on their appearance; powdered and lacquered and corseted, they sail about the community like stately barges, inspecting the young and maintaining the old. This prestige is their reward for years of apprenticeship and subservience; they acquire it simply by growing old. As they reach the age of 70, they once more slip into soup-stains and old shoes. The old men wander about with ashes on their shirts and their flies undone. But it doesn't matter now, because they are revered. They have survived.

As Miami gets smaller and older, the job of maintaining the festivities becomes exhausting. The UCW is down to ten active members, all of whom are old and feeble. Only five are strong enough to serve at banquets. "Our top price for a banquet is $1.25 a plate," sighs the social convener, who's a spry 65. "It's a lot of hard work for a little bit of money."

"If a community like this is going to survive, everyone has to work real hard and really *try*," says an earnest young woman, "but it's getting so difficult. People are suffering from meeting exhaustion. One night last winter my husband had four meetings and I had one. He stayed home. People are giving up."

It's astonishing in such a sleepy village to find everyone constantly rushing off in all directions. "Oh," they shriek, "I'm too busy! I'm much too busy to talk today. Come back some other time." The pace increases as the people get older; pensioners are almost never home. You have to make an appointment days in advance and even then they'll probably stand you up. "Oooh," says an 80-year-old widow, throwing her hands in the air, "we're organized up to our ears! We're organized to death!"

Miami is working to preserve a rural culture which doesn't exist. Although it has remained a backwater, Miami has been industrialized, mechanized, absorbed into an alien urban society. The principal agent of destruction has been its most precious institution, the school. The old rituals are hollow and meaningless, serving not to preserve and perpetuate the community, but to destroy it. The young people avoid them like the plague.

"The social things are so *antiquated*," rages a farm wife. "I was the first to go to church without a hat. Everybody nearly fell out of their pews! I wore a pantsuit to church. *That* rocked the boat. I thought maybe there was something you could do to shake people up. The organizations are in such a *rut*. But people just said, 'Oh, she's a kook. From the city.' I could do anything and they'd laugh it off.

"Women are segregated. It's so stifling. You're supposed to scrub floors and vote the way your husband votes. You're not supposed to have an idea of your own. Women don't challenge it. They sit around and talk about their husbands! *Theirs* is the best. They're just the shadow of the guy they married. I've talked to women about it. 'Couldn't we get together and do *something*, something that wasn't tied up with the church?' Boy, they sure need women's lib out here!"

Conformity is enforced by gossip, which is taken very seriously in Miami. News from the outside is unreal, mythical. It lacks the validity of information transmitted by word of mouth. Communication is highly personal in the country. Family trivia is of paramount importance, issues and abstractions are of no interest whatsoever. Even the newspapers don't publish news; they print gossip. Old people are able to maintain their power because they have more tidbits stored away on other people than anybody else. Embroidered with complicated family trees, local traditions, and personal anecdotes, gossip gradually becomes folklore.

"You can't fart without somebody knowing all about it," snorts a young man. "Everyone knows each other's bank accounts, how often they get drunk, how often they screw their wives. It's terrible. I hate it. Of course gossip is always negative. It's always bad news. There's always that little gasp, that tsk tsk of disapproval.

"Saturday night is the big session. People gather in groups, at the store, in the post office. Boy, once they start talking, they'll talk all night! Women do the shopping, then they sit in the car and watch everyone walking down the sidewalk. Like hawks they sit there. People thought it was their 'duty' to tell my mom and dad if they saw me smoking. They're a bunch of do-goody nosy bastards.

"There are two kinds of people in Miami, those who drink and those who don't. Alcoholism is a great sin. There's a lot of alcoholics. Before mixed drinking the poor wife would end up sitting in the front of the pub for two, three hours. Got blisters on her ass from sitting in the car. Laziness was a great sin. I gather there's more screwing now than when I was a kid. Beats me. How can you screw someone in a little town without everyone knowing? Everyone knows your truck. Every so often a pair of teachers gets caught necking in the teachers' room. Once every five years two unmarried people live together. Every ten years someone runs off. Most people don't have the guts to do those things. The divorce rate is zero. There's always some old s.o.b. sitting in the window or out in the yard listening and watching, listening and watching. Nothing better to do.

"Party lines are the major vehicle. People make no bones about listening in. A guy will get on to a friend of his and say, 'I wonder if Jake's cultivator will be free tomorrow?' If this doesn't get a response he'll say, 'Hey, you there, Jake?' Then you hear Jake's wife on the line yelling, 'Hey Jake, you're wanted on the phone!' People just assume everyone is listening. It causes terrible feuds between families. Brothers, old friends will fight over a quarter section of land, sometimes for the most obscure reason in the world. They won't speak to each other for five years."

Gossip is a kind of voodoo. It has the viciousness and single-minded passion of witchcraft and gives its practitioners the power to will people harm. It requires elaborate defences. Miami people laugh a lot. The men are always kidding around, playfully poking each other in the ribs with a lot of winks and nods. The women are constantly smiling. But its a funny, nervous kind of laughter, intensely secretive, a polite way of parrying embarrassing confrontations, a habit, a social convenience which greases the wheels of human contact. Miami people work hard to get along with one another; it requires a great deal of self-control and very formalized conventions. People gather around themselves what few shreds of privacy they can piece together. Silence and politeness are the best defences. Words are hardly necessary between old enemies, and silence offends no one. Only the most banal stock phrases are required; the real conversation takes place with a flick of the hand, a fleeting glint in the eyes, a small change in the tone of voice, a blush, a nervous drumming of the foot. Minute gradations in expression are all noted with careful accuracy. Rural people communicate through a highly sophisticated and complex diplomatic language. Words are few and simple, but they carry a heavy weight of emotional overtone. People work their way slowly, carefully, into a topic, prefacing a question or a request with a long palaver designed to put the listener at ease. Farmers call it "fishing." "People never come right out with anything," says one farmer. "They always fish around for it, angling, sidling up to it. When you know what they're after you keep 'em dangling for awhile, play 'em around." Good guys who laugh a lot and agree with everybody are admired because they help relieve the tension.

"They treat you so *elegantly*," says a newcomer. "If they'd crucify me on the spot I'd appreciate that. It's that sick-sweet smile! I went to one meeting of every lodge. One. The meeting is conducted so stiffly when there's a stranger present that you felt you'll never get to know a soul in that room."

Politeness stifles attempts to change Miami. Troublemakers leave, or they conform. "Everybody *has* to get along," says a farmer's wife; "you have to live with these people. Forever."

The old ladies are gathered in a little white bungalow opposite the school. The furniture has been shoved out of the living room to make space for the quilting frame, which takes up just about the whole room. It's a widow's house, full of dark oak curlicue furniture and those obese, overstuffed maroon plush chesterfield sets that everybody in Canada owned in the Forties. The chesterfield and armchair have a white lace doily on the back and one on each arm. The small windows are piled high with house plants. All the widows in Miami peer out through a screen of luxuriant foliage; healthy house plants are a source of great pride and social prestige, although one lady, Mrs. Marshall (who is also the champion quilt maker), is by far the best house plant grower; her house is a miniature rain forest. The plants give a restful, murky, undersea quality to the house.

The ladies are seated around the quilting frame, three or four to a side, each in her appointed place. The quilt is spread out taut on the frame, a huge pink and white trampoline destined to be a wedding present for a local girl. A baroque pattern of swirls and whorls has been traced on in pencil; the ladies stitch it in with fine white thread. They stitch quickly, methodically, relentlessly, scarcely glancing at the material. Their wrinkled, liver-spotted hands move delicately over the surface, like moths; when they come to the end of a thread they snip it off neatly with a pair of tiny sharp sewing scissors. Stitch stitch snip stitch snip stitch stitch. The rhythm of their needles keeps pace with the flicker of their tongues, as they spin the web of life, measure it, and snip it off. They are the Fates, these white old ladies with hairnets and goggle glasses like the bottoms of pop bottles; Miami's reputations rest in their withered, ruthless fingers. They rule Miami like a cartel of aged queens, setting the standards in dress, conduct, and moral behavior; their decision, once given, is absolute. News is heard here long before it gets to Vern's; it is mulled over, evaluated and passed along, complete with the quilting bee's editorial opinion. Their judgments are reached quickly, since their standards have remained unchanged for 50 years.

"We have a nice lunch and a little gossip," beams one of the matriarchs.

"Oh yes," pipes another, "if we didn't come here, we'd miss all the news!"

"Sometimes the men say it's just. . . ." The first woman trails off, not wanting to use a word like dirt or muck.

"Well I think that when my husband goes to his card games they're worse than we are," booms the second lady, who speaks very loudly because she is deaf. Several of the women are quite deaf, which means that all the news has to be repeated two or three times. They can see lips moving out of the corner of their eyes and demand to be told what was said. This makes the other ladies frown and go white around the mouth.

The quilting club is sponsored by the United Church, although the ladies seem to spend more time making quilts for weddings and showers than they do for sale. Crib quilts are their specialty. "Every time somebody is having a baby, we sell a quilt to the grandmother," states the hostess with satisfaction. The quilts are superb. They come in a galaxy of colors and any one of dozens of patterns from patchwork to appliqué; they are made with great taste and painstaking workmanship. The going price is $70; most are sold to Americans. One was hung in the Winnipeg Art Gallery. The ladies have a sharp sense of the financial value of their past; they cackle with delight at their ability to thwart American bargain hunters who want to make off with their antique furniture.

One of the ladies is left-handed and is causing a problem, because she keeps running into other people's territory on the quilt. This observation leads to an extended discussion of left-handedness and its effect on children, based on the personal experience of several of the ladies who have had or taught left-handed children. It includes a complete list of everyone in the Miami area who is left-handed.

"Both our bankers are left-handed," states one woman emphatically, as if to clinch the argument.

"Has the new banker any children?" queries another woman, not missing a stitch or raising her eyes from the quilt.

"Yes, two," pipes the hostess, looking around in triumph at being the first with the information. The other ladies look grumpy.

"Are they old enough to go to school?"

There is a general nodding of heads and a cacophony of affirmatives around the quilt. The stitching picks up speed.

"Have they moved in yet?"

"Oh yes!" says the hostess. "They were here on Friday. They were uptown for dinner Friday night."

"*Before* Friday," crows a woman across the quilt, striking like a snake. "I saw the children playing behind the house on Friday morning. They were up before I was."

"Yes, before I was too," adds the woman next to her.

They stitch for a while in silence. Only two children. "Terry Atkinson had four, didn't he?" asks a woman. Everyone nods. "And the station agent, he's leaving. He has four too, doesn't he?" They all nod. There is no melancholy in their voices, no gloom, but rather an un-expected and startling hint of satisfaction.

"Mrs. Sprott! You're on my square! Do you see where you are?" Mrs. Sprott, who wears magnifying glasses, has intruded about six inches into Mrs. Marshall's section of the quilt. Mrs. Sprott peers around, confused.

"Oh am I?" she chortles. "Well, what's the matter?"

Mrs. Marshall sets her jaw and looks daggers. Mrs. Sprott discreetly quilts her way back out.

"Mrs. Sprott is *eighty-four*," whispers the hostess loudly. "She mows her own lawn and has *beautiful* plants. Her house is so *clean!*" Mrs. Sprott beams with pleasure. "You must see her house," the hostess continues. "It's just down the street, near the Collingwood."

"That's the old folks home," says Mrs. Sprott conde-scendingly. "Our senior citizens live there."

The old people greet Miami's imminent demise with pleasure. They meticulously chronicle the progress of its decay, savoring each loss, each failure, with a small smile of triumph. "The town will die with the people who are in it," croaks an old crone, pursing her lips complacently. The old people built Miami. It is theirs. It is their right to take the community down with them. There is a casual cheerful-ness about it, as if everyone has reached a secret agreement to destroy the town rather than let it fall into the hands of the enemy.

"I tell you we're gettin' fewer and fewer," chortles the president of the Miami Legion, Branch 88, looking around at the six men in overalls gathered in the room. No one has bothered to wear his beret and medals. "Six. Is that enough to be legal?"

"Haw, haw," roar the men.

"Well, we're here," states the president, shuffling his papers. He clears his throat. "Comrades, we'll open the meeting." They scrape to their feet and bow their heads while the president reads from a little ·dog-eared book.

"They shall grow not old, as we that are left grow old. Age shall not weary them, nor the years condemn. At the going down of the sun, and in the morning, we will remember them." The men repeat in unison: "We will remember them." All together they say: "Lord God of hosts, be with us yet, Lest we forget, Lest we forget." They stand for a minute, heads bowed, in silence.

The business is haggling over liquor accounts from the World War I banquet. "It sure was a good supper!" beams one veteran, patting his paunch. "We all got filled up that night!" The testimonial ashtray for Emil Desjarlais cost $4. "Aw, don't bother writin' everything down!" the treasurer yells at the secretary, who is laboring along in a big round hand. "Our kitty men are all home and in good shape!" booms comrade president. Every month the men put in 25 cents to buy cards for members in the hospital. "We've had nobody in the hospital for the last two months, so we're home free!"

Mike Hofer, boss of the Miami Hutterite Colony, is seated proudly in front of his homemade plywood desk which, since it contains all the records of the colony's $500,000 annual business transactions and the colony's only telephone, is the seat of his power. A cherubic man with a bristly brown beard and apple cheeks who, at 36, has fathered the nine children who appear at intervals to grin shyly around the door, Hofer is outspoken, garrulous, a bubbling fountain of jokes, anecdotes, and strong opinions about everything. Sleek and prosperous in his sparkling clean checked shirt and baggy black homespun trousers, he tilts his chair back on two legs as he talks and rests his feet on the desk, waving his bottle of Labatt's Blue the way an executive waves a cigar.

"If there's anything new in farming to make a dollar easier, we sure try!" he beams, taking a mighty swig from his beer bottle which ends only when, Adam's apple working furiously, he has drained the bottle dry. He plunks it down on the desk and gestures to his wife, a stout woman swathed in a voluminous ankle-length print dress, who immediately produces another. I am seated across the room on a wooden pew plucked from a defunct rural church drinking dandelion wine. Yellow as piss and strong as whiskey, it is, without a doubt, the best wine I have ever tasted. Mr. Hofer makes it himself according to a recipe passed along from boss man to boss man as a kind of ceremonial badge of office. Mr. Hofer also possesses the only key to the colony's wine cellar.

The Miami Hutterite Colony is a commune, a Protestant community based on Christ's teaching that his followers live in a state of material poverty and brotherly love. A small commune with only 85 people — most of them children — and 3,000 acres of land located south of Miami near the site of old Nelsonville, the colony looks much like a camp, which in fact it is since everyone lives in identical white bunkhouses purchased cheap from a government construction camp when the colony was established in 1966. Divided into duplexes and furnished with yellow varnished wooden furniture made by the commune carpenter, the bunkhouses stick out like spokes from the simple church and communal dining hall at the hub. Mr. Hofer takes me on a tour. The spring wind is cold and the yard is very quiet. It's siesta time, says Mr. Hofer with a big yawn. A handful of giggly girls in long dresses and kerchiefs are in school, a small one-room country school scavenged from a dead village, but nobody cares if the kids play hooky since as far as the Hutterites are concerned the school, which goes only to grade eight, is just a token concession to the worldly corruption of the provincial government. It's not in the centre of the community but stuck off to one side in the scrub.

We walk towards the dairy and the pig barns past a rippling field of geese, followed by a fuzzy, frolicking puppy. I pat it. "Wanna buy the dog?" queries Mr. Hofer. No. Huge, modern, and automated, the barns reveal acres of squealing piglets, endless rows of Holsteins, and cacophonies of chickens. The colony produces 5,000 geese a year, 3,500 hogs, 6,000 chickens, and milk from the cows is sold to a cheese factory. The Hutterites do their own butchering, and the grain from their 3,000 acres is used for feed. Each department is in charge of an overseer — the goose man, the pig man, the milk man, etc. — who, like the boss himself, is elected by the adult men of the community. Farming decisions are made by a council of all the overseers, including the minister, who, with the boss, approves all major purchases. The boss takes charge of all negotiations with the outside. "We were in Winnipeg buying shoes for everybody," he moans, waving his arms in despair. "Last year they were $9.75 a pair. This year we had to pay $10.90." The shoes are distributed from house to house by the minister, who is also the shoe man. Everybody gets the same kind. The women make all the clothes and knit the socks on a knitting machine, but the boss goes along on their trips to buy material to make sure they don't get anything too expensive or too bright. "If women's lib gets in here we'll lock 'em all out," he chortles. The boss pays all the bills and supervises the community bank account, which is called the Miami Holding Company. No individual Hutterite has any money; even pension cheques and the Family Allowance are turned over to Mike.

The commune earns $1,200 a day, a gross annual income of almost $6,000 per capita, substantially more than the average independent Miami farmer makes. The frugal habits and spartan style of the Hutterites keep expenses to a minimum: radios and television are forbidden, although kids smuggle transistors around in their baggy medieval pockets and a fair amount of hell is raised whenever the elders are away on a buying spree. The whole colony travels around in a single International van. All money which is not invested in the farm is saved. In another ten years, when the colony has doubled in size, the boss will be able to plunk down between $250,000 and $500,000 in cash to buy land for some of his families to set up a new Hutterite commune in Manitoba.

We head towards the dining hall for dinner. The men, curious but self-effacing, are seated on benches at long trestle tables, and the women are in the kitchen spooning soup and vegetables out of enormous stainless steel vats. The boss buys all the colony's food, a year's supply at a time, and supervises its preparation. His wife bustles around the kitchen. "My wife Justina, she's the chief cook and bottle washer!" Mike says proudly. The food is plain but nourishing — salad and pickles, roast chicken, mixed vegetables, and a lumpy glob of potatoes and flour oozing grease that looks like tapioca which the boss, gobbling it down with relish, calls "little grey fellas."

The last stop after lunch is the wine cellar, a small cool room in the basement of the dining hall beyond the shelves of tinned peaches piled up to the ceiling. The boss unlocks it carefully with one of the keys on his jangling chain. The room is ringed with stained wooden kegs filled with half a dozen different kinds of wine. One of the kegs is sitting on a beautiful carved wooden table. I pat it. "Wanna buy the table?" asks Mike, his eyes flashing like cash registers. Unfortunately he won't sell the wine.

You often see Hutterites in Winnipeg, where it looks as if every Hutterite in the province comes to town on the same day, but never in Miami. They don't shop there. They don't send their kids to the Miami school or enrol them in hockey or CGIT or Scouts. They don't vote or curl or join the Rebekahs. "For all they do for the community they might as well have smallpox," snarls a farmer. Almost everybody, not just in Miami but throughout the prairies, hates the Hutterites. They are universally slandered, persecuted, discriminated against. "Aw, they're a crooked bunch of buggers," a respected Miami citizen tells me. "The police don't lay charges against Hutterites. They get away with everything. They steal pigs, strip cars. If they want to buy a farmer's land they'll irritate the guy until he has to sell. I know one guy, they dumped a shit wagon right at his gate!" People gleefully spread rumors about Hutterite children stealing candies from Leathers' store or peddling the colony's weed spray door to door or their fondness for midnight visits to a bachelor farmer to get a little high on color TV. "You set up a colony, look how many votes you'd get," scoffs Reeve Rudy Hink, "and look how many you'd lose." Although there are fewer than 10,000 Hutterites in the three prairie provinces out of a total population of almost 3.5 million, rural people talk about them as if they were about to take over the West. Communism works. Not only have the Hutterites survived as an autonomous culture and economy, they have grown and multiplied, working like bees with the most advanced machinery and technology yet maintaining their 400-year-old religion, antique dress, and communal system. Many of the established colonies are worth more than $1 million with $1 million in gross annual sales. The Hutterites' wealth is as obvious as their contempt for it. They are a living reproof to the independent farmer who, unwilling to admit that a Hutterite may be richer than he is, gnashes his teeth with rage and spits vituperation. He sells out and leaves the land; the Hutterites buy the land he leaves. "Pretty soon," grumbles an elderly farmer, "the Hutterites will be the only farmers left in western Canada."

Chapter 8
Winkler

Honk if you Love Jesus!

(Bumper sticker, Winkler, Manitoba)

It's a bad night for a sale, but the flyers have been out for days now, stuffed into 20,000 mailboxes in Winkler, Morden, Horndean, Rosenfeld, St. Jean, Gretna, Altona, Manitou, and Plum Coulee. In fact, just about every household in southern Manitoba has received a fat flyer announcing Winkler's second January

MOONLIGHT SALE!
Open Til 11 p.m.!   First Come First Served!
Keep your eyes open to get the
FANTASTIC BUYS
BACON ENDS!   BANANAS!
19¢ lb.   9¢ lb. (6 p.m. to 9 p.m.)
Check These Hourly Specials!
Starting at 10 p.m. to 11 p.m.
Wide Angle
DUST PANS!
15 inches   Reg. 98¢
39¢ ea.
ALL ITEMS ARE AS STOCK LASTS!
The Moonlight Sale will be opened by a
Torchlight Parade of Snowmobiles
Down Winkler's Main Street at 7:00 p.m.
THURS. JAN. 20th
(Prices Good Only at Time Listed)

The temperature in Winkler at 7 p.m. on Thursday, January 20, 1972, is 35 below zero and dropping. The air is frozen into little slivers of glass which pierce the lungs. The light from the full moon reflected in the crystallized air makes the night fluorescent. People scurry through the neon streets beneath small white clouds of congealed breath like the balloons in comic strips. Tears run down their cheeks. The cold freezes hands and feet to blocks of wood. It hurts to walk more than a few feet; even the cars scream and groan. The snowmobile parade has been cancelled because there's no snow.

Hundreds of cars begin to pour into Winkler just after suppertime, drawn like maggots to the smell of 20 per cent off. They come from all directions, strung out in long cavalcades, their lights visible on the highways for miles around, an encircling army on the march. Before 7 p.m. every parking space in Winkler is taken, not only on Main Street but on all the side streets for three and four blocks in every direction. All the church parking lots are full. The streets are choked with cars going round and round in hopeless circles, sending up blinding plumes of frozen exhaust which glow hellfire red from the brake lights. All the cars converge on the corner of Main Street and Mountain Avenue, Winkler's principal intersection, and create a monumental traffic jam, since Winkler's principal intersection, like all its other intersections, lacks a traffic light — a source of great humiliation to Winkler. Every car disgorges a horde of people swaddled in scarves, who run for the nearest store. They have waited a year for Winkler's Moonlight Sale and they're not going to miss it.

The stores are jammed. Knots of people spill out onto the sidewalks. They saunter casually from store to store as if it were a hot day in July and poke their heads in the windows of parked cars to say hello to the old women in babushkas huddled inside. Main Street is sunny, bathed in yellow lamplight streaming from the store windows; the headlights on the stalled cars make the street as bright as noon. The music store is piping cheerful accordian music into the street to entice people in towards the electric organs and color TVs. Even the Bible book store, which sells evangelical bumper stickers ("Have a Nice Eternity!"), is doing a thumping trade in sacred records and religious tracts.

The centre of excitement, and really the only reason for

coming to Winkler, is Gladstone's store, a fabulous empo-
rium of goods rescued from fire sales and bankruptcies
across western Canada which takes up almost a full block
on Main Street. Tension increases as 7:30 p.m. approaches,
because that's the time of Gladstone's first Treasure Spot.
The person standing closest to the hidden Treasure Spot
receives his choice of any dress in the store for $1; if he
has a Gladstone's sales slip for January 20, he gets another
$25 worth of merchandise for another $1. The crowd in
Gladstone's at 7:30 p.m. is so dense it's impossible to see
who wins the Treasure Spot. The name of the winner is
announced over the loud speaker; it's a man from a town
65 miles away.

People come at 7 p.m., because that's when apples go on
sale for $2.09 a bushel and the Co-op has girls' blouses for
77 cents. But the featured items are cunningly spaced out to
ensure that customers will spend as many hours as possible
in Winkler. Pantyhose is 25 cents a pair at 8 p.m., but the
orange juice doesn't go on sale until 9 p.m., and butter is
cheap at 10 p.m. To save on all the specials a family has
to spend between four and five hours in Winkler, and
during that time, of course, they buy a whole lot of other
stuff. The entranceways to the store are crammed with
people standing guard over mounds of flour (100 pounds
for $5.99), toilet paper, and tin cans. Waiting.

Eventually the crush pushes them out into the street,
because in Winkler there's nowhere else to go. Winkler has
a beer parlor, a dingy place in the old hotel still restricted
to men only, and the Harvest Inn, a spartan arborite coffee
shop. That's all. Squeezed out of the popular bargain
basement stores, shoppers are forced to take refuge in the
empty, higher-priced stores, much to the delight of the
businessmen who are able to turn a 30-cent saving on a bag
of bananas into an $800 three-room group.

The sale is joyless. Women paw desultorily through piles
of cheap chiffon scarves and odd shoes and, frowning,
burrow among the bruised tomatoes and the wilted lettuce.
There is no shoving or pushing, no screaming or snatching
or clawing, no bellows of anger or shrill arguments over
merchandise. No laughter. Everyone is polite. People speak
quietly in low voices, almost whispers. They stand patiently

to be waited on, oblivious of the mob. In Penner's Dry
Goods Store, where women have come for flannelette, the
silence is almost reverent. It's a while before the low dull
roar becomes noticeable. It's the steady oppressive sound
of a million grasshoppers munching. Unsmiling, expressionless, methodical, the swarm of customers grinds its way
through the store; they pick the shelves clean and devastate
the fruit and vegetables. Some people have backed their
cars and trucks up to the front door of Gladstone's grocery
store; bent double like ants, they lug out bags of flour, cases
of apples, and dozens of paper cartons full of groceries.
They work with concentration, with passionate, single-
minded intensity.

Shopping in Winkler is taken very seriously. There is
nothing else to do. Winkler has no movies (movies are evil),
no bars, no bowling alley, no clubs or lodges or fraternal
organizations (except the Chamber of Commerce). Dancing
is forbidden. Drinking is disapproved of. Sex is frowned
upon. Shopping is recreation, an acceptable orgy. Women
often apologize afterwards, saying, "Oh, I didn't really need
anything, I just went for the outing."

Winkler is the Shopping Centre of Southern Manitoba.
It's also one of the most religious towns in the province.

Winkler is ugly, a low rambling mud hole obscured by dust
in summer and blowing snow in winter, whose most distinguishing feature is its green metal water tower. It is built
in a wallow on the CPR railway line about 80 miles southwest of Winnipeg in what is somewhat euphemistically
called the "garden valley" of Manitoba. Because the highway bypasses Winkler a mile to the north, it's one of those
prairie towns you enter by the back door, down back alleys,
past potato sheds, seed plants, trailer factories, and junk
yards. On the east is a hideous black garbage dump, which
spreads torn paper and blown garbage over the fields for
hundreds of yards in every direction; on days when it's
burned, a pall of stinking smoke hangs over the area.
Nobody has bothered much with trees in Winkler. Those
there are are scattered and weedy; the town has so little
water that until the waterworks began to pipe it in during

the Fifties, it had to be trucked in from a distance of 15
miles. "Those Mennonite towns never had any aesthetic
values," grunts an old man who grew up in several. "They're
pretty crummy."

But Winkler is rich. Or at least it thinks rich. Winkler is
a phenomenon, one of the few prairie towns that is growing,
booming, prospering. Its growth is so unusual, so incredible
that Winkler is spoken about in hushed tones by agrarian
economists and is written up respectfully in publications
issued by the provincial department of industry and commerce. "A growing community with a glowing future," says
the mayor, H. F. Wiebe. The town's amazing success is
usually treated as something mysterious, a miraculous act
of God beyond comprehension or explanation. "The town
caught private enterprisitis," volunteers Ralph King, owner
of the local garment factory and the only black man for a
hundred miles.

Winkler is still a small town of fewer than 3,200 people,
but its population has doubled in 20 years and grows at a
steady rate of 60 people a year. Not only is Winkler growing
faster than most towns in Manitoba, but also it is growing
faster than its prosperous rival, Morden, a smug WASPville
nine miles west that Winkler hates like poison. Drawing
on a trading area of about 25,000 people, which increases
to 40,000 during sales, Winkler's retail stores do an annual
trade of $5 million. (The Winkler Chamber of Commerce
claims 85 retail outlets with annual sales of $15.5 million;
these figures are probably inflated, for the Chamber tends
to count each department in a store as a separate business
and then to add on the store itself. It was claiming a
population of 3,200 as early as 1970, when the real figure
was closer to 2,900. Every moonlighting electrician and
housewife who curls hair is considered a business; in 1971,
a drive-in hamburger stand that was moved to a larger
building in a different location was hailed as a fabulous
new business and had its picture published in the local
newspaper.)

Winkler is the only town for miles around that has an
industrial park with industries in it. It has 17 industries
making everything from fiberglass golf carts to pre-fab
homes, with an annual production worth $8 million and a

combined payroll of $2.1 million. Most are small, new (nine have been built since 1961), and owned by local people, although three of the most successful — Triple-E Trailers, Triple-E Motor Homes and Dutch Mobile Homes — were bought out by the Canadian conglomerate Neonex in 1972, after a fire destroyed the Triple-E plant and killed the manager. Building permits in Winkler in 1972 topped $1.5 million; since 1966 annual construction has never fallen below $500,000. The assessed value of the town is more than $7 million, an increase of more than $5 million in ten years. It's the kind of town to which the Department of Industry and Commerce points and says, "Look how industry can save a rural community."

Winkler is to a certain extent the product of the government ideology of the Sixties that industrial development in small towns would stem the tide of rural depopulation and preserve the towns from obliteration. Towns, like the farmers around them, were urged to modernize and mechanize, to become aggressive, efficient, rich, and big, to turn themselves, in other words, into cities. Revenue from agriculture, previously their principal income, was played down in favor of high-powered salesmanship and the prospect of a large American manufacturer. The government created the Manitoba Development Fund (now the Manitoba Development Corporation) to lend money to prospective developers in the hope that the financial incentives would be sufficient to entice them to locate in rural areas. Regional development offices were opened in various parts of the agricultural hinterland to offer information and assistance to potential investors. Some towns' problems were solved instantly, if a factory or cannery located there; the rest have had to scramble. Industries have proved to be very few and far between. General Motors did not move to Plum Coulee. The financial incentives served to attract a host of fly-by-night enterprises that went belly-up after a year or two and some that were outright swindles. In many cases townspeople had backed these ventures by purchasing debentures and lost several thousand dollars; they became suspicious of the next venture and soon soured on the whole idea. (The government still tends to be undiscriminating: in 1972 the NDP minister of industry and commerce announced a pending deal with the Kraft corporation to build a rapeseed crushing plant in western Manitoba in spite of the fact that several cabinet ministers had publicly declared their support of the NFU boycott of Kraft. The deal was called off.)

"We get very few enquiries," says Jack Bender, manager of the Pembina Valley regional development office, which includes Winkler. "If we get one a month we're doing very good." Since the industrialization program got into full swing about 1966, rural depopulation has intensified, the majority of towns have shrunk, and the agricultural economy has been in a prolonged slump. The government has virtually abandoned the program; in 1972 it was busy making another survey to find out what was wrong with rural Manitoba. In the midst of this retrenchment and disillusionment, Winkler remains a runaway success, a grubby, backward town with no natural advantages which industrialized and commercialized itself in a little over ten years. Winkler's Main Street is always jammed with cars (except on Monday when the town is closed), and flocks of people shop in its smart new stores with plate glass windows and plastic neon signs which are full to the brim with the very latest in garish modern merchandise. Between 7 a.m. and 8 a.m., the roads to town are choked with the cars of people going to work. New buildings are going up all over town. The credit union is bursting with money; the young people outnumber the old. Why Winkler? The reasons for Winkler's success are complex, but there's only one that's important: Winkler believes in God.

On September 6, 1883, Isaac Wiens received title to his homestead beside the CPR track, which ran through the northern fringe of the Mennonite Reserve. Wiens was one of more than 7,000 Mennonites who migrated to Manitoba between 1874 and 1880 to escape military conscription and religious persecution in Russia. A pacifist Protestant sect originating in Holland and Germany during the Reformation, the Mennonites had lived in Russia since the eighteenth century in autonomous agricultural colonies where they were allowed to speak Low German and to practice their puritan religious beliefs on the condition they did not attempt to convert Russian Orthodox peasants in neighbouring villages. Highly organized, industrious, and fertile, the Mennonites soon became wealthy growing wheat, which they marketed through ports on the Black Sea. The Mennonites had been enticed to Russia by Catherine the Great, who was looking for people to inhabit the barren steppes from which she had driven the Turks; their wealth soon caused the czars to cast covetous eyes on the colonies, and by 1870 they were threatened with expropriation. At this time the Canadian government, like Catherine the Great, was advertising for people to inhabit the Western prairies. It offered the Mennonites two parcels of land, one of eight townships (288 sq. mi.) in swampy bush country east of the Red River and another of 17 townships (612 sq. mi.) west of the river on the open prairie north of the American border, within which settlement would be reserved for Mennonite immigrants. The Canadian government saw the Mennonites not only as good colonists but also as a buffer against American invasion. The government needed a lot of people fast; it promised the Mennonites exemption from military service, religious freedom, and permission to educate their children from the Bible in the German language. Since the province at that time had no public schools and no system of municipal government, the Mennonites were allowed to assume that within the confines of their reserves they would be able to re-establish the system of local government they had had in their villages in Russia.

The immigrants who came were the very religious*and the very poor; the rich Mennonites who owned estates, herds of cattle, and flour mills stayed in Russia to protect their investments. The immigrants were what the Mennonites called *die Anwohner* , the landless people, the excess population of the Russian colonies who, since all the land had been taken up, made a meager living laboring for Mennonite landlords. Some were seeking a religious utopia where they could establish a society of perfect peace and humility; most just wanted land. They came in family groups, several hundred friends and relatives from the same Russian village, bringing only a few small belongings wrapped in a quilt and the little money they earned from selling their possessions to those who remained behind. In

1874 the first group of settlers borrowed $215,000 — approximately $1,000 per family — from the Canadian government to pay for their passage and to buy their homesteading outfits.

Paddlewheel steamers brought them down the Red River from St. Paul, Minnesota, to Winnipeg, where they attempted to purchase homesteading equipment before making the five-day trip by ox cart to the reserves. Instantly recognizable in their homemade black homespun clothes, the women swathed in long skirts, aprons, and babushkas, the Mennonites created quite a stir in Winnipeg. They were the first "foreigners" to set foot in western Canada. The patronizing and bigoted attitude of the British residents is reflected in the report of their arrival by the *Manitoba Free Press*, August 8, 1874:

Who They Are and What They Are

'ARRIVAL OF THE ADVANCE GUARD'
The first installment of the Mennonites, consisting of sixty-five families or three hundred and eighty persons arrived last Friday by the International. The accommodations of the
KITTSON'S LINE
were put to their utmost capacity by this influx but passable accommodation was afforded by means of a canvas-roofed barge, which the immigrants, after this ocean voyage, do not complain of. The individuals of the party seem to be composed of exactly the

RIGHT KIND OF STUFF
physically, for pioneer life, and this taken in connection with the well-known frugal habits and thriftiness of the Germans, ensure their prosperity here. An idea has gotten abroad that
FOREIGN IMMIGRATION
or, in other words an influx of large bodies of people not speaking the English language, is not desirable here, but it must be remembered that this Province must of necessity depend upon

agriculture to a great extent for its prosperity and, that being the case, no more desirable people can be persuaded to make their homes here than these.

THE SCENE IN THE CITY
during the greater part of the day was lively in the extreme, shops, particularly hardware stores, places where agricultural tools and implements are sold, and those of dealers in provisions were besieged by crowds of these new comers.

PLENTY OF MONEY
seems to be one of the characteristics of Mennonites, but notwithstanding this they have fallen, through being accustomed to dealing with the Jews into a habit of
BEATING DOWN PRICES
and a stand would be made for a reduction of five cents on an article worth fifty dollars. Large sales were made, one hardware establishment selling close to four thousand dollars worth of goods today, and the purchasers might have been seen all day long wending their way back to headquarters with
HEAVY LOADS
of hay forks, scythes, stones, coffee mills, frying pans, groceries, provisions, tin-ware, potatoes, and sundry odds and ends, useful and pleasant to have by the Manitoba pioneer.

Out on the Canadian steppe, the colonists re-established their villages and gave them the same German names — Rosenfeld, Blumenort, Reinland, Chortiza, Hoffnungsfeld — as the names of the villages they had left in Russia. Each village was laid out in the medieval Russian pattern — two rows of 10 or 15 farmhouses facing a single street which ended in the community pasture. The houses were frame cottages with high peaked roofs for storing grain and a big brick stove in the middle which heated the house and served as an oven. The barn was attached to the house at the back, a cozy and efficient custom which shocked British farmers' respect for cleanliness. Painted white with green trim and a red barn, each house was set in a neatly fenced ten-acre yard with a big orchard and vegetable garden in front and grazing space for a cow behind. The church had the place of honor in the centre of the village. Like the houses, it was a long, low building with two rows of small windows, unadorned except for heavy handhewn pews with little pegs on the back where farmers hung their hats. Cottonwood trees from the creek beds were carefully planted in the yards and along both sides of the street where, as the years passed, they framed each Russian village in a picturesque arch.

The Mennonite village was efficient, autonomous, and perfectly adapted to the frontier. It was not a commune but a theocracy, a community of God's chosen people who had banded together for salvation and self-defence, a society which had evolved through centuries of persecution. The first Mennonites were Dutch artisans and small businessmen, urban people of comfortable means who specialized in weaving silk and making brandy; burned and slaughtered as heretics by the Catholic Church, they fled to the barren marshes of the Vistula delta, where they settled in villages to isolate themselves from the violence and corruption of the civilized world. They made the marsh bloom; the world moved in and forced them onward to the Russian steppes and then to the Canadian West. During this pilgrimage they became an agricultural people, not only for independence and survival, but also because the land came to form the basis for their fundamentalist Christian theology. Yet they remained bourgeois. Although the farmers in a village pooled their land to form a large area of four or five sections around the village, each retained ownership of his own property and exercised complete financial control over it. Every section of land was divided into equal strips to ensure that each farmer got a fair share of good and bad land, so individual holdings were scattered in three or four different places; one section was set aside as community pasture with a village cowherd who went down the street every morning blowing his horn to round up the cattle, but each farmer owned his own herd.

The village was governed by a mayor and council elected
from among the local landowners. The council hired the
schoolteachers and cowherd, appointed the fire chief, and
levied taxes to pay for the maintenance of the school and
the street. A detailed account was kept of every farmer's
cattle and machinery for assessment purposes. All children
between six and 13 were required to attend the village
school, where they learned reading, writing, and simple
arithmetic; the Bible was the basic curriculum and the sole
textbook, the language of instruction was German, and the
teacher's main job was to enforce discipline and obedience
in the children and to prepare them for church membership
by instructing them in the catechism. The school term ran
from October 15 to the commencement of spring seeding,
then for four weeks after spring seeding. It was designed
not only to free the children for farm work but also to give
the teacher time to get his crop in.

The real political and financial power in the village
rested in the church. Like the mayor, the minister was a
village farmer elected by the congregation for his intelligence, moral rectitude, and Biblical scholarship. He had no
formal training in theology, but that was not considered a
handicap, since the written sermons were handed down
over the generations. It helped if he had some financial
acumen, because the church was also the village bank. To
prevent individual farmers from destroying the village's
autonomy by contracting debts to outsiders, the church
board of elders negotiated all major loans and guaranteed
individual mortgages on behalf of the whole village. Mutual
liability not only tied the village together but made the
Mennonites renowned far and wide for the amazing
rapidity with which they paid off their debts. Debt was an
obligation to an alien commercial society from which the
Mennonites strove to isolate themselves. Not only were
they automatically segregated by their German tongue and
Russian peasant dress, but also the churches laid down
strict rules forbidding any intercourse with the enemy.
Land could not be sold to outsiders, children were not to
attend public school, Mennonites were not to go into business or accept employment from *die Englanda*, the Mennonite equivalent of *maudits Anglais*. Liquor, cigarettes, frivol-

ous dress, and entertainment were forbidden, and towns, where these luxuries could be obtained, were to be shunned. Some of the more conservative ministers made lavish and indiscriminate use of excommunication for such sins as riding a bicycle, driving a buggy, or using sleigh bells. Offending children were whipped by the village cowherd.

Since within the womb of the village no distinction was made between sacred and secular, the line separating religious ideology from folk customs became blurred, and the Mennonite way of life came to be based not only on traditional religious beliefs but also on agricultural concepts of productivity and thrift. The preservation of the old customs was considered absolutely essential to a holy life. Frugality, made necessary through the exigencies of survival, became a religious imperative, and prosperity was a sign of God's blessing. Although they were formed by people seeking to live a simple life according to the teachings of Christ, the Mennonite colonies became increasingly capitalist. If hard work and a clean life are to the greater glory of God, then the harder a man worked and the more strictly he adhered to the moral strictures of the Bible, the more Christian he was. In a rich land, hard work and no vices usually brought wealth; the rich men became both the economic and moral power in the community. Their riches were a sign not of worldliness but of sanctity. Since there were so few people in each village, the same men usually served as the village council and the church elders, and these men were the wealthiest men in the community. (One bishop who controlled several churches south of Winkler owned 3,000 acres.) These men were often able to manipulate the rules of the colony to their advantage and to place poorer farmers in their debt by lending them money or paying them wages for village chores. (It was, for instance, possible to contribute $1.70 a day in lieu of doing volunteer labor repairing the roads. The money was paid to a poorer farmer, who did the work.) As a man who grew up in a village describes it:

"They were always pursuing money, but on Sunday morning they'd sit there in church and the minister would incite them to higher virtues — be good to thy neighbour and don't screw him and all this kind of stuff — and of course on Monday morning they all went back at it as hard as they could. It was almost a self-justification to steal a little bit around the edges or to pull a fast one if you could get away with it, you know, be a used car dealer. Of course no one would ever admit they were doing that. They'd say, 'Well, I'm just trying to get the best deal possible.' There was nothing wrong with being a good businessman. In fact, some of the people who did the most people wrong, the worst, were the ones sitting in the front row Sunday morning. They were the real shysters; they'd steal land off old widows in their weakest moments. The minister didn't disapprove. Frequently the people who did it were the elders in the church. The minister isn't going to rant and rave about that too much."

Every village developed a social and economic hierarchy which was reflected in its geography. The most prosperous and influential farmer often lived closest to the church, because he had donated or sold the land on which the church was built. At the bottom of the social scale were *die Anwohner*, the landless people; they were the waifs and strays, the extra people, those who were too poor or shiftless to set up farms of their own. They lived in shacks on small garden plots at the end of the village; they paid rent and taxes, but they had no vote and no voice in village affairs. Unable to leave the village for religious reasons, most of them worked at odd jobs around the community and did manual labor for the farmers. The skilled became the village artisans — the blacksmith, harnessmaker, and peddlar. (Prosperous farmers customarily purchased extra land, which they sold to their sons as they came of age, so as to prevent them from falling to *Anwohner* status or becoming a burden on the family.) Once a Mennonite had sunk to *Anwohner* status, he was paid so poorly and taxed so heavily it was almost impossible for him to get out. He was cruelly scorned by a community which considered material wealth to be evidence of virtue:

"A lot of people went to great lengths to extol the virtues of being poor, but they desperately tried not to be," comments an ex-villager. "Poverty was never cherished by anybody. It wasn't the kind of thing they strove for. They tried to get out of it if they possibly could. The poor were the brunt of local jokes. If somebody was going to be picked on, if somebody was going to have his garden raided, they'd be the first. They were the lower class. The wealthier ones people stayed away from. You wouldn't go into his garden and bust a watermelon."

Below the *Anwohner* were the teacher ("If you can't farm, teach," said the Mennonites) and the cowherd.

Hierarchical, authoritarian, and profitable, the Mennonite villages certainly weren't communes, nor were they traditional feudal villages: they were corporations.

Isaac Wiens was in trouble in the spring of 1892. For ten years the trains had chugged through the West Reserve without stopping. Wiens, like most Mennonites, didn't really mind, since towns were depraved centres of violence, lust, and corruption, destined like Sodom and Gomorrah to be blasted off the face of the earth. For this view he had ample evidence in Morden, the hard-drinking, high-living CPR boom town down the line, where he was forced to sell his grain and purchase his few staple provisions. But in 1892 the CPR, perceiving profit to be made from the prosperous Mennonites, made Wiens an offer. The railway proposed to purchase half his property and to build a station by the track. A station meant a town. As owner of half the townsite, Wiens would be a wealthy man. It was an appalling dilemma. Not only would he profit from the spread of the vice and wickedness which he abhorred, but the CPR proposed to name the new townsite Wiens.

The Mennonite church threatened to excommunicate Wiens.

Isaac Wiens was a godly man. He agreed to trade land with a German lumber merchant who owned a homestead on the other side of the railway track. The merchant's name was Valentine Winkler. Winkler was one of a number of German-speaking entrepreneurs who had come to Manitoba to make their fortunes from the Mennonite immigration. Because the Mennonites morally disapproved of trade and commerce, there were no Mennonite businessmen; but when they had to purchase equipment and supplies, the Mennonites preferred to deal with heretics who spoke German, so the handful of German merchants had a virtual monopoly on the lucrative Mennonite trade. Valentine Winkler had prospered as part owner of a lumber yard, and by 1892 he was a Liberal member of the Manitoba legislature. Winkler was not johnny-on-the-spot by accident; not only did he have access to railway rumors as a politician, but his father-in-law was the surveyor in charge of selecting all the CPR townsites in southern Manitoba. Winkler's buffalo wallow was divided into neat rectangular blocks; the CPR bought every second block, and Valentine Winkler owned the rest.

Valentine Winkler opened a lumber yard. He put up a grain elevator. He built a splendid house in Morden. In 1915 he became minister of agriculture in the provincial government. A charming, gregarious man, Winkler was all commerce to the Mennonites — interpreter, lawyer, civil servant, moneylender, letter-writer, grain buyer, consultant, and newspaper; until his death in 1920, he was also their sole contact with the Canadian political system, an arrangement which suited both sides equally well.

Winkler was an orphan town, neglected by the government, unloved and unwanted by the Mennonites. Not even its own founder would live there. As one contemporary observer described it: "Unpainted buildings of all shapes and sizes, frequently of ramshackle construction, straggled along the business street. Some stores were sheathed with tin; the false fronts were visible from all sides." The stores were interspersed with vacant lots and stables, and horse dung was piled in the streets. The merchants finally had to request that the huge stacks of hay heaped in the trading area on Main Street be removed because they interfered with business when the hay blew into the customers' mouths. In spring the run-off from the fields turned the business area into a swamp. Even the Mennonites shopped in Morden, a smug WASP "government" town where they were gypped by the storekeepers and insulted on the streets. The Anglo-Saxons and the Mennonites enjoyed a relationship of mutual loathing. The Mennonites were shocked at Morden's greed and licentiousness; the English disapproved of the Mennonites' "closeness," their "foreign" language, their "communal" system, and most of all their prosperity. The grassland proved to be exceptionally fertile and the Mennonites' agricultural economy highly productive; the Mennonites were taking off big crops while the British were still clearing brush. The British retaliated by cutting off the Mennonites' supply of wood in the hills, which forced them to burn dried cow dung. The Mennonites' prosperity was attributed to the willingness of their women to do hard work in the fields. Shrugs an elderly Mennonite: "An Anglo-Saxon woman won't work in the fields because she feels like a Russian peasant. Heck, the Mennonites *are* Russian peasants." (The Mennonites still laugh about the dignified British lady who drank tea during the day and hung out her wash and scrubbed her floors in the middle of the night.) An outpost of Empire, Morden was brimming with jingoistic fervor and British racism; as Britain became more deeply embroiled in military conflicts, Morden's flag-waving became more enthusiastic and the town's dislike of German-speaking pacifists more intense. The Mennonites built Winkler as a defence and revenge. Nobody imagined that it would turn into a Jewish town.

A sprinkling of Jews in the North-West would do
good. They would at once go in for peddling and
politics and be of much use in the New Country
as Cheap Jacks and Chapmen.

(Sir John A. Macdonald, 1882)

Jewish wagon peddlars began to flock to the Mennonite reserve around the turn of the century, each one staking out a small circuit of five or six villages which he visited once a week. Accustomed to dealing with Jewish middlemen in Russia, the Mennonites welcomed them with open arms. The peddlars provided convenient shopping and relieved the Mennonites of the awkward choice of having either to deal with the English or go into trade themselves: the Jews were so obviously beyond salvation that it was less sinful to do business with them than with a fellow Christian. The Jews quickly established themselves as go-betweens linking

the heathen towns with the Mennonite villages — exactly
the same position they had occupied in Russia — and the
pattern of their little ghetto villages which had dotted the
Russian steppe was reproduced almost intact. It was a
happy relationship based on mutual experience and trust;
the Jews quickly acquired almost all the Mennonite
business.

The peddlars set out from Winkler every Monday morning
at sunrise, their wagons loaded with yard goods, needles,
pins, soap, pots and pans, and household trinkets; these
they bartered in the villages for chickens and eggs, clopping
back clucking and crowing every Friday afternoon in time
for the Sabbath. Each peddlar had his own territory and his
own regular customers. The weekly arrival of the peddlar
caused great excitement in the village, since for many
Mennonite women the Jew was virtually their only contact
with the world; it was also the only business transaction
they could make on their own, and they relished the
haggling. As he made his way from yard to yard, women
and girls rushed out, surrounded the wagon, and peered
in to see what new and interesting curiosities he had added
since the previous week. "The peddlar was a great event!"
recalls a village wife. "We called ours the 'Russian peddlar.'
He must have been poor since he had only one horse. The
wagon had a little box in front to sit on and put the eggs
in and a big box behind made of that flimsy wainscotting
wood and painted green. It had his name printed on the side
— FLEISCHMAN. The box was divided into compartments
with different sets of doors. There were little doors on the
side where he kept the thread and novelties; the cotton
prints were at the back, and then there was a compartment
at the bottom with a grating where he put the chickens.

"He'd drive onto the yard and open the doors and you'd
start dickering. 'And Mutter, what will you have today?'
he'd say in Yiddish. You argued over everything, trying to
drive the price down. He dickered pretty well. There was
no cash so you paid in eggs and chickens. He liked to catch
the chickens himself so he'd get the nice fat ones; he had no
scale so he'd hold them up by the legs to test the weight.
The women always wanted to give him the hens that weren't
laying. Everything was incredibly cheap. Print was seventeen

cents a yard; you could make a dress for fifty cents. He always had the same material, navy print with white flowers for dresses and white cotton with pink and blue flowers for quilts. Everyone in the village bought from him; it was cheaper than the stores, if you didn't mind all having the same apron."

The peddlar's life was not easy. "Our peddlar was a little shrimp of a guy," laughs a farmer. "His pants were too long and he used to trip all over them when he was chasing the chickens. We kids used to run after his wagon and stick our fingers through the grate to pull the feathers on the chickens and make them yowl. Boy, he got mad! He'd take his whip to us, lashing about and yelling at us 'Young 'uns, young 'uns!' " Whenever the peddlar's cart overturned in a yard, some farm women ran out to gather up the eggs that spilled out of the box. Most of the peddlars were extremely poor; they persisted well into the Forties, trading apples and oranges for old car batteries and other bits and pieces of scrap metal. At night they bunked in with a Mennonite family who would agree to cook them a kosher meal in exchange for a couple of spools of thread.

As soon as a peddlar got a little capital together, he opened a store. Winkler was an ideal location, since there was almost no competition. Most Mennonites who dared dabble in trade were dealt with swiftly and harshly; one of Winkler's first Mennonite merchants was excommunicated and boycotted by members of his church because he moved to town and sent his children to a public school. Although his store was patronized by compassionate Jews and Anglo-Saxons, he was quickly forced out of business and sold his store to a Jew. Soon Winkler had a large and thriving Jewish bourgeoisie which, including the itinerant peddlars in the neighbourhood and travelling salesmen from Winnipeg, must have numbered more than 50 people. The Jewish children attended the Presbyterian Sunday school, which was conducted in the CPR station, but later a small synagogue was built in Winkler, and a rabbi was employed to slaughter the chickens and teach the boys Hebrew. Although in many rural communities the Jews more or less abandoned religion ("We had religion once a year, on the High Holidays," snorts a former Plum Coulee clerk. "We were too

busy, too busy making money."), the Winkler merchants
tried hard to maintain the customs. "The stores were kept
open on a Saturday," recalls the son of one Jewish storekeeper, "but you never saw any Jewish people ride on a
Saturday or smoke on a Saturday. My mother was very
Orthodox. If she saw anyone desecrating the Sabbath she'd
more than bawl them out, she'd bring the wrath of God
down upon them. The holidays were carefully observed.
The stores were closed."

Competition among the peddlar-merchants was cutthroat
because everyone was selling the same stuff. While
each merchant depended on his regulars, people from the
villages where he had peddled, he offered incredible bargains to lure newcomers away from his competitors; the
customer hotfooted it back to his regular merchant and
forced him to meet the opposition's price or lose his business. To avoid cash the storekeepers took almost everything
in trade — chickens, eggs, butter, lard, hams, homemade
sausage, cucumbers, and watermelons, which they shipped
to Winnipeg by the railway carload. Once a week the
Mennonites lugged in crates of live chickens and tubs of
lard; in return they were given tokens stamped with the
merchant's name to use in the store.

"We sold a lot of kerchiefs," sighs a retired storekeeper.
"And coats. The Mennonites wore dogskin coats. Sold 'em
in July. I could hardly get 'em out of the box, they sold
like hotcakes. We sold dozens of spools of thread, *carloads*
of thread. They used so much thread they made beds out of
the spools. And carloads of Raymond sewing machines, that
was the big brand name then. The men wore homemade
suits, black with black peaked caps. Even the little kids
wore suits — black pants and jackets, all the same. They
made 'em. We never sold ready-made clothes for women or
children. We sold a few ready-made suits here and there.
Mostly for funerals. When they died, they'd get a black suit.
I don't recall ever seeing a necktie."

Because the Mennonites abhorred frivolity, the range of
merchandise in the Winkler stores was extremely limited.
It was also cheaper for the merchant to buy in bulk. "There
was a tremendous difference in the styling that you found
in the small town and in Winnipeg," says a merchant's son.

"People bought from Eaton's catalogue. And they bought
the suits that the merchant bought from the wholesale
houses. They didn't go in for any extremes. It was a very
staple, basic garment. Your hat was a felt hat or a straw
hat. Overalls were the staple. You didn't have various
brands to choose from. One merchant would have the Pick
overall and the others would have something else. And
that's what you bought. The shoes were good solid shoes.
You had your Sunday shoes that were a little finer but still
a good wearing boot."

But the merchants made up in quantity what they lacked
in fashion: "We bought carloads of salt, carloads of nails.
People bought whole bolts of flannelette; we ordered 2,000,
3,000 yards at a time. Everything came in bulk. There was
no packaged stuff. You'd come in and say, 'Gimme ten
cents' worth of pepper' and we had to put this all up. Sugar,
cookies, soda crackers, all came in barrels. We had to weigh
everything. There'd be five, six clerks in the store goin' like
mad.

"We opened the store at seven a.m. and closed at eleven
p.m. Saturday night we'd close up at midnight. I sold more
shoes on a Saturday than the stores do now in six months.
Now a pair of shoes will last me seven years, but in those
days they had horses and cattle and they'd be walking in
the manure and the manure used to eat up the leather. Any
farm boy would have to have about two pairs of shoes a
year. Sold 'em for one twenty-five a pair and made thirty-
five cents.

"There was a print called PP print, Potter's print from
England. The Mennonites were great users of print and it
was a must for them to have their quilts covered with a big
flowered PP print. We used every tactic known in the book
to get hold of some of this print, even bribing other storekeepers in faraway places. The man that had the PP print
cheaper, he was the one that did business. It cost about
seventeen cents a yard. Very cheap. That was the big thing.
Everybody tried to give a better bargain and build up their
customers through credit. We had lots of fun. If I saw that
one merchant was doing something, I'd try to go him one
better. One day we'd sell sugar cheaper and the next day
someone else. There was one gentleman who always used

to sell sugar for less but he never had any."

The general stores were cozy, crowded, sensual places where the joys of haggling could consume the better part of a day. Here the men did the bargaining; the women waited. "The women made their skirts with big pockets that they used to fill up with sunflower seeds," recalls one Jew. "All the women would come in and they'd sit and gossip and crack the sunflower seeds until the floor was just covered with sunflower seeds! On a muddy day we'd have to sprinkle sawdust on the floor. Between the sawdust and the sunflower seeds, we'd have to clean the place out with shovels."

The successful Jewish peddlars grew rich. They invested in real estate, drove expensive cars, and sent their sons away to Winnipeg, where they subsequently became lawyers, professors, judges, and millionaires and gave Winkler a Horatio Alger myth. (It is still reverently reported in Winkler that one of these millionaires used to walk nine miles to school in January, barefoot.) "It was a good business town," reflects one of the sons who's now a judge in Winnipeg. "They were a very honest group of people. Crime was almost non-existent. A criminal lawyer would have starved in Winkler. If the Mennonite people got into trouble, they'd go to the minister and the minister would work it out for them. I remember once in the store my uncle was threatened physically by a Mennonite during some dispute. There was a bit of a ruckus, some pushing and shoving. Well, when the minister found out, he marched that man back in and made him apologize. Of course the ultimate threat was excommunication. If a man got excommunicated, he'd had it. He was finished. They were good people, honest people, peaceful people. The farmers were industrious. The land was good. They were saving, frugal in their habits. And they bought."

The only Jew still in business in Winkler is Max Gladstone, although he now lives in Winnipeg and Gladstone's Winkler store is just one of a profitable chain of clothing stores that stretches across western Canada. Gladstone's store completely dominates Winkler's retail trade. People don't come to shop in Winkler, they come to shop at Gladstone's; the rest of the merchants just pick up the crumbs. Gladstone's store is a giant peddlar's wagon, a discount heaven of kerchiefs, longjohns, zippers, overalls, and white enamel pots stretching in wild chaotic disorder over acres of tables and shelves. Although the store is modern, it's still comfortably tacky, like an old-fashioned general store. Grocery specials are dumped into huge wire bins or heaped up in cardboard cartons in the aisles. The selection is plain and limited. "We don't sell avocadoes here," says store manager Abe Friesen, but you can buy a double-breasted blue serge suit with brass buttons for $12. "We never went into what you would call quality merchandise," says Max Gladstone. The blue serge suits are made in Hungary, the frying pans come from France, the enamelware is Polish and the garish metal dishes are a product of the People's Republic of China. You get the feeling that Gladstone's is the end of the road, the last chance for the world's merchandise. Gladstone's gives a lot of it away as loss leaders to attract customers to the higher priced goods: bargains on one or two items are made up for by big mark-ups on half a dozen other things. Max Gladstone is a bargain basement Timothy Eaton: "We had to be good merchants," he says, "and we still are. It's the same method of fast selling, good aggressive advertising, honesty to our customers, never giving an argument on exchanges or refunds and a good price. Even when things were rough, we always sold cheaper."

Gladstone's average volume of business is estimated to be more than $30,000 a week, and during a sale it will quadruple to over $120,000. Total annual sales probably run to more than $2 million — about half the total retail business in Winkler. Its closest rival is the Co-op with annual sales of $1.3 million. By applying brilliant and sophisticated urban marketing techniques to his little country store (Gladstone's started advertising on radio in southern Manitoba in the early Sixties, when most rural merchants still considered advertising a waste of money and some Mennonite churches were not altogether convinced that radio was not an instrument of the devil.), Max Gladstone undersold his competition and revolutionized the old credit slavery system of rural merchandizing, which allowed each storekeeper to stake out his small but reliable constituency of customers. His success was so enormous that he could have destroyed the store and the town. But by forcing other merchants out of business he would have lost customers, and the town, full of gloomy boarded-up stores, would have gone into a precipitate decline. (Rural people speak with despair of the "Co-op town," the shabby village where everyone has been driven away by a co-op monopoly; no one goes there except the co-op members.) But Max Gladstone made the ultimate leap of capitalism. Rather than starting a ruinous price war, he helped organize the other merchants into a retail merchants' association, which organizes Winkler's sales. All the stores have their sales at the same time, gigantic four-day blow-outs which always occur during the third week of the month, the week the family allowance cheques come out. All the store-keepers co-operate on getting out the flyers, though every-body has different deals to offer. (The Co-op has the apples, Gladstone's gets the pears and the best price on flour, and Sirluck and Janzen have the best deal on instant coffee.) By making big wholesale purchases (Abe Friesen buys a carload of Easter goodies and sells 25 trailer loads of watermelons a year.), Winkler merchants get a better price and are able to sell cheaper. "We're competing with Winnipeg," says Friesen. "We're not concerned with the other towns." Because Gladstone's is the largest store, it gets the lion's share of the business; but the other merchants get their fair share.

Instead of a summer fair, Winkler has a sale. Billed as Old Time Value Days (a slogan which fools many outsiders into thinking it a celebration of Mennonite pioneer virtues), the mercantile blast is held during the third week of August, when things are slow and it's warm enough for the business-men to haul out their weirder items into little booths in the street and to pitch people, in good carny style, into the stores. Aside from the crowning of a teen-age queen and sporadic entertainment by various gospel singers and country-western groups, absolutely nothing happens during Old Time Value Days to interfere with the frenzy of buying. (The sole events in 1971 were a money-raising swimathon and a flour-carrying contest which rewarded the winner with all the free flour he could carry.) Old Time Value

Days is tremendously successful. The gimmick used to lure 40,000 people into Winkler stores over two days is a series of raffles, for which tickets are sold in the stores during the preceding weeks. The fair begins with a draw for a free vacuum cleaner and builds up to power lawn mowers and chesterfield sets; the grand finale is a "Win Your Weight in Silver Dollars" draw sponsored by the Chamber of Commerce which raises enough money to pay for all the other prizes.

Old Time Value Days, like almost everything else in Winkler, is a product of Gladstone's; Abe Friesen picked up the idea in the States. "In the States they were selling garbage," he says, "stuff they were trying to get rid of. We tried that here. We had no success for the first couple of years. People here don't go for that kind of merchandise." The giveaways have been expanded into a year-round program, an endless succession of lotteries for free snow-mobiles, canoes, vacations, and groceries donated by the Winkler merchants. The hucksterism is oppressive. For making money in Winkler is an obsession born of poverty just as the story of Winkler's wealth is really a story of poverty. It's Max Gladstone's story.

Max's father Harry went into business in Winkler in 1913 with his brother Morris. "They started repairing shoes," says Max, a gregarious, energetic millionaire of about 60. "The old-time Mennonite people used to wear a type of leather slippers, a kind of morning slipper without a back on it, and he started building these slippers. He'd never been a shoemaker in his life before. He bought hides and fur in Plum Coulee and opened a store in the shoemaker shop. It was a little bit of store, a little bit of shoes. It was a very small business.

"The partnership didn't work out. So they cut the building in half, put a wall down the centre so that each one was in his own store. It was a very big store, about twelve feet wide and twenty feet long. They made two doors side by side. One had a sign that said 'H. Gladstone' which was my dad and the other said 'Morris Gladstone.' They were both in the same business.

"I was working in the store by the time I was nine. My

dad couldn't read or write a word of anything. But he had a tremendous memory for figures. A customer would come in and whatever he'd buy, my dad would do the sums in his head. My sister and I would come home from school and we'd make out the charge slip on a little counter cheque book; my dad would tell us the customer's name and whether he'd bought moccasins or sugar or whatever and we'd write up the account. Everything in those days was on charge. The farmers only paid once a year, twice at most."

When the Depression completely destroyed the modest prosperity which Winkler merchants had achieved, the Gladstones turned their business back-to-front; instead of buying in Winnipeg and selling locally, they bought locally and sold in Winnipeg.

"We bought chickens and poultry and eggs and butter and cattle and you name it. Anything the farmers had. I'd load up the truck every Monday morning and run it into Winnipeg. First we tried to sell to the small dealers because we got a few cents a pound more. In those days in Winnipeg every Jewish area had a little chicken dealer. In the back of his house he'd have a little barn and he'd be selling chickens. We used to sell a coop here and a coop there and whatever we had left over would go to the big firms, Swifts, Canada Packers.

"In the Thirties we tried everything under the sun to make a buck. In one Mennonite village south of Winkler there was a gentleman who had a farm right on the American border. He had potatoes, and there was a shortage of potatoes in Manitoba. I'd go down there in the morning and load up a truckload of potatoes and go back in the afternoon for another load. The bins would be empty at night and the next morning I'd come back and there were the bins full of potatoes! The Americans were throwing them across the border in the night. There was a story going around Winkler that Gladstones were smuggling potatoes, which of course wasn't true. We bought them; whatever deals this gentleman had with the Americans I didn't know and didn't care. We were making ten of fifteen cents a bushel and we were very happy.

"I bought wool in Winnipeg. I'd buy about four thousand pounds for thirteen, fourteen cents a pound. We'd haul it to the border. There was a farmer there with a great big scale who bought the wool. It was always done in the middle of the night. The Americans would come across with four horses pulling a great big flatbed trailer with rubber tires. It was like a western movie. They had fellows working for them as outriders, fellows on horses with big five-cell flashlights. It was one of the greatest thrills of my life to see those fellows come riding up there. We'd weigh out the wool and they would load it. We got paid by the farmer. We'd make $100, $120 or about $50 to $60 clear; that was a tremendous amount of money. For me it was a tremendous thrill, thinking every night 'Gee, I'm making $50 or $60 to help our family along.' I made enough money that season to trade the old truck of ours in on a brand new 1934 GMC."

A truck was an incredible advantage at a time when no one else could afford either a truck or gasoline. The Gladstones virtually monopolized trade with Winnipeg through a network of extraordinary deals.

"I used to get up about four a.m. and go out to the farmers, pick up a load of grain and haul it into Winnipeg. Everyone in the area was on relief so it was strictly a barter system. We'd bring in a load of grain and trade it for a load of flour; a farmer would get twenty bags of flour for a load of grain, we got five bags. That was our profit. Those five bags we put in our store for resale. We sold the flour on vouchers."

Max Gladstone was still going to school when he wasn't wheeling and dealing, shovelling grain into his truck, or carrying 100-pound bags of flour up into farmers' attics. "It was mankilling work," he says, "and I weighed about 110 pounds. At the end of a day my partner and I'd have $25 between the two of us. My dad allowed me to keep $5 a month for myself, which was exciting because that's more than anyone around the area got!"

Most of the Jewish merchants had left Winkler before the Thirties. They had all sold out to the Mennonites.

The Mennonite agricultural tradition, nurtured through four centuries of flight and tribulation, collapsed in Manitoba in the Twenties, the victim not only of deceit and persecution but of subversion by an aggressive free enterprise ethic which it found both attractive and compatible. In the German lowlands and in Russia, Mennonite survival had been based on absolute isolation from the surrounding society. As long as the host nation was Catholic, autocratic, and feudal, it was not difficult for them to preserve their independent peasant status. Their tactic was to lie low, to keep their heads down and avoid any word or action which would call attention to them. They recognized no government except that of the colony; the sole authority was the church, which acted also as police force, judge, and jury. They tried, with their plain dress and passive demeanor, to make themselves as unobtrusive as possible. They were known as *die Stillen im Lande*, the silent people.

The Canadian government's promise of a reserve where the Mennonites could maintain their moral and economic independence was a fraud. The land had already been surveyed and divided into townships; in 1881 the West Reserve was transformed into the municipalities of Rhineland and Douglas. The Mennonites, overtaken by a government from which they had been promised immunity, were shaken. A fierce dispute split the colony; conservative Mennonites refused to have anything to do with the new government; others proposed taking it over by electing Mennonites to all the offices. The conservatives won. They refused to participate in an election, and the government appointed a Baptist machinery agent from Ontario as the first reeve of Rhineland. In 1898 the Mennonite reserve was thrown open to general settlement. As outside intrusion increased, the colony was rent by internal feuds and schisms. In 1902 several hundred Mennonites packed up and emigrated to the North-West Territories. In 1907 the government made it compulsory to fly the Union Jack over all schools in the province. In 1916 English was decreed to be the sole language of instruction. Mennonite parents who refused to send their children to English-speaking schools were fined and jailed. In 1917 the Mennonites were disenfranchised as conscientious objectors and in 1919 all further Mennonite immigration was prohibited. Within 45 years of their arrival, the Mennonites found that all their guarantees had been whittled away. The authority of the church was eroded by internal schisms and feuds triggered by the outside pressures; sales of land to outsiders, debts contracted by individual Mennonite farmers, and the temptation of free homesteads undermined the old village system. Determined to preserve their traditions, more than 4,000 Mennonites — half the population of the reserve — emigrated to Mexico in 1922.

The fleeing Mennonites sold their land to the Jewish merchants for $15 to $25 an acre; they also purchased from the merchants all the provisions and equipment they needed to start farming in Mexico. "We kept the store open night after night after night when the Mennonites were going to Mexico," says Max Gladstone. "Many nights we stayed open all night long." Train after train bulging with refugees steamed out of Winkler; the land was left silent and deserted. In 1923 the regulations against Mennonite immigration were lifted to permit the arrival of another 10,000 Russian Mennonites, wealthy landowners who had prudently stayed behind in 1874 only to be expropriated by the Bolshevik revolution. They paid the merchants $75 to $100 an acre for land and set off another splurge of grubstake buying.

Long before 1922, the Mennonites realized that their moral scruples were being systematically exploited. Refusal to engage in the usury of trade made them a captive market for a sympathetic merchant, and their scrupulous honesty made them valuable customers in a frontier society where honesty was a liability. Mennonites always paid their debts; nobody else bothered. The Mennonites found all their money draining away to the hostile society from which they were trying to separate themselves; the 1922 exodus was only the most extreme example of a long process by which they had financed their own impoverishment. Relieved of the pressure to conform to the old-fashioned pastoral values, the remaining Mennonites quickly decided that to survive as a religious and ethnic minority they would have to develop a self-sufficient economy, and to do that they would have to go into business. To preserve themselves from the enemy, they adopted the enemy's weapons; to maintain their religious identity, they sacrificed the principles on which it was built.

The transformation was essentially a conservative reaction, a return to petit bourgeois and artisan traditions, a logical outcome of the hierarchical, corporate system which had developed in the villages, spurred on by the pragmatic and aggressively anti-Communist new immigrants. The sanctified materialism which passed as religion among the neighbouring Baptists and Presbyterians was not far removed from the Mennonites' own Protestant roots, and the success of the pious English was seductive. "There were always half a dozen people in Mennonite towns who aped the English and adopted Canadian mannerisms," recalls one old man. Winkler had a substantial English population and its share of swinging Mennonites who drank, entertained at tea, and cavorted about in sophisticated English clothes. Most were millers, lumber dealers, and machinery salesmen, agricultural occupations which the Mennonites looked on with more favor than banking or law. The luxuries of a booming industrial economy made early inroads in the colony: in 1879 a miller named Johann Wall threw his village into an uproar by buying his wife a sewing machine; the other women were so jealous that Mrs. Wall refused to sew with it until everyone in the village had one.

Relaxation of religious sanctions allowed many Mennonites to expand small businesses and trades which they had begun as village moonlighters. Almost every village had its little storekeeper, a mechanic, a blacksmith, a folk doctor, and a dentist — farmers who practiced these trades on the side. Many of the landless people, forced to live by their wits performing a variety of menial tasks, had developed sophisticated and specialized skills as butchers, carpenters, repairmen, and mechanics. As their business expanded, they moved into town. Most of Winkler's industries — a creamery, a bakery, a building company, machine shops — grew out of modest, family-owned backyard businesses or village-style co-ops. The collapse of the old agricultural system released a surge of commercial creativity. Peter Enns, a self-taught village mechanic, transformed his plumbing and heating business into a multi-million-dollar trailer factory; Jake Neufeld, another mechanical genius, invented a cheap, pre-fab steel building to house Winkler's industries. Since the Fifties, the Mennonites have undergone a self-contained industrial revolution which has transformed their way of life. As Max Gladstone explains it: "The Mennonites are a little bit like the Jews, they've never really had their own home. They are known as wanderers. They've had to shift for themselves. They've had to fight for everything. Not being fighting people with a gun, they've had to survive by doing everything a little better than the next guy."

No Mennonite has done it better than Abe Kroeker.

A. A. Kroeker and Sons of Winkler is one of the biggest agribusiness corporations in western Canada. A family company, the Kroekers are as big as the rest of Winkler's industry put together. They control 9,000 acres of prime vegetable-growing land in southern Manitoba and harvest more than a million bushels of potatoes and onions a year; they also run subsidiary operations on irrigated land near Portage la Prairie, Manitoba, and Outlook, Saskatchewan, to which they commute by private plane. The Kroekers are a model of corporate self-sufficiency. They rent most of their land, which enables them to increase or cut back their acreage as markets fluctuate, and they grow only those crops which can be constantly rotated, so not an acre of Kroeker land lies fallow. Waste vegetables and greens are processed through cattle in Kroeker's feed lot, the Kroekers buy their seed from their own seed plant (the substandard seed grain from Kroeker's seed cleaning plant is fed to Kroeker's hogs in Kroeker's pig barn), their machinery comes from their own machinery agency, and their fertilizers and pesticides are purchased from Kroeker's fertilizer agency. Kroeker's army invades Winkler every fall. All day the big khaki transport trucks thunder up and down the roads leading into town. "They're army surplus," explains A. A. Kroeker. "We got them cheap." The trucks are carrying onions and potatoes from Kroeker's fields into Kroeker's storage warehouses. The army hums over the countryside with the passionate efficiency of a swarm of bees; every truck is connected to the company office by intercom, so the Kroekers know at all hours the exact location of every onion. Kroeker's spectacular success has given Winkler its enviable reputation as a town full of shrewd and brilliant businessmen. Abe Kroeker was the first Mennonite to succeed in business in the Winkler area, and his legendary achievement is a direct product of Mennonite values and the unique opportunities presented by a disintegrating society to a man of unusual imagination.

"I was born a businessman," smiles Abe Kroeker, a gentle, soft-spoken man of exceptional personal charm who was born 80 years ago on his father's homestead just outside Winkler. Proximity to town gave him opportunities other farm boys didn't have. At the age of nine he started work as a printer's devil in his brother-in-law's print shop.

"I had to pedal the press with my feet and I could really make it go! My brother-in-law was very proud of how fast I could operate that machine. He always showed me off when visitors came. Before I went to school in the morning I came in and started a fire in the shop. Then I went from business to business asking, 'What do you want printed?' I took the orders. By noon the printery would be warm and I would print the orders and in the evening I'd deliver the goods. Oh, did I ever work!" At twelve, his mother bought him a camera from Sears catalogue. It was a box camera with plates and a big black hood. There was no photographer in Winkler in 1904, so Abe Kroeker went about taking everyone's picture.

"It was customary then to have pictures taken at a funeral. A nice clear picture of the person in the coffin, that's what they generally wanted, and then, of course, the relatives standing around the coffin. I was invited to quite a few funerals and weddings to take pictures; I took some pretty good ones. Once when I was going through the village of Reinland, I took a couple of pictures of the young people all gathered on the porch of a farmhouse. I developed them and took them to the drugstore in Winkler, put them on a rack on display, with the prices on them, postcard size and larger ones. When I came back a week later they were all gone. So I made some more. When I came back another week later they were all gone again. My brother-in-law said, 'Yes, they're all gone but it's on the definite instructions that you won't make any more.' The ministers had bought them all. Photography was definitely against the rules of the churches. Vanity. The ministers couldn't figure out how I kept making more after they'd bought them all up."

When he had finished grade eight, which was all the little Winkler school could offer, Abe Kroeker ran away to high school. "In general, when I was a boy and a young man," he recalls, "we boys got two horses, a set of harness, and a wagon and that would start us off. The girls got a cow. And then you were ready to set up your own house. And that's probably what I would have got. I went to my father and I said, 'I don't want the horses and I don't want the wagon and I don't want the harness. I only want permission to leave, that's all!' And I borrowed money from my older brother to go to school. Teaching was a stepping stone in general for a lot of working-class boys so I went into teaching. That was in the days when teachers didn't need an education. I started teaching with grade nine. I taught for a couple of years in a little school near Winkler. I was very glad to get away from the farm, very glad."

As a teacher, Abe's salary was so low he supported himself taking photographs. As his children multiplied, he was persuaded to go into business with his brother, J. A. Kroeker, who had started a general store and harness shop in Winkler in 1900. "We were the only Mennonites who had a store in town," says Abe. "A lot of the old Mennonites would rather deal with a Jew than with a Mennonite who had fallen by the way. So we had to get our customers through sales. You know, it wasn't *that* wrong if you could buy something at half price. Hee hee hee."

Abe Kroeker brought the first sale to Winkler. "We went on a buying trip to Montreal and we sent information back about how the buying was coming along, what kind of bargains we were getting and that we were going to have a great big sale when we got home. By the time we got back, circulars had been printed and distributed to all the villages.

"We announced that on such and such a day we would not sell anything. We only wanted people to come and see what we had bought. We filled the whole store full of counters and displayed goods. It really looked as though we had bought out Montreal! We announced that there'd be door prizes. That was something unbelievable to ordinary people, the idea that we give something away! We displayed the prizes in the windows. That day at noon, from our store to the hotel, the people were standing just as thick as they could stand. We gave a lot of door prizes away, mostly hardware like aluminium kettles. It was a big success.

"The Jews thought it was all in the writing up. We sold out our store eventually to one of the Winkler Jews on the condition that I would write the advertising! The Jews never got the idea that you've got to give people a bargain and people have to know that it's a bargain. People know bargains. We gave people half price very often. People came by buggy from miles around. When Kroekers have a sale, it's a sale!

"We timed our sales for the Jewish holidays. And that really got under their skin! Oh, it was mean, yes! Because I had been a printer's devil I could do a job fast. We just printed the circulars to go out into the villages two days ahead of time. The Jews wouldn't know about it. Then I would go out with packages of candy for every village and the first boys that I met I said, 'Boys, will you take a circular to every home? Here are thirty circulars and here's a bag of candy for taking them out.' Then on to the next village and I covered the whole of southern Manitoba in one day. Of course the next day the Jews would know about the sale but what could they do? They *had* to close up. Hee hee hee. That was a lot of fun."

In 1928 Abe Kroeker quit the store and moved his family out to the farm, because he felt that life in town was corrupting his children. It was a religious decision. And it was a bad time to go farming. After enduring seven years of famine, Abe Kroeker gambled on corn. He scrounged some free seed and second-hand machinery and put his children to work weeding the crop. He raised 1,500 bushels of corn and enough stalks to feed his cattle over the winter. He sold 300 bushels of seed corn for $3 a bushel. "I could have jumped through the ceiling!" he says. "That was big money!" He planted the rest. Within four years, Kroeker's had 700 acres of corn, which were weeded and picked by bankrupt farmers looking for work. Abe Kroeker was the only farmer in Manitoba growing corn. As soon as the seven lean years ended, he switched to potatoes. He was the only farmer in Manitoba growing registered potatoes. The world beat a path to his door.

By combining his business acumen with Mennonite peasant labor, Abe Kroeker revolutionized farming in southern Manitoba. He grew into Joseph in a Biblically conscious community, a man of awesome wealth and power when everyone around him was poor. Taking advantage of the easy credit of the Fifties and Sixties, Kroeker's expanded; they bought and rented land, replaced family labor with hired workers, and turned the Winkler area into a private fiefdom which they govern with benevolent paternalism. The Kroekers are religious people, pillars of the Mennonite Brethern Church in Winkler of which Abe Kroeker is an ordained minister.

"We tried to apply Christian principles to business," he says, "but our principles have changed. In some areas they have weakened a bit. For instance, we never sold tobacco. The Jews, all of them had tobacco."

It's a very religious community of course. You might say bigoted. Yes, bigoted might be the right word, but then any people who are very orthodox I suppose are always bigoted.

(Winkler Jew)

Winkler is quaint, with a whiff of nostalgia about it, like a picture of a medieval town from a childhood storybook. Stout peasant women in ankle-length Potter's print skirts and cardigan sweaters buttoned up tight across their ample sagging bosoms waddle down Main Street with big paper shopping bags. Their faces are brown and leathery, crinkly around the eyes from sun and pain; their straight iron-grey hair, parted severely in the middle, is drawn back under black wool kerchiefs printed with bright pink flowers, and their thick legs, cased in wrinkled brown wool stockings, are bowed. The old men lounge in the sun in black suits with white shirts and narrow ties, too-small felt hats perched on top of their round, pale heads. These ancient gnomes bomb around town in brand new Buicks and Chryslers; their wizened necks strain to peer over the padded dashboard. The language of commerce and conversation is mainly Low German, a melodious and graphic folk tongue which the Mennonites speak with great expressiveness. As soon as they switch to English, their voices fade to a flat monotone and their faces go blank. They speak very softly, sedately; there's none of the hooting and hollering and rib-poking guffaws or wild waving of arms that you find in an English community like Miami where, among the men at least, everyone is engaged in perpetual strident joking and argument. The Mennonites evade arguments. You never hear a shout in Winkler or a big knee-slapping belly laugh that shows the teeth right back to the tonsils and you never, never hear a profanity. The Mennonites are still the silent people, cautious, self-deprecating; even their smiles are thin and shy. The women wear almost no makeup; to an outsider their faces seem pale and featureless. This low, elusive style is reflected in the town, which is flat and shapeless. Winkler has no easily identifiable centre, no big stone courthouse or old brick post office with a clock tower, no landmark from which the whole community takes direction. The Winkler town office is a humble stucco shack next to a gas station, which the council shares with the jail, the police, and the filthiest public washrooms in western Canada. It's Winkler's plainness, its lack of civic monuments which brings the sense of *déjà vu* to any Protestant. Winkler is Geneva in the time of John Calvin, a disciplined, rigidly controlled theocracy, self-sufficient both economically and morally, dedicated to the hot pursuit of worldly wealth strictly interpreted by the church as the greater glory of God. The air in Winkler is heavy with righteousness.

The churches are everywhere. They are Winkler's monuments, plain, impressive structures set off by acres of gravel parking lots. Winkler is busier on a Sunday morning than during a sale. All of the churches are Mennonite except one, a tiny old Lutheran church tucked shamefacedly away on a side street. The rest are the product of the schisms which have rent the Mennonite community over the past hundred years. The Mennonite faith, which recognizes only the authority of the Bible, is highly democratic; any group of parishioners annoyed with the minister simply hive off and start their own church. Most of the disputes have erupted over the introduction of modern innovations — choir singing, organs, Sunday school, and English language services — which the traditional believers consider to be worldly and corrupt. One village church broke apart in 1894 over the issue of Sunday school; the building was sawed in half and each congregation moved its half to a new location. The churches are more a product of personal grudges and family feuds than doctrinal differences, and the passion of the old village ministers for excommunication provided fertile ground for itinerant evangelists who harvested the strays. The new churches also provided rebels like the Kroekers with a socially acceptable escape from the old village ethic and with a growing pool of new customers.

Everybody goes to church in Winkler, if only out of self-defence. A person's religion is considered to be the most crucial thing about him, aside from whether or not he's on welfare. It's not uncommon for a stranger in town to be asked, after his name and occupation, whether or not he's been saved. Salvation is considered public information. Disapproval of agnosticism is so intense that outsiders who have lapsed are afraid to admit it; if they do, they are shunned or hounded to convert. Although the older people have seldom gone past grade six or eight, their Biblical literacy is formidable and hundreds of adults attend Sunday school classes every week to bone up on their New Testament. Everyday conversation is liberally sprinkled with Biblical quotations, chapter and verse; the extent of their use is a mark of both piety and social prestige. The supreme one-upmanship, of course, is to quote *only* chapter and verse, leaving your antagonist to supply the passage for himself. The Mennonites are very strong on St. Paul, the most rigid and repressive of the apostles, but the most important passage, the one that keeps recurring as a theme in Winkler, is Matthew 25:15-30, the parable of the talents, the story of the servant who invested and multiplied his silver coins and won the whole pot. Literally interpreted, it is the metaphysical bedrock of the capitalist system and the religious cornerstone of Winkler's economy.

Only two Winkler churches really count, the Bergthaler, named after a village in Russia, and the Mennonite Brethern. The principal difference between them appears to be that the Bergthaler believe in baptism by sprinkling while the Brethern practice total immersion in a tank in the attic. (Baptisms used to take place in Dead Horse Creek. A 1928 photo shows a huge crowd gathered on the river bank dressed in their Sunday best as if for a picnic. The baptismal candidates, most of them middle-aged couples, are lined up on a wooden ramp leading into the water, the men in dark suits and the women in white dresses, while those already baptized swim about, fully clothed, in the creek.) The rivalry between the two churches is keen. The Brethern built the first stone church in Winkler. (The first churches were just frame country buildings moved to town for convenience, a concession to urbanization which created an immense furor within the congregations.) The Bergthaler countered in 1970 with a fabulous $190,000 limestone structure that makes the Brethern church look hideous and decrepit. The congregation paid for it in one year. Since the new church was built, the Bergthaler congregation has increased steadily by 20 to 30 people a year until it's now close to 700 and the minister has an assistant. The Brethern, with only 375, are completely overshadowed. They are, however, very strong on crusades, the religious equivalent of a sale. People in Winkler are still talking about the spectacular in 1969 which packed the Brethern church for eight straight days and saw more than 700 young people declare for Christ, 200 for the first time. The minister wasn't greedy. "I gave the list of young people who made decisions back to their pastors," he says. "I didn't want to sheep steal."

The Bergthaler church looks like any posh suburban Protestant church, all carpet and wood panelling and subdued lighting from Swedish modern lamps hanging from a beamed cathedral ceiling. The service too is a similar melange of Bible texts, hymns, prayers, and bland, inoffensive preaching; the prayers are long and the singing is superb. The Bergthaler is the "establishment" church in Winkler; its membership contains, with a handful of exceptions, all the rich and influential people in town. No coins clink into its collection plate; all that's heard is the swish of bills and envelopes. The Sunday collection averages over $700, plus $50 from the Sunday school. But that's only the beginning. In 1970, in addition to paying off the building, the church collected $50,000 in donations: in 1971, donations rose to $88,000 (about $125 per member) and half the money was sent to missions or seminaries. "All of us are busy building the kingdom of God," beamed the minister at the annual meeting in 1971, "although it seems to me that the churches have reached their climax in giving." However, most of the money comes from a small group of people, the 20 members who gave over $1,000 each to the building fund on top of their regular contributions. "The same people that run the businesses in town are the church people," says Abe Friesen of Gladstone's, who's on the finance committee along with Peter Enns, founder of Triple-E trailers. The general manager of Neonex leads the choir, and the Sunday school superintendent is the mayor, H. F. Wiebe. The churches have joined together in a ministerial association which is an exact reproduction of the retail merchants' association; the ministerial association issues joint press releases on controversial issues and ensures that no two churches have crusades at the same time.

Religion in Winkler is militant and aggressive. Church members are expected to devote almost all their spare time to church activities and to participate in a continual round of Bible study groups and prayer meetings, where individuals offer up extemporaneous prayers on behalf of the group. Praying is open and public. Every event in Winkler opens with a prayer, and people are encouraged to witness verbally to their faith at every opportunity. They deliver little personal testimonials on their relations with God without embarrassment; the testimonials are often actively solicited by church authorities, such as this one from a Sunday school teacher published in the 1970 annual report of the Bergthaler church:

Why do I still teach a Sunday school class? . . .
Mainly I teach
To impress people.
To impress pupils with the fact
That Jesus Christ and his Father are the greatest!

There's no other product that can compare!
Therefore on Sunday morning I don my sales-
man's garb;
"The Jesus Story" is my sales pitch.
What did you say was *your* reason for teaching
Sunday school?
You don't teach at all! !
Why not . . . Nothing to sell? ?

People who don't attend church regularly are chastized by the minister. If they fail to improve, their membership is cancelled. For sinners, excommunication is still popular.

The church rules Winkler with an iron fist in a silken glove of piety. The man who wears the glove is the mayor. Mayor Henry Wiebe is manager of the Winkler Credit Union, the second wealthiest credit union in Manitoba with assets of over $14 million. (The wealthiest is in another Mennonite town.) Mr. Wiebe took over the credit union in 1950, after the previous manager had been arrested for embezzling the profits, an event which is referred to in official Winkler history as "the untimely recession of 1950." Because of the Mennonites' healthy distrust of banks, almost everyone in the area deals with the credit union; the Bank of Commerce is a little building off on a side street. The credit union has been largely responsible for Winkler's industrial boom; it lent money to local entrepreneurs at low rates of interest when the banks wouldn't touch them. As mayor, Henry Wiebe has been able to take credit for the smart investments he has made as credit union manager, and many of the people who have profited from his loans are fellow church members. Not only does Mayor Wiebe decide who receives loans, but, as mayor, he also has authority over who is allowed to build in the industrial park, what kind of business they go into, how much they pay for land, and whether they receive any tax concessions. The council also, of course, polices development in town through building regulations and licences.

Besides the credit union he manages, holding the mort-gages on most of the businesses in the town, the mayor also has a powerful influence over private citizens whose finan-cial status he knows intimately. This knowledge makes his job as a fund raiser for the church a lot easier. The mayor is himself a prominent landowner and shareholder in several Winkler enterprises; in recent years he has bought up old decrepit houses and torn them down or moved them out of town. This prevented poor people on welfare from moving in. Through his influence in the church, the mayor has been able to promote charitable projects, such as the construction of the old folks home, which have been sound investments for the credit union. Religious homilies ("To err is human, to forgive divine") are posted on a big signboard in front of the new credit union building; the signboard, like a movie theatre marquee, is changed once a week.

In the person of the mayor, Winkler has recreated the old village hierarchical system where municipal, sacred, and financial matters were all in the hands of the same small group of people. Winkler is a theocratic corporation. "Our people are accustomed to working together," says the mayor. "And as you can see we help each other. We benefit as well from our belief: I know we have been helped by our spiritual dimension. . .if things go wrong with a religious man he has an additional resource." Or as the tour guide puts it, sweeping his arm over the gleaming contents of one of Winkler's new factories, "Here we see Christianity at work!"

The church exercises its authority through a doctrine of self-discipline and a rigid system of moral restrictions. As one lapsed Mennonite puts it: "Anything that defiles the body, like booze and cigarettes, is bad. Dancing is evil because of the sexual overtones. It implies that you're coveting another woman. In the village there was very little opportunity for coveting your neighbour's wife because, well, most guys wouldn't want to because they were so ugly. A lot of women couldn't afford to get very prissy and they had no need to. Their Sunday best was one dress. A lot of the women who got dressed up for church were dressed quite nattily except, of course, that they were all fourteen axe handles across the beam. Movies were evil also but we all went. You'd never tell your folks where you'd been. We'd say we were going to town for coffee or we went to bowl. Bowling was accepted, barely."

As the fundamentalist influence increased in the Mennonite churches, many of the old folk customs were suppressed. It had been common for farmers to crack open a keg of beer to celebrate harvest; now everyone hides the beer in the basement and keeps the rye under the combine in the machine shed. The country dances with which villagers used to celebrate weddings had been banished by the Forties. A movie theatre opened in Winkler in 1946; it was forced to close a few months later, after the ministers circulated a petition stating it would undermine the morals of the people. Winkler's bowling alley and poolroom fortuitously burned down. The town exudes a gloomy and self-righteous puritanism.

Winkler is dry. At least half a dozen liquor referendums have gone down to smashing defeat since the first one was squelched in 1957. The latest attempt, in the fall of 1971, was beaten by a vote of 2 to 1; all the churches issued little printed tracts condemning booze as the root of all evil, and a passionate argument was carried on through letters to the local newspaper (which was in favor of liquor on the grounds that it was good for business). The mayor, a shareholder in the local motel, which is dry, came out against booze; some critics suggested he was more fearful of competition than of demon rum. Public abstinence does not, however, prevent a lot of jolly drunken farmers from rolling out of the Stanley Hotel beer parlor every night, and Winkler has a thriving Alcoholics Anonymous. "The liquor store in Morden would go broke if it weren't for Winkler," scoffs a Morden resident, and the newspaper suggested widening the highway to accommodate the steady flow of traffic to Morden's numerous watering holes. Certainly something must be responsible for the bizarre accidents which take place on the roads around Winkler. The junction where the main road into Winkler meets the highway has been named "Killer Korner" because between 150 and 200 people have been injured in accidents there in the last five years. On some weekends there'll be two or three cars completely demolished and whole families taken to hospital. Miraculously most people walk away unscathed.

The petition in favor of the liquor referendum was taken up

by Frank Rietze, a descendent of Winkler's first druggist
and one of those jacks-of-all-trades that are found in every
small town. Mr. Rietze deals in real estate, insurance,
mortgages, and houses; he also sells drivers' licences and
does the driver testing. Mr. Rietze is building inspector and
chairman of the town planning board, a position he holds
on the strength of his reputation as an engineer and survey-
or, skills he picked up informally as a worker on various
government construction projects around southern Manitoba. "I was promised a job in the highways department if
I voted for the right man," he explains. Mr. Rietze produced
a town plan for Winkler in 1961 which rezoned the town
into areas specifically designated for residential and industrial development; he also became an advocate of government subsidized low-cost housing. Mr. Rietze purchased 100
lots of residential property on the north side of town which
he is now developing as a housing project; a substantial
number of dwellings are to be low-cost housing.

We meet in the Green Diamond Club Room, a small,
dark room at the back of Mr. Rietze's office which is the
closest thing Winkler has to a cabaret. The room is painted
green and the ceiling is black with little stars that blink on
and off when the lights are turned out. A moth-eaten stuffed
deer head is mounted on the back wall over a painted
cardboard fireplace, an electric organ, and a color photo of
the Winkler hockey team. The room is draped with dusty
pink and white crepe streamers left over from somebody's
wedding, and the tile floor is polished to a high shine for
dancing.

Mr. Rietze locks the door, turns out the lights so the stars
come out, and produces a bottle of rye from a cupboard in
the pantry at the back. He pours a shot into two glass
tumblers and puts a dance record on the scratchy old
portable record player. We sit on a couple of the cold metal
chairs that are stacked against the wall.

"This building used to be Winkler theatre, the Crystal
Hall," says Mr. Rietze sadly. "Winkler used to be much
more wide open, years ago. We had a more mixed population, Poles, Germans, English. I had a bowling alley and
a poolroom from 1947 until it burned down in 1961. People
said it was a good thing to burn down. I couldn't make

money on the bowling alley. People wouldn't come because the poolroom was next door." A German Lutheran, Mr. Rietze is one of the few outsiders still left in Winkler, a village renegade. "Everybody's left," he says. "People don't feel at home here. They'll be your best of friends in church, but they'll be talking about you because your ways are not the same as theirs. They judge you." Outsiders who work in Winkler live in Morden to escape scrutiny. The hospital has a hard time keeping single nurses because of the total dearth of fun or prospects; rumor has it that one doctor was forced to leave after he was called to an emergency from a party and the patient complained of liquor on his breath. A Kinsmen club lasted long enough to build the swimming pool and then collapsed for lack of members. The churches have moved in to control baseball and hockey; the kids have dropped out. Mr. Rietze is Winkler's only sports promoter and a keen tennis player; he plays every summer evening after work, a lonely tribute to Winkler's golden age, when it had the best tennis players in all Manitoba. Winkler's huge new sports arena stands empty most of the time because council refuses to issue liquor permits for banquets or sporting events. Everyone calls it the Blue Elephant.

"We're a real cutthroat shopping town," says Mr. Rietze. "Wages are kept as low as possible to give people a good price on goods. We've got a lot of people coming into town and nothing to offer them after they've spent their shopping dollar. We tried to get a liquor store. Council turned it down. They're afraid. People don't want to be seen buying liquor. They're nice people here. Their way of making a buck is behind someone else's back. You know what one fellow who used to live here calls Winkler? The town with the high white walls."

He makes his way through the gloom to the organ, plugs it in, and runs his hands tenderly over the keyboard. Mr. Rietze plays for most of the dances and receptions in the Green Diamond Club Room. He spends many evenings here alone, playing to fill the black hours. As his fingers touch the keys, the familiar dance tunes of the Fifties swell out to fill the dingy, empty room. Mr. Rietze is wrapped up, eyes closed, swaying back and forth on the piano bench to the romantic rhythm of "Stranger in Paradise."

"It's a peaceful community, very peaceful," says a resident. "We didn't know about revolvers or shotguns or anything. They were basically foreign to the community. It was a good, honest farming community. The most exciting thing that happened there was when there was a fire and the fire bell rang and everybody ran to help with the hand pump."

When the Union Bank of Canada on Main Street was robbed in 1920, the town policeman cowered in bed while the bandits blew up the vault, shot the blacksmith in the legs, and made off with $21,000 in cash. Winkler has had its share of local thieves, bums, crooks, and roustabouts like any prairie town (the bank robbers were believed to be American whiskey runners in cahoots with the Winkler hotel owner who bootlegged booze out of the livery stable) as well as some unique and embarrassing characters. "The only time there was discrimination," says Max Gladstone, "was during the Hitler regime. There were two fellows running around in high leather boots, brown shirts, the whole thing. There were a fair amount of problems in those years, 1933 to 1935. We were discriminated against by a few. There was a bunch of literature, all this Hitler literature that was around in the area. One night the police came out and they had a great big bonfire and they burnt it all up. One fellow was sent away to a concentration camp."

Winkler has a three-man police force including the chief, Walter Nauer, a dignified, middle-aged man who's renowned in the area as a duck hunter. The police force takes itself very seriously. They always work in full uniform, complete with cap and gun. There is a new steel jail cell in the town office, but it's hardly ever used. "We've only had two break-and-enters in the last twelve years," says Mr. Nauer. When the beer parlor closes, the police drive the drunks home. "It's the same group every day," disapproves Mr. Nauer. "They're the type of people that give you trouble. Most are older married men. Ninety per cent are welfare cases." The police make a tidy sum in fines for traffic violations. "It's the old people," says Mr. Nauer, shaking his head. "They drive too slow and too carefully." The police are on duty until 4 a.m. "We check every door in the business section by hand," says Mr. Nauer.

The problems of maintaining the peace in a Christian community have made Winkler hypersensitive about law and order; the police are always dunning council for another constable, a trained dog, new guns. The atmosphere is almost militaristic. In 1969 the police triggered a Hallowe'en riot when they turned the fire hoses on a crowd of teen-age pranksters after one of them let the air out of a constable's tires. (The boys fought the volunteer fire department with cream cans, two of which went through the windows of a restaurant owned by a company which the mayor has shares in. The mayor praised the action of the police and fire brigade as "necessary to keep order and protect private property.") Since then the police have hired three extra men and a trained dog to police the town on Hallowe'en, but there have been no further incidents. The police also served as Winkler's dog catcher until they were forced to report they were unable to apprehend any dogs. The town has a host of regulations governing dogs, but nobody bothers with them in spite of a barrage of threatening letters from the town council during its periodic dog purges. This breach of discipline drives the council into a rage. Their obsession with dogs is surpassed only by their obsession with garbage. Although the town's own garbage dump is a stinking eyesore overrun with rats, council is constantly harassing the citizens to clean up their garbage cans, even to the point of distributing free to every household five plastic garbage bags with instructions that more are available, cheap, at the town office. People who dump garbage at the wrong time or in the wrong place at the town dump are fined. Even death offers no escape. Death is perhaps Winkler's biggest industry.

Mourners start to arrive at the church an hour before the funeral begins. Half an hour later the church is full, and the ushers are frantically setting up folding chairs in the basement. With fifteen minutes to go, the crowd spills out of the basement into the lobby and jostles for a good vantage point near the door. The ushers set up more folding chairs in the aisles and squeeze people into the open space in front of the pulpit, where they will have a bird's-eye view of the cadaver. Buzzing in the July heat, red round faces shining with sweat, the congregation seethes like a swarm of flies.

When Nick Wiebe, the undertaker, arrives with the body, the lobby is jammed and a small respectful crowd is gathered in the yard. Pulling the casket on a dolly, Nick elbows his way through the mob and clears a path to the main aisle; the crowd reforms like an honor guard on either side. Word of the deceased's arrival crackles through the congregation; heads turn and crane to catch a glimpse. The dead man's relatives march down the aisle in a procession and take their seats at the front; heads turn slowly to follow them. Nick trundles the casket down the aisle, places it in the centre of a circle of observers, and opens it.

The funeral is very cheerful. It's an old-fashioned service, mostly in German. The church is stark and bare and the hymns are droned unaccompanied. The young minister wears a black suit and a black silk shirt with no collar. He is flanked by the church deacons who, seated all in a row like six ravens, lead the singing. The sermon is simple and quietly spoken. The minister describes the dead man floating in an azure sky surrounded by a joyful host of departed friends and relatives. He speaks with such calm reassurance and such conviction that on this sunny summer afternoon he almost compels belief in a radiant eternal life. Death is the beginning, not the end; the funeral is a celebration. The crux of the service is the obituary. Read by the minister, it is a lengthy, detailed account of the dead man's accomplishments, his baptism and marriage, the highlights of his career, the strengths of his character, his love for his family and for God, and his last thoughts before he died; it includes a history of his last illness, minutely chronicling the time, nature, and extent of all his operations as the agony of the cancer took hold. Crude and direct, the obituary is very powerful; for a few moments it gives the dead man mythic stature. Lying up there in his coffin, he is the focus of all eyes and his character is the subject of all thoughts; the church becomes a theatre for the tiny human drama of which he is the star.

The service is very long, over an hour. The air in the church becomes foetid, and people begin to fan themselves with their hymn books, waving them like so many small white wings. At the end everyone files out past the open coffin; the line winds round and round the church and reaches down into the basement where people have been listening on the intercom. The corpse looks very yellow and waxy. Turning back towards the congregation, I can see that people's glistening faces are beatific; it's been a good service.

Funerals are Winkler's most popular mass entertainment. They are advertised all over southern Manitoba on radio CFAM, a Mennonite station partly owned by the Kroekers which specializes in religious broadcasts, classical music, and commercials. Hundreds of people come 30 and 40 miles to attend the funeral of someone they didn't know. Most funerals are spectaculars requiring a cast of thousands, and the lunch of coffee and buns served in the basement later parallels the parable of the loaves and the fishes. Winkler shuts up tight during a funeral; an eerie silence descends on the town and the streets are deserted. The only clue to everyone's whereabouts is the mass of cars around the church. A particularly grotesque suicide or a gruesome accident will draw an especially big crowd.

"I had a young couple once who were killed in a car accident shortly after they were marrried," says Nick Wiebe. "We laid her out in her wedding dress. It was very sad. I figure between 4,000 and 5,000 people went through the funeral home on the weekend, just to look. They made a complete shambles of the place."

An especially long and impressive funeral is a symbol of community status. "I remember when a minister died," smiles Nick. "The funeral lasted three hours. Thirteen ministers spoke. They went on so long it got dark. We ran into a blizzard on our way to the cemetery and had to turn back. On Sunday we had another service at the little country church by the cemetery. That service lasted three hours. It got so dark by the time we buried him we had to turn on the lights of the hearse to light the grave."

Funerals are big business in Winkler. They bring thousands of people into town, and the funeral is often just an excuse to do some shopping. Winkler funerals never seem to be held on Mondays, when the stores are closed. Death has also been good to Wiebe's Funeral Homes Ltd., which is now the biggest undertaking firm in southern Manitoba with branches in three towns; as the number of old people has increased in rural areas, Wiebe's, like most rural mortuaries, has prospered. Nick Wiebe, a shaggy, good-natured man with a glass eye and a Clark Gable moustache, owns one of Winkler's newest and most expensive homes opposite the funeral parlor which, because all the funerals are held in church, is a small concrete building where he does the embalming. Like many wealthy rural undertakers, he has risen to a position of prominence on the town council. An ex-soldier and reformed alcoholic, with a roguish swagger and a mischievous glint in his eye, Nick presents a startling contrast to the mayor, who is smooth as a porpoise and sweet with shaving lotion. Nick is Winkler's Esau, a rough and hairy everyman whom people respect for his sins and his honesty. God of the underworld, he guards the dark passions which lurk beneath Winkler's bland white face. The people constantly make him suffer ghastly jokes about his profession ("Nick'll be the last man in the world to let you down! Haw Haw Haw!"), but everyone calls him Lovable Nick. They don't say that about the mayor.

Nick went into the funeral business in 1949. Prior to that, the dead were simply planted in the front garden, close to the road so the headstones would be visible to passersby. The body was washed by the local women, stitched into a white cotton shroud, and laid out for a day or two in the parlor; caskets were made by the village cabinet maker. Funeral invitations were circulated like chain letters; the first name on the list delivered it to the second, the second to the third, and so on until everyone had been contacted. People were very hostile to any change in this simple, civilized custom; old women threatened to rise from the dead if their bodies were taken to the undertaker. "Refrigeration changed all that," says Nick. "People used to get a block of ice to keep the body cool. Once refrigeration came in, there were no more icehouses."

"Winkler," says Frank Rietze, "is where people come to die." Winkler was one of the first prairie towns to recognize the economic potential of old people. A senior citizens home was built by public subscription in the Fifties and a 14-unit light housekeeping complex was added in 1966. A six-storey apartment building constructed in 1970 made Winkler the first town in western Canada where the old folks live high-rise. ("The elevator is so small we can't get a stretcher in," complains Nick Wiebe. "We have to take the bodies down in a chair.") The high-rise cost $545,000; the bulk of the money was subscribed by members of the Kroeker family. Abe Kroeker is president of the board. "I am no good with old people," he says, shaking his head. "Of course, with age it is more difficult for me to get to Winkler to spend time with them." In 1972 the town added a 65-bed intensive-care home for the aged. It cost $600,000; $60,000 was raised in the community and the rest was put up by the provincial government.

There is a waiting list of 75 people for the high-rise; every time a resident dies, the phone rings off the hook with people asking who's next to get in. The mayor and council decide. The units are a bargain — $50 a month for a single, $76 for a double. The buildings are a product of the Mennonites' social conscience and desire to care for their own; they also signal widespread rural poverty and social upheaval. Many elderly people are virtually abandoned in the villages. When they become feeble or their money runs out, they have to sell their house and move into the old folks home, where their children come to visit them on weekends and holidays. (Every week the local newspaper carries a short column listing the names of all the visitors each resident has received. Competition for the most names is keen.) Because the homes are government subsidized, they accept only people who are destitute or severely disabled, and they carry, therefore, a stigma of poverty, helplessness, and abandonment. Most old people try to maintain themselves independently as long as possible; to go to the home is to give up. Winkler has 538 people over the age of 65; fewer than 100 live in the senior citizens homes. Pensioners of means usually purchase a new bungalow in town when they retire from the farm, bringing a boost to the construction industry and the town's taxes.

The illnesses of Winkler's old people help support a thriving medical establishment. Winkler has four doctors but no dentist (old people wear dentures or do without), a 57-bed hospital, and the Eden mental home, a psychiatric institution which averages 50 inmates and 300 outpatients. "We have to be terribly careful this doesn't turn into an old folks home," says the director. Institutions are part of the bedrock of Winkler's economy. They provide Winkler with a core of high-income professionals, hundreds of jobs, and millions of dollars in government subsidies. The aged are perpetually shunted around from high-rise to hospital to nursing home. By dying, they perform their last economic function.

In a community totally dedicated to productivity and the Protestant work ethic, the old exist only to provide work for others. "They treat you like you're in your second childhood!" snaps an 83-year-old great-grandmother who lives alone. The old women sit on the balconies of the high-rise like a flock of sparrows; their only recreation is to squabble with one another. To maintain order, a long list of rules and regulations is posted in the elevator. Television is banned from the recreation room. Clergymen prowl the halls in search of likely subjects to ease into the hereafter; church services are piped in on Sundays, and the ministers have even recorded ten-minute messages on tapes for patients in the hospitals. The churches are happiest when the school choir can be persuaded to sing at the old folks home — a simultaneous exercise in discipline for the old and young alike.

Half a dozen bikes are thrown down in the dried mud in the school yard. The old one-room white schoolhouse faces the road; a tattered red and white flag snaps in the strong west wind. It's only 8:30 a.m. on a cool spring morning, but all the children are already inside. "Some come at eight a.m.," says the teacher. "They like school." Edward School #1134 is the last of the one-room country schools. In the spring of 1972 it has nine pupils; within a year it will vanish, swallowed up by a unitary school division, and the children will be bussed to Winkler.

Edward School is halfway between Kroeker's hog barn and Kroeker's feed lot just north of Winkler. It serves the residents of 21 quarter sections; most of the people are employees of Kroeker's. The enrolment fluctuates between eight and 15 students. "The Kroekers are always hiring people, it depends on that," explains an elderly farmer, the chairman of the board. He says the school is over 67 years old, since it was there before he was born. "I went here myself," he says. "It was almost the same. Except we didn't have a piano. There were forty-four students in eight grades when I went here; we had bigger families then." The farmer's grandchildren attend Edward School. He's proud of it. "The town school is too crowded. We have more control over what's going on in school. If there's trouble with the children, we take care of that at home." He grins slowly, casting his eye about at the nine little faces. "If you get it in school, you'll get it another time at home. That works pretty good."

Edward School is cheap. The farmer estimates it costs him $70 a quarter section less than sending the children to town. The teacher is paid $4,900 a year. She lives next to the school in a little frame teacherage with a hand pump in the yard which is supplied, free, by the board. The farmers prefer to hire young women teachers because they're better at Christmas pageants. "We had a Christmas program last year with nine children that lasted over an hour!" says the chairman, his voice full of admiration. "Some was in German, some was in English. The children were dressed in costumes and put on a play on a little stage in front. The school was packed!"

I enter through the porch which is also the washroom; a closet in a corner contains a dirty chemical toilet, a civilized innovation since the days of outdoor biffies when children who waited too long to brave the cold found their underwear frozen to them by the time they made it to the toilet. The schoolroom is fragrant with the reek of the oiled wooden floor, stained and deeply scarred with the marks of hob-nailed boots. Posters showing six different ways to brush your teeth cover the soiled green walls, crayon drawings are taped to the blackboard, and a ragged paper Easter Bunny decorates the front of the teacher's desk. Over the upright piano a mildewed brown globe hangs by a wire from the ceiling. Rough plank shelves along the walls are crammed with dog-eared books, and on a shelf in the corner red and yellow plastic lunch pails are ranged in a row next to a stone crock full of drinking water. The wooden desks face the teacher in a semicircle. The sun streams in the eastern windows.

Precisely at 9 a.m., the only boy in the school goes to the door and rings the old-fashioned school bell. When he returns, one of the two girls in grade seven sits down at the tinny, tuneless piano and bangs out "O Canada." She rattles along lickety-split in triple time; the students gasp to keep up, until the tune sounds like a lot of spoons hitting a pot. The Lord's Prayer follows, then a double-quick "God Save the Queen." The teacher reads from the Bible, the passage about Joseph and the seven lean years and the seven fat years, then the students scrounge for their battered hymn books in big wooden boxes under their seats. They lead off with a familiar old favorite, their faces smiling as they yell out:

> I'm so glad that Jesus loves me,
> Jesus loves me, Jesus loves me;
> I'm so glad that Jesus love me,
> Jesus loves even me.

They sing six hymns, all verses, in a high falsetto. The religious exercises last 20 minutes. "You asked me yesterday if astronauts are circling around the moon," the teacher says. "I promised I'd try to find out today. Yes, they are. They're coming home tomorrow. Has anybody got any news?"

There is a long silence. All the faces look blank. "I can't think of any news," says the teacher. "Well, I guess that's all."

"I heard it was to go to sixty above today," volunteers a girl.

The teacher gives out the day's lessons. Since there are

no students in grades two, three, or eight, she has only five grades to teach. Some grades have only one pupil. Most of the students are brothers and sisters. It's a very intimate kind of education. Each child works away in silence as the teacher calls the grades, one by one, up to her desk for spelling: the words are printed on the blackboard or whispered. When the children finish their assignments they haul out a coloring book or stare out the window until the teacher gives them something else to do; the two grade fives spend their time smirking at each other. A steady, silent procession tramps back and forth to the single green metal wastebasket in the corner and then winds its way to the teacher's desk for a fresh sheet of paper. At recess the girls bring out their Barbie dolls and trade clothes; when it's warm they go outside and just stand around. The swings in the school yard are too broken and rusty to be of much use and there aren't enough kids in the school for a baseball game; the absence of concrete eliminates the pleasures of skipping and hopscotch. Someone has built a tree house in the back, a relic of the days when the school had boys, and there are a few old oil drums buried in the brush.

"Kathy, how many eights in twenty-four?" the teacher asks patiently, for the eleventh time. Kathy, a girl of eleven or twelve, hasn't a clue. Giggling, sniggering, grandstanding for attention, Kathy consumes almost all the teacher's time yet her mind remains pure as a fresh sheet of paper.

"P-u-p-l-e," Kathy has spelled on the board. "Pupil," says the teacher, gritting her teeth. "Pupil." Kathy grins and tries another. "F-a-v-e-r." "No," says the teacher, "fa-vor, Kathy, fa-*vor*." She gets up and writes on the board with a neat, round, schoolteacher script. As soon as the teacher passes on to the next grade, Kathy sashays back to her desk and pulls out a Harlequin romance.

Edward is one of twelve one- or two-room village and country schools still operating in the Winkler area in 1972; they are the only one-room schools left in the province outside of Hutterite colonies and Indian reserves. Although the Bible has long since been replaced as the textbook and German has been restricted to half an hour a day, the schools represent the Mennonites' last-ditch stand to preserve the independence and integrity of the village. They bitterly resent increasing control by a secular government and they resist the state's efforts to acculturate and homogenize their children. The village school is the linchpin of village cultural life; not only are the children taught according to Mennonite values but the teacher is expected to be the intellectual and social organizer of the entire community, to labor day and night to entertain and inform the parents as well as to keep a sharp eye on the morals of the responsible to the community; the school is an extension of home.

The young, like the old, are unable to escape the ministrations of the community. Singing, which was once considered sinful, is now encouraged in the schools on the grounds that it prevents juvenile delinquency. A questionnaire sent to parents in 1970 suggested that all high school students be compelled to participate in the choir. Next to the geriatric centre, Garden Valley Collegiate is the biggest institution in Winkler. Although it is tax-supported and follows the provincial curriculum, the school is essentially parochial, with as much emphasis on religion as on education. Almost all the teachers are Mennonite ("We hire Mennonites if at all possible," says the secretary of the school board. "Why pay an outsider to flout the traditions students. As a member of the community the teacher is of your church?"), and several of them are ministers and church elders. Rural trustees grill the teachers about their religious beliefs, moral conduct, and private lives as well as about the habits and reputations of fellow teachers, and those judged to be corrupt or subversive are dismissed. In June 1972, the school board passed a regulation limiting the length of male teachers' hair. Evolution is still a hot controversy in the school. Teachers get around Darwin by teaching Genesis: the Bible is still regarded as the basic text.

Many conservative Mennonites remain fundamentally opposed to secular education; they believe the old saying "the more learned, the more corrupted" and cite Genesis as incontrovertible evidence. They encourage their children to fail and pressure them to drop out of school as soon as possible. "When you have kids you put them to work, because that's what they're there for," comments a village school graduate. School is expected to be a moral authority;

it is not encouraged to put controversial ideas into the students' heads. (In a community where free enterprise is sanctified, anything new is immediately labelled "Communist," a very powerful smear word around Winkler, which, in 1972, is the only area of Manitoba that votes Social Credit.)

Although Winkler's young people are exceptionally docile and obedient ("We've never encountered drugs in the school," says a teacher. "Drinking is not a problem. Long hair is not an issue. There are no religious problems here. Cleanliness is the big issue I guess."), Winkler is almost hysterical about juvenile delinquency. "The youth problem has become a great burden on my heart," sighs Rev. Froese. In 1970 he and Mrs. Froeze counted 181 young people over the age of 14 who had not yet been won for Christ. "If you don't belong to the church you can't get married," says a village youth. "That's the real pressure. I know guys who got baptized because that's the only way they could get married. They never paid attention to church again." The better Winkler's kids behave, the more intensively they are policed and the more pious they are expected to be. At the slightest provocation, parents of exemplary teen-agers will launch into a furious tirade about the viciousness of youth. Because of their exaggerated terror of vice, parents treat school as a place of incarceration. There are no school dances. In 1970 the school play was cancelled at the last minute because the board thought it too sexy. The only place in town where kids are welcome is the Bible College. For fun Winkler's teen-agers hang out at the laundromat.

Most kids accept the hostility, the intellectual sterility, and the punitive discipline. Those who don't practice passive resistance; they keep their heads down and their mouths shut, and as soon as possible, they leave.

"It's the ones who do well that leave," sighs a trustee. "There's nothing for them here but dead-end jobs."

The work of caring for the young and the old is done by the women. Since the foundation of the Winkler economy is dedicated consumerism, the job of women in the Winkler area is to buy. In this they are no different from women in

any other Canadian community; the exceptional thing about
Winkler is the old-fashioned nature of the things they purchase. The staple goods available in Winkler stores — flour,
sugar, pots and pans, fabric, work clothes, vegetables, pins
— have not changed since 1900, although the goods themselves are up-to-date. Cheapness is still the criterion of
value; the style is still Eaton's catalogue. Although rural
women have acquired all the labor-saving devices of postwar technology, they feel a strong nostalgia for the homely
tasks and rituals performed by pioneer housewives. It's not
the hard work they want, although there is considerable
satisfaction in physical labor and an intense pleasure to
grubbing in the garden, but rather the sense of creativity
and dignity that came from doing well work which was
considered important. Most farm women supported their
families on the weekly cream cheque, and the woman's
labor determined not only how well the family ate but
whether they ate at all. The job of surviving on the frontier
required a physical, intellectual, and emotional commitment
which was both exhilarating and exhausting; the family was
an economic unit which she produced, mobilized, and sustained. She made most of the decisions governing the
children and possessed supreme moral authority. Although
her husband exercised titular control over the farm, she
usually kept the accounts and volunteered plenty of advice;
within the family corporation she was both janitor and
general manager. Although farm women endured the hard-
ships out of necessity, they were sustained by their power
and by the belief that they were building the New Jeru-
salem: their labor had both personal and social significance
and for many it meant salvation.

As the power of the rural matriarchs has been eroded,
respect for their intelligence and independence has diminished and the importance of their menial labor has been
grotesquely exaggerated; chores women once did out of
physical and financial necessity have been elevated to the
level of a sacred calling, a life, as Rev. Froese eloquently
put it in a Sunday sermon, of "pure and Biblical motherhood." This confusion of agricultural folk customs with
religious dogma has trapped many women in rituals which
have become meaningless and absurd. "A generation ago a

Mennonite mother who did not sew at least some of her family's clothing was considered an enigma. Unchristian, almost," says a rural Manitoba housewife. "The same held true of gardening and baking bread. Even today in many rural communities the woman who does not plant a garden and bake her own bread is looked upon as lazy, queer, or both. Rarely have I seen a woman serve purchased pastry without apology...instead of being freed from domestic duties, women now spend hours polishing already shining floors, baking calorie-rich dainties for dieting friends, and sewing yet another garment to add to bulging closets. Mennonite women in particular have clung almost desperately to domesticity as though there were intrinsic virtue in zwieback and home-sewn housedresses."

The problem of domestic overproduction is particularly acute for middle-aged women who have moved to town or whose families have grown up and left, depriving them of a market for their noodle soup and quilt covers. Yet so strong is habit and social pressure that production continues unabated. Winkler has a thriving Goodwill Store, where cast-off clothing is sold to the poor for ten cents or a quarter. (It is rumored that some of the poor buy up large quantities of this clothing and resell it at higher prices.) Outdated mini-skirts and old housedresses are donated to the Mennonite Central Committee, a mission agency which sends them to Africa. Even in town, many women maintain a huge vegetable garden and on summer Sundays they drive around solemnly inspecting the vitality of one another's vegetables. Social prestige is measured by the quantity of one's apples and the size of one's tomatoes. After putting up tons of preserves, they generously give their extra bushels of apples and pecks of cucumbers to a neighbour who has deliberately not planted a garden because she loathes canning. "I *never* want to see another pickle recipe!" screams a Winkler woman who has since fled to Winnipeg.

Prevented by custom and prejudice from taking part in civic affairs (None of the school boards, municipal or town councils around Winkler have women members, nor do the boards of the prominent churches. A local woman foolhardy enough to run for the NDP in a provincial election was bombarded with threatening and obscene telephone calls.)

and restricted by religious convention from social frivolities other than the occasional Tupperware party, Winkler women devote their excess domestic energy to missions. The Winkler ladies are clothing the black and brown peoples of the world. They produce a staggering tonnage of shirts, afghans, and children's clothes from material which is usually sent, pre-cut, from mission headquarters; one woman alone made 1,168 garments for the Red Cross in 1971. The favorite mission garment is the "Vietnam suit," a two-piece pyjama-style outfit in bright floral PP print. "They like bright colors," one lady explained. Like everything else in Winkler, the ladies' achievement is measured in terms of output. The 1970 Work Report for one small church group listed: 408 lbs. old clothing for MCC; 520 lbs. used clothing for Salvation Army; 60 lbs. (used) soap; 41 oz. stamps, 93 blankets; 142 baby blankets; 83 Vietnam suits; 3 shirts; 19 lbs. (used) Christmas cards; 124 rolls bandages; 51 school kits (toothpaste, wash cloth, soap, safety pins, nail clippers in a drawstring bag); 26 prs. knitted mittens; 24 stuffed toys; 12 leper shirts; 66 booklets; and 16 diapers. Each woman has a missionary "prayer pal" to whom she sends money and encouragement; the missionary writes back detailing the circumstances of each heathen conversion.

The church groups are segregated according to age and meet separately: the old sew, the middle-aged sing, the young marrieds talk about their children, and the single women are strong on Bible study. (Every patient in the Winkler hospital gets a card with a Bible verse printed on it on his breakfast tray every Sunday.) The women are separated for greater efficiency. In Winkler, even the weak and afflicted pay their way.

The noise is oppressive, a steady thunk thunk thunk of machinery punctuated by the anxious howls and bellows of the workers as they mill about the room, their grotesquely misshapen bodies contorted into futile gestures of uncomprehending helpfulness. Dressed all alike in blue-grey work clothes, heads shaved close to the skull, they stand and stare at the somnolent repetition of the machines or play vacantly with bits of rubber. As soon as the manager enters the room, they gallop around him, pulling at his sleeve and clamoring with loud, garbled cries. Their faces, vacuous and fluid as jellyfish, glow with childlike sweetness, which at a rebuff dissolves into black, shrieking rage as they scurry off, crying, to hide behind a machine. There are about 15 men in the room ranging in age from about 20 to 65. Nodding and grinning, they redouble their frenetic, haphazard activity in an effort to please, shambling and flapping about the heaps of old tires piled up in the room. Production at Winkler's Valley Rehab Centre is in full swing. The retarded are making rubber mats.

The Shurfoot Mat Co. of Winnipeg pays Valley Rehab 80 cents a square foot for the rubber link mats which it resells for $1.56 a square foot; the retarded churn out 18,000 square feet of mats a year for an income of $14,400. The money goes to pay the expenses of the centre. The retarded are paid on a point system. "They get points for the quality of work, personal care, appearance, and general attitude," says the manager, Ed Peters. "We pay them five cents per point. Most of them earn between $1.50 and $6 a week. The maximum is twenty-five points a day. Nobody's perfect."

The tires are supplied free by a Winkler trucking company that hauls potatoes into Winnipeg and brings the tires back; Shurfoot supplies the machinery to trim the tires and punch out the little rubber links. The machinery is so dangerous that only one or two of the retarded are able to use it; paid instructors took over after one man punched a hole through his finger. In another room, more retarded men thread the little links on wire spokes. "We are the only ones in western Canada making these mats," says Mr. Peters proudly. "Two of our mats are in the Canadian Embassy in Warsaw." The retarded got the contract because Shurfoot couldn't find anyone else willing to do the job.

In a third room, a couple of women laboriously weave small floor mats out of colorful strips of orlon pile donated by the local garment factory. The mats, which sell for $4.70, are not popular. "The local stores haven't sold a mat," complains Mr. Peters, a former straw boss at the garment factory who's very keen on increasing production. Valley

Rehab advertises that the services of the retarded are available to industries and businesses for packaging, collating,
assembling, and sewing. A group of women are busy turning
cuffs for parkas. The garment factory pays ten cents per
dozen pair of cuffs. "We did 345,000 cuffs last year," beams
Mr. Peters, smiling on the shy, fumbling women. The trailer
factories get the men to cut lumber for half a cent per two-
by-four.

About 55 retarded people work at the Rehab Centre.
They live at home or board in the town, reporting in each
morning at nine and quitting at 4 p.m. The centre was set
up in 1968 as a joint venture between Winkler and Morden
to cope with the large population of mentally handicapped
children and adults who were locked up in sheds and attics
on the farms. The $100,000 to build the workshop — which
is officially classified as an "industry" by the Department
of Industry and Commerce — was raised locally. $35,000 of
the centre's $49,000 annual budget is supplied by the provin-
cial government, which pays a grant of $50 a month for
each retarded "trainee." This is enough to pay the salaries
of the six supervisors; the retarded are expected to cover
the operating expenses themselves. Most of the women are
put to work in the kitchen preparing and serving the noon
meal, and the bulk of the food is grown in the Rehab's
garden, where the retarded do the hoeing and weeding.

"We designate people to go out in the garden," says Mr.
Peters sternly, pointing his finger. "You, you, and you. We
force them to go. 'You'll go until you like it!' We have to
do this. They don't like to work." Discipline is no problem.
Workers who behave badly are sent over to the Eden mental
hospital for two or three months of reassessment.

We walk past a table where a young man with the
hermaphrodite, pear-like shape of a mongoloid is bent in
deep concentration over a piece of paper. His head, mangy
where the hair has fallen out in big patches, is almost
resting on the page as he labors to print words with a tiny
stub of a pencil. His rubber mat lies neglected to one side.
Walking softly, Mr. Peters suddenly bangs his hand down
loudly on the table in front of the boy's head. The boy
jumps and looks up, frightened. In a low, threatening voice,
Mr. Peters demands to know what he's doing. The boy

mutters something about writing a letter. "I *told* you you're not allowed to do that!" Mr. Peters shouts. "*Now get back to work!*" The boy's face purples and his lower lip juts out with sullen rage. He fumbles with the paper. Mr. Peters yells again and bangs his hand on the table several times. The boy's tiny, close-set eyes glare with hate. Reluctantly, he picks up a rubber link and begins to thread it on to the wire spokes.

Valley Rehab is Winkler's triumph. By combining waste people and waste tires, the town not only solved a shameful social problem but also created a large and stable pool of cheap labor. And Winkler is a cheap labor town. Its highly touted prosperity is a fragile superstructure built on a broad base of poverty; the young, the old, the women, and the handicapped are linked together in a theocratic corporation for the greater glory of God and the greater profit of the handful of Winkler businessmen at the top. The social and religious life of the town is structured to extort the most money and the greatest efficiency from the working class; in spite of its superb organization and discipline, there are indications that Winkler's capitalist success is illusory and that it will, like many Canadian conglomerates, evaporate.

All of Winkler's industries, including the hospitals and other institutions, are built on a large supply of low-wage, unskilled, part-time, and seasonal labor. Without this labor, the industries wouldn't exist, since they would be unable to compete with larger, more efficient plants in Winnipeg. Winkler has no unions. Unions are considered to be "Communist." Anyone talking union is promptly fired. Everyone in Winkler except the professionals works for the minimum wage (The school board has been trying for years to reduce the wages of the teachers.). Since the professionals are usually paid by the province, the contrast between their wages and those of the rest of Winkler is astonishing. In 1972 a census of the town's 1,035 employees showed that 89 people, or 8.5 per cent of the work force, earned more than $8,000 a year; 609 people, or 60 per cent, earned less than $5,000. At the top was an elite of 53 people who made more than $10,000 a year; at the bottom were 117 people who earned less than $3,500. Winkler is clearly divided into two classes of people, the majority of whom are poor.

Skilled and experienced craftsmen work in Winkler for $2 an hour (compared with $6 or more in Winnipeg); Winkler factories hire welders and carpenters as "laborers" to avoid paying more than the minimum wage of $1.75 an hour. Some industries get around the minimum wage law by "training programs" in which the government subsidizes the work of inexperienced men for a number of weeks; at the end of this period, they are dismissed and a new batch of untrained men is hired. All employees are hired and fired at a moment's notice, according to fluctuations in the markets. Much of the work is seasonal; the potato companies employ a couple of hundred farm hands in the spring and fall, other people find summer jobs in the Morden cannery. Winter unemployment in the Winkler area is nine per cent; the slack is taken up by winter works, government training programs, and unemployment insurance.

Winkler's largest employer is the garment factory, which located in Winkler in 1958 on the suggestion of Max Gladstone. The town put up the money for the building. Based on a large supply of cheap, hard-working, and domestically skilled Mennonite labor, the garment factory has expanded to a staff of 120. The manager, Ralph King, has no illusions. "The women are working because they need the money, otherwise they wouldn't be working." Many of the women are wives and mothers of men employed full or part-time in Winkler's other industries; by paying low wages, Winkler is able to expand its industrial base because more people are forced to go to work. The garment factory is a tough place. The work is hard and the discipline stern. The turnover is 90 per cent. All the women have to meet certain qualifications: "I'm lookin' for a girl who needs money." Mr. King says bluntly. "I don't want women with kids under six and they can't be more than twenty pounds overweight." The high turnover works to Mr. King's advantage, because it enables him to take advantage of government-subsidized training programs.

The working women spell each other off: one works while another looks after her children for a small baby-sitting fee and in a year or two they switch around. The

baby-sitting industry is so entrenched that an attempt to
start a church-sponsored day care centre collapsed for lack
of children. Wages for office help and store clerks are so
low that it pays women to quit before they reach the level
of taxable income. So a job in Winkler, rather than providing one woman with a decent income, provides two or three
with pin money.

Who are these people who are willing to accept menial,
low-paying jobs without complaint? They are, of course, *die
Anwohner*, the landless ones. As it has modernized and
expanded, the Mennonite village corporation has brought its
own labor force along with it, and the village working class
continues to supply the sweat and muscle of Christian
capitalism. As the land has been taken over by the Kroekers
and other large Mennonite farm corporations, the displaced
farmers have been reduced to peasants who live in the
landlord's village and work for him for wages. The younger
ones live at home with their parents, and as the old people
move into nursing homes in Winkler, the young couples buy
up the village farmhouses. The ten-acre yard still provides
enough room for a cow, some chickens, and a vegetable
garden; another quarter section can be rented for grain.
Supplemented by wages earned in town, the little homestead
will sustain itself. More than half of Winkler's labor force
lives in the surrounding farm communities and villages.
Winkler's industries are supported by agriculture.

Unlike the English, who urged their children into the
cities, the Mennonites encouraged their children to stay on
the farm. Although the villages have decayed, the Mennonites have retained a strong sense of alienation and ethnic
solidarity; in Winkler it is still common to speak of "our
people." Ethnic loyalty is often a justification for exploitation: Mennonite businessmen may charge high prices, but
Mennonites will deal with them out of a vague feeling that
the money is somehow staying in the family. Wages are not
supposed to be high, because the Mennonite worker is
laboring for love of God.

Many young Mennonites who quit school early to work
on the farm are too poorly educated to find a good job. The
smart and aggressive go to Winnipeg; the rest go to work
in Winkler. The Winkler school system continues to provide

the community with a steady pool of cheap, unskilled labor — imaginative kids flee to the city, the slow and obedient are left. Because work is considered the universal remedy for juvenile delinquency, Winkler's continual hullabaloo about delinquency pressures the kids into low-paying, unwanted jobs. Although Winkler loudly protests the loss of its best young people, it deliberately creates the intolerable conditions which force them to leave.

An old man totters down the street pushing a cream can in a rusty white baby carriage. "Oh, that's water," laughs the garage attendant. "He's hauling it from the well over there. Been at it all week now."

Thirty per cent of Winkler's population have no running water, ten per cent have neither water nor sewer. Most of these people live in old, dilapidated houses on the southeast side of town, towards the garbage dump. The houses are wrapped in plastic to keep out the wind, and bales of straw are stacked around the foundations. Some of them are served by a well and cistern, and they all have a big garden out back. The homes of the poorest people are immediately identified by their outdoor privies. With more than 900 people living in substandard housing, Winkler has one of the biggest slums of any town its size in western Canada.

The poorest people in Winkler are the "Mexicans." Descendents of Mennonites who emigrated to Mexico in the Twenties, they have drifted back destitute in search of a utopia that has always eluded them. With all their possessions loaded into the back of an old car, they travel from farm to farm, accept the meanest jobs, and live in derelict shanties abandoned by other people. Many of them drive up in the spring, work in the fields, and commute back to Mexico for the winter; the old people, some of whom still have Canadian citizenship, come back for medical care and the old age pension. Virtually illiterate, fluent only in Low German, the Mexicans are treated with loathing and contempt by the prosperous bourgeoisie who are occupying their land. Everything that goes wrong in Winkler is usually blamed on the "Mexics." Their greatest sin is going on welfare. Since they have large families and very little money, they have been quick to discover the generosity of the Canadian state; Winkler's annual bill for health and welfare is $17,500. Sighs the mayor, who is death on welfare, "In Mexico the Mennonites say, 'Go to Winkler and ask for Mr. Will Fehr. He will give you lots of money.' "

Not many people can afford to live in Winkler. Residential taxes are extremely high — about $400 a year on a house worth $13,000 — and yet the town is poor. Winkler's churches are tax-exempt, as are the old folks homes and a church college, the Winkler Bible Institute. These institutions take up prime land in the centre of town and force the town to spread out around them, which raises the cost of roads and waterworks. The bulk of the town's $306,500 income from residential taxation is paid by a small number of middle-class people. They receive very little for their investment. "The roads in Winkler are worse than a cultivated field!" snaps one taxpayer. The needs of the town have been sacrificed to industry. Winkler has invested almost all its public works budget into providing services for the industrial park. The industries all have running water and sewer and are connected by excellent gravel roads. Yet for their superior services the industries pay substantially less taxes than the residents — Winkler's retail stores and factories together contribute only $182,500 a year. The low business and industrial taxes reflect a low assessment, and the assessment is low because many of the factories are cheaply constructed and most of the commercial buildings in town are old and run-down. In addition, Winkler gives each new industry a two-year tax write-off as an incentive. "We've got fifteen new industries in town that are paying $35,000 taxes a year," says Nick Wiebe. "They have cost us a lot of money." Winkler paved the road in front of the potato warehouses before it paved the principal streets in town, and every autumn Main Street is closed off at the railway tracks for six weeks so the CPR can stockpile vegetable cars. The industries' contribution to Winkler is an annual payroll of about $2 million, most of which passes through the hands of the retail merchants.

Although Winkler has been growing faster, Morden has been growing richer. An average family earns $400 more in Morden than in Winkler; Morden's retail trade ($8 million a year) is double Winkler's (The statistics brought cries of disbelief from the Winkler council, who are obviously unaware of the value of booze.) and is drawn from a trading area half as large. Morden's payroll is also double Winkler's, although the value of its industrial output is less and the town's assessment is $8 million compared to $5 million for Winkler.

Winkler's prosperity dwindles even more when seen in relation to what it's missing. In 1970, the 25,000 people in Winkler's trading area earned almost $48 million, but they spent only $4 million in Winkler; 92 per cent of the area's income went somewhere else. Of that $48 million gross income, only $2 million came from Winkler's industries. The rest was made from agriculture.

Winkler's commercial and industrial success is an illusion, supported by the labor, faith, and money of its citizens. Winkler is not a bastion of free enterprise. It's a corporate welfare bum. Winkler's most successful industries — the school, the hospitals, the aged — are those which are most heavily government subsidized. Neonex and Triple-E have received more than $275,000 in grants from the Department of Regional Economic Expansion since 1966, and two other Winkler industries have received smaller grants.

Such prosperity as Winkler has achieved is based on rural poverty: Winkler has grown as the villages and farms around have declined. Winkler's population increased by 1,236 between 1951 and 1971, but the population of the surrounding Rural Municipality of Stanley decreased by 2,956. Winkler just took up part of the slack. Only one family in ten in the municipality of Stanley makes enough money to pay income tax; according to tax forms in 1969, their average family income was $2,848, a drop of ten per cent since 1966. (Winkler's average income was $3,489.) It is a widespread myth that the Mennonite farmers are more prosperous than others, yet the average farm is small — less than 300 acres — with a gross annual income of less than $8,000. Twenty per cent of the farmers in Stanley sell more than $10,000 worth of produce a year, but 28 per cent sell less than $2,500. This makes them substantially poorer than the farmers around Miami, only nine per cent of whom sell less than $2,500. In 1971, the farmers of

Stanley were almost $175,000 in arrears on their taxes.

The Winkler economy is geared to depriving the rural people of their meager resources as efficiently as possible. Poor people buy cheap goods and fall for phoney bargains; poor people buy raffle tickets and chances on door prizes. Poor people work hard for the minimum wage. Poor people smuggle. By the time Winkler people have paid their taxes, donated to the church, and done their shopping, they have very little left. Bargain hunting is a way of life sanctioned by the church, which keeps entertainment at a minimum so as not to distract people from their job of spending money and exhorts them to greater efforts with evangelical bumper stickers which trumpet: "Things Go Better With Christ!" The air in Winkler is full of the sound of clinking coins.

"Go to now, ye rich men, weep and howl for the miseries that shall come upon you!" preached Menno Simons in sixteenth-century Germany. "Woe unto you that are rich!"

"I think if we had five or six years of good depression people would remember God," muses Peter Enns, who sold his trailer factory to Neonex for a small fortune. "Now everybody is too rich. They don't need God, they have everything. Sure, we still go to church on Sundays, but it's just a fad now, you know. We go and we give money, but what does that mean?"

Winkler is troubled by a sense of spiritual desolation, an awareness of hollowness and loss. "Our attitudes changed in Canada," reflects a villager. "The soil was no longer precious gold to be handed down but something to be exploited. We lost our feeling for the land."

Chapter 9

Bienfait

The bootlegger sits in the window of the poolroom. He gazes out absently across the dusty street towards the faded wooden hotel where old men in soiled overalls come and go through the little side door leading into the Eagle's Nest. His thick, stubby fingers move swiftly, shuttles weaving the cards together, shuffling, cutting, dealing, almost faster than the eye can follow. He barely glances at his cards, rapping out his score in a flat staccato voice as he pegs furiously along the board. His eyes, two brown stones, are fixed on his opponent, a skinny, twitchy young man who cracks his knuckles as he crows triumphantly at his own skill and shouts a steady patter of insults at the bootlegger. They've been playing cribbage for more than two hours; it's the twelfth game, the stake is five dollars a game, and the bootlegger is down 20 dollars.

Two freckled boys of 12 or 13 hover over the table, their tough faces serious and absorbed. It is a hot spring afternoon, but the poolroom is cool and dark. Three large green billiard tables stretch away into the gloom. There's an old wooden bench scavenged from a railway station along one wall and a pile of soft drink cases almost up to the ceiling. On the far wall is a crude, hand-lettered sign which reads "No Profane Language Please" and a little government notice: "Minors Under 16 Not Allowed." Two teen-age boys are fooling around at the last table; their cues make clean little "pock" sounds. "Oh fuck," says one. "That goddam cocksucker."

Across the street, Albert Cuddington comes out of the old brown store that says A. H. Cuddington General Merchant in big black letters across the false front, carefully locks the door, and walks slowly off down the street. Next door, Fred Liskowich rolls down the bamboo blinds in his grocery store. It's six o'clock. Main Street in Bienfait, Saskatchewan, is deserted.

233

"OK, you babies, you go home now, I'm going to supper," says the bootlegger, shooing the kids out the door and forking over 20 dollars to the cribbage hustler. He locks the door from the inside. "Come on," he says with a wink, "I'll cook you the best piece of steak you've ever eaten." He leads the way to the back of the poolroom. We go past a tiny, windowless room which contains half a dozen broken chairs and a small round table covered with a ragged piece of green felt. Poker is only one of Alex Ronyk's many skills. He points across Main Street to a small, brick-faced building next to the hotel. "I bought that cafe when the Chinaman hung himself in it. Went crazy. The town took it over for taxes. I paid $2,000 for it, fixed it up, sold it for $9,000. It's hard work, a cafe. You got to do too much running around. Jeez, did those people eat french fries! I peeled seven bags of potatoes on a Saturday alone. And after you put out your best meal some asshole tells you that it's no good. Chinamen can stand the racket. Not too many white men can stand it. A Chinaman can't make a living in this town if there's a white man cooking. Chinamen could never cook. I can cook better than any of them."

We enter a small back room. The furnace takes up most of the space. A bed and matching dresser fill the other corner. The bed has pink sheets. The walls are papered with naked girls from *Playboy* and old calendars, and an NDP election poster blocks the window. Mr. Ronyk's clothes are hung on a rack behind the furnace. Opposite the bed are a big white stove and some shelves jumbled with jars of jam and marmalade, toothbrushes, razor blades and tinned fruit. Mr. Ronyk's slippers are under the color TV, which is placed in the corner by the door so he can keep one eye on the TV and one eye on the poolroom at the same time. Everything is brown with grime, and the chrome table is littered with stale crusts of toast. I move the thick dirt around on the table with a filthy rag while he rinses off the breakfast plates and glasses under the cold water tap and rummages for some pots on the floor behind the furnace. He warns me against eating in the cafe next door. It's dirty, he says. Somebody once found a hair in his sandwich. He used to own it, but he sold it to a Chinaman. "That Chinaman," he says, mopping up the grease on top of the stove, "was dirtier 'n hell."

He reaches under the bed, pulls out a cardboard carton, and gingerly removes a rusty sawed-off shotgun, its butt nearly rotted away. "I found this in 1967 when I tore up the floor. Somebody had dug a hole and slipped it under." He lowers his voice and leans closer. "You know what this place used to be? Harry Bronfman's liquor warehouse. He kept all his booze here for running across the border. It had little wee windows, just like jail windows, with bars on them. We called it the boozorium. It had no real name. It wasn't supposed to be. They were all in the outlaw business. You can't have no name in the outlaw business. I'm sure this is the murder weapon, the gun that shot the Jew up at the station here."

Paul Matoff's bald head gleams in the light from the kerosene lamp as he leans over to count the money. It's almost two o'clock in the morning, October 4, 1922. Matoff has been at the CPR station since nine, when the cargo of liquor came in. He's nervous and impatient as he riffles through the bills done up in wads of $500. The station is dark and quiet, shrouded by thick clumps of trees and separated from the town by a wide set of tracks. Black strings of boxcars block off all view from the town. Standing in the station agent's bow window, Matoff can just see the lights on the top floor of the King Edward Hotel, where the Saturday night poker games are going full blast. Bienfait is full of miners and farmers looking for winter work. It's a good place to sell whiskey.

A faint clinking and the sound of low voices come from the side of the station near the express shed. Matoff's men are loading bottles into gunnysacks and stowing them carefully in the back of a truck. The driver is a big blond Frenchman with a broken nose, Jimmy Lacoste. He keeps a watchful eye on the shadows. A police patrol has passed through Bienfait ten minutes ago, but turned without crossing the tracks.

Lee Dillege, small and wiry, impatiently watches Matoff count the $6,000 he's paid him for the load of whiskey.

"You've given me five dollars too much," says Matoff, going through it again. Dillege is a regular customer of the Regina Wine and Spirit Company. He takes the liquor across the border, hides it on his farm in North Dakota, and sells it to contacts in the United States. His hands are soft and slender with long, delicate fingers, a gambler's hands. As he leans over to light a cigarette from the lamp, his eye catches the glitter of the diamond in Matoff's tiepin. "Hurry up," he says. "What's that?" asks Matoff, looking up. There's the small sound of footsteps crunching on cinders. Dillege goes to the door and peers out. "Hell, just a couple of harvesters." The telegraph operator, Colin Rawcliffe, sits on the edge of the table swinging his legs and apologizes for having had to be hauled out of the poolroom to take delivery of the booze.

There's a sharp, sudden sound of smashing glass. The barrel of a sawed-off shotgun pokes through the station window and fires point-blank into Matoff's back. He lurches forward, and blood gushes from a gaping hole in his right side. Rawcliffe scampers up the stairs. When he returns moments later, Dillege is bent over the body. "You stay here," he tells Rawcliffe. "You might get shot." As Dillege runs out the door towards his Cadillac he calls out, "Come on boys, let's get this booze away!"

Moments later, the high-powered Cadillac roars past the police patrol in a hail of bullets. By the time the police chug into the next town, the telephone wires have been cut. A few days later the liquor is found in a straw stack near the U.S. border — 18 sacks of rye, four sacks of cognac, 40 cases of gin, a sack of port, and one case of cocktails. A search of Dillege's farm uncovers a further 22 gallons of pure alcohol and 18 more sacks of rye in an underground chamber. Dillege is arrested and charged with conspiracy to commit murder. He is acquitted. The $6,000 and Paul Matoff's diamond tiepin are never found.

"Want a drink?" asks the bootlegger, opening a door at the back of the room. It leads into a garage where there's a big new red Buick. "I only got eight thousand miles on her," he says proudly. "All I do is drive to Estevan to buy the booze." He unlocks the trunk and takes out a bottle of Seagram's Five Star rye whiskey. "This is all I sell," he says. "It's not the best, but everybody likes it." He knocks the star off into a drawer. "I like to keep track of how much I sell." The drawer has about 500 little tin stars in it. "I'm open seven days a week but I do most of my business here on Sundays. Last week I made $144. I sell it for forty cents a beer, fifty cents a drink, same as in the pub. I take three dollars on a bottle of rye. I carry a lot of money on me. I have $500, $600 in my pocket. I have a gun. Nobody bothers me. I tell 'em I'll shoot first."

After our drink, Mr. Ronyk rummages in the oven and produces a big iron pot full of chunks of beef, potatoes, carrots, and onions. The stew is delicious.

Bienfait is a tough, bleak little town of about 800 people just east of Estevan, Saskatchewan, and ten miles north of the United States border. It has seen more than its share of trouble. People on this desolate stretch of prairie have had to scramble to make a living and they aren't too fussy about the law; bootlegging has provided the only big money Bienfait has ever seen. The faded, grinding poverty which is everywhere in rural western Canada is plain and undisguised in Bienfait; the place is bleached and desiccated like the skeleton of a buffalo picked clean by the birds.

Bienfait is set in an immense moonscape. Clay hills, each one exactly like the others, stretch off in symmetrical rows as far as the eye can see in all directions. The hills are brown and barren; nothing grows on them except a bit of sagebrush and a few wisps of dry grass, and pools of stagnant water form at their base. They're spillpiles, the refuse from 40 years of strip mining, which has been Bienfait's only reason for existence. The sandy, stony soil is ripped away to expose the thick seams of soft coal that is scooped up by mechanical shovels and trucked off. The mine operation is almost entirely automated; a handful of men run enormous Caterpillars and draglines that move tons of earth at a time. The mayor of Bienfait runs a dragline; it's considered the most prestigious job in the community. He makes $3.79 a hour and figures that's good money.

Bienfait is sandwiched between two mining operations —
Manitoba and Saskatchewan Coal to the south, owned by
Luscar Ltd. of Edmonton, and Battle River Coal to the
northwest, owned by Mannix, a conglomerate based in
Calgary which also owns Utility Coal, a mine south of
Estevan which supplies coal for Saskatchewan Power's
electricity generating plant. The miners resent the fact that
the profits go out of Saskatchewan. The mayor would like
to see the mines taken over by the Saskatchewan government.

Because the land is thin and poor for farming, the assessment is low and the taxes paid by the mining companies to
the municipality are miniscule. The land that has been
stripped and turned over is worthless. Most of it has been
turned into community pasture; the municipality charges
one cent per day for each cow using the field. Total income
from the pasture is about $5,000 a year. As more and more
land is stripped, the municipality is progressively impoverished. There are only 140 resident farmers left in the entire
municipality, and much of the land is owned by absentee
landlords who let it lie fallow or rent it out. Several parcels
of land are still owned by the Jewish Colonization Society,
although the little village of Hirsch, east of Bienfait, where
60 years ago everybody spoke Yiddish and kept kosher, is
now only a handful of unpainted shacks and a general store
owned by people called Campbell. The Jews did not last
long on their farms. As one Jew put it to me: " 'To hell with
Canada,' we said, 'we're going to Winnipeg!' "

Sparrows nest in the cab of a black steam locomotive
parked at the end of Bienfait's Main Street beside the CPR
tracks like a forgotten piece of scrap iron. A plaque on the
side ways: "Dedicated, Sept. 5, 1968 to the memory of the
mine workers, both deepseam and strip, who worked the
lignite coal seams in the Bienfait-Coalfields area since the
turn of the century." The engine was donated by one of the
mine companies. It dominates the town, an ominous and
ugly reminder of what one toothless old miner snortingly
calls "the bad old days," before everybody retired.

Bienfait was created one day in 1895, when, as local
legend claims, a French railway worker hammered in his
last spike at this particular spot, turned to his friend, and

said, *"Ah, bien fait.* " Ever since, the town has been called Beanfate. Bienfait has been a town only since 1958, when it had to incorporate to put in water and sewer. Before that, everybody hauled their own water from a well in the middle of the village on amazing water wagons rigged up out of old buggy and bicycle wheels with wash boilers, barrels, and cream cans mounted in the middle. Every day a bizarre procession made its way to the well from all corners of the village. Slop was thrown out into the back alleys, where flies swarmed around it, and the stench hung over the town. People burned their garbage in the back yard and payed the drayman $1.50 to haul away their old tin cans. Everybody had an outhouse in the back yard; when the hole filled up, the outhouse was moved over a few feet. Bienfait had wooden sidewalks until 1962. In spring the snow turned to mud; by July the earth had dried to dust and the gardens had shrivelled away. Dust storms swirled through the town, and swarms of grasshoppers ate their way methodically through the vegetables. "It was horrible, horrible!" cries Mrs. Wing Wong, who came from Victoria in 1952, the bride of the only Chinaman still left in town. "Skunks and sewage," says Wing Wong cheerfully. "That's Bienfait in the summer!"

Railway tracks are everywhere in Bienfait; you get the feeling you're always on the wrong side. Bienfait is one big shantytown. The houses are small clapboard cottages, many little more than shacks painted bright blue and pink and orange in the Ukrainian style, jammed close together on tiny lots. Many have been moved in from farms and mining camps. "Bienfait is a cheap place to live," Wing Wong explains. "That's why Bienfait will exist. Taxes aren't high. The highest rent is about $75 a month. We don't have paved streets, but. . . ." When the streets develop potholes, Frank, the town handyman, simply puts up a barricade and everybody drives around it on the boulevard until he gets it fixed. Packs of mangy dogs roam the town scavenging in the garbage and snapping at passing cars.

Bienfait has no bank, but a man from the Estevan Credit Union comes in twice a week. Everything on Main Street is small and narrow and crowded up to the sidewalk; even the newer stores, a spillover from the oil boom of the

Fifties, have a faded tackiness typical of prairie towns where everything is taken for granted. The most impressive building in Bienfait is the Legion, which is new and shiny with plate glass and yellow paint and set back from the street in a little patch of manicured lawn opposite the hotel. The white Victorian veranda which gave the hotel a touch of style in the days when it was called the King Edward has long since been torn down. The hotel is now painted robin's-egg blue and called the Plainsman. There's a big wooden cutout of Davy Crockett over the front door and an Indian's head with feathers over the Eagle's Nest. The hotel is at the end of Main Street, facing the station, a reminder of the days when the entire population of Bienfait gathered on the platform at 8:40 p.m. to meet the train from Regina and peddlars, land speculators, and homesteaders galloped across the tracks for a one-dollar room and a hot meal.

Down the street in A. H. Cuddington's general store, built by one of Bienfait's first merchants, Mr. Cuddington presides over a collection of rubber boots and popsicles. The oiled wooden floor heaves and sags in great waves. At noon Mr. Cuddington hangs a little cardboard sign on the door with a pencilled message: "Out to Dinner."

The plastic sign over Fred Liskowich's store says FRED LISKO ICH, but you don't notice it after a couple of days. Fred Liskowich is a fierce man with a bristly grey brushcut who started selling groceries to miners in the Twenties and has built up a big business. I ask him for the secret of his success. "Welfare!" he shouts. "It used to be just relief. Now you get a steady income coming in."

Main Street runs one short block north from the highway to dead-end at the CPR tracks. The street is very wide and cars and trucks are still allowed to park in the middle, forming a divider strip, except in the winter when the snow is piled up there. Cars full of greasers bomb up one side of Main Street, make a screaming U-turn at the tracks, and bomb down the other side to the pool hall. Main Street in summer is a cloud of dust except when it rains; then it's a bog. Half the stores are boarded up and the rest are for sale if there was anyone to buy. Holes appear in both sides of the street where buildings have been torn down. (The butcher, for example, demolished his meat market and moved into the old post office to save taxes.) The blank, abandoned buildings scattered in weedy lots look like over-turned cardboard boxes. One kick would bring them all tumbling down. "They look like cowboy days stores," says Mrs. Wong. Bienfait is a western town, a gamblers' town, a gunfighters' town. Bienfait is ashamed of its reputation. Nobody wants to talk about the three murdered men in the graveyard.

South of town, the Souris River twists its way through a magnificent wooded ravine, cutting a massive scar across the face of the plains. Indians camped in its hidden coulees when they hunted the buffalo on the high prairie and drove the herds over the bluffs. They camped around an arched hoodoo the river had eroded from sandstone and carved small pictures of animals into the soft rock. The French explorers called it Roche Percée. When the buffalo disap-peared, the Indians trekked out of the valley. A coal mine operated for years in the valley at the base of "Ross Percy." Twenty years ago it closed down and the dragline, like a giant scarecrow, was abandoned on top of the hill. The silent, isolated coulees are full of hill people, squatters who have built themselves little tar-paper shacks and surrounded them with tin sheds, rusty oil drums, biffies, scrap iron, wooden wagons, refrigerators, and whatever else they could pick up from a derelict mining camp. Like fossils in stone, the valley has carefully preserved the junk of successive civilizations. High on the bluffs overlooking the river, the deep ruts formed by caravans of Métis Red River carts are still visible in the prairie grass and a stone cairn marks the spot where the North West Mounted Police camped on the banks of the Souris at Roche Percée on their first trip west in 1874. Long before the CPR arrived, the Souris River was a commercial highway, and from traffic on it, which reached its peak during prohibition, Bienfait has made its living.

The first settlers walked overland from the end of steel at Moosomin and settled in the valley near water. One farmer digging into the side of the hill to make a stable hit coal. As he enlarged his stable, he sold fuel to the neigh-bourhood homesteaders. Each man dug his own with a pick

and shovel, and a winter's supply cost $1. Soon the bluffs
and hillsides were pocked with little tunnels leading into
the coal seams: gopher holes, people called them. The first
commercial mine, the Souris Valley Coal Company, was
opened by a homesteader called Hazzard in 1891. He hired
other farmers to dig coal during the winter and sold the
surplus to Winnipeg businessmen. A small camp grew up
in the valley at the mouth of the mine. In 1905 the mine
was bought by a Winnipeg company, Western Dominion
Collieries, and the camp was moved to the top of the bluff.
The CPR opened a second mine in Bienfait in 1906, and a
third company, Manitoba and Saskatchewan Coal, was
started by a rival Winnipeg syndicate headed by Sir William
Whyte of the CPR. Bienfait was industrialized. The CPR
shipped in men and shipped out coal. The profits went to
Winnipeg and from there to the banks and brokerage
houses of eastern Canada. No money stayed in Bienfait.

The mines opened in August and shut down in March.
Homesteaders trying to prove up their few ploughed acres
went underground in the coal mines to tide themselves over
the winter. "We homesteaded on a pile of rock," says Archie
MacQuarrie. "When I was sixteen I started in the mines.
I worked all the mines, right around. The working conditions in all were the same, rotten. I looked after the horses.
All the coal cars underground were pulled by horses. They
lived down there. We had stables and everything underground. The horses went blind from being in the dark." Pay
was $1.50 a day or $4 a week with board (about ten or
twelve cents an hour). The men worked as many hours as
they were able; an 80-hour week was average. Farmers
who found their land poor and barren sold out their farms
and moved close to the mines; they squatted in little
shanties in the ravines with a horse, a cow, and a handful
of chickens. Long after all the free land had been taken up,
immigrants continued to come west, hungry, penniless,
anxious to work. "We dropped off the train in Bienfait,"
says Morrell Edwardson, who arrived in 1907. "All around
was prairie and we seemed to be encircled by prairie fires.
It was like a scene from the *Inferno*. I was fifteen and both
my father and I worked at the mine. That fall many of the
mine workers joined the United Mine Workers Union, so

the mine owners fired us all and closed down. We were hard pressed to save ourselves from starvation." Most of the latecomers were central Europeans or Ukrainians. "We called them Gallicians, Ruskies," remembers an old man. "They didn't talk English. All they needed was a loaf of bread and a ring of bologna. They started all the trouble." "Bohunk" was the word most popularly used by the Anglo-Saxons who had gotten to Bienfait first and had a stranglehold on the commercial life of the town. "My father hated it," growls Metro Katrusik, mayor of Bienfait. "If anybody called me a bohunk now, he'd get a pop in the nose."

The babel that was Bienfait quickly sorted itself out. At the old Hazzard mine, renamed Taylorton in honor of its Winnipeg owner, the Ukrainians lived in one valley, the Germans in another, and the Englishmen lived in the company houses on top of the hill by the pit. The Ukrainians plastered their houses with mud and whitewashed them brilliant shades of blue and orange; they flattened out the tin kegs that blasting powder came in and used them for siding. Their barns, and even many of their houses, were dug into the side of the hill; the floors of both were mud. The valley people kept pigs and made their own sausage in outdoor smokehouses; they earned extra money by selling chickens, geese, and milk to the people on the hill. The company houses, identical with white siding with green trim, were laid out in neat rows as if, said one miner, they expected an Indian attack. Everybody had a cow and a little garden and everybody took in boarders. There were three electric lights in camp — one at the church, one at the store, and one in front of the lice-infested Blue Goose boardinghouse, where the single men lived in a single room. The church was non-denominational. The service varied from Roman Catholic to Salvation Army depending on which clergyman they could coax out from Estevan. School at the mine went to grade eight, at which point the boys went to work underground as "trappers," opening and closing doors for the horse-drawn coal caravans. The school also taught night classes in English which were very popular. "I could swear in pretty nearly every language in the world," one miner told me proudly.

The miners lived in the dark, went down at 7 a.m. or earlier, before the sun was up, and came up again after sunset; their lamps bobbed like fireflies as they walked home in the dark. A blast on the whistle signaled the end of the workday; they listened carefully, because a long blast meant no work the following day. "The mine managers said that if you didn't have a union you could work longer hours and make more money," says Archie MacQuarrie. "The silly buggers fell for it." Men bribed the manager to get a job. Equipped with tools, lamps, rubber boots, and blasting powder purchased from the company store, they worked in water that was knee-deep; they drank it and peed in it. They shovelled coal by hand, heaving it six feet up into the cars. "I loaded forty tons of coal a day for ten cents a ton," boasts the bootlegger, who's done everything. "Hell, if you couldn't load forty tons a day, why you weren't a man! We'd load our $4 worth and quit. Often we'd quit as early as two-thirty p.m. I was young then."

In the spring the single men drifted off to work on railroad section gangs or as hired hands on local farms; the married men sat idle in the sun. "We'd go uptown and squat outside the store," Bert Hitchen reminisces, "and the first thing you'd know, somebody would have out an ol' pack o' cards. We'd play for pennies, matches even, to kill the time. There wasn't nothin' else to do." The company store was the centre of every mine camp. The miners were dependent on it for their provisions, and their store bill was automatically deducted from their wages at the end of every month. Unemployed for four or five months every summer, the miners ran up huge debts at the store which were paid off from their winter's wages. Many men were perpetually in the hole. "We lived off fresh air!" cackles Hitchen. The miners hunted rabbits and prairie chicken in the valley and fished in the river, and on winter nights they cleared the snow from the ice and skated in the light from their carbide lamps hung in the trees. Poker games ran all weekend in the bunkhouses, where homemade wine was 25 cents a glass. Once a winter the company loaded everybody into a railway boxcar, and they all steamed off to a dance in Bienfait.

Bienfait was a rowdy town, an overgrown mining camp

thrown up around a welter of poolrooms, bars, dance halls, cafes, and the Bienfait Boarding House, which was also a livery barn, movie theatre and community dining hall where the miners ate off oilcloth, the travelling salesmen were served on white linen, and the mine executives ate in a separate room. But the heart of Bienfait, as of every Saskatchewan town, was the Chinese cafe; Bienfait's was owned by "Sandy McTavish" Wong, as he was called by the miners. Brought to western Canada as coolie labor to build the CPR, the Chinese found themselves much in demand as cooks and houseboys in the hotels, brothels, and private residences of the rich, where they lent a certain snob appeal to the raw new frontier towns scattered along the track. Having learned to cook and wash and wait on tables, all the Chinese, barred by legal and racial restrictions from other forms of enterprise, went into the restaurant and laundry business, a choice dictated by force of circumstance rather than inclination. "As long as you can butter a piece of toast you're in the cafe business," says Sandy's son Wing Wong cynically.

Mysterious, exotic, alien, tainted with a hint of vice and corruption, the Chinese cafe was an institution, a place of immense fascination and almost mythic significance. "I was really too young to know what went on there," says a Saskatchewan boy. "The Chinese were very much a community unto themselves. Who could explain the relationship of one Chinese to another? Some were adopted, some were illegal immigrants. You didn't ask questions. It was always dirty, always full of people. God, you went into the kitchen and you almost threw up. The Chinese cafe usually had a very unsavory reputation. There was gambling and rumors of fights with butcher knives. It was a hangout. You could buy anything there. It was the birth control centre. You were too embarrassed to go to the doctor or the drugstore but with the Chinaman it didn't matter who knew. People told terrible stories about the Chinaman. He was a kind of bogeyman. Mothers used to threaten us that if we didn't behave, the Chinaman would come after us with a meat cleaver."

"I never really had a father," says Wing Wong, who started to work in the cafe in 1923 when he was ten. "I was never really taught anything. His father made him work so I had to work for him. I worked in the cafe and went to school. I had to get up early to get the miners to work. They roomed with us, upstairs. We had four rooms and they were all rented out in the winter. I had to get them breakfast at five a.m. Then I went back to bed. There was no running water, no bath houses. The miners got awfully dirty. They'd bring out the washtub and bathe in the kitchen; they'd just hang up their dirty clothes till the next day. Their clothes were stiff as boards. The miners all wore Stanfields. They'd turn brown from the sulphur when you washed them, no matter how much Sunlight soap you used. For a toilet we just had a hole in the ground. We got Eaton's and Simpson's catalogues; you read one and used the other.

"Our cafe was called the Bienfait Cafe. You could get a meal for twenty-five cents. Our top price dinner was forty-five cents. The hotel got the more refined trade. We got the rougher crowd. Saturday nights they'd have a show at the Legion, you'd sell the odd bottle of pop and ice-cream cone. Dance nights were the worst. You'd get the rowdies from out of town and they were the worst. Most dances ended in a fight or two. The dance hall was in the Legion, right next to the cafe. They almost wrecked the place. There were about three thousand miners around then. The miners worked hard and drank hard and played hard; if there wasn't a fight in town on a Saturday night, it was a miracle. It was rough. We used to call the police, but it was kind of mob violence in a way. One or two would start it and everybody else would jump in. They'd be drinking all day; when they drink, miners have a tendency to fight. A Frenchman would insult a Scotchman about the bagpipes and in a second one of them would have a black eye. The fight was on! You'd have three fights going at the same time, one at the Legion, one at the Ukrainian hall and one at the Labor Hall. There was always a poker game. Sometimes they would play all week in back of the corner store. We'd make coffee in a washtub and pack sandwiches in a boiler and carry it over to them.

"It was rough. It had its bright moments, but there's a lot of bad features about a small-town cafe. Credit really killed it. Everybody's owing you. My dad had quite a bit of money owed and he died broke. We worked seven days a week, long hours. You'd be ready to close and a ball team would come back and they'd want to get fed. They'd charge it up and never pay. You closed for the night when the last soul left. If he was drunk, he was harder to please. Of course we took a lot of verbal abuse. To them we were Chinks."

In a tough mining town which had no money and a talent for leisure, bootlegging offered an attractive source of income. When Saskatchewan went dry in 1915, bootlegging became Bienfait's principal industry. The economy of the West is built on booze. Whiskey was the cash of the fur trade and it established the fortunes of the businessmen who were later to build the CPR. The North West Mounted Police were sent west for the express purpose of closing down Fort Whoop-Up, an American whiskey post that was creating suicidal drunkenness among the Indians with a brew containing tea, pepper, gunpowder, and laudanum, as well as a little diluted rum. Until 1891 liquor was available in the North-West Territories only by government permit. Since permits were routinely given to doctors and druggists, every little railway shack town had three doctors and five druggists. Liquor was also made freely available to politicians and local merchants who made appropriate campaign contributions. They in turn entertained their friends at lavish stags and card parties, especially before elections. Whiskey made men popular. It also made them rich and solidified the rigid social stratifications which have been the most durable feature of western provincial life. The history of the West is the battle between the settler's thirst for whiskey and his passion for money. Prohibition successfully combined the two: it made the drunks rich, especially in Bienfait. The only really profitable economy Bienfait has ever had is disorganized crime.

"Every second house in town was a bootlegger," says the postmaster. "You'd get a big water glass full of wine for twenty-five cents. The competition was fierce. Guys would drum up customers by offering a free garlic sausage or a lunch. You drank right in the house. There'd always be a big gang in playing cards. You'd win a pot and buy a round for everybody. You got everybody lit up on their own money."

Most Bienfait businessmen sold home brew which they made from a simple, inexpensive recipe — one quart whiskey, one quart pure alcohol, one quart water, and a dash of burnt sugar — and sold for about $10 a quart. "I used to bootleg over the doctor's office," says Alex Ronyk. "This doctor was an awful drunk. He was my best customer. Millions his name was, Doc Millions. Women would bring their babies in and he'd be drunker 'n hell. The babies would twitch and he'd tell them what was wrong. He was pretty good. He never operated when he was drunk."

Bootlegging was a community recreation which bound the miners together in a conspiracy of silence: if a man wasn't bootlegging, chances were that his mother or brother was, so he kept his mouth shut. Warnings of police raids were flashed along telephone party lines, and neighbours were roused out in the middle of the night to help pull a wagonload of booze out of the mud. These fly-by-night family operations depended on selling small quantities of homemade stuff to a local clientele; Bienfait's best customers were Americans. The Souris Valley became a freeway for channelling illegal booze across the border; the winding coulees provided perfect hiding places for stills. Liquor was stored in grain bins, hay stacks, and cisterns, and half the gopher holes in the valley held caches of booze; police discovered one still in a barn when they noticed that all the pigs were drunk. Miners with cars poured whiskey in their fuel tanks and filled their tires with it; one farmer herded his bottles across the border stuffed in blankets wrapped around his cattle. They say one rumrunner with a daughter named Nellie who could drive like a demon made so much money he had to push the door of his safe shut with his feet.

The Bienfait whiskey trade was dominated by the Bienfait boozorium, a huge warehouse in the middle of Main Street owned, like all the other warehouses dotted across southern Saskatchewan, by Harry Bronfman. Although it was illegal to sell liquor in Saskatchewan, it was not illegal to export it to the United States. The boozorium was an export house, a subsidiary of the Regina Wine and Spirit Co. and the Yorkton Distributing Co. The liquor was made in

Yorkton to the same recipe that the Bienfait moonlighters used and disguised as imported whiskey by false labels. The boozorium's stock of expensive Canadian and imported liquors was inspected regularly by the government, and a list was sent to the Saskatchewan Liquor Commission. The inventory for December 1920 shows 1,471 cases of assorted rye, gin, rum, and scotch, 260 gallons of unlabelled liquor, and a few barrels of beer.

"The front office looked just like a druggist's store," says one old man. "All the different brands were displayed along the wall. The buys would come in, sample it and make a deal for how many cases they wanted." The boozorium usually sold a case of twelve bottles for about $50; in the United States it sold for $300. The transactions were very formal, complete with a billing of lading from the Trans-Canada Transportation Company, another Bronfman subsidiary. At the peak of the export traffic in 1922, the Bronfman warehouses were earning an estimated $500,000 a month. "All we handled was $100 or $1,000 bills," says Harry Zellickson, a farm boy from Hirsch who managed the Bienfait boozorium. "We made about $10,000 to $20,000 a day. It all depended on the customers. The money had to be on the counter before they drew out. No cheques. It had to be cash. As soon as I had about $10,000 or $15,000 it went right away into the bank.

"I used to deliver liquor to the USA in a truck. A lot of the boys got jobs doing that. We were salesmen. I could come as far as the boundary. Then I handed it over. I had to get the money first — they were tough. Everybody was trying to make an easy dollar. Oh sure, we were held up lots of times. I didn't give a goddam. 'Come on, take it!' I said. 'I'll never shoot. You can have all the revolvers.' We was insured.

"Police would come by and say, 'I hear you were held up last night.' 'Were we?' I'd say. We didn't want it publicized. Then every Tom, Dick and Harry would come and try to hold us up. It was a big racket. Lee Dillege, he was a big gangster but a hell of a fine fella. They were all gentlemen. The nicest people were the biggest gangsters."

Most of the Americans who came up for the booze were small-time hoods, farmers and transients looking for kicks who unloaded their cargo to another middleman as soon as they were over the border. They drove up in their fast bulletproof cars complete with machine guns and whiled away the time until dark pitching silver dollars at cracks in the barroom floor. "You wouldn't know 'em from anyone else," says Ken John, who had the distinction of sharing a hotel room with Jimmy Lacoste. "They looked just the same." They ran the border at night, not for fear of the police, who were hopelessly outclassed in their old tin lizzies, but to avoid hijackers lurking in the dark gullies of the Souris Valley. The smuggling ran both ways:

"You could order any type of car you wanted," says Ken John. "It would be a hot car, of course. They'd steal a car off the street in Omaha and drive it into town and try to sell it. They'd start off asking $1,500. The price would come down pretty quick; they couldn't afford to stick around too long. You could get a good car for $500. But you had to watch out. They'd turn up in a week or two and steal it back from you.

"Most of the guys wore guns, shoulder holsters. In the hotel there'd be a holster on every table. I remember one poker game in my room, a guy stuck ten-dollar bills into the lamp chimney to light his cigars. There was a lot of money around. The station agent made big money. He got a cut on the liquor, a commission on all the express. We just went to the back door of the boozorium any time we wanted whiskey.

"The laws were very loose. The police would raid us at midnight. They tried us right there and then at one a.m. They'd fine us, grab ten dollars a piece off the poker players and the boys would go back to playing. There was a saying among the poker players: 'One day, eighty dollars; eighty days, no dollars.' I don't know one who ever finished up with a dollar. Nobody saved their money. There was nothing to spend it on."

"Everyone died poor," says Alex Ronyk, who quit the mine to make his living playing poker. "There was one guy, Bob Hazzard, he was worth half a million. Sold his coal mine. He was so dumb the guys would get him to sign a blank cheque. Then they'd make it out for whatever they wanted. He lived in a little shack next to the hotel. The

outfit got all his money. Fleeced him. They went to Vegas
and Reno and lost the whole damn bunch. One of them's
dealing cards in Vegas. In them days guys didn't fool
around. One guy who was runnin' whiskey, they electro-
cuted him. Found him up a hydro pole. People say they
killed the Jew, Matoff, because he'd given 'em a load of tea
once instead of whiskey. Humph. A dirty trick. I remember
once in the poolroom these two guys come in. 'I'll shoot you
a game of pool for your Buick,' says one. So the guy had
both Buicks, bam, just like that. This was the biggest town
in the West then. They gambled in the cafe and in the
bowling alley. Hell, they were gamblin' all over the place.
In this room here a poker game never quit, night and day.
We took twenty-five cents out of a pot, it worked out to
about ten dollars an hour. Some nights I'd win $500. One
guy got so damn rich he went crazy."

Like the coal companies, Harry Bronfman and his brothers
took their profits out of Bienfait. The Bienfait Export Liquor
Co. was run very efficiently, a respectable business, with a
lot of cheap labor and friends in high places. "The police
were all paid off," shrugs Harry Zellickson. "They'd look
the other way. A Mountie would jump on your running
board, you'd hand him a quart of whiskey and he'd jump
off. The government wanted to make the money. Harry
Bronfman had to go to the government to get in. The
government knew there was money in it. We had a lot of
good friends in parliament. There'd be a little contract
coming up. Gardiner would say, 'You do a little favor for
me.' Then he used to come to my father and do a little thing
for him. We had a little contract with the highway. I made
a few pennies. [James G. Gardiner was Saskatchewan
Minister of Highways, Labor and Industries from 1922 to
1926, and Premier of Saskatchewan from 1926 to 1929. A
schoolteacher in Hirsch at the turn of the century, Gardiner
boarded on the Zellickson farm. He later lived next door to
Harry Bronfman in Regina.]

"Jimmy Gardiner teached me. He wasn't there wanting
to be a teacher. He was a politician. Politics was in him.
He was so well-liked, everybody was good strong Liberals.
Gardiner done a lot for the newcomers. He'd get them a
quarter section, a loan. So when he was running they didn't

care who the other candidate was. They didn't even know
his name. All they knew was 'Gardiner.' Then he moved to
Ottawa. We were in Saskatchewan. We had to get something out of the government so we switched to the Conservative Party. I got more out of the Conservatives than I did
out of the Liberals.

"We made a living. People wanted to make a living. We
had no money. We was on relief on the farm. You wanted
a drink, we gave you a drink. Who doesn't want a drink of
liquor? I got paid. Those Bronfmans became millionaires. . .
so what the hell?"

The end of prohibition and the beginning of the Depression
knocked the bottom out of Bienfait's whiskey economy. The
price of coal slipped and the mines cut back. Men were laid
off; wages were cut in half. By the spring of 1931, when the
mines shut down for the summer most men were taking
home less than $2 a day. The mine companies, however,
still managed a profit of almost $1 million. The men were
responsible for laying track, pumping water out of the mine,
and timbering the rooms, for which they received no pay.
Many would go underground at 3 a.m. in order to get a
head start on the day's work. False weights cheated them
out of tons of coal; this same coal was later sold to them to
heat their houses. Hours were wasted waiting for coal cars
or repairing broken machinery; the men worked in a haze
of fumes and smoke from blasting powder. Smaller mines
closed down as the demand for coal decreased. Only 600
men were working in the winter of 1930-31, and by August
the number had dwindled to 200. By trying to spread the
work among all the men, managers wound up employing
each for only a few hours a week. Competition for jobs was
fierce as farmers fled the land. Any miner who complained
was immediately fired. "Heck, if you abused a horse you
were fired!" says Bert Hitchen. " 'That bloody horse cost
me $300,' yells the manager. 'You can get a man any time,
but you can't get a good horse. You can get a good man for
nothing!' "

"The mine manager was a tough son-of-a-bitch," reflects
Alex Ronyk. "Jeez was he mean! He'd yell and swear at the

guys. Hit them even. Those immigrants would run like hell
when they smelled him coming. He used to smoke a big
cigar. The smoke would drift through the mine, you could
smell it as soon as he was down the shaft. Those immigrants
got one whiff and they'd clear the tracks. They were scared.
I wasn't scared of him. He fired me. That's why I'm here in
the poolroom."

Poverty made conditions in the deteriorating mine camps
unendurable. There was a $7 fine for allowing livestock to
run at large in the mine camp. Standing in the wrong place
in the mine cost $5; one man was charged $8 for a cave-in
he didn't cause. Prices at the company stores were grossly
inflated — a pair of rubber boots cost $5 — and mysterious
"mistakes" were made in the miners' bills which cost them
$5 to $10 extra a month. One clerk was convicted of
tampering with the mail. "If a woman dared to buy a cheap
dress from Eaton's mail order, she was a marked woman
and faced the wrath of the mine owner," stated one woman.
Every month, $1.25 was deducted from each miner's pay
cheque for medical expenses. When he wanted to see the
doctor, he wrote his name in a book in the mine office; the
doctor came once a week. Often he didn't bother to show
up at all. The doctors made about $1,500 a year from the
mine rake-offs.

The pressure of unemployment and poverty turned the
mines into concentration camps. Everybody took in boarders
to make a few extra pennies, and many of the small,
draughty company houses became filthy and overcrowded.
Eleven men paid 25 cents a day to share six beds in a
company bunkhouse that was full of bedbugs. They supplied
their own blankets. The charge at the boardinghouse was
$1.05 a day. Single men who did not stay in the boarding-
house paid $1 a month tax. The drinking water was pol-
luted; pigs rooted amongst the cow dung and garbage in the
yards. Annie Baryluk's company house was typical:

"We have one bedroom. There's two beds in there. A
dining room, no beds in there, and a kitchen with one bed.
There's eleven in the family... I think we need a bigger
place than that. When it's raining the rain comes in the
kitchen. There is only one ply of paper, cardboard paper,
nailed to about two inch boards...It's all coming down and

cracked. When the weather is frosty, you wake up in the
morning and you can't walk on the floor because it's all
full of snow, right around the room." Although the company
houses rented for from $5 to $10 a month, the miners were
anxious to live in them: a company house meant a miner
was recognized as a permanent employee and would be
guaranteed work.

Peddlars — farm wives and women from the valley
selling eggs and meat — were forbidden to enter the mine
camps. The Manitoba and Saskatchewan mine erected a
barbed wire fence around the camp and stationed a guard
at the gate. The following edict was posted in the mine
office:

"All employees are forbidden to purchase anything from
Mrs. A. Molyneaux while peddling around the mine. Anyone
doing so will be disobeying the wishes of the management
and will be inviting trouble for themselves. Management has
decided that it is not in the best interests of the Company
to allow Mrs. Molyneaux to peddle around the mine,
furthermore, are determined to stop same."

Mrs. Molyneaux was selling milk.

So onerous were the fines and check-offs that many
miners had only $5 to $10 left on their month's pay cheque.
Some got a bill telling them how much they owed the company. Protests were laughed down or met with a torrent of
abusive language. Miners were threatened with black-
listing. They were told to take what they could get or they'd
get a damn sight less.

In Bienfait, where the miners rented shacks from Estevan
businessmen, the bill for relief threatened to bankrupt the
village. A pathetic appeal for help was sent to the provincial
government on July 8, 1931, by the town clerk:

"This is principally a mining Village with a population at
the present time of 526. Since Spring we have had on our
hands 22 cases of destitution the Council have had to take
care of. Eighteen of whom are married with families. All
last winter they were employed on an average of two days
per week, and the Mines contiguous [sic] to Bienfait all
closed down on April 1st, at which time the miners had
nothing to fall back on as it was a wrestle to keep body
and soul together up to that time. The Council has endea-

voured to keep these people alive, amploying [sic] them in
the nuisance grounds, streets, cemetery etc. sufficiently
enough to give them a bare living, and they have held
strictly to the idea of furnishing work in order to hold back
the bums. In doing this service they have spent to date
$454.15 and are now at the end of their resources... As this
is a case of emergency, kindly let us know what assistance
you can give us and when you can give such assistance as
the present conditions are desperate."

The entire commerce of the Bienfait community was
carried on by welfare vouchers, which were handed out at
the municipal office after rigorous examination and scolding
by the clerk. The farmers traded their vouchers for coal at
one of the small gopher hole mines and the mine owners
paid their employees with the vouchers. The miners took
the vouchers to a storekeeper in exchange for groceries. The
storekeeper sent all his vouchers to his wholesaler in Winnipeg to pay for his supplies. When the wholesaler cashed
the vouchers in, each one bore half a dozen signatures.

The vouchers caused tremendous stress and bad feeling
within the community since each voucher was made out to
a particular store and the entire sum of money had to be
spent in that store. The system was not above political
pressure and patronage. Competing desperately for vouchers,
the storekeepers tried to obligate their customers by extending credit and soon found themselves trapped in a credit
war. With the security of a guaranteed government income,
merchants felt no need to lower prices. "You'd see a pair of
shoes cheaper in the other store and you couldn't get them,"
lamented one woman. "The next month you'd take your
voucher to the other store and he'd charge you more for
something else."

"My mother kept six or seven boarders in the mine
camp," says Metro Katrusik. "They saved their money and
bought a farm in 1929. Not everybody could save up for a
farm. You had to have cash. There were no finance companies. Hard times come along. They sold the farm. You
could grow stuff but you couldn't sell it. But we never did
take relief. If you could keep off the relief rolls you were
doing pretty good. There was a lot of stuff goin' on in the
Thirties. People beatin' the municipality and living like

kings. The council covered up. You think the guy is such a goody-goody. People would go into the municipal office and raise hell about relief. They kept it back on purpose. The clerk would tell you you were a Communist. Try to scare you off. Mrs. Dzuba went to the welfare office once. She was an awful big woman. The clerk called her a Communist. She reached across the counter, pulled him over and gave him a darn good lickin'. She got six months. Most men would have been too ashamed to lay charges. He hung himself. The municipality was short of funds. He hung himself with baling wire, right there in the office."

In the summer of 1931, the miners invite organizers of the Mine Workers Union of Canada to come to Bienfait. The last attempt to form a union ended in disaster on June 30, 1920, when an organizer for the One Big Union was kidnapped before he could give his first speech. He was spirited away at midnight in a rumrunner's car and dumped across the American border. His abductors told him that if he attempted to return to Canada he would be tarred and feathered. Seven men were arrested and charged with kidnapping. They included the president of the Estevan Great War Veterans Association and Corporal George Hunter of the Saskatchewan Provincial Police. All were acquitted and fifty miners were laid off for supposedly paying membership fees to the OBU.

The union organizers are Communists. They make no secret of the fact. At rallies in the mine camps and during meetings in Estevan and on the street corners in Bienfait, they speak openly of support from the Red International. The miners are receptive. By the middle of August, committees of miners are organized in every camp. Every last miner in the coalfields has signed up with the union when John Adams is fired by Crescent Collieries on August 21. The miners strike. Adams is reinstated within three days. When the big mine companies, joined together in a marketing cartel since 1924, fail to show up for a grievance meeting on September 7, the miners strike again. Every mine is shut down.

The strike drags on for three weeks, and feelings grow

increasingly bitter. The miners, their gardens wiped out by drought, are all on relief. The municipality cuts them off after a week, but is forced to reinstate them. The mine cartel refuses to recognize the union and fails to show up for two meetings with union negotiators. The mines hire 13 private guards to protect the pitheads and a special detail of RCMP is assigned to patrol the mine camps. Enraged by the hostility of the companies, the miners' anger is fanned by the fiery rhetoric of organizer Annie Buller, who harangues the crowds of strikers on the corner of Main Street in Bienfait. A scuffle breaks out when the Taylorton mine hires transient farmers as scab labor; 30 striking miners rush the boardinghouse at dawn and throw the farmers out. In a full-page newspaper ad in the Estevan *Mercury*, the mine owners claim that a riot has taken place and clamor for more police protection. Claiming that the miners' side of the story has been ignored, the union rents the Estevan town hall and advertises that the miners will hold a demonstration in Estevan on September 29 which will culminate in a public meeting in the town hall where union organizers will state the reasons for the miners' strike. By September 29, 47 RCMP policemen are stationed in Estevan.

The strikers begin to gather in Bienfait just after noon. They clatter in from the valleys and mine camps in old cars or on the backs of coal trucks. By two o'clock, more than 400 people are milling around outside the union hall on Railway Avenue. They are dressed in their best clothes, as if it were Sunday. The men, their eyes still ringed with black in their pale scrubbed faces, all look alike in shiny black suits and cloth caps, and the women, winter coats buttoned up over their shabby dresses, wear hats. It's a bright Indian summer day; the crowd is tense, excited, full of anticipation. Young women carry squalling babies and children play tag around the cars. Everyone has brought a lunch. People say it is just like the big union picnic at Taylorton last summer.

The parade starts to form up, and everybody clambers into the cars and trucks. Horns tooting, the cavalcade rattles off south to Crescent Collieries to pick up the rest of the miners. There it turns west and starts slowly towards Estevan. Strung out on the dirt road for more than a mile, the caravan kicks up a cloud of dust that can be seen for miles. As the trucks lumber towards Estevan, the men bring out large banners with hand-lettered slogans: "We Won't Work for Starvation Wages"; "We Want Houses, Not Piano Boxes"; "Down With Company Stores." One car is draped in the white ensign of the British navy. The parade is led by a big truck carrying the members of the miners' strike committee. The mayor of Estevan has telephoned at noon to say that the miners' parade is forbidden. They have decided to go ahead anyway. In the trucks the miners are laughing and singing. As they pass Big Butte School, children playing in the school yard stop and wave. The miners shout and wave back. On the outskirts of Estevan, more cars dash in from side roads and men run out of their houses to climb aboard the trucks.

At first the red coats look like dots in the distance. "Police!" shouts the truck driver. The RCMP are drawn up in a single line across the road in front of the town hall. In the centre is the fat blue form of Estevan Police Chief A. E. McCutcheon. "The bastards," whispers Martin Day, the strikers' spokesman. The mayor has not mentioned police.

The truck puts on speed. A block away from the cordon, it turns suddenly and darts up a side street. Astonished, the RCMP chase after it, trying to head it off at the next corner. As soon as they take up their new position, the truck wheels again. Tires squealing, it roars back to the main street and brakes to a stop in front of the town hall. The miners cheer and tumble out of the truck. Chief McCutcheon puffs up, shouting that the parade is illegal. The RCMP group in front of the town hall. "Get out of town or I'll arrest the whole damn bunch of you!" yells McCutcheon. The miners shout and curse back at him. The crowd grows as more and more cars and trucks pull into town. "Arrest this man!" yells McCutcheon, pointing his nightstick at Martin Day. The police move in on the group of miners; they shove with their sticks as the men gather around Day. "Come on, break it up!"orders one policeman. He brings his riding crop down hard across a miner's shoulders. The miner wheels and smashes his fist into the policeman's face. The police begin to flail at the mob with their riding crops.

"Come on, boys!" yells a miner. "Let's get 'em!" As the women scream insults and invective from the sidewalks, the strikers pelt the police with stones and bits of broken concrete from the road. Scouring the streets for sticks and scrap metal, they find a pile of large iron washers in a vacant lot opposite the town hall. Their withering fire forces the police back against the brick wall. Ma Davis, the fat and eccentric old woman who runs the boardinghouse at the Manitoba and Saskatchewan mine, kicks a Mountie's hat down the middle of the road. Shrilling choice oaths at the police, she rips open her coat and bares her breasts to them. "Here I am!" she taunts. "Come and get me!"

The Mounties open fire. The sound of the shots is drowned in the shouts of the crowd and the wail of the fire siren in the town hall. The bullets make little puffs in the gravel on the road. Firing over the heads of the mob, one Mountie shoots a little old lady who's watching the riot from an upstairs window. Soon all the windows in the shops lining the street are shot out. The Estevan music teacher, running along the street towards the fire hall, is shot in the leg. The police begin to fire at random into the crowd. Julian Gryshko, a miner, is shot in the stomach. Carried into a nearby livery barn, he bleeds to death in a few moments.

Siren blaring, the shiny new Estevan fire engine roars into the street. The volunteer fire brigade hitches up the single hose and aims a stream of water at the miners.

"We were holding 'em back behind a building with the high pressure hose," says one member of the fire brigade. "It got so hot for us we couldn't take it. There was so much stuff coming at us from behind the building and guns poppin' off what we got outa there. We just couldn't take it. Even if we did have helmets on. One poor Mountie was standing in the middle of the road in a trance. Gun in his hand. His hat was knocked off. He was weaving. The blood! He was covered in blood from his head right down to his boots, his tunic, his pants, everything. He didn't even know what was going on. He was standing up to the last straw. Maybe he nailed some of 'em strikers. Some of 'em was shot and he'd be the one to do it."

The miners rush the fire engine and turn the hose on the

police. Nick Nargan, a young miner just out from the Ukraine, jumps on top of the engine. Opening his shirt, he shouts to the police, "Shoot me! Shoot me!" A Mountie takes careful aim and shoots him through the heart.

The riot is over in less than an hour. Armed with rifles, the RCMP detail arrives from the mine camps. The miners and their families run to the trucks and flee back to Bienfait. In the Bienfait Cafe, Wing Wong pours on the iodine as Sandy Wong wraps the men in bandages made from old bedsheets. The Estevan drayman loads the bodies of the two strikers onto his wagon and drives them to the undertaker. The Estevan hospital is full of Mounties bruised and bleeding from deep head cuts.

Two miners arrive at the hospital. They're carrying Pete Markunas who is bleeding from a bullet wound in the stomach.

"Hey, who's paying for this?" asks Dr. J. A. Creighton, one of the mine doctors.

"The union is," replies one of the miners.

"The union is not!" says Dr. Creighton. "Nobody gets into this hospital unless there's payment a week in advance. You put your money down before you bring that man in."

The miner nods towards the policemen milling in the hall.

"The government pays for men in uniform," says Dr. Creighton.

The miners drive Markunas 50 miles to the Weyburn hospital. He dies on Thursday.

Sixty RCMP with a mounted machine gun in the back of a truck raid Bienfait the following day. Fourteen miners are arrested, including a man found lying in bed with a bullet in his back. They are committed to stand trial in Estevan on charges of rioting. The arsenal of miners' weapons produced in court includes: one old rifle with a broken butt, an axe, a loaded club, a stick, heaps of iron washers, and assorted pieces of metal. No policemen are charged.

In a letter to the Estevan newspaper on Thursday, October 1, Edmund Osler, president of the Estevan Legion, calls on all ex-servicemen among the miners to dissociate themselves from the riot and strike. "It surely must be apparent," says Mr. Osler, "that considerations of loyalty to British institutions and respect for British law must override all questions at issue." The newspaper launches a Red scare. "Red propaganda is busy everywhere adverse conditions create unrest and discontent," says the editor. "Unless it is hit, and hit hard right now, there will be troublous times for good citizens this coming winter. . . If it is necessary to that end for blood to be spilled in the streets, blood will be spilled." These sentiments are echoed by the attorney-general of the province and by the premier.

The three dead miners are buried on Sunday. A procession of more than 600 men and women walks silently from the union hall to the Bienfait cemetery just across the tracks beside the CPR station. The women with babies come first, then the men four abreast, tears streaming down their faces. The black caskets, covered with flowers, are carried by 18 veterans. The crowd stands quietly around the communal grave. A few banners hoisted high over their heads crackle in the wind: "They Fought for Bread, They Got Bullets Instead"; "Murdered by the Bosses' Hired Police Thugs"; "Honor to the Martyrs for the Workers' Cause." A group of women chants Ukrainian funeral hymns, and the veterans lead the crowd in singing "Nearer My God to Thee." Their voices sound high and thin. A simple working-man's service is read at the graveside. Later at the union hall, a band from Moose Jaw plays a short selection of hymns.

The Bienfait branch of the Legion is organized on Monday. Publically repudiating revolutionary principles at a Legion meeting in Estevan, the veterans claim that the "Reds" are only a small percentage of the miners. The violence, they say, was caused by "outside agitators" who have since disappeared. "The disturbances," testifies one miner, "are deeply deplored by the better elements." An offer of generous financial assistance to the Legion is made by Dr. J. A. Creighton.

The provincial government deliberately attempts to intimidate the strikers and to isolate them from outside support. On October 3, Premier J. M. T. Anderson declares that the union organizers are "outside agitators" and the attorney-general labels the union "communistic." The provincial civil servant sent to mediate between the men and the companies states that the union is revolutionary and forces the union to compromise on its terms. The day the miners are to vote on the proposed settlement one of the union's organizers is arrested.

The miners vote to return to work October 8. The vote is held in the union hall, closely scrutinized by 40 members of the RCMP. Only miners who were employed at the time of the strike are allowed to vote. Flanked by two Union Jacks, 40 Bienfait legionnaires, battle ribbons pinned to their best blue suits, are massed at attention on the stage; almost all are miners and union members. The vote is 130 to 41 in favor of returning to work. No mention is made of recognition for the union.

May Day, 1972. The dry grass in the Bienfait cemetery is a carpet of crocuses. The big concrete headstone stands off in a corner.

LEST WE FORGET
MURDERED
ESTEVAN Sept. 29, 1931
BY ....

P. MARKUNAS
  AGE 28

N. NARGAN
AGE 28

J. GRYSHKO
AGE 29

IN MEMORY OF
DISTRICT MINERS #7606

The inscription originally read: "Murdered by RCMP." The Bienfait town council launched a strong campaign to have the headstone removed. Eventually someone painted out "RCMP" with a streak of yellow paint. Later the letters were chiselled out of the concrete. An attempt has been made to fill in the rest of the inscription with cement.

The anniversary of the massacre passes each year unremarked. Strangers in Bienfait are not directed to the grave. Bienfait people do not talk about the riot. If it is mentioned, a shadow of alarm flashes across their faces and they speak in whispers. It's hard to find anyone who will admit to having been there, and if they were, they saw and did nothing. The official story, put out by the Legion and the Estevan Chamber of Commerce, is that the riot was a Communist plot, a crime for which the miners were totally to blame. Many miners have accepted this view; others have retreated into silence. There is no honor for the martyrs in Bienfait.

Only two of the arrested miners were fined. The rest were released on bond or with suspended sentences. The stiffest sentences — from one to two years at hard labor — were reserved for the Communist organizers, none of whom had been in Estevan on the day of the riot. Blacklisted by the mine companies, the union leaders drifted away to other jobs. After making token improvements and raising wages, the companies quickly reverted to their old habits. The union was ignored. Men suspected of being radical were not hired, and dozens of them returned to the valleys to open their own little mines. Enticed by high wages and good jobs, many of the legionnaires suddenly remembered they had suspected the union all along. "They were Communists, but the workers didn't know," says Archie MacQuarrie, who describes himself as a good union man. "It was a Communist union, that's why it didn't hold up. They crept in here in the dead of night. That's when the fellow was going to show us how to knock out a Mountie. But I figured 'em out. I could see the Red flag! Most of the miners were in favor until they started to catch on to what kind of an outfit it was. I challenged 'em at one meeting. 'You're no turning yellow, Archie?' the fellas said to me. 'I fought those beggars in France,' I said, 'and I'll do it again if I have to.' " Archie MacQuarrie had a flat tire on the day of the parade. "That saved us from goin' with the rest of 'em," he grins.

"No miner was against the union," explains Dan Bozak, who started his own mine in 1933. "They were afraid. The union was pretty weak; the big mines did as they pleased. Some guys were getting jobs. The fellows that got jobs were so damn quiet! A lot of fellows never were taken back. You were scared to speak in those days. If you done a little too much talking. . . it didn't take much to annoy the companies. If they couldn't brand you anything else, they'd brand you

a Communist. If you said a few words that were a little
radical, you were a Communist. You were a radical if you
opened your mouth. Everybody got scared. The arrests
scared a lot of people out. They were scared pretty easy."

The Ukrainians, many only recently arrived in Canada,
were particularly vulnerable.

" A lot of people were threatened with deportation," says
Paul Rohatyn, a Bienfait miner whose whole family was
blacklisted. "There was no such thing as unemployment
insurance, welfare. People had to knuckle under. The strike
was smashed very ruthlessly by the government. You get
Kent State now. Estevan was the same thing. People were
chased and shot at on the road. People had their fingers
shot off the trucks. Maybe it was a mistake to go to Estevan
that day but unions have to do these things sometimes. They
smashed the union but good."

Following a second bloody strike in 1939 which was
ended by the outbreak of war, the Bienfait miners were
finally organized in 1945. Relations between the companies
and the union are now quite cordial. "We have an annual
banquet in the Legion Hall," says Paul Rohatyn. "We all
have a very nice time."

The old men gather in front of the poolroom when the early
morning sun has warmed the little piece of sidewalk by the
door. Bent and gnarled like tiny figurines in a clock, they
emerge every day at exactly the same time, shuffling
urgently down the road in their rusty black shoes, their
stained, baggy trousers held high over rounded potbellies
by wide, pale suspenders. Some still affect the workingman's
soiled striped overalls, their caps pulled low over red-
rimmed eyes white with cataracts, their jowls fuzzy with
three days' growth of white stubble. The first ones there
laboriously haul out some battered kitchen chairs with
broken rungs and no backs and tilt them back so they can
lean against the delicious warmth of the plate glass windows.
The latecomers lean on their crutches and canes or hunker
down on the concrete with their backs against the building.
Gumming away at plugs of tobacco and spitting rhythmi-
cally on the sidewalk, they gnaw over yesterday's trivia in
voices high and shrill with alarm.

"It was on TV," pipes one old man in a pinstripe blue shirt and straw boater as the group draws closer with attention. "I heard it myself. They found this fella who's one hundred and fifty!" His voice cracks with excitement. "One hundred and fifty years old! And his wife is one hundred and his *son* is ninety-nine!" He leans back in triumph. "It's true. This guy on TV is gonna go down and visit him!" There's a lot of spitting and low mumbling among the group. Suddenly several of them break into broad, toothless grins; they guffaw and pound their canes on the ground, bellies jiggling. One thin, nostalgic voice floats high and clear over the crowd: "Jeez, I'd fuck all night if I was one hundred and fifty!"

At exactly ten o'clock, Alex Ronyk emerges from his little furnace room at the back of Centennial Billiards (which he named and painted lavender in honor of Canada's birthday), and the old miners shuffle in for their morning round of gin rummy. Balanced precariously on the broken chairs around a small table by the door, they play for 25 cents a hand. The house rake is ten cents a game. Every so often Ronyk will give one of them a haircut, perching him high in an antique white barber's chair in the corner by the window as he attacks the grey wisps with an enormous pair of electric clippers. The floor is strewn with last week's hair. Short and squat, with the puffy face of someone who never sees the sun, Ronyk is a man of artistic sensibilities. He's always impeccably dressed in the latest colored shirts with coordinated slacks. He's suave and sociable, but sensitive about his age, which must be about 65, and about the fact that he's bald as a billiard ball. He stocks a collection of three wigs — a red one, a black one, and a grey one — which he keeps on styrofoam heads in his kitchen and alternates according to his mood. It takes a while to recognize Mr. Ronyk with red hair in the morning and black hair in the afternoon; the grey one is reserved for very dignified occasions: he wore it in May to his son's graduation from the University of Saskatchewan. The wigs are very bright and synthetic, and the stitching shows in the part, especially when they're not on quite straight. He buys them across the border in the States for $15 apiece and lends them out "on trial" to his cronies, who clown around town in them. He takes them very seriously and is embarrassed at being caught without a wig on. They're a badge of his financial success and his status as Bienfait's leading businessman.

"You got to have nerves of steel in this business," he says. "I do all the baby-sitting for the old and the young and the crazy and the smart. I look after them all. All the old fogies are always waitin' for me to play rummy with them for ten cents a game." A look of weariness crosses his wrinkled face. "Jeez, those old guys are a lotta laughs, fightin' with each other, swearin' and callin' each other names all over a crummy twenty-five cents. Christ, you should see 'em go at it. They do everything but hit each other. Naw, you can't make a go of a place like this without gambling and booze. We still have the odd game in here after I lock the door. There's more money now in town than there ever was but they're not as keen on gambling as they used to be. The only time you gamble is when you're short of money. Two thousand men with twenty dollars is better than one man with a million. Once in a while they all get tanked up and come in here late at night. It's a real job running the games with a lot of drunks around. I've felt guilty a lot of times about the guys losing so much. Ah, they probably would have lost it some place else anyway. Most of these miners aren't smart guys. Otherwise they wouldn't be in the mine.

"Wives are the biggest problem. Sometimes they report me to the police. The Mounties'll try to get me. But I got two men on the beat all the time, one old guy out front, one old guy in the back alley. These old guys'll walk up and down for a couple of bucks. I got a bell on the counter. It rings and we clear the table. I never been caught once. What would those old coots do if I closed down? Christ, they'd die!"

The town policeman, Joe Pryznyk, is a beefy, good-natured guy with a big beer gut and a short brushcut that makes his head look perfectly round. A big blue anchor is tattooed on each bulging forearm. During the day, Pryznyk's function seems to be to lean against the front of the fire hall and mop sweat from his brow. He's a bit nervous about going back to work on May 15; he's been off with a broken leg since October when, Mr. Cuddington the town clerk observes acidly, "compensation set in." Joe doesn't bother with a uniform. In the summer he wears shirt sleeves, in the winter a parka. He carries his gun in a pocket of the parka. The only time he has ever used it was to shoot 50 dogs during the rabies scare. A lot of people refuse to believe that he is a policeman. They laugh at him and chew him out when he pulls them over for drunken driving.

"There's not a window in a church in town that hasn't been shot out," says Bert Hitchen. "You talk to the parents but it doesn't do no good. The kids won't listen. When Joe started his patrol today, they were out there cussin' him out. Swearin' right to his face. Well, if Joe can't do something about it we'll just have to get another policeman. The one we had before was no good. Spent all his time in the pub chasin' the girl in there. Had to get rid of him."

"Every winter the curling rink and the skating rink are ransacked," sighs Joe. "Just about every place in town has been hit at some time — Fred's grocery store, the hotel, the Legion, the post office. Unemployment causes a lot of the trouble. The Legion was hit at Christmas. A bunch of kids stole $1,000 worth of booze. They were out of work, no money. They wanted a good time. You get two or three a year and then it quietens down until the scare is off. Last year there was a big fight on Main Street. The Estevan gang and the Bienfait gang. I was just one guy. I wasn't going to take on fifty guys. The mayor says, 'Go chase 'em, Joe.' So I told them to break it up and they did." He sounds surprised. Ever since Joe was beaten up a few years ago by a gang of local hard rocks, he's taken the attitude that it's better to ignore trouble than to fight it.

"There's a few assaults every year," he says philosophically. "They don't amount to much, the husband beating up the wife, the wife beating up the husband. I quit going to these family fights. I'd get two or three calls in the middle of the night. They feel you're a marriage counsellor. I'd go and calm 'em down and say I'd come around in the morning for a statement. Well, it would all be forgotten! Now I just tell them I won't get involved and hang up. The guy's usually been drinking. I figure that if he's at the stage

where he's gonna beat up on his wife, he's at the stage
where he can't do too much harm."

Joe's on call 24 hours a day and helps out Frank the
Utility when necessary. He earns $4,496.16 a year plus car
allowance. The town considers his salary to be very generous. "In some towns," says Mr. Cuddington, "they pay a
policeman according to the number of fines he brings in.
They figure that if they're paying him $400 a month he
should bring in some money to cover it." The town policeman has always been a bone of contention in Bienfait.

"If somebody is raising heck in town, if I can get him to
leave town, that's the main thing," says Joe. "I hate like
heck to send anybody to jail."

During Joe's convalescence, Bienfait was policed by the
RCMP from Estevan. The greasers went to jail and half the
male population of Bienfait lost their drivers' licences for
drunken driving. Bienfait people don't much like the RCMP.
As long as Joe Pryznyk is on the job, the RCMP cannot
enter the town unless specifically requested by him to do so.
The town is safe; Joe protects it against law and order.
Bienfait remains a subversive little town.

An old woman in a babushka tramps into the town office
banging the door open and shut. She is short and stout with
a long brown overcoat that reaches almost to her ankles;
her red, wrinkled face is wreathed in smiles. She carries a
giant shopping bag.

"I come here Saturday and you are not open!" she shouts
at the town clerk, Fred Cuddington. A look of pain crosses
Mr. Cuddington's face. He explains how the office is now
closed Saturdays and open Wednesdays.

"Ah!" says the old lady, her eyes lighting up. "You go
to drink beer all day! You get a big stomach!" She pats her
own stomach, beaming. "No can bend if you have big
stomach! Hee hee hee!"

Mr. Cuddington looks wounded.

"Maybe you no like me talking to you like that?" says
the woman, suddenly contrite. She plunks herself down on
a wooden bench and begins to rummage through the
shopping bag.

She produces a little white envelope full of money. After counting through it carefully, she hands over a $20 bill and a $1 bill to Mr. Cuddington to pay her heat and power for April. As Mr. Cuddington laboriously enters the sum in his account book, she begins a loud harangue in rapid, broken English about her plum trees. Some boys have broken down her fence and stolen all her plums. Mr. Cuddington banters with her, teasing her about getting her plums into jars before they get into the kids. The old lady laughs so hard she almost rolls off the bench.

"Whatchyou gonna do about it?" she suddenly demands, as she packs her shopping bag to leave. Mr. Cuddington allows that the town will probably do nothing.

"I shoot you! I shoot you!" shouts the old lady, laughing uproariously. "Some day I bring gun and shoot you!" She slams the door as she leaves.

Mr. Cuddington looks weary. The phone rings. A shrill voice screams that there's a dead dog in her yard and when is he going to do something about it? "Yes ma'am," says Mr. Cuddington. "We'll fix it up right away." Frank the Utility is summoned from next door where he's fixing the town lawn mower. With a sigh, he jumps into the 1947 Town of Bienfait truck and rattles off. A steady procession of old people bangs in the door with their little envelopes full of money. Mr. Cuddington deals with them all with great dignity and politeness.

"A lot of these old people aren't well, you know," confides Mr. Cuddington. "They get excited. You don't want them to have a heart attack. Heck, there's one old guy comes in here and wants to talk politics. He's got a heart condition, in and out of the hospital. There's no way I'm gonna incite him and have him drop down dead right here on the floor in front of me! So I say nothing. He just wants to argue anyway." At the political hub of town, Mr. Cuddington is very sensitive to the nuances of Bienfait diplomacy.

Bienfait is full of pensioners. Most of them get by on $113 a month from the government, and live in green and white cottages moved in from the mines when the camps closed down 20 or more years ago. The mines sold the houses for $1. Well-off people moved to Estevan, which banned the old mine shanties; the poor people brought their houses to Bienfait. The houses are no bargain — heat and power bills run as high as $50 a month in winter and taxes, even at less than $100 a year, are a great burden to the old people.

Bienfait is a town of moonlighters. Everybody has one or two or three little extra jobs to rake in a few bucks. All over town houses and picket fences are posted with home-made signs. One man repairs shoes, another does upholstery, someone else carpenters or paints or cuts hair in his basement, and women give each other perms in the kitchen. No professional can survive this devastating free-lance competition. The businessmen don't really seem to mind. Most of them are waiting to die and hoping that the town and their customers won't beat them to it. The younger ones are the kind of men who have done a dozen better jobs and failed at them all. There's one rich man in town who's big in construction and one executive, a retired mine manager who drives down from Estevan for his daily cribbage game in the poolroom. Bienfait is a plain town. "Hick town! Hick town!" says Mrs. Wong, banging down her load of groceries. Gordie Howe wasn't born there. It has produced no fabulously rich or successful people who have made it big down East. Bienfait has no movie theatre, no park, no bowling alley, no library, no swimming pool, no band. The teenagers hang out in Estevan, gunning their engines at the A & W. Even the union hall is closed down; all union business is now conducted out of Regina. Bienfait local president is Ron Dzuba, a big friendly man in his late twenties with a flock of small children and a brand new house just outside the town limits. He's an oiler on a dragline. "I never went to school long enough to do anything else," he shrugs. "I worked in a grocery store before. This is easier than working in the store." Ron makes $2.20 an hour; like a lot of the oilers, he rents land from the company and farms on the side when grain is moving. "Oiling's not that hard a job. You haven't got no responsibility." Ron is president of the local more or less by default. "Nobody," he says, "really wants to be bothered with it."

The pleasures of Bienfait are simple. On warm evenings, the light from the poolroom makes a golden puddle on the street; drawn to its warmth, the townspeople cluster in it like moths. They stand quietly, soaking up the smell of the grass, lulled by the hum of the night insects. Boys are playing baseball in the corner of the school yard under a big maple tree, and little girls sitting all in a row cheer them on. A few parents lean over the fence or stop briefly on the sidewalk, smiling. The Anglican ladies are busy preparing a strawberry social. Every day the town closes down for half an hour after the post office opens as everybody scampers off to see if he got any mail. Approached leisurely, with a chat here and there with someone on the street, going for the mail can consume most of a morning. It is a masculine activity, one of the few chores many of the old miners have left. Their steps quicken as they approach the post office and their faces brighten a little with hope and expectation. Getting the mail is usually followed by coffee row, so business in Bienfait seldom gets under way much before 11 a.m., just in time for lunch. Bienfait has no chamber of commerce. There's never been enough money in town to create an elite, that clique of haberdashers and shoe salesmen who have a stranglehold on every prairie town where there's a dollar to be made. Bienfait businessmen are loners, separated by ancient ethnic hatreds, fiercely guarding a dwindling clientele they have painstakingly built up through credit. Everywhere, you hear: "I always shop at Liskowich's because he carried us in the Depression." To be respectable in Bienfait is to be poor. Bienfait has no money. Poverty defines the town. Life in Bienfait is the thin satisfaction of scrimping, and politics is the art of scraping by. Politicians are unfailingly elected on a poverty ticket, and numerous and ingenious new ways are found not to spend money. "We didn't spend a nickel on snow removal!" crows Mr. Cuddington triumphantly. Mr. Cuddington's annual salary of $4,770 is the town's biggest single expenditure. He is watched carefully; you can set your watch by the time Mr. Cuddington takes for his coffee breaks. One minute too long and half a dozen people are on the phone to the mayor. The council has refused to buy him a new filing cabinet. They have told him to use cardboard boxes. Mr. Cuddington is also a justice of the peace. He used to hear a lot of local cases directed to him by the town police. "I don't get the calls I used to," he says sadly. "Most of them go to the magistrate in Estevan." Traffic fines, amounting to about $750 a year, are an important source of income for Bienfait.

Bienfait's total budget is $60,185 a year. A little over $23,000 comes from taxes, the rest comes from assorted other sources, mainly water bills. Unlike other Saskatchewan towns whose businesses have gone broke, Bienfait has grown in population; it has twice as many residents as it had in the heyday of the Twenties. Elderly people have moved in expecting services for which they cannot pay. Taxes are $85,000 in arrears. Only a handful of the ramshackle businesses pay taxes, and the Legion is tax-exempt. The town is reluctant to foreclose because it can't sell the impounded property. Bienfait is essentially worthless. Attempts at progress force it deeper into the hole: after water and sewer were installed, the union hall was found to be unsanitary; rather than spend money to fix it up, the union decided to close it.

The cemetery is a big money-maker for the town. Plots sell for $20 and $35. Foreseeing an increase in business, the council has drawn up a detailed plan of cemetery expansion. It fits in well with the plans of Marathon Realty, which is trying to unload all the CPR property next door, including the station. Business licences for all the moonlighters bring in a substantial $600 a year, and the fire brigade earns $50 for every fire it attends in the surrounding RM of Coalfields. Even tax arrears can be profitable, since the town makes more than $1,000 a year in penalties. The income is doled out parsimoniously — $200 for the nuisance ground, $1,350 for charity, $952 for gravel, $1,400 to fix the sidewalks, $1,300 for telephone and postage. Each sum is chewed over by the council of the Town of Bienfait, which meets twice a month in the back of the town office, where a map of Bienfait hangs on one wall and on the other, a huge diagram in a glass frame which says, "Bienfait Cemetery Plot Directory."

The mayor, scowling, presides at the end of the table. There are no spectators or petitioners. Mr. Cuddington announces that the week of May 22 is Official Clean Up Week in Bienfait. A long silence. The mayor suggests that people be reminded not to burn garbage after 6 p.m. Carried.

Children, says the schoolteacher, are all over the highway. "Why don't they use the sidewalk?" snaps the mayor.

"The sidewalk is disintegrating," says the schoolteacher. "That's why they're walking on the road."

"There will be no new sidewalks this year," growls the mayor. Silence.

The hotel owner wants a list of all the children in the area. There is talk of a swimming pool. He wants permission to go through the hospitalization cards for names.

"To hell with him," says the mayor. "Let him knock on doors." The swimming pool had started out as a Homecoming project in 1971 but the majority of people wanted artificial ice. "Aw, they talk in the beer parlor but nobody wants to go on the committee," says the mayor. "Sure they'll build it, but they're gonna expect the town to pick up the tab." He glares balefully around the table as this information sinks in. Silence.

People are complaining about dogs. Bienfait has no pound and no dogcatcher. A pound would cost $4,000. It's out of the question. A suggestion to lock the dogs up in the abandoned garage on Main Street is rejected.

"You build a pound in town and if these dogs howl you're gonna have lots of complaints," says the mayor. The councillors wince. "If you put the pound out too far, people are gonna break it down. Some guy wants his dog outa there so he lets 'em *all* out."

"In Lampman the first dog impounded was the mayor's," volunteers the schoolteacher. "The pound keeper got fired." Silence. "I could take care of the problem easy," says Frank the Utility. He squints one eye shut and makes a little motion with his trigger finger. "Shoot 'em. Bang. Bang."

"Oh then I'll get some more eggs thrown on my house," says the schoolteacher. Silence.

Mr. Cuddington reports that his attempts to tax the single trailer in the Bienfait trailer park have failed. The trailer was moved away in the dead of night. "Here today and gone tomorrow," shrugs the mayor. "We can't bank on any of 'em." The vacant garage, valued at $4,200, is removed from the assessment roll.

"Are we going to have any extra decorations for July 1?" demands a stout lady. Silence.

"The town's supposed to have decorations," says the mayor. "I don't know where they are." Bert Hitchen says someone should paint the old steam engine. Maybe, he suggests, the mine would donate the paint. The mayor looks bored.

Frank the Utility gives notice that the lawn mower is worn out and he wants a raise. The council stares sadly at the table. Frank plows the snow, grades the streets, mows the grass, collects the garbage, repairs the machinery, fixes the waterworks, and washes and waxes the floor of the town office. He does everything, in fact, except dig the graves. He is paid $380 a month.

"That's welfare wages," grumbles the mayor. One of the councillors protests that Frank also picks up odd jobs at the hospital and does chores for the school and the municipality and in his off hours shovels snow and fixes fences for private citizens. "It's not," argues the councillor, "as if he didn't have some extra income."

The stout lady, pondering Frank, calls the attention of council to the dull condition of the office floor. Council is quickly absorbed in a heated debate about various brands of floor wax. The argument is resolved in a loud voice by the schoolteacher. "I use Future myself," he says. "I've given up on Bravo." Frank is instructed to use Future.

The meeting adjourns.

The male councillors, plainly satisfied with their three hours of work, head for the beer parlor. Government in Bienfait, as in all dying prairie towns, is government by inertia. It is a holding action, a ritual which fends off the encroaching grass.

Mr. Cuddington apologizes. "No councillor is gonna hold back progress, but. . . ."

There is nothing to be done.

Metro Katrusik is a shrewd, forthright man with a quick temper and a weathered, leathery face. He was born in a mine camp and started working in the mines at 14. He now lives in a big, modern house, the finest house in Bienfait, and drives an Oldsmobile. Every morning at 9:30 he drives three blocks to Main Street, makes a big U-turn at the old steam engine, and parks in front of the pool hall. His car is a signal that he is open for business. After two cups of thin, bitter coffee in the cafe, he moves next door to play a hand of rummy with the old men. Within an hour, Katrusik has picked up every shred of gossip in town. He wears his striped engineer's cap as a badge of office and a weather vane; if it is soiled and greasy, it means he has just come off shift at the mine and is liable to be grumpy; if it is clean and starched, he's had a good night's sleep and is on his way to work. It is his sixth year as mayor of Bienfait.

"Why, I don't know. It's just a headache. All complaints come to the mayor. It's like being skip on a curling rink. Most of the councillors don't hang around town too much. Keep outa sight. Our biggest complaint is dogs. And ponies. This being a smaller town, the kids like to bring them in; they ride them to school. Well, the first thing you know there's crap all over the yard and some kid falls in it and there's hell to pay. You tell the kids and they just thumb their nose at you. The cafe people are the worst. The kids tether their ponies behind the cafe; they leave 'em for two or three hours and there's a mess. He's a miserable son-of-a-gun. You tell him about it and he gets mad! Starts yelling at me. One guy hid his horse in the garage. He cleaned up the mess and put it in the garbage. Frank was hauling it away. We didn't even know about it until Frank come in and says, 'It's not my job to haul horse manure.' Well, as soon as you write to people they're peeved." He sighs.

"Credit killed a lot of the businesses. Like the hardware merchant. Some people owed him $200, $300. Wouldn't pay their bills. Fred's got thousands on the books that he'll never hope to collect. The butcher shop is strictly cash now and he's making a go of it. The stores here seem to have the idea that there's no competition here. Like our service station here, his gas is five cents higher than Estevan! Dozens of Bienfait people are filling up in Estevan. I don't blame them. You can buy cheaper in the grocery stores here but you can buy nicer stuff in Estevan. It turns you off to shop here. It's not their fault. A guy gets some stuff in, nobody buys it, it starts to go bad, he throws it out. The only time people shop here is when they've run out; then they're peeved if the stuff isn't there. I can see the day coming when we'll have only one store."

Metro Katrusik is a socialist. He runs Bienfait like a union. As long as he's president, he expects solidarity. Voices of dissent and criticism are treated as scabs. He loathes them. He tries hard to reflect the wishes of the majority of the town membership. Katrusik is a man of strong convictions and great personal dignity; he protects Bienfait, shields it, allows people to live the way they always have. Bienfait is a closed shop.

"I'm just a common workingman," the mayor states suddenly, his eyes glittering with defiance. Much of his political power is based on his status at the mine. "Oh I like strippin'," he says. He caresses the levers which control the giant shovel dangling on its long chain. "I like running the machine. I sit here for eight hours a day. It's nice and quiet. The seat is soft. It's a lot dirtier down in the pit." It's also a lot dirtier down in the guts of the machine, where Katrusik's son keeps the parts oiled. The dragline is as big as a house; on its edge is a white washing machine where they rinse out their coveralls in solvent and hang them over the rail to dry. "Mining today is a joke," says Metro. He grins like a benign pumpkin. He made 17.5 cents an hour driving a horse-drawn coal wagon in 1933. "Many people considered I was fortunate. That was big wages for a young kid. You were lucky to be able to get a job like that. We even had a schoolteacher working in the mine. I told my dad, 'What's the point of my getting an education if I'm gonna end up in the mine anyway?' In 1937 I was getting forty-five cents an hour and that was *big* money!"

He shifts levers. The shovel swings through the air and bites out a ten-ton scoop of earth. Far below, a bulldozer as big as a dinky toy is scraping at the exposed coal seam which winds away to the west like a black river.

"It's a funny thing," the mayor reflects, "just about all the mine managers are alkies, or used to be, you know. I guess they drank with the right people. That's how they got ahead. I always said it's not what you know, it's who you know. I could never do that, suckholing, buying a guy drinks. Sure I'll drink with the manager, but he buys his round, I buy

my round. A lot of miners used to toady to the manager.
Wine him and dine him. Christ, the manager could even
take a guy's wife and he'd look the other way. I guess they
got ahead. I dunno. I argue with the manager. He'll come
up to the dragline just looking for an argument. He has no
use for unions. So we really go at it. A lot of guys say, 'Why
do you talk to him like that? I'd never do that.' Well hell,
he can't fire me. I do my job. He can't sack me for what I
say.

"All the bosses in the mines were English. Never a
Ukrainian. All the heavy work would be Ukrainian. The
dumb ones, they did the hard work. We had a lot of Mennonites during the war. They were very religious. Some of
the smart-alecky guys would swear at them on purpose.
There was a lot of swearing. Something seems to go better
if you swear at it. I didn't go to war. We were froze in the
mine. I didn't mind. I don't believe in killing. I'm a pacifist.
I watch the news on TV. A lot of times when I see what
they're doing in Vietnam, my eyes fill up with tears. I figure
if we ever get out of line, the Americans'll do the same
thing to Canada."

The mayor is fighting for his political life in the summer
of 1972. The big issue is whether or not to pave Main Street.
The controversy waxes fierce and passionate and the town
is split into two warring camps. The suggestion was made
by the new hotel owner, who's been in Bienfait less than a
year. An upstart, says the mayor's faction. The mayor's
position is clear: since Main Street has never been paved in
the past, there is therefore no good reason why it should be
paved in the future. However, the hotel owner, as one of
Bienfait's two major taxpayers (the mayor is the other), has
a certain amount of clout. Presiding over the beer parlor
every afternoon, he never misses a chance to stick it to the
mayor; the old fogies cackle with delight. The mayor,
brooding over his revenge high in the little glass house on
the dragline, is miserable. And he is worried.

"He has big ideas," scoffs Metro. "If I don't have Main
Street blacktopped by July first, he tells me, he's running
for mayor! He expects people to come to that crummy old
hotel! You gotta fool them, he says. Offer 'em something
that'll fool 'em into coming to Bienfait. He wants to start

a museum. Put a couple of dead cats in it, he says, and the Americans will come. Then they'll buy a bottle of beer in the hotel. I go in there a lot, just to argue with him. I give it to him and he gives it to me. It's a real picnic. Hell, I wouldn't have decided to run for mayor again until he said he was gonna run.

"The old hotel keeper, he used to be mayor here. He was a sly fellow. He was just a farmer, poor like the rest of us, then he bought the hotel. We always figured there was someone behind him, a syndicate. Where else would he get the money? He bootlegged of course. He never took the rap either. He always had someone else working for him. He'd get knocked over by the cops, this other guy would take the blame. He paid the fine of course. But his record was clean. So after prohibition ended, he opened a beer parlor. Ran that for years. You couldn't get a licence if you didn't have a clean record. He made quite a lot of money. He was mayor for years and years. Never did a damn thing for Bienfait. He held it back on purpose. He figured that if the town grew, somebody might move in and build another hotel, open another beer parlor, and it would hurt his business.

"Why did people elect him? He had a lot of power. In those days, the hotel keeper was usually the richest man in town. Men with money didn't ask people what to do, they *told* them."

Wilf Gardiner, the hotel owner, presides over the bar in the Eagle's Nest, a dark, cavernous place with cheap arborite tables and chrome chairs. The bar is draped with a Saskatchewan flag designed by Wilf, who also serves the beer. Wilf bought the Bienfait hotel in the summer of 1971, shortly after he was fired as chairman of Homecoming '71 after a big row with Premier Ross Thatcher. Bienfait was the last resort. "Usually a man who's been in government can get a big job with business," says Gardiner. "Thatcher had enough power to freeze me out of any job." Wilf was a Liberal MLA and minister of public works in Thatcher's government. He's Jimmy Gardiner's son.

Wilf and his family run the hotel themselves. His wife

cooks and cleans, he hustles beer, and his kids mop up the pub on Sundays. "We had to let all the help go," he says. "They were getting all the profits." A huge, dark man in a flame red shirt that matches the flag, Gardiner is a wheeler-dealer, a promotor with a dozen schemes up his sleeve and all the angles figured. After the mayor leaves for work in the morning, the political hub of Bienfait shifts to the Eagle's Nest where Gardiner harangues the assembled pensioners in a dull, monotonous drone. He's out to promote Bienfait, to turn the town on its ear. Already he's organized a shuffleboard tournament and an Indian pow-wow in the beer parlor. "I'm an honorary chief of the Crees," he booms. "I have the complete outfit, white buckskin jacket, feather headdress; my wife has a wig with long braids. We're gonna dress in the outfits all summer for the tourist business. I've been working for seven years to get tourists into this province. The people say the only reason I'm doing it is because I'm gonna benefit, being in the hotel business. Most of them don't recognize it as history. They're not old enough. Some people will always figure that anything you do is gonna cost money. Why, you could get an old building in town, gather up the relics and have a museum. You could have a talking museum with tape recordings from the old citizens. Put a bottle out for donations. Like Deadwood, Wild Bill Hickok's town. Most people would only go to Deadwood once, but once you get them there, you'd got their dollar. You could exaggerate things a little, sell the place."

Gardiner has detected that Metro Katrusik is not too enthusiastic about advertising Bienfait's illicit past. His eyes twinkle wickedly and a slow smile spreads across his face from ear to ear. "The mayor was one of the biggest bootleggers in the area! He admits it. Heck, everybody's bought a case from him. He got caught. Now he says he's reformed. Haw haw haw." Gardiner's sly laugh booms through the pub.

July 1 is Bienfait's big day. Bienfait's Dominion Day celebration has always outclassed the fairs and sports days of towns for miles around, but never was it more spectacular than on Homecoming Day, July 1, 1971, when a pancake breakfast on Main Street followed by a parade of decorated floats led by the Estevan Legion color party and the famous Estevan Consolidated High School Band was climaxed by a flypast of jets from the Canadian air force base at Moose Jaw.

It's a black, rainy night late in April 1972 when the people of Bienfait meet to decide what they're going to do this year. Most of the 20-odd people gathered in the curling rink are in their thirties and forties. Several of the women wear athletic jackets, and the men are almost identical with double chins, beerbellies, and red baseball caps. One has a maroon jacket with "Bienfait Fire Dept." across the chest. Everybody arrives right on time. They wait patiently for 20 minutes for the mayor to show up. He doesn't.

The firemen are assigned the crown and anchor game; the Knights of Columbus get the bingo. Profit on last year's raffle of a $100 bill was $189.

"We kinda lost on popcorn last year," somebody reports.

"The bags were too big," says a voice.

"Why not have a horseshoe tournament? That's always a big thing," pipes another voice.

"Every year we've had horseshoes we've gone in the hole," states the chairman flatly.

A wet, grizzled face appears in the door. "There's a big fire in the nuisance grounds!" it shouts.

"Where's the phone?" asks somebody.

"It's disconnected."

"Give us twenty minutes, then blow the whistle and we'll come," says the big guy in the Bienfait Fire Dept. jacket.

The face disappears, muttering.

"Are we going to have a bar on the sports grounds again this year?" asks a woman.

"If you ask me we got enough refreshments in town that day without having them on the sports ground," says a man. "It's supposed to be a day for the kids." The bar is voted down.

The butcher proposes a barbecue.

"Are we gonna ask the Estevan band?" demands a voice.

"We got a band," says somebody.

"Sure," says the chairman. "All eight pieces." The

Estevan band will be invited again in spite of the fact that Estevan has treacherously decided to have its festival on the same day. Three hundred dollars is voted for fireworks. "What's July without fireworks?" yells a voice to quieten objections.

"Why not have a Mardi Gras on Friday night?" suggests Wilf Gardiner. "Both the Legion and my place could stay open all night. I think we could get a permit. There's a possibility of the street being paved before that. It could be a big opening for the street."

"Are you talking about serving liquor in the *street*?" asks a voice. Silence.

"OK," says the Bienfait Fire Dept. "How many firemen want to go?"

"Aw, let 'er burn, Tommy!" a guy shouts back. The fat man sits down.

"Nobody has seized on the 'Homecoming' theme yet," pursues Gardiner. "We could get the name registered. We could get exclusive rights to it. We could pick up all the souvenirs and stuff left over from last year, get it half-price and make some money on it. The minister of industry has promised to give me all the leftover stuff."

The Bienfait volunteer fire brigade gets up and tramps out. "Jeez, it's raining!" hollers the fat man as he goes out the door, "Why am I going to put out a fire?"

"Bienfait could be the Homecoming Capital of the World!" booms Gardiner.

The fire engine gives a desultory groan of its siren, a single flash of its light, and, with the men clinging to it like wet leaves, chugs off through the rain to the garbage dump.

Chapter 10

Biggar

A light, freezing rain is falling on Biggar as the legionnaires form up for the Remembrance Day parade. Row on row of wizened grey men in blue blazers, grey trousers, and blue berets, they come pouring out of the Legion Hall and mill around at the bottom of Main Street near the railway station, where they wait for the Air Cadet band, which is still practicing drum rolls in the parking lot behind the post office. The band, a dozen gawky youths with slicked-down hair in World War II air force uniforms, finally marches up and takes its place behind the Legion color party. A roll of drums and the mob of men, four abreast, moves up Main Street towards the Majestic Theatre, Biggar's movie theatre, where the service will be held.

The parade is led by two members of the Biggar RCMP in red coats and spurs. They look very awkward and embarrassed as they grin sideways at the handful of forlorn spectators huddled on the sidewalk. Sergeant Zorn's red jacket is stretched tight as a drum across his substantial gut. Arms swinging high, he sails along like a big red balloon. Behind him are four flags carried by two middle-aged women from the Legion Auxiliary and a pair of beefy veterans whose bright rows of war medals clank over their hearts. The crowd of men follow, trying to keep in step, holding themselves as erect as they can in the icy slush. Their rubbers are tied on with string, and their long tweed topcoats flap in the wind. The only sounds are the lonely rat-tat-tat of the drums and the shuffle of hundreds of shoes through the snow. The men stare straight ahead. They are followed by the women of the Legion Auxiliary in matching blue blazers and berets, their thin blue legs sticking like matchsticks out of their heavy winter boots, then by ranks of Elks in purple fezzes with white tassels and the ladies of the Royal Purple in purple blazers and white skirts. On and on they come, phalanx after phalanx, Cubs, Scouts, Brownies, Guides, kids of al lages and all sizes, pushing and giggling, herded by solemn Brown Owls and stern scoutmasters. Each group is in uniform and carries its own banner or flag.

The parade quickly covers the two blocks to the Majestic Theatre, and the marchers file inside past the little glass ticket window. Soon the theatre is full, and some people have to stand at the back by the doors. The Majestic is very old and very dingy, and the dust rises in fine clouds as the chair seats are thumped down. The wooden floor sags under the weight of the crowd. Up on the stage, three of Biggar's dozen or so clergymen are ranged on chairs between the crumpled flags and potted ferns, along with the RCMP and the Biggar Mother, a frail old lady in a black dress; in the centre is a cardboard cenotaph. The service used to be held at the real cenotaph in Queen Elizabeth Park, until the ladies of the I.O.D.E. complained of having to stand in the cold.

After "O Canada" and "O God Our Help in Ages Past," the names of the dead men are read out by a legionnaire. There are only 22 names. The legionnaire mispronounces some of them. A trumpeter up in the balcony plays the "Last Post" and then "Reveille" after the Silence. He launches into "Abide With Me" as the Biggar Mother places the first wreath at the base of the cardboard cenotaph. Wreaths are then laid on behalf of the provincial government and the Town of Biggar. A lady from the Legion Auxiliary makes her way down the aisle and up to the stage to lay a wreath. She is followed by a member of the I.O.D.E., then an Elk, two Brownies, the Knights of Columbus, the Lady Trainmen, a member of the student council at Biggar Composite High, two Cubs, two Scouts, a representative of the Rural Municipality of Biggar...the procession goes on and on. The trumpeter keeps playing. He plays the simple melody over once, twice, three times. Still the wreaths keep coming. The trumpeting takes on an air of urgency and desperation, and phrases bleat and slur as the trumpeter gasps for breath. He hits false notes and then misses notes altogether. Soon his breathing is as audible as the hymn, and the audience is transfixed by the unseen agony in the balcony. "Abide With Me" grows weaker and weaker, spluttering, stuttering until, just as the president of the Chamber of Commerce reaches the stage with his wreath, it fades away. The balcony is silent.

The Anglican minister gives the scripture lesson, the United Church minister says a very long prayer, and the sermon is delivered by the pastor from the Church of God. The collection is taken in round metal film cans. A couple more hymns, a prayer, "God Save the Queen," and everyone rushes thankfully out into the fresh air. In disarray, the legionnaires retreat to the basement of the Legion Hall, where they will toast their fallen comrades with rye and ginger ale.

"Jeez, I bet you'd never guess that was me!" grins a stout, balding veteran with tiny purple veins in his cheeks, pointing at a photo pinned to the wall of the Legion pub which shows a young, very pale and slender boy with curly blond hair under a heavy army officer's cap. The wall is covered with faded snapshots of shy, skinny teen-agers in old-fashioned uniforms. The legionnaires get a big bang out of comparing the boys in the photos with the wrinkled and paunchy men clustered around the tables.

"I wouldn't miss this parade for anythin'," crows a toothless old scarecrow who is gulping down his whiskey a glass at a time. A veteran of World War I, he lives in a shack on the farm he homesteaded in 1913. "Got m' son t' drive me in t' day," he grins. "Lost m' driver's licence. The police here got m' twice for drunkin drivin'." He casts a sly, sidelong look at Sgt. Zorn over in the corner, and his brown, rubbery face crinkles into a broad, gummy smile. He swallows another glass of whiskey. "Fined me $175 and took away m' licence. I only paid $100 of the fine though. 'Can't afford to pay the rest,' I told 'em. 'I got no money.'" He bends over the table in a silent, wheezing cackle. "They caught m' drivin' again last week. Sneakin' down Main Street. Hee hee hee. There's nothin' they can do t' me. I can't pay the fine an' they won't send me to jail, cause I'm too old!"

Someone launches into a chorus of "The White Cliffs of Dover." Red faces glistening with sweat, the legionnaires raise their glasses in salute and start to sing.

"This was always a whiskey town," says a tiny old rail-roader bent over almost double. "Nowadays the guys take one or two ounces and fill it up with ginger ale. In the old days they'd pour a whole tumbler full and drink it down. I remember pouring guys on the caboose. They'd be dead to the world for half the trip. Railroadin' in the early days was based on a bottle of whiskey. Bootleggers were thrivin', poker joints were thrivin'. There were four or five poker games goin' all the time around town. Goin' steady twenty-four hours a day. You could walk in there any time of the day or night and find a game. The Chinese cafe had a game, in the basement, and there was one in the Eden Hotel. Then there was the old ram pasture next to the Biggar Hotel. There was usually a game goin' there. Oh, it was an old rooming house. We called it the ram pasture. Biggar was full of roomin' houses 'cause of all the single fellas on the railroad. There was the Western and the Royal Alex as well. The Royal Alex was a sort of clean, decent place to live but the other two, you could commit murder in them and if you didn't let the blood run out under the door nobody'd say anything. The town police knew these places were runnin' but they just let them go. I don't know if the police got a rake-off or anything. The whole West was pretty well the same. Even the doctors and the dentist, they was big drinkers. Heavy drinkers. At one party this guy complained of having a toothache. The dentist, Doc McKay, says, 'Sit up in the chair, we'll pull your G. D. tooth for ya. Which one is it? You guys hold 'im in the chair, I'll pull that bloody tooth.' He takes hold of his goldarn old forceps and pulls every tooth in his head! Took 'em all out!

"Prostitutes rode the trains and a lot of them'd come in on paydays. Stay around three or four days and then they'd be gone. They never stuck around. No, there was one. I remember the town council was goin' to run her out. She showed up at the meeting and said, 'You can't get rid of me. I've got too much on all you guys.' And that was all that was heard of that. Oh, everybody had a lot of money then. We had runnin' water. And we had a local power plant here that come on about four p.m. and run til ten or eleven o'clock at night. Then the street lights went off. Boy, it was dark! My first job was callin' train crews, runnin' up

and down the streets through the snowdrifts at night. Pitch
black. Ploughin' through the snow. When you wanted to
cross the street in the wintertime you had to climb over a
mound of manure. They used to pile manure over the water
mains to keep 'em from freezin' up in the wintertime. All
the manure from all the livery barns in town. They put an
extra big pile over the water hydrants and if there was a
fire, why they'd have to take a pick and shovel and pick
out the frozen manure around the hydrant to get the water
turned on!''

Early in the summer of 1908, William Hodgins Biggar, KC,
of Belleville, Ontario, was travelling leisurely across north-
western Saskatchewan in the private railway car of Charles
Melville Hays, president of the Grand Trunk Pacific Railway, for which Mr. Biggar was the solicitor. A former
Ontario MLA and sometime mayor of Belleville, Mr. Biggar
was accompanying other members of the board of directors
of the Grand Trunk Pacific Railway on an inspection tour
of their new railway line to the West Coast. To relieve the
tedium of the journey, the men amused themselves by
designating the buffalo wallows and patches of wolf willow
as the new stations and divisional points on the railway.
Not surprisingly, they named the stations after themselves.
Mr. Hays went first, naming his townsite Melville. The
next divisional point went to Mr. Biggar. It turned out to be
a large alkali slough on a featureless stretch of prairie 60
miles due west of Saskatoon. Before the train arrived, the
slough was nameless; after the train pulled out, it was
Biggar. William Wainwright, chief accountant for the Grand
Trunk, took the next divisional point and set the limits
which were to govern the lives of the thousands of railway
men who have spent the last 65 years shuttling endlessly
between Biggar and Wainwright. Mr. Biggar never saw his
town. A photo of him as a distinguished, white-haired old
gentleman hangs in the Biggar town hall, but aside from a
couple of old-timers, no one in town knows or cares who
he is.
  The townside for Biggar was originally laid out on the
slough on the south side of the tracks, but it was changed

in the nick of time to the hill on the north. The incline makes Main Street a little precipitous in the winter, but it gives Biggar good drainage, of which the town is proud. "Ya gotta remember that Biggar's a very cheap town to operate," says a town councillor, wagging his finger. "Water drainage is nothin'. We can have a cloudburst and there isn't a puddle around, only a little birdbath here and there."

Biggar really got going in 1912, when it had two large hotels, an immigration shed, the ram pasture, a dozen stores, a brick school, and a lot of nerve. The fact that Biggar was miles from nowhere, with a population of about 200 people, perched on a dusty, windblown plain of dubious economic value, did not deter the town fathers. They purchased another section of land north of town, subdivided it into lots, and named it Boulevard Heights. A blueprint was drawn up showing winding drives facing a lake, and the area was advertised in the Biggar *Independent* as "the high class residential section of Biggar." Lots sold for $75 and $50 and faced streets named after all the town councillors and prominent citizens. In reality, however, the high-class district was nothing more than a seedy pasture surrounding a slough. Some people were rumored to have made fortunes selling the phoney lots, but in 1912 the mayor was arrested by the North West Mounted Police and the whole scheme collapsed. Any lots that had been sold gradually reverted to the town for taxes. The municipal map still shows the Town of Biggar occupying a section and a half of which two-thirds are cow pasture.

Biggar is a working-class town. The railway attracted men from the shipyards and industrial slums of Europe and Great Britain. Some were skilled, some not; to the Grand Trunk it made little difference. "Everyone who worked in the roundhouse was looked on as unskilled labor," says retired railroader Leo Campbell, who worked for 17 cents an hour. The railway contained its own pecking order: the men on the trains — brakemen, conductors, engineers — were a cut above the roundhouse workers. "You had to pass a physical exam to get in the running service," says Leo, "and you had to be able to read and write very good." The train crews earned twice as much money. At the top were the yard master and the station agent, who issued the orders and bossed the crews. The agent had to be a skilled telegrapher and janitor. "It was up to the agent to keep the station clean," explains agent Tom Sutherland. "We got five dollars a month for cleanin' the place up. I used to scrub it myself once a week. Cleaned the windows twice a year. Ah, there was lots of dirty agents!"

Because of the language and education requirements, the railway hierarchy filtered out along ethnic and racial lines. Eastern European immigrants usually ended up on the section gang, the most menial and poorly paid jobs on the railway. Every tiny whistle-stop had its two-storey section house for the foreman and a clapboard bunkhouse for the men. Armed with picks and shovels and hoes, the gangs shuffled laboriously up and down their seven miles of track, repairing ties and hacking out the weeds from between the rails. Poor, foreign-speaking, blackened by the sun and the cinders, the section men were a caste apart, respected only by the village children, who would have given their right arm for a chance to zip up and down the track on the little handcar that took the men back and forth to work. The section men who stayed around town usually squatted on free land near the tracks, forming the nucleus of what came to be known as "shanty town," or "the wrong side of the tracks," which derived its moral reputation from the gang's bachelor fondness for poker and booze.

The working people of Biggar built their new houses on the prairie the way they had been accustomed to living in the old country. Biggar is all squished together, tiny Victorian frame bungalows with skirted verandas and knick-knacks in the windows set cheek-by-jowl on 25-foot lots enclosed by wire and picket fences. A miniature metropolis of painted shutters and plastic flowers, Biggar is crowded and claustrophobic, as if its population were two million instead of 2,600. Protected by the railway to the south and the highway on the north and west, Biggar is a walled city, a respectable, proletarian little town set incongruously in the middle of a windswept wilderness. Biggar's niggardliness about land is not the product of geography, which offers endless acres of empty rolling grassland, but of an urban tradition which equates land with wealth. Biggar thinks small and thinks cheap. The little old bungalows are full of railroaders earning $10,000 a year. One of them is town councillor Ken Foster. "Sure I could live in a new house," he says. "The taxes would be $390. My taxes here are $189. When that sewer pipe goes by and that paving machine, I only pay half as much."

Small lots made the town easier to service and gave Biggar certain civilized amenities. Before the waterworks were installed, the town was served by a horse-drawn water wagon which made the rounds of the houses twice a week. Water cost 25 cents a barrel (five barrels for $1), and customers signalled by hanging a red rag out the window or on the clothesline. The water was kept in an open barrel in the kitchen, and each householder had to lug it pail by pail from the wagon to his barrel. Everybody bathed in the washtub except the mayor, Dr. S. E. Shaw, who rigged up an outdoor shower with a metal tank and copper pipes, which warmed the water in the sun. Milk was kept cool in pails of water, and food was stored in tin boxes outside or in a hole under the floor. In the winter, frozen carcasses of meat were strung up in the trees out of reach of the dogs, and the Ukrainians smoked their sausage by hanging it down the chimney. Garbage was thrown to the pigs and chickens in the back yards, and the town was too poor to haul away the piles of offal that swarmed with rats and flies in the summer heat. Destitute railroaders and bankrupt homesteaders too poor to afford the town's services camped out in filthy shacks and crowded boardinghouses near the tracks. As a result of this primitive sanitation, epidemics of typhoid, cholera, and diphtheria decimated the little community. The sick were quarantined in a shack northwest of town known as the "pest house," where their meals were delivered in pails thrust through the door on the end of a long stick and the doctor paid his infrequent visits wrapped in a bedsheet with two holes cut out for his eyes.

In the spring of 1918, influenza swept like wildfire through the area. There were 19 funerals a day in Biggar at the height of the epidemic. The picture show and the poolroom were closed, and the immigration hall was turned into a hospital. "The homesteaders would drive in, put their team in the barn behind the shed and climb into bed," recalls Hugh Buchanan. "Most of them were bachelors and

they were all alone on the farm. The pest house was full
and they had beds up in the school too. Whole families
were in bed. The doctor, he'd pretty near cry. There was
nothing he could do for them. The doctor didn't know
what to give. He'd hand them a prescription for Epsom
salts.

"I was an official pallbearer. We had two black horses
and a hearse with glass doors. We'd load the rough wooden
boxes into the dray and go out to the cemetery on Sundays.
In the winter we couldn't bury 'em because the ground was
frozen, so we piled 'em up like cordwood in a little shed
out at the cemetery. Saturday night we'd put on face masks
and get all stinked up with eucalyptus and go out in the
country and dance with the girls."

To people for whom life has been cheap, a hospital
becomes a place of both physical and symbolic importance.
The first building you notice as you come into Biggar from
the north past the famous sign which announces: NEW
YORK IS BIG BUT THIS IS BIGGAR is the Biggar
Union Hospital, an ugly grey stucco building on top of the
rise overlooking the town with its old name, St. Margaret's,
spelled out in wrought-iron script over the gate. St.
Margaret's was the centre of a substantial Roman Catholic
establishment in Biggar. St. Gabriel's Roman Catholic
Church is down the street, a modest but spanking new
frame building with an attached rectory for Father "Bill,"
Biggar's hip young priest, and St. Gabriel's parochial school
is across the street in the ramshackle old convent marked
by a mouldy plaster statue of the Virgin.

Main Street runs downhill to the CNR station and rail
yards past a welter of aged gas stations, vacant lots, and
slum houses. The salmon pink Kingdom Hall of Jehovah's
Witnesses sticks out like a sore thumb. Across the street and
a little farther down, the Biggar Citizens' Clinic occupies an
old Safeway store; its empty windows are soaped from
Hallowe'en, and a sign on the door says "Closed." Most of
Biggar's three-block business section is built of red brick,
which gives the town a substantial, established appearance
but makes it seem older than its 60 years, perhaps because
all the buildings are very shabby and run down. Urban
blight has overtaken Biggar before the town has had a
chance to grow. The biggest building is the three-storey

Eamon Block, an ancient brick office building with a poker den in the basement, a color TV salesman on the main floor, and scores of penniless widows living on the top floors. A plaque on the post office next door says it was built by Louis St. Laurent in 1955, which makes it just about the newest building on Main Street. The post office is also the busiest place in town, next to the Canton Cafe across the street and the beer parlor of the Eden Hotel, which is down at the end of Main Street facing the station. The beer parlor of the Eden Hotel is always full, and it's jammed to the rafters on Saturday night. With its sophisticated bordello-red-and-black decor, two shuffleboard tables, and plush red carpet, the beer parlor is the most lavish establishment in Biggar. A sign pasted to the green door leading to the pub announces:

AN IRRESISTIBLE DEAL!
For November Only
To coincide with the month-end opening of
the Biggar Denture Clinic — Prairie Denture
Service offers:
25% SAVINGS TO ALL NEW DENTURE PATIENTS
10% SAVINGS TO RELINE, REMAKE OR REPAIR
DENTURES
Take Advantage of This Month-Long Savings
by Making Your Appointment Today!
phone 244-0753 Saskatoon
PRAIRIE DENTURE SERVICE

You can tell a lot about a town from its teeth. Biggar is very big in dentures. The Prairie Denture Clinic is open three days a week in the Eamon Block on Main Street. Since the entire population of the district is less there 8,000, a substantial number of them must be wearing false teeth to justify this volume of business. One reason is that Biggar has no resident dentist, and has been without one ever since Doc McKay took off some time in the Twenties.

Teeth are a luxury in rural western Canada. Many people have learned to do without. There just isn't much business for a dentist in Biggar, not only because dental work is

expensive, but also because beautiful teeth are not considered
very important. Teeth are utilitarian; when they rot, they're
pulled. They are seldom replaced until the whole mouthful
is gone. Many people get along happily with two or three
rotted stumps and feel no embarrassment at a smile that's
stained and chipped as a broken picket fence. Snaggle teeth
are as much a part of the farmer's image as his short hair
and windburned neck. Who is there to impress?

Store teeth are an indication of social status. They represent money, pride, and self-esteem. "Even in the old days
people had false teeth," says an old railroader. "Wore 'em
in their hip pocket most of the time." Most of the businessmen in Biggar have dentures. False teeth are a badge of
office, like a suit and tie, a visible line of social demarcation
which separates the farm from the town. Having sold the
farm and moved to town, many retired farmers invest in
teeth, a social gesture equivalent to that of the farm
children who, sensitive to urban social pressures from
school and TV, brush with Crest.

False teeth give Biggar businessmen a shark-like quality.
Their smiles are startlingly bright and glittering; their rows
of pearly white teeth glow with a peculiar plastic lumines-
cence. It's a community of Cheshire cats. The teeth are
overwhelming, an ultimate reality which will remain long
after the rest of the body has faded away. The effect is
menacing and sad, for false teeth are only noticeable when
they're cheap.

Biggar thinks poor. The town has never recovered from
the Depression. It looks much the same as it did in the
Twenties, only older, and now instead of being optimistic,
it is cautious and depressed, a faded photograph of its old
self. Too late for the railway boom, Biggar was less than 20
years old in 1930. The crash was not a sudden catastrophe
but rather the culmination of a series of depressions which
had washed over Saskatchewan after the war and had kept
Biggar teetering on the verge of bankruptcy. The farmers
dug in their heels and carried on. Train service was cut, and
hundreds of railroaders were laid off. "Ninety per cent of
the area was on relief," says Max Hock, Biggar's Jewish
general merchant, whose son Lloyd has now taken over the
family business on Main Street. "The kids were going bare-

foot. It made you cry to see them. We traded eggs and butter for groceries and meat. Some farmers would phone in and say they had no vehicle to come in with and they couldn't waste feed on a horse..We'd bring them in in a truck and send them back home. Nobody starved to death here. There was always a little cash around. Some people left the land, not too many. This area wasn't hit as bad as the South. I can still see the string of wagons coming through town going north. Day after day they came through, all the family's stuff piled up with the kids sitting on top and the cow tied up behind."

Trainloads of relief supplies were shipped into Saskatchewan from eastern Canada — potatoes, turnips, apples, cheese, beans, and carloads of salt cod. "They were flat and yellow and stiff as boards," says a farm boy. "Nobody knew what to do with them. Who in Saskatchewan had ever seen a salt cod? Not even the storekeepers would take the damned things in trade. In the Maritimes the women soak them in water overnight so the salt comes out. But we didn't know that. So some people boiled them, some people fried them. They were totally inedible. And the stink was terrible! My father would eat anything. He would eat the most disgusting parts of the cattle — everything. But he wouldn't eat the cod. So we gave it to the pigs. The pigs couldn't eat it. So we gathered the cod up and buried it, like a dead thing. Some people are reported to have used them as shingles to repair their roofs, but I can't imagine that. The stink when it rained would make the house unlivable. But of course it never rained in Saskatchewan in those years. We used to get big barrels of clothes too — attic clothes I called them since they obviously came from people's attics. Lots of bowler hats and umbrellas. Black umbrellas. It was funny, because of course the only reason we had to take these cast-off clothes in the first place was because there was no rain in Saskatchewan!"

The younger men went on the bum, scrounging what they could from the land. "I hit the boxcars and rode all around," says Biggar farmer and municipal councillor Joe Boisvert. "You heard a lot of different stories. Some guy was goin' back to see his honey, some guy was goin' to rob a jewelry store. We rode on top of the boxcars on nice days. If you felt like having a little sleep you'd tie yourself down. The police gave us a hard time. We thought they had nothing else to do. We used to get tough. We'd do almost anything for excitement. We'd get a basket of rotten eggs and throw 'em at the section men as we rode along."

"They were sitting on the tops of the freights just solid," says station agent Tom Sutherland. "When the train stopped the bums would get off and stretch their legs. The trainman would have to stand on a fence post to wave signals because there was guys all over the tracks. 'Why don't you tell 'em to git off?' people'd say. Hell, we were outnumbered by the bums! They had the forces. 'Throw 'em in the army,' people said. 'We're not afraid of goin' in the army,' they replied. 'We're not gun-shy. We've been shot at by every RCMP in the country!'"

"You used the old bum deal," says Boisvert. "You'd offer to do some little job for something to eat. Religious institutions were the only place to go to keep you from starving."

"You'd kill pigs, put up ice," says Sutherland. "Everybody was makin' home brew. There was five bootleggers per hundred people. There were quite some experts. Some was quite good. You'd boil it up in an old cream can. Sometimes it would explode, scald people all to hell. The druggist used to bootleg. He was sellin' 'Spirits of Nitre' at $4.50 a gallon. 'What's that?' said the RCMP. 'Just a horse medicine,' he says. Hell, it was mostly alcohol. The RCMP had a waiting list. There was so many guys going to jail that we had to wait our turn to go to Prince Albert. You didn't have any money, so you had to go to jail. They'd tell you when your turn was and come and take you away."

"We made up songs about the cheese and beans at the Christmas concert," says an old lady, crippled now with arthritis. "Don't you ever think we didn't have any fun! The dances started at midnight and went until dawn. I'll always remember them because of the long table at the end of the hall, all across the hall. People would put their coats there. You'd look closely and the coats were full of little babies, rows and rows of them, from two months to two years, stacked like cordwood. At six o'clock in the morning the women would come and pick up their parcels and go home. The country was young then. When you're young, you think life's a heck of a nice thing. You don't give a hoot what happens!"

Biggar is entering another depression. In 1971 the town's population dropped by 150 to 2,607, the first drop since Biggar lost 18 per cent of its population in the Thirties. Biggar is now the same size it was in 1929. The town's decline reflects the diminished importance of the railway as automation makes Biggar irrelevant. When the roundhouse closed in 1960, the town lost 32 families. The town lives in fear of losing its status as a divisional point. "Guys are scared to build a house," says Glen Clements, the lone real estate agent. "Every year the rumor comes down the track that they're going to pull the point. Nobody wants to be stuck with a house he can't sell." The railway has given Biggar a transient mentality. Although most of the railroaders remain rooted in Biggar, they are always mentally preparing for the big trip down the road. They have little interest in material possessions; their houses are plain, their furniture utilitarian. They are reluctant to invest in anything that's too big to load in the trunk of the family car. As they grow old, their houses accumulate a staggering quantity of little things — bric-a-brac, souvenir ashtrays, photos, memorabilia of all kinds whose main attraction, outside of sentimental value, is portability. Eventually they accumulate so much stuff they can't possibly move. Biggar's a railway waiting room, a cozy, ramshackle, shabby place with brown varnished walls and cardboard reproductions of the Rockies, where everyone is camped out like refugees surrounded by their family possessions, waiting for the train. As they wait, the town grows older and older. Between 1956 and 1966, the number of people over 65 almost doubled. "There was a big retirement boom," says Clements. The people who created Biggar's second boom were the people who had created the first boom — a homesteader who was 20 in 1910 turned 65 in 1955. That boom is not likely to happen again. The land around Biggar is empty; the villages and hamlets are ghost towns. In 1941 the rural population around Biggar was 8,778; now it's barely 4,000. You can drive 15 miles without seeing a farmhouse. Biggar has sucked the countryside dry.

The CNR has not been an unmixed blessing. The railway pays less than $2,000 a year in taxes, since most of its holdings lie outside the town limits, and the reasonably good wages are a recent phenomenon; until the late Fifties, wages and pensions were low. As a result, Biggar is full of impoverished widows living in old houses or cramped apartments over the stores. Transients and unemployed laborers have moved into the cheap houses abandoned by transferred railroaders; many are Indians looking for work off the reserve. In 1961, half the town population earned less than ₃3,000 a year.

But the railway has made Biggar much wealthier than most prairie towns. In 1961 the average income for a male worker in Biggar was $4,042, $43 higher than the Canadian average and $450 higher than the Saskatchewan average. Even women's wages — $1,716 — were well above the average. Ten per cent of the town's population earned more than $6,000 a year. The relatively high wages are reflected in Biggar's enormous volume of retail trade. With a trading area of only 8,000 people, the town took in more than $6 million in retail business in 1971. (Winkler, with 600 more people and a trading area of 25,000, took in only $5 million.) Biggar people are big spenders — the credit union has $2.3 million out on loan and only $420,000 in long-term savings accounts — and Biggar gets a big slice of the local dollar, because competing towns and villages have died. This wealth is divided among a very small number of businessmen. Biggar's merchants are very wealthy men, but you'd never know it to look at the town.

In the last 15 years, only two new commercial buildings have been built in downtown Biggar; and nobody bothers with renovations. The stores are dingy and overcrowded, some little more than holes in the wall and people live upstairs over most of them. The town is a rabbit warren, with people living in attics, basements, garages, back rooms, closets, and old offices; even the hotels are full of pensioners and welfare cases, permanent guests of the government. Overcrowding creates traffic problems on shopping days. "I like to see where they can't park on Main Street," says the mayor Lloyd Hock. "It makes the town look busy. People get into the beat of it. The town that's dead, that's where there's no one on the street." The same kind of thinking applies to the stores: a store that's small and cramped looks busier than one that's large and modern. The merchants are conservative and complacent; accustomed to good, steady trade from the railroaders and pensioners, they see no need to compete or expand. Reluctant to do anything which might initiate a price war, they seldom advertise and almost never have sales. This image of genteel impoverishment is cheap and smart. Crummy buildings keep taxes low; renovations are expensive and could set off a chain reaction which might force some merchants out of business. Shabby stores reassure customers that the businessman is not making much profit; high prices go unnoticed. In spite of their big slice of business, most Biggar merchants live modestly, even humbly, to avoid criticism or embarrassing speculation. With their profits, they are able to buy up old houses and rent them out to poor people. They get an additional rake-off by renting the rooms over their stores (old buildings are more valuable because the rents are low enough to attract widows and pensioners who cannot afford to buy a house), and many widows clerk in the stores for low wages to make enough money to pay the rent. Welfare people are a bonus; their rent is paid by the provincial government. "The old people are the first ones we have to think about," says Lloyd Hock. Biggar businessmen long ago learned the value of poverty: poor people shop locally, the rich go to Saskatoon. Their attitude is essentially that of the slum landlord, and it is graphically reflected in the government of the town.

NOTICE
RAT CONTROL
The town of Biggar has been carrying out
a program to eliminate the rat problem
in our area. If you have any evidence that
you or anyone else have rats
PLEASE CONTACT THIS TOWN OFFICE
AND THE TOWN WILL SUPPLY THE RAT
POISON FREE OF CHARGE.

Biggar is grubby. The town budget in 1971 was a paltry $386,882, and half of it was school tax. The total assessed value of the town is only $3.8 million, and the business assessment actually dropped by $10,000 between 1969 and 1971. The sewage plant is obsolete, the swimming pool is dangerous. "The town spent $10,000 in repairs to the pool," says Ken Foster. "Last year a guy dived off the board and hit the bottom. Broke his neck. Paralyzed from the neck down. Turns out the pool is too shallow for a two-metre board. We're gonna get sued." To save money, the town has stopped ploughing snow from the sidewalks, so the sidewalks are treacherous and almost impassable. "We hoped people would clean off their own stretch of sidewalk," says the mayor. The pensioners, too feeble to shovel their walk or negotiate the drifts, complain equally bitterly about the snow and the taxes. The town is thinking of closing some streets to save maintenance. Building regulations are lax, zoning restrictions are inadequate, a proliferation of garages, sheds, and commercial buildings has lowered property values in most residential areas. The cemetery is a disgrace. The town has profiteered from the dead; it takes in more than $1,500 a year from the sale of plots and spends almost nothing on maintenance. In 1972, a citizens' clean-up committee headed by the undertaker volunteered to cut the weeds and repair the broken headstones. They advertised for a caretaker for the summer months: "We invite tenders for this position which will require a great deal of self-motivation, initiative and a willingness to work on your own. The applicant must own his own lawn mower, some small tools and a truck or trailer." The cheapest applicant was hired; the cost of repairing the graves was billed to the next-of-kin. "This is the cheapest town I've ever been in in my life," mutters a railroader. "It stinks."

The town's niggardliness is not a necessity but the result of deliberate civic policy. Until 1969, Biggar's tax rate was one of the lowest in Saskatchewan. Terrified of debt, the town council refused to invest in anything more than piece-meal public works, although the civic debt was far below what the town could afford to carry. "It was an old man's council," says Ken Foster, a railroader who was the first reform councillor to be elected before the former mayor and

council were swept out of office in 1970. "You'd say something and you'd know they were wrong and they wouldn't
listen to you. They got madder than hell if you criticized
them. Oh no, you couldn't do that! You'd finally get an OK
to do something, you'd go down to the town shed and the
guy would say OK but nothing would get done!" The new
council's sole reform has been a clean-up of the garbage
dump and the vacant lots. To save money, 250 school
children were mobilized to pick up litter. But businessmen
dominate town council, and Biggar's aura of civic decay is
essentially camouflage. A town that looks ugly and poor
frightens rival businessmen away. The merchants use Biggar
as a kind of bogeyman to protect their comfortable monopoly from intruders. "They're afraid," comments a resident
caustically, "that the town might progress."

Biggar discourages visitors. Hotel accommodation offers
a choice of three — the Biggar Hotel, the Eden Hotel, and
Al's Motel. The hotels are dark and creaky and full of
crippled, pathetic old men; everyone shares the toilet down
the hall. Al's Motel is a beaverboard shack near the highway
built by Al, who owns the service station across the road.
The rooms are drab and bare with a minimum of cheap
furniture, a toilet and shower. Al didn't bother to water-
proof the shower stall, so the beaverboard is leprous and
mouldy. The rooms have no telephones, so the guests have
to use the pay phone in Al's Diner next door. Messages are
taken by the cook and waitress, a sullen, snoopy woman
who also keeps the guest register. The telephone is encrust-
ed with grease from the cadaverous hamburgers the sad
woman fries up on the grill behind the lunch counter. Men
in work clothes bang in and out of the screen door for a
cup of acid coffee, and little boys come by after school to
buy cigarettes. Al's relies on travelling salesmen and motor-
ists blown in by blizzards. Al charges only $4 a night.

Strangers in Biggar are stared at relentlessly, shamelessly,
like sideshow freaks. It grates on the nerves. There is a
strong undercurrent of tension in the town, a tremor of
hostility and fear. People on the street are aggressive and
outspoken, blunt to the point of rudeness. The businessmen
are nervous and evasive. When I introduce myself to the
druggist, he turns pale as a ghost. Lloyd Hock blanches and

looks sideways. Bitter and uncommunicative, the retiring editor of the Biggar *Independent* is packing to leave. Biggar is cruel and defensive, an armed camp whose warring factions have reached an uneasy truce, a town still bleeding from wounds inflicted during the doctors' strike in 1962.

The battleground is the beer parlor of the Eden Hotel. It's the hot stove league, as the townspeople say, committee room for half the organizations in town, political head-quarters for Biggar's most powerful faction, the railroaders, who congregate there all afternoon not primarily to drink but to argue. "Railroaders are very outspoken," says train-man Ken Foster. "They're the biggest bellyachers in the world. They're the greatest ones for wanting something. They don't contribute too much, except their advice. They're knowledgeable people, very knowledgeable. They can take any topic and they know all about it. This is what you find down in the pub when they all get together. This pub deal, you know, the railroad tolerated it till after the war, then they tightened down. No liquor on the job. Like myself: I'll never go near the railroad with liquor on me. I don't drink on board and I don't drink at the other end of the road, but twenty years ago, hell, when you got off that train you had to go and make that run all over again in the beer parlor!"

The "rails" form a separate caste in Biggar, a craft guild united by its own ritual, jargon, and mystique. "Back in the steam engine days," says a yardmaster, "the railroad men, they'd stick together. They used to swear by one another and swear at one another. They'd lie for ya and do every-thing else to keep ya outta trouble. Sometimes they'd bend over backwards to get ya into trouble! A lot of them lived the railroad. They still do."

"There was something about a steam locomotive that was almost human," muses Leo Campbell with a tender smile. "They were alive, part of the establishment. You treated them as one of your own family. You could tell them apart as they were coming into the station. You'd hear their whistle, hear their bell, the laboring of their exhaust as they climbed the hill. They didn't have names, just numbers, but those numbers were as familiar as Tom or Harry or Jim. Just mention a number and a picture of that locomotive would flash in front of your mind. When a collision occurred those numbers became fixed in your memory."

"At night the old steam engines would talk away to themselves even if no one was on them," says Tom Sutherland, who spent many winter nights alone in the station. "They was the only things that was alive besides me. They'd make noises just like when you're asleep. Not all the same sounds either. There was a breathing to them. Poommph."

Held together by their mysterious servitude to the steam engine and the arcane routine of CNR timetables, the railroaders have formed big family clans in Biggar in which members are identified by special railroad nicknames. "My brother was known as Clinker Jim," says Ken Foster. "When a fire clinkered, you know, he wasn't firin' it right. It was always clinkered. There was a guy called Lord McKay and another we named Vinegar Face McKay. A conductor was Flat Wheel McCallum. Then there was Whistler Wright. He was always whistlin' until we threatened to throw him out the window. My name is Cash Register. There's nobody after the buck like me!"

The camaraderie hides deep jealousies within the railway hierarchy, which is rigidly stratified according to status and income. The brakemen resent the conductor, who's their boss, and the conductor hates the engineer, who makes more money and rides up front. "The engineer is God," sneers one young brakeman. "The working men are just bums." The engineers love to play Casey Jones; they swagger around in their striped caps which they starch and dry over a tin can to make them stand up straight. Everyone pities the fireman, whose job is redundant, and hates the station agent, who treats the blue collar workers with contempt. "In the olden days," says Tom Sutherland, "some of the agents wouldn't even speak to an engineer or trainman. You had to guard your territory. Doing a favor for a trainman, he figured it was cowardice. He'd be dirty to you. If they figured you was the least bit weak, they'd sneer at you, call you everything, and any kind of language goes on the railroad. They figured the agent was their whipping post. You know what the motto of the railroad is? 'Do unto others before they do it unto you.'"

Disputes over train orders sometimes broke out into fist fights in the station, but the railroaders usually contented themselves with scrawling "F-off" on the agent's fence with shit on Hallowe'en. Threats and harassment were a kind of guerrilla warfare the railroaders used to protect themselves from the prying eyes of the CNR management. It worked. "You had to keep quiet unless you wanted feuds," says Sutherland. Intimidated local management would cover for the trainmen, overlook drunkenness, and fail to report flagrant violations of rules and regulations. Pranks and arguments were not only a way to relieve the tedium of the trip but also a form of revenge against the CNR. A wild collection of drifters, alcoholics, and rangytangs, the rails formed a Robin Hood brotherhood locked in mortal combat with the railway moguls. Their weapon was the train.

"Oh there were lots of wrecks!" chortles Sutherland. "I seen train wrecks right at the station! We'd hold out bamboo hoops with the train orders in 'em and the engineers would take 'em on the fly. It was kinda a contest. An engineer would open 'er up and go through like hell when he was supposed to stop. The track was very bad. The ties would come loose and derail the trains. The engines didn't derail, it was the cars behind. They'd jump the track and come rollin' along in front of the station. A lot of station agents' kids have been killed by trains. And trains have hit a lot of stations. Two trains collided once right at the station. Oil car exploded. Agent and his wife burned to death."

Automation ended the fun. "Hell," says Ken Foster, "now you just climb on and away you go. What is there to do?" The world of Biggar trainmen is bounded on the west by Wainwright and on the east by Watrous. They never go any farther. Watrous is considered the better run, because the train has to shunt through Saskatoon, which provides a small break in the monotony. Everything is handled by computer; the crew mostly sits in the caboose playing cards and telling dirty stories. They all admit they're bored. "It's bread and butter," shrugs a young brakeman. "For what you do, it's a big paying job." It's also a glum future for a young man. A railroader's income and status are related not to ability but to seniority. Most of the men are veterans who hired on after the war, and they still have 15 or 20 years to go before retirement. "They haven't hired an engineer here since 1956," says the brakeman. "I'm qualified to be a conductor but there are so many guys ahead of me I'll be a brakeman for another twenty years." He smiles wanly. "There's nothing you can do. You go along or cry a lot." The young men resent the bottleneck at the top. They are bored by the traditions and arguments left over from the days of steam; mention the romance of railroading and they look blank or laugh out loud. Diesels aren't people. They haven't been in a wreck or played chicken with an oncoming train; their only thrill on the endless journey to Wainwright is watching the train demolish the occasional unsuspecting cow at a level crossing. Small town boys lured out of high school by the promise of big wages, their only justification for their job is money, and the new railway mystique revolves around the spending of it.

Biggar's gambling den does a big business on paydays, when the cars and pickup trucks are lined up on Main Street for blocks. The poker game is run by a professional, a young ex-railroader who now makes a weekly circuit of the neighbouring towns. Once a year, a planeload of Biggar Elks takes off for a week in Las Vegas.

"A railroader's got a pocket full of money and lots of free time," says a poker player who quit railroading to go farming. "I quit because I was getting to be a bum. The evenings were all the same, in the beer parlor or the pool hall. Alcoholism's a big problem in Biggar. For alcoholism you've got to have a good economic base, I don't mean for the deadbeats but for the guys that are still carrying on as family men. The railroaders are the economic elite of Biggar, but they've developed a beer parlor culture."

There's not much waiting for a railroader at the end of the line. Retiring employees are honored at an annual CNR retirement banquet. "All the old retirees come back," says Leo Campbell. "They stand up and tell what they were on the railway and how many years they served. The men get a wallet embossed with their railway order and $25 cash." The ladies, says Mrs. Campbell, "get a real good cup and saucer, one worth about $3.50."

"Biggar's a tough town," says one of the boys in the cafe,

lowering his voice with respect. "Just say 'Biggar' and everybody runs! The guys from here can beat up everybody in all the other towns." The two boys are about 13, small and slight, long hair hanging in their eyes. They're sitting in the Canton Cafe drinking Cokes before going to lacrosse practice. "We're known as the 'sports,'" one of them explains with a tinge of regret. "The rocks call us the boppers, the fairies. The rocks, they're the same as greasers. They're the big guys." Each group has its gangs, usually based on where they live in town. The little guys fight with rocks, eggs, and snowballs, going all out with spray paint on Hallowe'en; the big guys use their fists and fight almost any time. Life for the boppers is hazardous, since they get shoved around a lot and viciously by the rocks, whom they worship. The centre of action for everybody is the school dance, a monthly Friday night rock session in the school gym where 400 kids in dirty jeans and long hair stand around awkwardly waiting for someone to ask them to dance. The rocks have a monopoly of everything that matters — cars, booze, girls, and drugs. "Boy, there's gonna be a lot of kids picked up after Friday night," whispers one of the little guys. "You know there was $140,000 in drugs here in town one night!" His eyes are big and round with wonder. He doesn't take drugs, he says proudly, because his girl friend doesn't approve. His parents don't even approve of his smoking, so he doesn't smoke in front of them, out of consideration for their feelings.

The small town greaser's macho fantasy is flamboyant but brief. He grows old as soon as he gets a job, which in Biggar happens at 18 or 20. He throws away his boots and leather jacket, cuts his hair, and wears a cheap suit to his job at the hardware store. He gets married and his wife has a baby. He is suddenly diminished, shrivelled, a nothing. A man without personality or reputation, he fades away in the collective imagination, his drunks and his trips to court forgotten. The fate of these pale, callow young clerks frightens the little guys, who see it waiting for them on the other side. "Jeez, this guy Norm Jones," says one of them sadly, "you see him walking down the street. He had a reputation as a big rock! He's only twenty-five. Jeez."

There's a lot of vandalism and petty theft in Biggar, beer

parlor arguments erupt into brawls, and a few wives get knocked around when their husbands come home drunk and broke. Grain theft is common when wheat is worth something, and cattle rustling is a chronic problem. (Rustlers can drive up to feedlot in a Cadillac, kill and butcher a steer, and make off with the meat right under the farmer's nose.) Few of the serious crimes ever come to court. (In 1971, charges were laid in only two out of 12 assaults and six out of 34 cases of theft.) The police are too taken up with trivia.

Sgt. Zorn is head of a nine-man RCMP detachment in Biggar; five of them are highway patrol, who work the road between Biggar and Saskatoon, and the other four police the town. Biggar has one policeman for every 650 people, and the Mounties are particularly zealous. Sgt. Zorn is a TV cop. A super-efficient crime-stopper who is determined to "clean up" Biggar, he scours the streets searching for potential crooks under every bush. Even small children are not immune; he hauls them in for driving tractors underage and for riding bicycles on the sidewalk.

Sgt. Zorn's unusual diligence has financial implications for the police and the town. Fines for traffic violations are paid to the town; in 1971, Sgt. Zorn raked in a whopping $7,265. When the town council at one point considered reducing the number of police, Sgt. Zorn pointed out the consequent reduction in fines and the council quickly changed its mind. The council is assisted in its money-raising by the justice of the peace, who handles the overflow of traffic cases. The town clerk used to be the JP. Now Glen Clements, a town councillor, is. In the first year Sgt. Zorn came to Biggar, the number of prosecutions almost doubled, although the incidence of crime decreased slightly. Most of the charges were for offences which are almost absurd: $10 for backing while unsafe; $20 for an inadequate exhaust; $25 for transporting uncovered cattle when it was below 32 degrees above zero; $25 for unnecessary spinning of tires; $10 for failure to dim headlights; $10 for trespass· ing on railway property. In most towns, these infractions rate a warning or a reprimand; in Biggar they go to court, along with the drunks and the bums and the other people grabbed for speeding and dangerous driving, and the names are all published in *The Independent*. Nobody feels the humiliation anymore; just about everybody in the Biggar area has been arrested for something. Court is a community picnic.

Court in Biggar is a casual affair held in the vestibule of the old town hall on the second and fourth Mondays of the month. A circuit judge comes out from a neighbouring town for the day. Dressed in a dark suit, he presides at a little table on wheels facing rows of metal folding chairs crowded with the accused, their friends and relatives, and curious spectators. For all but the most serious cases the Crown dispenses with the services of a prosecutor. This function is performed by Sgt. Zorn, and the defendants are coached by the judge, who tells them how to plead and gives them free legal advice. Biggar has no lawyer. The court also gets along without the services of a court reporter, who has been replaced by a tape recorder the judge carries around with him and sets up on the table in front. The judge also collects the fines and roots about in his wallet for the correct change.

Court is very informal. The cases are the usual collection of country crimes — drunk driving, stealing purple gas, having liquor in the car, petty theft. Most people plead guilty, tromp up and pay their fines, and walk out grinning. Occasionally a lawyer from Saskatoon swoops in like Perry Mason to defend a local client, but city lawyers are expensive and reluctant to come out to Biggar for a run-of-the-mill case. Out of anger and wounded pride, many local people defend themselves. Inarticulate and bereft of legal knowledge, they stumble along without a leg to stand on, offering a string of sullen excuses or tearful pleas for mercy. Their speeches have the quality of religious testimonials, little capsule histories of all the misfortunes which have led up to their present trouble. With sad faces and wringing hands, they tell of their poverty, their ignorance of the law, their heart conditions and diabetes. Some are quite eloquent, others defend themselves by waving their fists and screaming at Sgt. Zorn, who huffs and puffs and gets very red in the face. The redder he gets, the more the audience smacks its lips with delight and the more the accused redoubles his charges of deceit and corruption, looking around every so often in triumph. The judge is very understanding and sympathetic; he lets the defendant rant and rave for several minutes before fining him and sending him home.

The judge, however, is no match for Biggar's unofficial citizen advocate, Dave Kissick, who, free of charge, takes on all the most desperate and impoverished cases, particularly his own. An eccentric old cowboy with grey hair and bristly black eyebrows, Kissick keeps a few head of horses on a small piece of land on the outskirts of town and lives on welfare. Twenty years ago he did two years for rape and used the time to bone up on the law, of which his knowledge is as extensive as Sgt. Zorn's. For 17 years he has been engaged in a hopeless battle to get the municipality to build a road to his farm and is currently embroiled in a vicious range war with the farmer next door, who wants his land. When the neighbour built a fence across Kissick's land, he tore it up and was hauled into court on a charge of wilful damage. Sgt. Zorn prosecuted; Kissick defended himself.

"I called that Zorn a liar five times!" he chortles. "I told him I hoped the next time he lied that the floor would open up and he'd drop right through it and break his cotton-pickin' neck!" Kissick became so enraged that the trial was halted and the judge committed him to University Hospital in Saskatoon for a 30-day psychiatric examination. "The Mounties put a glass panel up in the car like I was a maniac," he snorts. He taunted them all the way to Saskatoon and then took on the psychiatrist. He refused to take tests and his wife got a lawyer. "I was out in two days," he says. "I'm gonna charge them all with kidnappin'!"

In Saskatoon the case was dismissed and the judge apologized. No charges were laid against the farmer who built the fence.

"You're caught up between the greed of the government and the indifference of the people," says Kissick. "I'm just a little farmer against the big farmer. If you're a little farmer, you're a nut."

Biggar is full of little farmers. The land is light and spotty with gravel pits and alkali sloughs full of deer which American hunters harvest in the fall. Sixty years of cultivation have made very little impact. For all their scrambling, most farmers aren't much ahead of where their fathers were. A new house is so rare it brings cries of envy and astonishment; some still make do with a wood stove, an oil heater in the living room, and a chemical can in the chicken shed. Biggar farmers play the land like a poker game, trying with all their skill and wizardry to trick or seduce the prairie into yielding them a living. They take a very relaxed attitude to the vagaries of fate and nobody gets very uptight about ethics. It's every man for himself and a little discreet intimidation, bootlegging, or bribery won't hurt a man's reputation unless he gets caught. It's a help to be either very tough or very mean. Some farmers chase unwanted visitors with shotguns, and the gentle pensioners on the rat patrol have been bitten numerous times by farm dogs. Rocks eroded by the wind, the farmers are tough and proud and independent. The countryside is dotted with the shacks of old homesteaders who are living out their last days in stubborn squalor because they're damned if they'll move into town. Biggar farmers seem to have an instinctive awareness that if they don't laugh at life it will destroy them. Outspoken, friendly, they drink a lot, curl a lot ("The curling broom," says an NFU organizer, "is our largest obstacle to progress."), and talk incessantly. Biggar farmers thrive on conversation, which they like to carry on at the tops of their lungs, preferably in the beer parlor. They are a community of Don Quixotes, men of keen intelligence and little education, passionate with grievance, overwhelmed by a knowledge of injustice, voluble, articulate, witty, bursting with ideas, profanity, theories, opinions, and insults, all accompanied by a passionate waving of arms and pounding of fists on the table. Flushed with beer and intellectual fire, they deliver incisive and devastating critiques of everything from the death of God to the decay of capitalism, saving their greatest vituperation for the sins of the government, of which they have encyclopaedic knowledge and absolute contempt. Politicians of all parties are eaten alive in Biggar.

Most of all the farmers love to fight with the railroaders, with whom they share a relationship of mutual suspicion. Each group accuses the other of being stupid, lazy, and rich. In the beer parlor they sit at separate tables and mutter about each other. Things come to a head in the classroom, where the farm kids and the rail kids fight tooth and claw. "I was in a fight a day," remembers a farm boy. "I whipped their asses. The farm kids were the big strong kids. You sling shit all day, pitch straw, milk cows, you're no goddam weakling. You really had to prove yourself to those goddam little town kids. The farm kids were a cut below in terms of the social ladder. The farm kid was always an outsider. He always came to town, he was always coming into someone else's world. They didn't go to the farm. The town kid, his father would be a minister or a businessman and wear a white shirt. The farmer would always have a bloody overall with shit up to his knees."

The distinctions of class in rural areas are very ambiguous. Status is based on style. Since style is essentially an urban concept, it is measured in terms of city things like concrete, street lights, running water, and sewer. The rarer and more expensive a commodity, the greater its value as a status symbol. Since water has always been both scarce and expensive on the high prairie, cleanliness is an obsession. Only townspeople who can afford dry-cleaning bills wear expensive clothes; rural culture is strictly wash-and-wear. (Set apart by their overalls and catalogue clothes, farmers avoid the gaucherie of the small town elite who hopelessly attempt to emulate Toronto, because somewhere on the trip between East and West urban fashions undergo a sea change, and by the time they reach rural Saskatchewan they are vulgarized beyond all recognition. The local swingers proudly swagger in their magenta shirts and solid white ties and show off their sideburns and flare pants, confident that they are the glass of fashion since everybody in town is wearing exactly the same outfit.)

Farmers have more wealth than townspeople and intensely middle-class attitudes, but the menial and dirty nature of their work marks them as working class. The considerable status which a farmer once derived from being an independent landowner has diminished as his land has become heavily mortgaged, but his greatest loss has been leisure. Even the big shots have had to give up the long winters of idleness which were the badge of their superiority. They've been pushed into cattle and hogs which are, by nature, grubby. On the white collar standard, a dirt farmer's way of

life, regardless of his intelligence or ambition, places him
at the bottom. His acute awareness of this is reflected in his
language, when he often half-mockingly refers to himself
as a "native" or a "peasant" from the "outback."

The closer a town is to major communications networks,
the more highly developed its awareness of civilized forms
of social distinctions. Biggar, on the main line of the CNR,
is very class-conscious. Because the urban style is based on
the triumphs of capitalism, it implies political views which
are either Liberal or Conservative. Biggar businessmen are
solidly Liberal; the farmers and most of the railroaders are
NDP. However, the dominance of agriculture in the economy of Saskatchewan and the political power of the NDP
have created an alternative elite; farmers may be at the
bottom of the urban capitalist hierarchy, but they're at the
top of the rural socialist hierarchy.

The enormous power of the rural establishment is reflected in the superstructure of the co-ops, credit unions, and
wheat pools which dominate Saskatchewan and which
provide the farmers with an alternative economy and give
them an exceptional sense of self-confidence and independence. The town is an alien presence which they regard
with deep suspicion and hostility. Like the railroaders, the
farmers often deliberately adopt subversive attitudes and
uncouth forms of behavior, not from shame or humility but
out of defiance and an obstreperous sense of their own
superiority.

Everybody argues politics. "Biggar," sighs a railroader's
wife, "is a CCF hotbed." The home constituency of both
M. J. Coldwell and former Saskatchewan Premier Woodrow
Lloyd, Biggar has voted CCF ever since the party was born.
The Depression radicalized Saskatchewan farmers. It proved
the Marxist analysis of the pioneer prairie radicals and
forced farmers to apply co-operative principles in a scramble
to save their skins. Many Biggar farmers look back on the
Depression with fond nostalgia. Deserted by the carpet-
baggers, ordinary farm people found themselves running
meetings, making speeches, and manipulating events which
controlled their own lives. The desert blossomed with
hundreds of little organizations that turned Saskatchewan
farmers into astute critics, clever debaters, and ruthless

infighters armed with a cynical but sophisticated analysis
of the Canadian system. Everything has been thought out
in Saskatchewan. Almost any farmer can sit down and give
you, in plain ungrammatical words, a complex and passionate assessment of the meaning of his own life and his
existential relationship with the rest of the world. There's
no bullshit in rural Saskatchewan, no fuzziness of thinking,
no smokescreen of meaningless platitudes. Biggar farmers
devour vast quantities of political tracts and thrive on
tedious meetings, triumphantly finding conspiracy and deceit
behind even the most obscure and innocuous statements.
With the obsession of medieval scholastics, they argue
endlessly about the fine points of agricultural legislation
and delight in calling down curses on the heads of their
political enemies. Iconoclastic, extreme, Biggar farmers are
far to the right of the Liberals and far to the left of the
NDP. "The Liberals," snorts one of them, "are the NDP in
slow motion." Looking with righteous contempt on the
strategems and compromises of the democratic process, they
occupy a political no-man's-land where the cross-fire of
mutually conflicting criticism is withering. "We believe in
reality!" thumps one very large, beefy farmer. "We don't
believe in fooling people. If I think something about you, I
tell you. We speak out. I don't do things because society
says I have to do it. I question everything. Call me an
individual anarchist, let's put it that way."

Many have dropped out of the National Farmers' Union
because they think it is too radical or not radical enough.
The local president, Doug Potter, runs around stamping
out brush fires of insurrection and calming wounded
feelings in the pub. "When we became militant," he says,
"it turned a lot of farmers off. Nobody wants to be obnoxious, you know, everybody wants to be friends. They won't
get on a tractor and go in a tractor demonstration. They're
embarrassed. Some farmer they know will point at them and
laugh. A lot of these guys, they came from European countries where they didn't have anything. They came out here,
got a piece of land and now they're going to hang on to
that piece of land if they have to kick and scratch and
tromp all over their neighbours.

"There's this old image of the farmer as a very peaceful,

passive individual with a great love for the land, for animals
and the growing of crops and a love for his fellow man.
Maybe that was true once, but that's all in the past. We
don't get tough enough. I'm opposed to violence myself, but
people will have to realize that not all of our farmers are
this way. They will use violence. Already there have been
things. . .tractors tampered with, a few burnings. This has
happened before in other countries. When you take the land
from the people, you have revolution."

A fat farmer strikes a chord on his guitar, and Doug
Potter breaks into a melodious chorus of "A White Sports
Coat and a Pink Carnation." The man next to him whispers,
"One of these nights, some of us are going to go out, we're
just going to go out and. . . ." The fat farmer raises his bottle
of beer. "To the Revolution!" he grins.

"Fuck Off" is scrawled in big black letters on the white
stucco wall of the Third Avenue United Church. It's been
there for weeks, since Hallowe'en. Nobody can be bothered
to wipe it off.

"Who cleaned the pumpkin off the church steps?"
demands a member of the board. No one knows.

Third Avenue United Church is very old and very dingy,
a cramped wooden building with a tiny, steep choir loft
and stained oak pews. The floor is tiled and the walls are
painted institutional blue. The membership is about 275,
but the congregation numbers a little more than 100. "It's
the church of the upper class," states a board member. "This
is where you can meet your boss. To many people it's
simply a business thing." The big shots are tightfisted. The
church struggles along on an annual budget of $16,000; the
minister is paid $6,000, but he gets a splendid new house
for free. It has no storm door. The minister is forced to
petition the board for one.

"It's not meant to have a storm door," states a member
of the board. The minister explains about the snow and the
wind. "A storm door would spoil the appearance," complains a tough-looking woman with henna hair and a determined jaw. The minister explains patiently about the flies.
A committee struck off at the previous meeting to inves-

tigate the problem reports that the local lumberyard is offering an aluminium door for $90. "Oh my word!" shrieks the woman. After a lengthy and detailed comparison of prices and models in both wood and aluminium, they decide on a standard model for $54; for another $5 they can have an angel on the door.

Third Avenue United Church has fallen on hard times. As a result of a deaf clergyman whom they finally pensioned off in 1970, they lost a lot of members to the Lutherans and the Church of God. In November 1971, the bank balance is $524.03, which is $300 more than the previous year.

"Men can't see the dirt the way a woman can," growls the tough woman looking around the basement with a beady eye, "but even a man can see the dirt down here!" The church janitor has been the principal topic at every board meeting for two years. The minister explains that the vacuum cleaner is broken.

"He either smartens up before the end of the year or we let him go," she grumbles.

The chairman of the maintenance committee reports that the janitor is paid only $1.50 an hour for ten hours a week. "It's his only source of income," pleads the chairman. "We've already cut his wages down once."

"It's a terrible weakness in a janitor if he can't see the dirt," states the woman emphatically.

"Is he a Jehovah's Witness?" asks a member of the board.

The town plumber and the furnace man refuse to do any work for the church or the Legion. "They say we're warmongering organizations," whispers a little old lady. "They're Jehovah's Witnesses."

Third Avenue United is one of about a dozen little churches which wage a ferocious religious war in Biggar. It's engaged in fierce competition with several fundamentalist sects who meet in converted schools and the Elks' Hall; the congregations shift from church to church depending on the personality of the minister but seldom number more than 50. Evangelistic pressure from the Witnesses has provoked the other ministers into an intense round of home visitations, prayer meetings, baptisms, solicitations, newsletters, counselling sessions, and kaffeeklatsches to seduce the lapsed and to prevent further defections. Each one has staked out his ground: the Lutheran pastor is good at music, the Church of God is strong on farmers, the Catholics have a big youth group, the Witnesses court the Indians, and the Baptist minister, Pastor Boymook, who tries to convert everyone he meets on the street, accosts even the United Church minister with "Are you *sure* that you know God?" The United Church minister, former railroader S. A. "Curly" Doan, faithfully attends coffee row every morning at the Canton Cafe. "I spend a lot of time with bereaved families," he says. He buries many people he has never met, because as the catch-all church, Third Avenue gets stuck with the funerals of the local unbelievers whose relatives, out of desperation, deal with the God who asks the least questions.

With the exception of the Anglican clergyman, who is cast in the Gothic mold, the competition has resulted in a glut of groovy ministers, intense, hip young men with white teeth and big smiles who are plugged into McLuhan and who talk reverently about "the media" as if it were the Holy Ghost. With an ingratiating style and a firm conviction that theology is public relations, they try to dazzle the community with pyrotechnic displays of relevance. The musical Lutheran writes a jivey column called "Creative Christianity" in *The Independent*, the young Catholic priest, Father "Bill," conducts a popular folk mass every Friday night, and Curly Doan broadcasts the Biggar news every day on the Rosetown radio station.

The United Church Women, seated in a prim circle of pastel pantsuits and peony prints, look with a jaundiced eye on Curly Doan as he bounds into the church basement lugging his huge tape recorder. Colorful posters pinned to the walls are ablaze with slogans: "What the World Needs Now Is — LOVE!" and "Come to Church — There's 'Soul Food' There!" Curly Doan beams and plugs in the tape recorder. "For our prayer," he says, "I'd like to play this song." The women dutifully bow their heads and close their eyes. A loud, up-tempo rock song bursts from the machine. "Come sing about looove," it wails, "chick-a-boom, chick-a-boom, chicka, chicka boom boom boom." The women never flinch or bat an eye. "We hush to Thee, hear us! Oh yeah!"

blares the song, "chick-a-boom, chick-a-boom, chicka, chicka boom."

Prayer over, the women get down to business. The president reports $5 in the bank. Surveying the meetings of the past year, she states that one member demonstrated candle making and another showed how to make a centrepiece out of used Christmas decorations. She urges the members to bring used clothing and stockings.

"Who is going to do the baking for the bazaar?" she demands. Bazaar business consumes more than an hour. The women are looking at their watches by the time Curly Doan is invited to give the lesson. He plays Simon and Garfunkel's "The Sound of Silence" on the tape recorder and distributes mimeographed sheets with the words. He asks them to discuss the meaning of loneliness, isolation, darkness. Silence. The women stare blankly at the sheets. Doan quotes McLuhan, talks about communication, and tries to get something going on the significance of the telephone. His words fall like pebbles into a pond. Silence. The women look at their watches. Upstairs the phone begins to ring. In desperation Doan turns to the CBC.

"All that filth!" cries one woman. "All that smutty language. That's our tax money that's paying for it! They should get rid of all that trash." The women mutter excitedly among themselves.

"If you'll excuse me, I must leave," apologises a middle-aged lady rising to her feet. "I'm late for my bridge game!" she whispers to a friend as she goes out. The meeting is over.

"I can't preach on deep theological subjects," says Curly Doan. "It's just a matter of discipline and exercise to attend worship." He announces a "contemporary" service for Sunday at 9:30 a.m. Nobody comes. However, he leaves the film projector up and takes his revenge by showing a dreadful little movie about mission work in Africa at the regular service at 11 a.m. The church is full. It's a special service. The local insurance salesman has donated an expensive gift to the church as a memorial to his late parents; this morning it is to be dedicated. The object rests at the front of the

church just to the right of the pulpit. It's on a metal trolley
and is covered with a grey plastic hood. The insurance agent
and his wife are seated nervously on special chairs against
the wall.

After the customary prayers and a tuneless hymn shrilled
by a choir of little girls in the loft, Curly Doan swishes
down from the pulpit in his black gown and stands beside
the object to be dedicated. He beckons the couple to
approach. They do so cautiously, almost on tiptoe, grouping
themselves around the metal trolley and gazing respectfully
at the grey plastic cover. The congregation is hushed. The
insurance agent clears his throat and produces a little slip
of white paper from his pocket. "Mr. Doan," he reads, "in
memory of Mr. and Mrs. J. C. Bielby, we ask you to receive
this Gestetner duplicating machine for the use of organizations within this church, and that you dedicate it for
service to Almighty God."

Laying his hands on the grey plastic cover, Curly Doan
replies: "On behalf of the church council and the congregation, I accept the Gestetner as a memorial to Mr. and
Mrs. Bielby and promise to use it in the church's service
to the glory of Almighty God." As he speaks, he slowly
raises the cover until with a flourish, he dramatically lifts
it and exposes the machine. "I dedicate this gift to the glory
of God, in the name of the Father and of the Son and of the
Holy Spirit! Amen!"

Class in Biggar is built on booze. Alcohol is a very sensitive
topic. People talk about it a lot, but with fear and suspicion.
The broken homes, violence, and poverty created by the
whiskey culture of the railroad have made liquor a powerful
taboo. Alcoholism is admitted to be a problem, but the local
AA is very much underground. Drinking is shameful. Since
everybody in Biggar drinks, it's not a matter of who does
and who doesn't, but where you are seen doing it. The big
shots do not go to the beer parlor; they drink at home. "I
know an 80-year-old alcoholic lady," sighs a minister. "I've
seen her sneaking bottles into her house. 'I don't drink,' she
says, 'I take pills that make me talk like thish.' " The line
of social demarcation is so clear it could be painted across

Main Street: a business or professional man will share a few drinks at the Legion, but he goes white at the thought of going to the pub. The problem with the pub is not drink, but the milling crowd of people that surges in and out. In order to preserve their position, the elite restrict themselves to private parties and clubs to which the membership is restricted. The most prominent businessmen and the influential farmers are Masons, descendents of the Orange Lodge, Biggar's most powerful organization in the days when the baker used to get dressed up in a uniform and a sword and ride his white pony down Main Street on the twelfth of July. The small merchants and clerks are Lions, and the railroaders are all Elks. "The Elks is just a poker dive," says one old railroader. "I joined 'em. Everybody did. If you want to go to dances and parties, you *have* to join."

"There's too damn many clubs," grumbles another railroader. "It's just an entertainment thing, a beer party. I used to belong to the Knights of Columbus. What a bunch of deadbeats! They'd sit around and discuss foolish things. Never did a bloody thing." Genteel social life in Biggar is limited to bridge parties and a winter round of club banquets, each one carefully restricted to its own exclusive membership.

The socialist farmers, of course, see the beer parlor as a bastion of proleterian equality. "The finest group of people you're likely to meet," says Doug Potter emphatically, "are in the beer parlor."

The social prestige of the United Church is derived from the temperance movement, which successfully combined the stigma of drunkenness with that of being poor, foreign and Catholic. Instigated by straight-laced Scotch Protestant clergymen who were shocked at the bawdiness and squalor of the frontier, the temperance crusade drew support from liberal social reformers who related drunkenness to poverty and inequality and who hoped, by stamping out booze, to stamp out the injustices of the capitalist system. The movement was taken up by evangelists who found it easier to rail against demon rum than to attack low wages, price gouging, and other forms of exploitation practiced by the corpulent businessmen who occupied their front pews. Supported by the rich and the powerful, who were able to profit from liquor through their influential contacts in time of drought, temperance was essentially an attack on the working class, an attempt to "clean up" the ruffians and to whip them into a semblance of respectability appropriate to a Christian and British nation. The prime motivation was profit. "We know that if the liquor business were abolished the people would buy more farm products, more of clothing, more of meat, more of flour, more of every commodity," wrote a business-man to the Biggar *Independent* in 1915. "The manufacturer of saloon bars will find his market gone but he will find a bigger market for household furniture opened. The man who makes beer and whiskey bottles will make milk bottles. People are going to buy more of the things they want, the necessities, comforts and luxuries of life and their buying will be enormously increased once the liquor traffic stops robbing them."

An economic crusade based on the theory that a sober man works harder than a drunk, temperance didn't take off until the outbreak of World War I, when as a result of defeats in France, it was convincingly argued that booze was sapping the vital bodily fluids of the nation. Abstinence became part of the war effort, a means of increasing effi-ciency and productivity, of saving money and bolstering morale, and the temperance cause was inextricably bound up with British imperialism: "At this time when the Empire is engaged in a titanic struggle for its very existence as well as for its honor," pleads the reeve of Mountain View municipality in *The Independent*, "it is our plain and sim-ple duty to banish the liquor store as a patriotic people."

By making drinking tantamount to treason, this kind of propaganda cast a glare of suspicion on the German, Slav, and other "foreign" immigrants who customarily drank wine or beer. Race prejudice formed a crucial argument in the Banish-the-Bar crusade, which, in a petition to the premier of Saskatchewan to close the bars, cited in addition to economy the following two reasons:

"On account of the mixed character of our population, brawls and riots are liable to break out in many places where these various nationalities frequent the bars.

"It is more than hinted that some of the bars are meeting places for our Empire's enemies and breeding places for sedition. This is intolerable. Surely the province cannot continue to license convenient centres for spies and plotters against the country's peace."

In Biggar, which had a large French, German, and Slavic population, the campaign to go dry was led by the Methodist Church and Dr. S. E. Shaw, who was also the mayor. Rousing meetings featuring musical entertainment and hell-fire speakers drew huge crowds to the Majestic Theatre and the little country schools. *The Independent* got on the bandwagon by putting out temperance "extras" and running testimonials from reformed drunks.

Temperance was a WASP movement and it played openly on the moral smugness of the British settlers by threatening their sense of racial purity and superiority. "The history of the liquor traffic teaches us that it has always corrupted and debased the physical, social, political, mental, domestic and moral life of men and nations!" wrote a Biggar resident in *The Independent*. But the doctors had the most convincing argument. "Science has shown that alcoholic liquors even in socalled moderation are causing degeneracy of the race," a medical expert stated in *The Independent*. "It means that every year we are breeding still more idiots, insane, feeble-minded, criminals etc. to be housed and fed. It is now an acknowledged fact that insanity started by drinking parents may spread to the third and fourth generations!"

Temperance hysteria profoundly split the Biggar community and initiated religious, ethnic, and class hatred which has kept the community tense and divided. Sensitive to the implied racial and moral slurs, the European immigrants correctly interpreted prohibition as a WASP grab for political power and economic control. They reacted with hostility. Since most of them were also working class and Catholic, the issue of drink contributed to labor solidarity (Biggar railroaders were unionized in 1917) and precipitated a feud between Protestant and Catholic which became increasingly bitter. As the Catholic paper *Le Patriote* put it: "The real suspicious feature of the whole affair comes when we consider the leaders of the Prohibition League. They are men, well-intentioned no doubt, and full of zeal for the cause, but at the same time they are in the main men filled with a virulent hatred for the Roman Catholic Church and all that belongs to it. They are those who have striven to destroy our Separate School System, who have assailed the doctrines of the Church, who have preached the 'one flag, one language' doctrine from the housetops, who class all Catholics as 'foreigners', who vaunt the superiority of the Anglo-Saxon, who parade their own loyalty and insinuatingly belittle the patriotism of the Catholics."

To combat the Protestant assault, the Catholics erected a rival establishment in Biggar which drew on solid support from a large French farming population. Biggar had a Catholic church as early as 1913, and the church ran a little seminary where a dozen promising sons of local farmers were trained for the priesthood. Four Grey Nuns opened a convent school in 1923. Along with the seminary and church, the convent was certainly the most impressive religious institution in Biggar. But the key to Catholic power was the hospital.

Aside from the pest house, Biggar had no hospital: maternity cases were boarded at the homes of midwives, and the sick were taken in by indigent housewives who claimed to have some experience in nursing. Biggar taxpayers had voted $10,000 for the construction of a hospital in 1911, but the proposal was shelved by the town council at the urging of the mayor, Dr. Shaw, on the grounds that hospitals do not pay. An attempt to organize a municipal hospital following the flu epidemic in 1919 was squelched for similar reasons before it came to a vote. The town's niggardliness paid off. In 1923 the Catholic priest converted the old Knights of Columbus hall into a 25-bed hospital, and it didn't cost the town a cent. Aside from the government grant — 50 cents per patient per day — St. Margaret's Hospital depended entirely on charity. Letters of solicitation were sent to surrounding towns and municipalities. "In my opinion," crowed Dr. Shaw, "it would pay the council of the town and those of the rural districts to make liberal and generous grants as they are lucky, since they got the best of the bargain." The town of Biggar came through with $200 for furnishings, but it hit the hospital with an annual tax bill. A little money came from patients and voluntary donations, but most of the revenue came from the Catholic Church, which financed the building and carried the debt.

The eleven nursing sisters were paid almost nothing, vegetables to feed both patients and staff were grown in the St. Gabriel's parish garden, the parish farm supplied the meat, and pillows were stuffed with feathers from the farm's chickens. The ladies' auxiliary raised the money to buy medical equipment through a barrage of bazaars, bake sales, flower sales, card parties, and begging.

St. Margaret's received no support from prominent Biggar Protestants, because most of them had joined the Ku Klux Klan. By 1928, the Klan had evolved into a predominantly anti-Catholic organization, an arm of the Orange Lodge and, through it, of the Conservative Party, dedicated to the extermination of parochial schools and the defeat of Jimmy Gardiner's Liberal government. It was essentially a political movement which used the tactics of religious and racial smear to destroy the credibility of the Liberals, who, since they had been in office during the influx of Catholic immigrants, were accused of being sell-outs to Rome. Since only 25 per cent of Saskatchewan's population was Roman Catholic, this tactic assured the Conservatives of the support of the majority of voters.

The recognized Klan leader in Saskatchewan was a defrocked priest named J. J. Maloney. Since Maloney was courting the daughter of Biggar's leading merchant, W. W. Miller, he made Biggar unofficial headquarters for the Klan. Maloney had come to Saskatchewan in 1926 to organize opposition to Prime Minister Mackenzie King, who was running in a by-election in Prince Albert; when the Klan's American organizers, Lewis Scott and Pat Emmons, absconded with the funds in 1927 and the principal speaker, Dr. J. H. Hawkins, was deported, Maloney took over Klan organization and rapidly built it up to a membership of about 40,000 in 109 Saskatchewan towns. Advertising himself as an "ex-priest" anxious to expose the corruption of the Catholic Church (his enemies claimed he had been expelled from an Ontario seminary for poor grades and "financial irregularities"), Maloney edited a newspaper called the *Western Freedman* and rocketed around Saskatchewan making speeches in movie theatres and community halls. A fiery and compelling orator, he held his audiences spellbound, lacing his rhetoric with enough sex and slander to titillate, but not offend, his listeners. His favorite topic was "The Dangers of the Confessional and the Unnatural Lives of Nuns and Priests."

"I went to one Klan meeting," recalls George Hindley, a CCF stalwart in Biggar. "It was in the hall in Watrous. It was a Sunday night. It was rather strange since in those days Sunday was more sacred than it is today. The hall was packed. Maloney got up to speak and he used all the tactics of a faker, a demagogue, a cheap evangelist, a cheap politician. He was just a cheap haranguer who knew how to appeal to a mob like old John Diefenbaker, and he's always a dangerous man. He would throw in enough religious phrases to make him sound as if he might be a man of God. He was fighting the Liberals, the Catholic Church and the Devil. He lumped them all together. He had a great gift of oratory. Why, he had Jimmy Gardiner literally by the throat, grasping him to death. You could see the old Tories chortling at Gardiner choking. Next, says Maloney, it will be the Pope. It was a masterful performance. He had the audience with him. I could see by the sparkle in their eyes how excited they were."

Maloney held numerous meetings in the Majestic Theatre and in the country halls around Biggar to incite prejudice against the French farmers and the Catholic school. "The feeling around here was very strong," says George Hindley. "It was a wicked feeling. Religion can really make things dirtier, muddier, stinking. Even the United Church minister was accused of being pro-Papist." The United Church minister, Rev. H. D. Ranns, was Maloney's most outspoken critic in Biggar. "They are making the most rash and extreme statements about public questions and about Jews, Catholics and foreigners," he wrote to Premier Gardiner in 1927. "The speaker on Monday evening told them that if they would join the Klan he would see to it that all Catholic teachers were out of the schools and all separate schools closed... They make the wildest statements about the Pope and some of our Roman Catholic people are boiling over and threatening reprisals." Rev. Ranns's opposition to the Klan so enraged the members of his congregation that he was forced to leave Biggar; the Orangemen broke away and opened the Presbyterian Church, a pretentious crumbling building on Main Street which is still known in Biggar as "the spite church."

Signs in Biggar windows declared: "We don't want Catholics"; "We don't want Jews." The Jews, who lived in a state of truce with both Protestants and Catholics, were afraid to send their children out into the streets. "Maloney drew them like honey," says a retired Jewish merchant bitterly. "It was all against Jews, Dogans, Niggers and Chinamen. There was no violence. No murders or anything like that. Just talk mostly. They had their meetings. It was quite open. The Orange Lodge had a sign in the window: 'Klansmen, I greet you.' "

"We all had our fire stations," says Joe Boisvert, who was a boarding student at the convent. "The nuns were afraid of the convent burning down."

The Klan became overtly political in 1928 with the selection of W. W. Miller, Biggar Klansman and now Maloney's father-in-law, as the Progressive Conservative candidate in the forthcoming provincial election. Owner of the town's largest general store, Miller was wealthy and powerful. "He was well-heeled," comments his Jewish rival, "but he had no brains. Catholics were some of his best customers. They stopped paying their bills. I talked to the priest about it. 'Father,' I said, 'what's going to happen to our town?' 'Oh, nothing at all,' he said. 'You just wait and see.' "

In the winter of 1928, Miller's store burned down. "I'm pretty sure it was set on fire," says Hugh Buchanan. "It was New Year's Eve," recalls a neighbouring merchant. "A cold night, about twenty below and a lot of snow. We heard the firebell ringing and the sirens going strong but we didn't pay much attention. Then we got a phone call that Miller's store was on fire. If we didn't get on top of our own building, it would burn down too. By twelve-thirty we were all at the store, trying to pour water over the roof to keep the sparks off. The fire chief begged Miller to let him break in and locate the source of the fire. 'No one breaks my place down,' says Miller. He was an obnoxious man. The place burned to the ground. Beaver coats, the best shoes, all in the water. He didn't know himself how much stuff he had." Another Biggar resident has a different version: "The fire chief was a prominent Catholic. A small fire broke out in the basement of Miller's store. The chief surveyed the situation and decided that it would be dangerous to open the doors or the whole block would go up in flames. He locked the building and posted guards. The building burned for three or four days. There was no insurance."

Miller put up a new store, a solid two-storey brick block that cost over $60,000 and is still the finest building in Biggar. It was a symbol of Klan power, which reached its peak in the election campaign of 1929. Although the Conservatives denied any association with the Ku Klux Klan, the Conservative leader, Dr. J. T. M. Anderson, was a frequent visitor to Klan gatherings, and the party's ties with the Orange Lodge were no secret. In Biggar, the Majestic Theatre was filled to overflowing with crowds anxious to hear Maloney speak on "Is it True that the Roman Catholic Church Runs the Liberal Party?" The Conservatives gained enormous popular support from ordinary people who found the moral righteousness of bigotry a way of punishing the Liberals for the hypocrisy of prohibition and the obvious patronage which greased the wheels of the party machine. "The Liberals had been in power for twenty years and never done anything!" snorts Joe Shepherd, owner of the Majestic. "They were so rotten — and they still are!"

On election night, a Conservative victory was celebrated in Biggar by the burning of a large cross in front of the Catholic convent. "The ringleaders wore sheets," recalls Leo Campbell, "white hoods with the eyes cut out. The others gathered to look on and cheer. They were not disguised. Some wore their Orange regalia."

W. W. Miller, MLA, went off to the legislature in Regina; the following year he was bankrupt. "Maloney borrowed money and Miller backed his notes," says Leo Campbell. "Money stopped coming in after 1930 and the Royal Bank foreclosed on Miller's store. They sold it to the hardware merchant, A. W. Mooney, for $10,000. Miller was so surprised I think he died of a heart attack."

Maloney, who had previously been hauled into court for non-payment of a printing bill, left town immediately after Miller's collapse. "He saw the Klan as a get-rich-quick scheme," says Leo Campbell. "Nobody knows what hap-

pened to the money that was collected." Between 1930 and
1933, Maloney successfully organized the Klan in Alberta.
In 1933 he was charged with theft and sentenced to two
months in jail. He returned to Saskatchewan in 1938 and
was arrested in Kitchener, Ontario, in 1940 on six charges
of false pretenses. According to M. J. Coldwell, CCF MP
for Biggar, Maloney "was picked up in British Columbia for
obtaining money by false pretenses, was jailed and I think
died under arrest or. . .a few years later."

The Klan collapsed in the Thirties, and the Conservatives
were defeated in 1935. "We had a good run and lots of fun
for a little over ten dollars," says one member. Although
it did little damage, the Ku Klux Klan was more than a
Hallowe'en prank. It was, in the words of one Klansman,
"the most complete political organization in the West." On
the framework of this organization was built the CCF.

*I once saw a codfish nailed to a telephone pole with
a couple of spikes and on it was written 'Vote CCF.'*

(Biggar farmer)

The CCF started organizing in the Biggar area early in the
Thirties. "The Thirties started people thinking, and that's
dynamite," says George Hindley, a Biggar farmer and
Congregationalist preacher who was one of the original
CCF organizers. "People were desperate. They were willing
to grasp at any straw. They were more tolerant of Communism than they are today. They realized that you have to
uproot the source of the trouble, and it was very plain that
the source was private enterprise."

Led by Anglo-Saxon socialists in the tradition of the
British labor movement, the CCF believed that enlightened
self-interest would lead to an almost immediate democratic
take-over of the Canadian government. The platform was
simple: socialization of all private industry in Canada,
including land. In the 1934 Saskatchewan election the CCF
gained 30 per cent of the rural vote and formed the official
opposition, yet the party leadership was devastated that they
had failed to win. When CCF support slipped the following

year in the face of inroads from Social Credit, the party adopted a program that contained no mention of socialism, and although many farmers welcomed state ownership of land as protection against the mortgage companies, the nationalization of land was dropped from the CCF platform. The socialist experiment in Saskatchewan was effectively dead by 1936, when the CCF established formal alliances with both Social Credit and the Conservatives. The party became a trade union, a farmers' pressure group out to win reforms.

"The CCF was built on fundamentalist religion and the demise of the old Conservative Party," states a doctor who is active in the Saskatchewan NDP. "A lot of people who had been active in Ku Klux Klan activities became quite active in the local CCF. I know of two people in the Biggar area."

"Oh, a lot of our supporters were Conservatives," says George Hindley. "You didn't have time to make converts. You had to get votes! That's one of the weaknesses of our movement. We haven't emphasized the slow buildup of an informed opinion."

The Ku Klux Klan taught Saskatchewan politicians a valuable lesson in community organizing. Klan rallies were a superb example of how, by great showmanship and tight control, a few men could gain power almost overnight. The CCF moved in and took over the grass-roots structure which the Klan had left almost intact; Tommy Douglas's campaign manager in the federal election of 1935 was a former Ku Klux Klan organizer, Daniel C. Grant. The CCF was at that time essentially a WASP movement. Douglas was a Baptist minister whose high moral tone and Biblical quotations went over well with a Protestant audience weaned on temperance meetings and Klan rhetoric. CCF leaders were preachers, teachers, and farm organizers who had risen to prominence in support of prohibition and social reform. The CCF was a middle-class movement. "A lot of people have the idea that a socialist is down and out," snaps George Hindley. "The wealthiest farmers I know are NDP. They're the thinking people."

The combination of Protestant and Communist overtones in the new CCF drove the Catholics into furious opposition and wedded them almost irrevocably to the Liberal Party. Like the Klan, the CCF championed the public school and Catholics were fearful that their parochial schools would be closed and Catholics fired from teaching jobs in the public schools. "A feeling built up that if the CCF got in, all the best of our heritage would be destroyed," laughs George Hindley. "The churches would be torn down, the convents would be closed and the nuns driven into the streets and forced to wear hot pants. A lotta people kind of believed it." This hostility provoked the CCF into a complete muffling of Marx and the substitution of a form of secular evangelism which cloaked the minor reforms of the CCF platform in the rhetoric of the Second Coming.

"The CCF was the greatest religious revival that ever took place," says George Hindley. "It made more impact on people's outlook than any religious effort. A lot of people would say I'm sacrilegious, but it's true."

The farmers' faith in the CCF deepened as the Depression worsened; the Liberals countered with hysterical threats about Communism. Since Liberal strength was centred in the small towns, whose merchants remained convinced that the source of their prestige lay somewhere in the mysterious East, political fundamentalism not only alienated Catholic and Protestant, businessman and working man, but also created profound antagonism between country and town. In spite of overwhelming CCF support in Biggar, this mistrust was not allayed by the CCF election victory in 1944 or by the personal popularity of Biggar's schoolteacher MLA, Woodrow Lloyd. Having precipitated a class war, the CCF had no means of eliminating the class structure, since all basic socialist principles had been deleted from their platform. Because they did not change the social structure, old hatreds have hardened and grudges inflamed by bitter election campaigns have been buried until circumstances offer an opportunity for revenge. Both sides have retreated into extreme positions from which they eye the enemy with baleful and passionate mistrust. Political debate has been submerged by a demand for absolute devotion to the cause and unswerving commitment to party ideology. Both Liberal and CCF factions are led by those people considered to be the most intransigent, the people who, in Biggar, are proudly known as "the hard core." Politics in Biggar is do or die, and everybody wears his party label loudly on his sleeve. "You can't talk to someone for ten minutes before they're trying to find out which way you're voting," says a disgusted newcomer. "The kids are fighting over politics on the school bus. With their fists! Some kids saw me going into a Liberal coffee party so they asked my little daughter if I was a Liberal. It's none of their damn business!" Although the boozing which used to enliven Biggar elections has disappeared, they're still dirty. Ken Foster describes his election to the town council: "The man running against me was another railroader. We was just two guys that had grown up in town, and I felt that when they counted the ballots there wouldn't be too many separating us one way or the other. I was a Liberal and he was NDP. Of course, they're very divided in this town and very dedicated. I like this. I like dedicated people. This is the thing that makes the wheels run. Well, I thought to myself, now we gotta do a lotta hustling around here. Every vote's gonna count. I'm lookin' around to figure out where I'm gonna get these votes and I thought, now I'm goin' up to the hospital and get the sisters down to vote. Make sure they get down there. And they won't get down unless you take them. So I got hold of a fellow, a hoghead [engineer] down here, and he went up and rounded up the sisters and sure enough, five minutes before the poll closed, in come the sisters from the hospital and the ones from the school. After the poll closed and they counted the votes, I was clappin' my hands. I only won by ten votes! Haw haw haw haw!"

Fueled on racial and religious grudges nursed for more than 40 years, political strife in Biggar erupted into a bitter class feud during the doctors' strike in 1962.

Small town medicine is primitive. The prairie frontier towns had plenty of doctors, but most of them were there because they had been run out of wherever they had been before. Drunks, charlatans, soldiers of fortune interested mainly in peddling prescription booze for "medicinal purposes," many of them drifted from village to village, enlivening the social life of the town with their penchant for gambling, horse racing, and good living. When they settled down they usually turned into town characters, highly respected for their eccentricity if not for their medical skill. Nobody put much faith in medical skill anyway. Most people relied on home remedies or the patent medicines which were advertised in the local newspaper:

> Miller's Worm Powders are par excellence the medicine for children who are found suffering from the ravages of worms. They immediately alter the stomach conditions under which worms subsist and drive them from the system.

An incredible array of pills, powders and nostrums was peddled to cure everything from flatulence and depression to old age:

> WOMEN WHO ARE ALWAYS TIRED
> May Find Help in this Letter:
> "I cannot speak too highly of your medecine. When through neglect or overwork I get run down and my appetite is poor and I have that weak, languid, always tired feeling, I get a bottle of Lydia E. Pinkham's Vegetable Compound and it builds me up, gives me strength and restores me to perfect health again. It is truly a great blessing to women."
> WOMEN FROM 45 TO 55 TESTIFY TO THE MERIT OF LYDIA E. PINKHAM'S VEGE-TABLE COMPOUND DURING CHANGE OF LIFE!

This kind of amateur competition was good for the druggist but not for the doctor, who seldom made much money and

was often forced into other schemes to acquire the standard
of living to which he felt he was entitled. Such a man was
Dr. Shaw. As well as being mayor of Biggar, Dr. Shaw was
a prime shareholder in the fraudulent Biggar land boom of
1912 and he actually built a few houses on the west end of
town in an area called Shawville. The development didn't
amount to much, so he ploughed most of his property under
to raise prize-winning alfalfa. Dr. Shaw was an unmistak-
able presence in Biggar. "He had a stomach on him like
that!" says Hugh Buchanan, holding his hand about three
feet out from his waist. "He was awful rough. I think he'd
been a doctor on a ship. He drove one of those old Fords
with the brass radiator and the crank. His wife would make
meals for him to take to the patients. You'd see him going
along, driving with one hand, the other arm hanging out
the window holding a pot of stew." Dr. Shaw also carried
a hot water bottle full of whiskey to sustain himself on his
rounds. "To tell you the truth, he wasn't much of a doctor,"
says Joe Shepherd. "Most people took care of themselves
or died quick."

In spite of his failings, or because of them, the country
doctor was much beloved. "If the doctor is great, there's
nothing he can't do," says a surgeon who used to practice
in Biggar. "If he can take out a gallbladder with his left
hand tied behind his back he's a greater hero. In most of
these small towns in Saskatchewan the biggest industry is
the hospital and health care, so it's one of the dominating
facts of life in a small town. This type of attitude leads
many small town doctors to do a lot of things they're really
not trained to do or capable of doing. And it makes for poor
medicine. They do operations they really don't have to do.
A professional man says something and who has any training to contradict him? When I was in Biggar there was
hardly anybody who had an appendix, a gallbladder, a
thyroid or tonsils. Even now there are areas in this province
where the hysterectomy rate is five and six times that of
Saskatoon and where the tonsillectomy rate is ten or twelve
times higher. There's an area of southern Saskatchewan
where the appendectomy rate must be the highest in the
world! Nobody can convince me that there's an area of this
province where acute appendices occur twelve times as

often as in Saskatoon. Where there is room for evil, evil is done." Prior to medicare, the difficulty of collecting their bills dampened doctors' enthusiasm for surgery, but it did not prevent many of them from "booming" certain types of unnecessary surgery when an epidemic scare ran through the community.

Because of the mysterious nature of his profession and his intimate personal relationship with his patients, a successful country doctor is elevated to a position of almost religious respect. His triumphs are hailed as miracles, his mistakes are forgotten. As he grows old and the children he has brought into the world have babies of their own, he becomes midwife and spiritual godfather to the entire community. "When a country doctor becomes isolated and pre-occupied with making money," says the surgeon, "he becomes a danger." His power extends to other areas of the community, to politics, the church, real estate, and education as people automatically make way for him, not so much out of regard for his medical diploma as from fear of death or the shame of unpaid bills. Medicare was introduced into Saskatchewan in 1962 not only to improve health standards but also to relieve the population of its indebtedness to the country doctor. Well-intentioned and accustomed to veneration, the doctor is usually oblivious to the fact that his patients possibly harbor resentment towards the empire he has constructed out of their misfortune.

Dr. Allan Hooge practiced in Biggar for 24 years before the medicare crisis destroyed his career in 1962. He came there in 1938 from Rosetown at the invitation of a citizens' committee. Dr. Shaw had died and Biggar had only two doctors. "Dr. Gardiner was dying of cirrhosis of the liver," reflects Dr. Hooge, "and Dr. Brace was not too capable. I went into practice on my own. There was more money in Biggar. It was a mixed farming area and people paid me with chickens or a side of beef or a little money from the cream and egg cheques. In Rosetown the pay was practically nothing. In 1937 the government paid all the doctors $100 a month. There was no other way that we could keep our offices open. Those years were really rough. Dr. Brace left in 1939 and from then until 1945 I was the only doctor in the area.

"People didn't go to the doctor with trivia. They were *really sick* . You didn't have an annual checkup. There were no antibiotics, no antihistamines or miracle drugs. Pneumonia was an almost fatal disease. People were not as concerned about their health. They relied on farmers' remedies — mustard plasters and poultices. The druggist was also a person who was held in great respect. There was no vet so the druggist carried all the vet's supplies and recommended treatment for cattle problems. So people would ask him what to do for a cough and he'd prescribe for them. A lot depended on how greedy he was.

"The hospital left a great deal to be desired. It was a converted Massey-Harris machine shed, a conglomeration of buildings thrown together down on Second Avenue where the liquor store is now. The roof leaked and when it rained water poured in all over the place. It had the oldest X-ray machine in Canada and a very old operating table. The operating room was just a little room on the second floor with a fifty-watt bulb. Patients were carried up the narrow stairwell on stretchers.

"Appendicitis was a very common disease. It would be rare if you didn't have an acute appendix once a week. It was a constant nightmare. People were very reluctant to go to doctors unless it was absolutely necessary. Children's tummyaches weren't taken very seriously and if you got them after perforation had taken place, you ran into very serious problems. Appendicitis was one of the commonest causes of death in young people.

"I never felt that the people had any fear of doctors. I felt that I was appreciated and respected. People were very loyal. If you looked after one generation you looked after the next; if you had treated a person well twenty-five years ago he was consistent in coming to you. Farmers were the most faithful and the most reliable and the best paying clientele I had in my practice. I got to know the background of practically every family. I knew whether they were neurotic, whether they ever went to a doctor, whether if they complained you'd better listen. You got to know the background and the tendencies of the whole country. You knew who was going to call you at midnight, on your afternoon off, at suppertime. Doctors were much happier before medicare, when people didn't have any insured service. I knew all my people. I knew if Jones came in, he was hard up. 'I know you can't afford it,' I'd say. He'd usually insist on paying something. 'Well,' I'd say, 'if you want to leave a buck, OK, but I won't bill you.' You never entered a minister's call on your ledger. Nurses, sisters, you just wouldn't charge.

"The knowledge tended to become terribly personal. It became personal to the point where you were close friends. If your patient developed gallstones, you felt so close that you hated like the dickens to do the gallbladder. Of course he insisted that he wouldn't have anyone else. People put you up on a pedestal. Whatever the problem was, alcoholism, a marriage on the rocks, they came to the family doctor. There was a lot of psychosomatic illness. People would come to you with physical complaints. You'd take a history, do the whole routine. After you were at the game for a while you'd find out that the symptoms didn't jibe at all. You'd come right out and say, 'Would you mind telling me what the problem is?' They'd open up and the whole story would pour out. Often the solution was simple and you could clear up a situation in one sitting. There were a tremendous number of psychological and psychiatric problems. I had to learn psychiatric techniques because there was no way I could get people to go to a psychiatrist in Battleford or Saskatoon. There wasn't the same stigma in coming to me. I was always a good listener. There were days when I never got home for supper. Once someone broke down and started to tell you all their problems, you couldn't shut it off in half an hour. I enjoyed surgery but I think my greatest contribution was in the field of psychological counselling. The concern for people and their problems was more important than taking out a gallbladder or doing a hysterectomy. Appendices, of course, were my bread and butter."

Dr. Hooge was popular and his practice thrived. By 1962 he had formed the Biggar Medical Clinic in partnership with Dr. L. G. Dunbar, the son of a local railroader, and two young doctors who were hired on salary. The Hooge clinic was the only medical service in Biggar. Dr. Hooge was also chairman of the school board, a position he had held for more than 20 years, a member of the United Church choir and board of stewards, a past Master of the Masonic Lodge, a Kinsman, and past president of the Biggar Liberal Association. The most powerful person in Biggar, he was the acknowledged leader of the small coterie of wealthy businessmen who dominated the school board, the town council, and the hospital board and who formed the nucleus of the embattled Liberal Party. The only man in the community who outranked Dr. Hooge was Premier Woodrow Lloyd, the Biggar MLA and education minister who had taken over leadership of the Saskatchewan NDP in 1960. "The only way that Woodrow Lloyd could lose an election was by running amok in the streets," snaps a Liberal.

Premier Lloyd announced in the spring of 1962 that medicare would go into effect on July 1, 1962. The doctors immediately threatened to strike. Sensing an opportunity to make political mileage, the Liberals latched on to the popularity of the family doctor and launched a "Red scare" campaign in the hopes of defeating the government and riding back into power on a wave of populist support. The strategy was familiar to those who had witnessed the Conservative victory of 1929, and the tactics were the same — racial smear, innuendo, and mob hysteria. Nowhere in Saskatchewan did the Keep Our Doctors campaign create more strife and bitterness than in Biggar, where Dr. Hooge had come to occupy the position of prestige and influence once enjoyed by W. W. Miller.

As the CNR declined, the economic importance of St. Margaret's hospital and the medical clinic to Biggar increased. When, in March and April of 1962, the doctors began threatening to pull out of Saskatchewan, Biggar residents foresaw the collapse of both the hospital and the clinic and, as a consequence, the death of the town. Biggar's Liberal businessmen stampeded into a passionate attack on the provincial government led by Lloyd Hock and the Biggar *Independent*, which inflamed public opinion with scurrilous rhetoric cloaking veiled threats in the language of racial hatred: "Just wait," warned the issue of April 19, 1962, "until sometime in the future when you go to see your doctor and find out he has left the province and in his place will be a coal black witch doctor from darkest Africa with his mumbo jumbo and rattles!"

Early in May, a sign went up in the Biggar clinic as it did in every doctor's office in Saskatchewan:

TO OUR PATIENTS
THIS OFFICE WILL BE CLOSED AFTER
JULY 1ST, 1962
WE DO NOT INTEND TO CARRY ON PRACTICE
UNDER
THE SASKATCHEWAN MEDICAL CARE
INSURANCE ACT.

"We simply can't work under a state controlled medical scheme," stated Dr. Hooge. "We will close the clinic. We will leave the province." Nobody took Dr. Hooge's threats too seriously. He had spent all his working life in Biggar. He had built St. Margaret's hospital into an institution which, while it wasn't accredited, was respectable and a place where people felt secure. He had encouraged his patients to depend on the doctor and cared for them conscientiously. People considered him to be their friend. Dr. Hooge knew that Biggar was an NDP hotbed and that most of his patients ardently supported medicare. He made no secret of his commitment to Biggar. "When I settled there," he says, "I settled there for good. It was not a matter of packing up and getting out after I'd made so much money. I wanted to live in Biggar." He assured his patients that after July 1, two doctors would be stationed in Biggar for emergency service.

By June, the anti-medicare campaign had been swept out of the doctors' control by the Keep Our Doctors committee, a grass-roots organization founded by a group of hysterical Regina housewives which quickly became a front for the Liberal Party and the anti-Communist rhetoric of Ross Thatcher. On June 10, a branch of the KOD was formed in Biggar. Its leading members were real estate agent Glen Clements, the two druggists, and Bill Morphy, the editor of *The Independent*. All were prominent Liberals and members of the Biggar Chamber of Commerce. Chairman was Lloyd Hock, the son of Max Hock, co-partner in Hock and Packer,

which, since the demise of W. W. Miller, had become
Biggar's largest general store. Armed with an 800-name
petition supporting the doctors, Hock presented a brief to
Premier Lloyd on June 13 which demanded that the government resign for "causing anxiety to expectant mothers."
The KOD strategy was to blame the government for the
mass panic which it was deliberately inciting through a
campaign of political vilification, intimidation, and racism.
(The KOD stress on motherhood reflected a familiar concern with racial purity and the "sanctity of white woman-
hood." One placard at a KOD rally featured a caricature of
a doctor with a large Semitic nose, a Chinese pigtail, and
Oriental clothing, which carried the slogan: "Sask. Gov't
Medicare Import.") "When a bunch of lying, two-bit politicians start to use their powers to threaten our honorable
and dedicated doctors...it is time we got rid of them,"
stated *The Independent*. The alternative, it said, was "some
strange gook doctor from a foreign country." The druggists
took out a bold-faced ad in the paper reminding people that,
after the strike was on, prescriptions for restricted and
essential drugs could not be refilled without the authority
of a physician. The ad created a run on the drugstores. "I
did the biggest business ever!" crowed pharmacist Ivan
Leslie. The financial advantages of the scare were not lost
on the doctors: the Biggar clinic was crowded every day
and every bed in St. Margaret's hospital was occupied.

As tension in the community increased, the doctors
became militant and hostile to their patients. On June 14,
Dr. Hooge announced that there would be no emergency
doctors in Biggar after July 1. On June 21, the doctors
tendered their resignations to St. Margaret's effective June
30. In a "farewell" statement June 28, the doctors stated
they deeply regretted "that we have no choice but to
withdraw our services. The disaster which threatens to
descend on July 1, 1962 is not of our making." On June 30,
22 patients were dismissed from St. Margaret's. Commented
one of them: "They chased me out of the hospital. Everyone
on his feet was chased out. Now I have to suffer and the
government is to blame!" The clinic closed at 6:30 p.m. At
midnight the doctors were on strike.

The farmers were shocked that Dr. Hooge would abandon them. At first they had blamed the KOD cabal for the political strife, but now everything fell into place. Said one farmer: "Ever since we settled these prairies sixty years ago we have been skinned by grain companies, fleeced by packing companies, cheated by farm machinery companies, tricked by politicians and plagued by drought and grasshoppers. These doctors are nothing new. We will win, the way we won the fight with the Grain Exchange."

An emergency doctor saw 20 patients at St. Margaret's over the Dominion Day weekend and made six house calls. "Some weren't sick at all," the doctor said. "They were simply afraid."

"The doctors had scared people," says Hazel Newton, a railroader's wife who had worked in Dr. Hooge's office. "Every time you saw them they would tell you the dreadful things that would happen. It was especially hard on the old people. One old lady had her car sitting out on the front street in case of emergency. It was an absolutely beastly time."

On July 4, Roy Atkinson, president of the Saskatchewan Farmers' Union, assembled 65 farmers at the Oxborough community hall just outside Biggar. The meeting unanimously agreed to form the Biggar and District Citizens' Medical Health Association with the intention of opening a citizens' clinic in Biggar staffed by doctors willing to work under medicare. A committee was appointed to canvass for the money needed to equip the clinic; $4,000 was pledged at the meeting. Within two days, the citizens' clinic had raised $40,000. The citizens immediately asked the doctors to practice under medicare.

All the doctors answered no. The citizens' clinic was endorsed by 250 people at a mass meeting in the Biggar town hall on July 9, and the following morning it opened an office in a dingy little room behind a barber shop on Main Street and began advertising for members. Dr. Hooge was astonished that Mrs. Newton, a friendly and mild-mannered woman, was on the board of directors. "My dad was from Sweden," she explains. "We heard medicare at home all the time. 'Who's going to pay this b——'s bills?' I remember how my parents used to dread calling the doctor. You had to be just about dead. I always said these guys would not pull out. I stuck up for them until they actually left."

In a letter to *The Independent* the doctors accused the citizens' clinic of raising money "by misrepresentation, falsehoods and by playing on the sympathies of the widowed and the elderly." On July 19, a KOD-sponsored "Doctors' Appreciation Night" drew a huge crowd to the town hall where the four Biggar doctors were the guests of honor. Stating that the strike was the only course open for those who "cherish freedom," Dr. Hooge thanked the KOD for their "magnificent support in this vicious struggle." He blamed the opposition on an "ill-informed minority" who refused to reject socialist dogma.

The clinic was a rallying point not only for the NDP hard core but for everyone who was offended by the doctors' attitudes and the KOD. Membership quickly grew to more than 400, and when Mrs. Adam Dunbar, the formidable president of the local I.O.D.E., offered to manage the office free of charge, the KOD faded away, leaving Lloyd Hock holding the bag. Glen Clements informed the citizens' group that the Biggar clinic would be available for purchase, but instead they took up the offer of a local railroader who volunteered to rent his new home as a temporary clinic for $125 a month. By July 19, the clinic was incorporated and the services of two British doctors had been secured.

The Biggar big shots were appalled that farmers and working men would have the audacity to openly rebel against their traditional authority. "Where would people like *you* ever get doctors?" scoffed Mayor Lionel Jones. With the establishment of the clinic, the medicare conflict in Biggar moved beyond a political squabble into a revolt. "There was a real clique in Biggar running things," says Mrs. Newton, "Dr. Hooge, Lionel Jones and all their friends. We were fighting against all the people who were leaders. They never dreamed we'd stand up to them."

"The old guard had run the town for years," says Earl Danychuk, chairman of the citizens' clinic. "It even hurt some of them to think they were challenged. Biggar had been stable for a lot of years. They had called the tune. Now here was this new group who had moved up economically and were out to try their wings. It was a confrontation that had to come." The strike gave the farmers and railroaders a sense of solidarity they had not shared since the Thirties, and the ferocity of the doctors' attack on the government heightened their awareness of democratic principles. The clinic became a symbol of democracy and, as its popularity increased, a power base from which they could potentially overthrow the social hierarchy and take over the town.

Panic-stricken by this threat to their power, the business elite reacted with a campaign of vicious slander and personal vilification. The citizens' clinic was called a "Red camp." Roy Atkinson was beaten up on Main Street and people canvassing for clinic memberships were met with threats and insults. A canvass of Main Street produced three donations — the shoemaker and two garage owners.

"I kept my mouth shut," says Hugh Buchanan, who owned the meat market on Main Street. "I would go down to the store and my stomach would be in a knot. I'd be afraid to say anything for fear of hurting someone's feelings and nobody would say anything to me. It was terrible. They were arguing even in the store, in front of the counter!

"Husbands were separated from their wives, old friends weren't speaking to each other. Oh, you have no idea how it was. Even in church. In church everyone always sits in the same seats. Well, the Liberals would go and sit in the CCF pews and the CCF would have to find another seat!"

The United Church minister, who supported medicare, accepted another call in June, and the new minister was chosen on the basis of his support for Dr. Hooge. "The church was deeply disturbed," says Curly Doan. "Many people left the church over medicare and they have never returned."

"There was a black shadow of hatred hanging over the community," says Leo Campbell. "You could feel it. You never knew just who you were talking to or whether they were death against you. It was very much the same as the Ku Klux Klan. I believe the animosity was a carry-over. There was enough of it still alive that they copied it and used it to their advantage. It will not die until all those old participants have died and it will have left a few roots that will carry on yet."

On July 23, the doctors accepted medicare. The strike was over. That evening the Biggar Citizens' Clinic opened its doors.

"This town has had many disputes in the past," said a farmer after the strike was over, "but this time the knife was in a little deeper." Biggar began to feel the pain when people quietly started to leave. The dentist, who had only just come, left. The three junior doctors in the Hooge clinic found jobs elsewhere. Harry Specter sold The Golden Rule clothing store on Main Street to the citizens' clinic and retired on the profits. Reuben Packer, distressed by the loss of customers during the strike, sold out to Max Hock and went to the West Coast. Business didn't pick up. Clinic supporters patronized drugstores in Saskatoon and dealt at the Biggar Co-op. One druggist left town. Max Hock was forced to close down his grocery section; Lloyd Hock was told to keep his mouth shut. Lionel Jones's hardware business, which occupied W. W. Miller's doomed building, dwindled by a third. "We *still* can't bring ourselves to go into Jones' store," says Hazel Newton, who has been secretary of the citizens' clinic since it was formed. *The Independent*, flooded with cancelled subscriptions, was hard hit by loss of advertising as a result of the business boycott. Caught flat-footed by the doctors' capitulation to medicare, the leading KOD spokesmen shamefacedly denied having had anything to do with the organization and looked with a certain cool reserve on Dr. Hooge, who had hung them out on a limb which threatened to plunge them into bankruptcy.

A lot of Dr. Hooge's oldest patients said they'd die on the street before they'd go back to him. His stature in the community destroyed and his practice eroded away by the handsome young doctor in the rival clinic, Dr. Hooge retired from Biggar for reasons of ill health in 1966. "My image certainly took an awful beating," he says bitterly. "The image of the doctor was very badly smeared and spoiled when medicare came in. It was the socialists that rammed it through. It was politics. It created an awful lot of unnecessary bitterness. There was nothing I could do about it. I felt like walking out on the whole thing.

"My practice didn't suffer. I did have mixed feelings about people I had befriended who suddenly became my enemies for nothing I had done. During the strike I worked at the hospital free of charge. I couldn't see my people suffer. Then I went back to work and I was a heel because I wouldn't work at a community clinic! As far as I was concerned the community clinic was some type of fuzzy ideology, the way the Communists have an ideology. In practice it doesn't work. Can you picture me after twenty-five years turning my office over to a group of *lay people*?"

A bewildered, lonely man, Dr. Hooge lives in a beautiful home in Saskatoon; he returns to Biggar occasionally for the funerals of close friends. He is puzzled about why his life in Biggar was ruined. "I burnt $40,000 in bad debts when I left," he offers. "I didn't turn one dollar over to a collection agency."

"I feel sorry for Dr. Hooge," says Hazel Newton, her freckled face full of anguish. "It was like Thatcher. We didn't want him around, but we didn't want him to *die*."

The citizens' clinic soon had more than half the business in Biggar. It reached the peak of its success in 1967, when it had three doctors and 700 members. But by then it was a community clinic in name only. "The doctors worked for wages at the beginning," explains Mrs. Newton, "but after they could see that they were bringing in a lot of business they wanted to buy our clinic. There was no way we wanted to have another private clinic sitting on the corner!" A compromise was reached: the clinic supplied the equipment and charged the doctors rent, and the doctors pocketed the profits.

To a certain extent the clinic board felt they had to offer the doctors an incentive, because Biggar was not a pleasant place to live. The clinic doctors were shunned or actively persecuted by half the town population. Two doctors were denied operating privileges at St. Margaret's, where the nuns remained fiercely loyal to Dr. Hooge. The clinic received no money and no administrative assistance from the provincial government, and there was no attempt to develop the

kind of services which distinguish a community clinic from
a private operation.

As a result the Biggar community clinic was ripped off by
a succession of young doctors who used its facilities and
ready-made practice to save enough money to buy a practice
of their own. Few of the doctors lasted more than two or
three years, some stayed only a few months. "These guys
were out for the money," says Mrs. Newton bitterly. "There
were no two ways about what they were here for." The
doctors' greed weakened popular faith in the clinic; some
board members began to advocate selling it. Intimidated by
the doctors, the citizens' committee was quickly reduced to
the humble position of landlord. "Lay people working with
medical people is a very, very difficult situation," says Mrs.
Newton. "Unless you can get a doctor who's a socialist-
minded man, it's just not going to work. And a socialist
doctor is a very rare bird."

The last doctor left in April 1971, taking most of the
clinic's equipment with him, and the Biggar citizens' clinic
closed its doors.

There is nothing in Biggar to indicate that the town is, or
ever has been, a socialist hotbed. "We muffed it," shrugs
Earl Danychuk. "It was all in our hands and we could have
carried on through. Even in terms of controlling the town
council. We ran a full slate of NDP candidates in 1963 but
none of them got in. A lot of blue-collar workers voted
against them. You have to recognize, you can change the
administration but it might cost you dollars. Railroaders
who are making $10,000 a year think conservative. They're
pretty shrewd. In the end, I had to admire the businessmen."

The co-ops, credit unions, and pools have become profit-
oriented enterprises; the Biggar co-op has refused to support
the Kraft boycott because the manager fears it would cut
into business. For a community which has voted passion-
ately CCF-NDP for almost 30 years, Biggar is lacking in
even rudimentary social services. St. Margaret's hospital is
a disgrace. In an attempt to force private hospitals out of
business, the CCF government began cutting back on its

grants to St. Margaret's in 1947. The sisters stubbornly hung on until St. Margaret's went bankrupt in 1967 and was refinanced as a tax-supported municipal hospital. The result of this financial squeeze is a crumbling, impoverished hospital and third-rate medical care for Premier Lloyd's loyal constituents. (In November 1962, twelve babies were born at St. Margaret's in one week. Since the hospital had only eight bassinets, one baby had to be placed in the incubator, two in plastic laundry baskets, and one in a wire grocery cart.) This callous policy created understandable bitterness among Catholics and supporters of St. Margaret's, who consequently heartily endorsed the doctors' strike.

Scrupulous about pork-barrelling, Woodrow Lloyd was careful not to locate any government offices in Biggar; therefore Biggar has no civil service establishment of the sort that has proved such a boon to small communities in Conservative and Social Credit provinces. Rather, the centralization of government in Regina and Saskatoon has accelerated the decline of rural Saskatchewan to an extent much greater than in the rest of the prairies. A strong advocate of school consolidation, Lloyd began to close down rural schools in 1944. The closing of the small schools encouraged the collapse of rural communities and brought on a vast rural exodus. The process of rural decay which is just beginning in Manitoba and Alberta is a generation ahead in Saskatchewan.

Consolidation did not give the CCF any control over local school boards, which were quickly taken over by Liberals who carefully screened the teachers to keep out "Reds" and made sure that nothing smacking of socialism was taught in the school. "The board's concern is mostly morals," says a Biggar teacher. "They're worried about immoral books in the school library. There was a big ruckus over *Barometer Rising*. I don't know if they're really concerned morally or if it's just prejudice. They feel the law is too lenient on young people. 'Throw 'em in jail!' they say. 'Hang 'em! Get rid of 'em.' No way could you ever raise the topic of the Ku Klux Klan or the strike in class! It's just not done. Hell, these kids can go all the way through school without even taking a course in Canadian history!"

The impact of socialism on the school system has been

considerably less than that of the I.O.D.E., which has made
sure that every school for miles around is equipped with a
flag and a large framed photograph of the current king or
queen. The Daughters of the Empire kept a particularly
close watch on schools in "foreign" areas around Biggar,
and a battalion of matrons descended on any little school
which seemed to be wavering in its allegiance. An investigating committee was sent out to Louvain School in 1938 to
help correct the unpatriotic feeling. "We had heard that a
local dance band had refused to play 'God Save the King,' "
says Helen Little who, at 80, is a 50-year charter member.
"We took them a flag and some books. We got them
straightened around." The chapter "adopted" the school and
immediately required an essay on "Patriotism" from all the
pupils. "It was a Ukrainian area," says Mrs. Little severely.
"They had lost all their patriotism!"

The present chairman of the school board, Jake Singer,
is also reeve of the municipality and chairman of the
hospital board, a monopoly which indicates the extent of
political apathy around Biggar. Municipal politicians are
just as reactionary and tightfisted around Biggar as they are
in the most conservative areas of the prairies and all of them
are elected by acclamation. The failure of the NDP to
change either the economic structure of Saskatchewan or
the attitudes of its residents has resulted in a rural population which is more conservative and more cynical than it
was 60 years ago. "We used to have men who were informed
socialists," says George Hindley wistfully. "They had excellent libraries. We haven't concerned ourselves with changing
people's minds, but just with the number of votes we could
get. Once the party was organized, we had to have some
objective and that objective was to get votes. We tried to
appear more respectable. I'm sure we didn't gain anything
by it."

The Biggar constituency NDP association has 900 members. After enormous struggle and much prompting from
head office, they managed to produce five insignificant
resolutions for the party's 1971 convention. "We haven't
got people educated to making resolutions," chirps Bea
Brown, constituency secretary and centre of the hard core.
"It's really not working." For an election, the Biggar NDP

can produce $10,000 overnight; between elections, the NDP Women's Club spends its time catering for weddings. "It's our social life," beams Mrs. Brown. "I never talk politics. I never 'politick.' If someone has a problem and wants to contact the MLA, then I hear from them. We don't want commotion. We want peace and quiet and let's get on with progress! I don't think the old hard core are as radical as at the start of the CCF. We learned quite a bit over the years. At one point we were going to take over everything! We've learned that there are only certain things you can nationalize. The rest has to be done on a free enterprise basis. We like to feel that we're very flexible."

The NDP is so flexible that all the farmers voted for the Liberals in 1964 because Ross Thatcher promised them purple gas. "The NDP is just a great big bureaucracy," scoffs Danychuk. "The word comes down from Father and everybody jumps. The NDP is a conservative party."

"I am a Waffle!" rumbles George Hindley, waving his gnarled old finger in the air. "For fifty years I've been a Waffle. For fifty years I've been hearing the same things — poverty, slums, unemployment. It never changes because the cause never changes. Radical socialism is the only answer. I don't mean Communism, but then it isn't so bad, and if it comes to that, then OK!"

Biggar is quiet on the surface, but its silence is based on the superstition that if you don't talk about something it will go away. The doctors' strike is still so fresh in Biggar's memory it might have happened yesterday. Many people talk of it in whispers; the Main Street businessmen who were active in the KOD almost faint when the topic is raised and refuse to discuss it under any circumstances. Business is continuing to drift away to Saskatoon, and many farmers, like the Taylors, make a point of going to Biggar as little as possible. A pathetic attempt has been made to improve relations through an annual Rural-Urban Day in which farmers and businessmen sit down to discuss their mutual problems; the seminar simply produces a torrent of grievances, and since most of the suggested improvements would require the town to spend money, they are quietly shelved.

The most radical organization in Biggar is the I.O.D.E.,
which, in between collecting white elephants and knitting
vests for Eskimo children, sent off a telegram condemning
the American nuclear blast on Amchitka Island. The most
popular group is the Mutual Benefit Society, a pre-paid
funeral plan. A lot of organizations have collapsed. "You
call a hundred people for a meeting," complains the president of the defunct chamber of commerce, "and nine or ten
show up. You decide to do something and the first thing you
know somebody who wasn't there is running around town
trying to change everything. There's no point in starting
anything if you just have to do it over." Most organizations
have not progressed beyond the routine of raising money
and wondering how to spend it. "I wonder if we shouldn't
be looking for a project?" queries Lion Ken. "Every organization needs a project." Money-raising is a way of life in
Biggar. The religious war is mainly a battle of bazaars.
Little card tables with white tablecloths are set up in the
church basement and Brownies serve the cheese, slice, and
pickles while their mothers sell the home baking and white
elephants from long tables ranged against the wall. "Wow,"
said an Anglican lady at the end of a hard afternoon, "we
made $59!" Not a week goes by in winter without a
Bavarian beer festival, turkey shoot, auction, raffle, or nut
drive. "God," groans a Lion, "you get tired of people
coming to your door." Squabbling over the same bits of
loose change does nothing to alleviate tension or dislike in
Biggar. "I've never met so many bigoted people!" exclaims
a teacher. "They're anti-French, anti-German, anti-Indian,
anti-everything!"

The most bigoted person around Biggar is the Prairie
Atheist, John Sarvas, a successful cattle farmer who, after
founding the Society of Prairie Atheists in 1970, launched
a vigorous and totally unsuccessful battle with the school
board to eliminate the morning prayer and the noon grace
in the Biggar elementary school. "They always got to be
sneakin' in there with this Christianity," he mutters. "It's an
infringement on my child's rights as an atheist." Armed with
literature from American atheist organizations, Sarvas and
his wife labor diligently over their battered typewriter to
churn out articulate and highly persuasive little pro-atheist

columns for *The Independent*. Six dollars buys them the
same amount of space as the Lutheran minister gets. "Boy,
there was an uproar in the school after my columns started
coming out!" grins Sarvas. "I said that Jesus' birthday
wasn't in the Bible. One of the teachers grabs the Bible and
starts leafin' through it. It wasn't there. Haw haw. I read
the Bible. My wife reads the Bible. There's nothin' in there
that tells you to be good, or moral or principled. The Bible's
full of pornography. It's full of uh. . . well, you name it, it's
in there. Sex fiends. They talk about sex. Even Lot, he
impregnated his daughter. It's all in there! Then they take
me to court and they make me stand and hold my hand on
it and pray to tell the truth, the whole truth and nothing
but the truth. Then I put my hand on this dirty book!"

The Society of Prairie Atheists has few members, but
Sarvas gets a lot of moral support from Biggar's great
unwashed, a large free-floating population of agnostics,
atheists, Marxists, and people who are just fed up with the
local churches which Sarvas cheerfully attacks with indiscriminate vengeance. "We've got more respect in the community than we've ever had," he says. "They pat me on the
back and say 'Give 'em hell, John. Don't stop now. Keep
rockin' the boat!' I daren't walk into the pub too often.
I'll sneak in with my hat down, see, because there's so many
guys sittin' around drinkin'. Some of them may like me and
some may not and why stir up trouble when you don't have
to? There's guys that'll stand up in there and yell, 'I'm an
atheist! Sarvas is right. I'm an atheist!' They been atheists
for years but they're afraid to say anything. I'm the only guy
that's openly admitted I'm an atheist and write about it and
sign my name to it. I took an awful chance. I have a big
farm here. I'm worth $150,000. They could have avoided
me, you understand, they could have boycotted me. They
could have done everything."

Sarvas's vehement attacks drive the clergy into a blind
rage, but there's nothing they can do about it. A friendly
bear of a man with a broad Slavic face, sky blue eyes, a
voice like a bull moose, and hands that could break a man
in two, Sarvas is known for his fierce temper, particularly
on the subject of Christianity. The only minister willing to
challenge it was little Pastor Boymook, a pale, slender young

man of equally passionate conviction who incurred Sarvas's wrath by placing a sign announcing a revival meeting on his property. Ordered to remove it, Pastor Boymook confronted Sarvas out by the feedlot, where he endured a torrent of abuse and finally fled when Sarvas, carried away by the force of his argument, began punching a hole in the ground with his crowbar. "The local ministers won't confront me!" he roars with injured pride. "I can't even stop 'em on the street. They just run! I'd love to have a confrontation."

Although Sarvas bases his argument for atheism on a cogent critique of the Christian church and an appeal to enlightened reason, underlying it is a bitter, irrational hostility to Catholicism. Along with a library of erudite religious history and atheist tracts, he has an incredible collection of anti-Catholic hate literature. "Sure I'm harder on the Catholics," he says, " 'cause they're the ones that are steppin' on me. The Protestants ain't botherin' me." Sarvas sees world events in terms of a Catholic conspiracy. His attitude parallels that of the CCF fundamentalists who see life in terms of a capitalist conspiracy and comes from basically the same deep personal experience of injustice:

"I can remember the first day I went to school and I can remember the second day I went to school because I shit myself. My parents could hardly speak any English and there was very little that I could talk. We were the only people in an area of thirty-three children who weren't Catholic. They used to call me a honky. I was a honky. There are people in Biggar right today, kids that I went to school with, that used to beat me up. They couldn't beat me up one at a time, they'd have to all gang up because I could look after myself one at a time, but when they all got after me...There's a guy works in the garage in Biggar. He used to beat me up many times with the other guys. I was a honky. I was a DP. I couldn't talk English very good. The first two years were bad. They used to beat me up black and blue and I was scared to say anything to my dad because I felt I should be able to carry my own end at school. Boy I used to take some awful poundings. My shoulders were just black and blue, my stomach. They tried to castrate me one time. They cut all my clothes up and everything. Right in the school yard."

Sarvas's rage, like that of other Saskatchewan anarchists and eccentrics, stems from deep frustration at the violence and indignity of life on the prairie. "If he's gonna be a God," queries Sarvas, "why couldn't he be a good God?" Rather than trying to shore up the battlements of common sense and human compassion to protect themselves against the silence of the land and the petty ugliness of everyday existence, they shun the Lions and the political meetings and choose instead to stand alone like Lear on the heath and rail at the wind. Because their outrage derives from a common experience, they are always driving Saskatchewan to extremes, pushing it beyond reason and tolerance into a primitive emotional fury. Sarvas's attacks on religion stem from a warm heart and a sound political analysis, yet they slip beyond commitment into prejudice, and somewhere in the turbulent storm of his language another cross in burning.

The nuns have gone. Only one is left, Sister Jean, who teaches at the parochial school. A new parochial school is being built in spite of the fact that even the principal predicts it will be empty in a few years. Enrollment has been cut heavily by the pill, and many Catholic parents have refused to send their children to the condemned convent. "Now many parents tend to play one school off against the other," says the principal. "If there is a squabble or a dispute with the teacher, they pull their children out and send them to the public school. There's a lot of feeling that we should fold."

The diminution of St. Gabriel's school reflects the almost total anglicization of the French-Canadian community. "I didn't know a damn bit of English when I came out to this country!" says an old lady who still speaks with a heavy French accent. "We always spoke French. It was forbidden to speak English in the house. For twenty years I fought so my children would learn French. Now, not one of their children speaks French. They haven't been smart enough to keep it up. The radio, the TV, it's all in English. When there is one person who don't understand French, you've got to speak English." For many Catholic railroaders who are now earning good money and who are eager to achieve

respectable status, St. Gabriel's is a stigma. "Our daughter
was beaten up because she went to a Catholic school," says
a young railroader's wife. "The kids would wait for her in
the alley and yell, 'Catholic! Catholic! nyaah! nyaah!
nyaah!' Everything they can do against our school they will
do."

"If you want to be a member of the exclusive society in
town," states the principal, "you send your children to the
public school."

So bitter are the personal hatreds in Biggar, so numerous
the mutually exclusive cliques and clubs, so hostile the
conflicting crosscurrents of ideologies, that everyone remains
essentially alone. Yet the people are not depressed by their
solitude. They seem to relish conflict. They slash at each
other with their tongues and pick enthusiastically at the
scabs of old sores. "It's a harsh society," shrugs a farmer
with pride in his voice. "It's cruel. People that hang on in a
rural society, they gotta be tough, you know. There's no
place to hide."

Chapter 11
Moose Jaw, 1972

I object to the city in which I live being declared an international belly-laugh.

(Moose Jaw woman)

Moose Jaw's skyline is impressive. Driving in from the north, I can pick out a couple of skyscrapers shimmering in the heat haze from a distance of 20 miles. As I get nearer, one of the high-rises turns out to be a government terminal elevator and the other, the smokestack on the Robin Hood Flour mill. Close up, both are empty. So is much of Moose Jaw. The big stone post office on Main Street is closed; its broad window ledges serve as a roost for bearded hippies basking like lizards in the sun. Dozens of round oil-storage tanks sprout like mushrooms around the Gulf and Husky oil refineries on the banks of Moose Jaw Creek, but there are no signs of activity. The waiting room of the CPR station is a vast echoing cavern, as cold and dank as a urinal. The restaurant is closed and only two trains are listed on the board. The long oak benches are crowded with dirty old men in shabby overcoats who reek of stale piss. River Street is blank and deserted. There is a spooky chill to Moose Jaw. "When I was a kid," explains a young man, "we lived in a small town just outside of Moose Jaw. The radio station used to have a very popular shut-in program on weekends. We always listened to it. I always associated Moose Jaw with sickness and death, a quiet shut-in place. Then I came here and it was true. It's full of quiet parks, with funeral homes all around the parks." Domed and pillared public edifices loom out of the city's streets like mausoleums. Moose Jaw is a city of monuments. Everybody in Moose Jaw is asked the same question: What's it like to be dying?

351

Moose Jaw lost 2,000 jobs and all its major industry in the five years between 1966 and 1971. Average personal income fell from $5,032 to $4,898, placing Moose Jaw 97th among Canada's 99 major cities. The population dropped from a peak of 33,900 in 1965 to 31,000 in 1972; this figure includes 200 residents of St. Anthony's Home for the Aged and more than 1,000 inmates of the Saskatchewan Training School for the mentally retarded. The actual decline does not reflect the more serious shift in population. Between 5,000 and 10,000 working people and children left Moose Jaw; their places were taken by rural immigrants, either elderly people who had retired from farms or those who had been forced off because of poverty. (A housing survey conducted in Moose Jaw in 1971 found that half the population had come from rural Saskatchewan and one-third were pensioners.) Moose Jaw's skilled workers have been replaced by unskilled laborers, its young people have been displaced by the old. Moose Jaw claims to have the highest percentage of old people of any city in Canada; it also has a staggering welfare bill of more than $1 million a year. Moose Jaw has regressed from an industrial city into an overgrown country town; its decay suggests that the industrialization of the prairies does not automatically bring prosperity.

In spite of the economic disasters of the Thirties which made Moose Jaw a byword for failure, the city never lost its cheery confidence that if it blew its own horn loud enough the world would sit up and take notice. The worse things got, the harder it blew. In 1936, in the very pit of the Depression, when Moose Jaw had to turn on its famous street lights at noon because the sky was black with blowing dirt, the board of trade issued a pamphlet praising Moose Jaw as "The Beauty Spot of the Prairies." The $750,000 left over from the sale of the electric light company was used to set up an industrial development commission which, through financial subsidies and other inducements, attempted to lure industry to Moose Jaw. Its first loan was to Indestructable Neckwear Ltd., which received $3,000 to manufacture celluloid shirt collars. It went broke in 1938, a fate which was to overtake many of Moose Jaw's forced-growth Depression industries, including a soap factory, a fire engine manufacturer, and a man who made houses out of wood-board and tar. Bankruptcy has always been an accepted way of doing business in the West. For every farmer who has gone broke, there's been a fly-by-night merchant who has simply closed his doors and taken off down the line. (In the days when business was bad and fire departments were non-existent, it was always convenient to set a match to your store and pocket the insurance. The fire publicized the town and the rush of new insurance capital brought a small rebuilding boom. Most prairie towns have been burned to the ground two or three times to the mutual profit and satisfaction of the merchants.) Moose Jaw's offer of free money attracted a flock of opportunists who had no intention of staying around after the loan ran out. The city also invested heavily in established local industries; forced to foreclose as one after the other went belly-up, the city, quite by accident, came into possession of virtually the entire industrial establishment of Moose Jaw. Embarrassed by this inadvertent socialism, it proceeded to unload the businesses as quickly as possible to the first buyer. The meat-packing plant was sold to Swifts for $1; British-American Oil purchased a small local oil refinery for $160,000. The sales were accompanied by gifts of land, generous tax concessions, and cheap utility rates; in exchange the companies agreed to provide several hundred jobs. Since only very large national and multinational corporations had money to invest during the Depression, control of Moose Jaw's economy passed out of the city and, in most cases, out of the country.

The industries brought a modest working-class prosperity to Moose Jaw. Swifts employed 450 men, Robin Hood Flour (a subsidiary of International Milling of Minneapolis) had 200 employees, British-American Oil (bought out in the Sixties by Gulf Oil of the United States) hired 160, and the CPR employed more than 2,000 men. Moose Jaw became a trade union town and, as a result, enjoyed the largesse of the CCF government which established an ill-fated shoe factory and woollen mill in the city during the Forties. Industrialization did not provoke another boom. The new industries invested almost nothing in Moose Jaw; the government factories soon went bankrupt. Although Moose

Jaw's population grew by 10,000, it continued to lag far behind Regina and became, in effect, an industrial suburb of the capital city. The elegant Victorian mansions were chopped up into rooming houses, and rows of cheap bungalows were thrown up on the outskirts of town beyond the water and sewer lines. Moose Jaw lost caste. The stores remained small and tacky; it became a city of cafes and car dealers. People earned their wages in Moose Jaw and spent their money in Regina.

Moose Jaw became a kind of plague spot, a city whose most distinguishing feature was a bad smell. The pattern was set by the CPR which, having first grab, built its rail yards on the banks of Moose Jaw Creek at the bottom of the gully. The railway dammed the creek, which created a cesspool in the middle of town and reduced the downstream flow to a trickle. All the other industries, snuggling up as close as they could to the CPR, used the creek as a common sewer. The creek was seriously polluted as early as 1890, when two citizens in tracing the source of a dreadful stench found that carcasses and offal from the meat-packing plant were being dumped directly into the water. The garbage floated north through Moose Jaw, where the creek water was used for both drinking and washing. The city was forced to find an alternative supply of water, running it in along an open trench from a slough 20 miles to the north. Whenever the slough dried up, the city faced a severe water shortage. Oil and chemicals dumped into the creek by the railway and refineries formed a four-foot sludge on the bottom and killed the trees along the banks; water in the pool by the CPR dam turned black and scummy. Public beaches and swimming holes were closed in 1966 when oil slicks were found on the sand; the city had just spent $11,000 building bathhouses and concessions. Whenever suggestions were made that the industries clean up the creek, they threatened to pull out of Moose Jaw and public protest was silenced. The city did not help by locating both its garbage dump and its sewage lagoon in the industrial core, which was not only upstream but upwind from the city. "The smell was incredible," recalls a resident. "The wind was always blowing up Main Street from the southwest. It was dusty and filthy. You could smell the refinery

from the southeast and from the southwest you got Robin
Hood Mills. They had just closed down and there was a lot
of grain going bad in the elevator. Whew."

Moose Jaw's industrial economy had barely become
established when it began to collapse. The CPR began to
pull out of Moose Jaw in the Fifties, as automation and
dwindling passenger service made its Moose Jaw establishment increasingly obsolete: approximately 1,500 men were
laid off between 1958 and 1966. Swifts closed in 1954,
putting 450 men out of work. The dilapidated building was
sold to a Winnipeg merchant who used it as a junk yard; it
burned to the ground in 1959, sticking Moose Jaw with
$25,000 in back taxes. Title to the property reverted to the
city, which sold it to the Saskatchewan Power Corporation
for the amount of arrears. Early in 1966, two bakeries and a
dairy closed their Moose Jaw operations and centralized in
Regina. On September 21, 1966, Robin Hood suddenly
announced that the flour mill would shut down at the end
of the month and company operations would be consolidated in Saskatoon. The closure was a shock to the city.
The mill had been established in 1900 with a $6,000 public
subscription; it was Moose Jaw's oldest industry and biggest
building, a huge shambling structure towering hundreds of
feet over the city. An impressive 80-foot, full-length portrait
of Robin Hood had been painted on the side of the mill to
match the picture on the flour bags, and the city had
written to Errol Flynn for permission to use his likeness
on the portrait. Robin Hood was a landmark; it gave the
city a sense of stature and importance. Moose Jaw liked to
call itself "The Mill City." In 1970 Robin Hood presented
its abandoned mill as a "gift" to the Saskatchewan Economic Development Commission to avoid paying its $45,000
annual taxes. As a provincial agency, SEDCO pays no taxes.
It promised to develop the property as an industrial site,
but the mill remains, its windows smashed and the portrait
fading, as a haven for rats and ghostly hideout where the
local kids go to smoke marijuana.

Robin Hood explained that the Moose Jaw mill was
closed because it was inefficient and operating at a loss.
Moose Jaw's remaining workers looked around and noticed
that all the city's industries were becoming gradually obso-

lete. The discovery precipitated a bitter four-month strike at British-American Oil in 1966 over the issue of job security. In 1968 the company announced that it would remain in Moose Jaw for "at least 15 years." The following year it stated that its Moose Jaw operations would be phased out by 1971. Husky Oil, an American company which had come to Moose Jaw in 1955, followed suit. Both said they were leaving for "economic reasons." Their loss cost Moose Jaw another 200 jobs and $70,000 a year in taxes. The industrial withdrawal precipitated a business depression. Several big stores, most of them owned by Regina and Winnipeg merchants, shut down, and plans for a $3 million shopping-centre complex were scrapped. In 1970 building permits fell to $2 million and construction came to a virtual standstill. The city was hurt and outraged. Having been so loyal and generous to its industries, it expected them to be loyal to Moose Jaw. "They abandoned us!" shouts an old man, his eyes wide with shock. Gifts of land and tax concessions had made Moose Jaw a cheap camping place until corporations found it more profitable to move elsewhere. To find the trouble, Moose Jaw had only to look west: drought and automation have depopulated the prairie as far as Calgary and Edmonton. Moose Jaw is a stranded outpost on the eastern edge of a wasteland. Once more it is a stopping place on the road to somewhere else.

"There is no economic crisis," announces Mayor Ernie Pascoe in February 1972, although the city has just submitted a pathetic brief to the provincial government begging for small government grants. Mayor Pascoe and the Moose Jaw business establishment believe in positive thinking. They do not blame the corporations for deserting Moose Jaw; anyone rude enough to mutter about branch plants and rip-offs is accused of poor-mouthing and disloyalty. All Moose Jaw's troubles are attributed to apathy and lack of civic spirit, faults which are usually equated with creeping socialism. The city's sole response to its industrial collapse has been a chamber of commerce booster campaign designed to promote a phoney image of prosperity. "They go around telling people we should smile, be proud of coming from Moose Jaw, quit running the city down," says a trade union leader cynically. "If everyone would just try harder we'd get industry." Between 1968 and 1972, the city spent $200,000 on promotional junkets, advertising, conferences, consultants' reports, housing studies, "think sessions," and a barrage of promotional literature about Moose Jaw which bore only a remote resemblance to the truth. Everything failed. The city's leading economic advisor was J. W. McCaig, a prominent citizen and president of Trimac trucking company, who had recently moved his head office to Calgary for economic reasons. Because of the city's tradition of seeing economic development as an exercise in public relations, Moose Jaw's decline is mirrored in the gradual diminution of its civic slogans: by 1970 the only thing Moose Jaw could find to promote was the annual Kinsmen High School band festival, and Moose Jaw is now known as the Band Capital of North America.

Mayor Pascoe sits behind a shiny hardwood desk in his office in the old Moose Jaw City Hall flanked by a Canadian flag and a portrait of the Queen. A dapper teetotaller in his sixties with a dark blue business suit and a small white toothbrush moustache, Mayor Pascoe is a former Diefenbaker Conservative MP and, appropriately for Moose Jaw, an ex-newspaperman. Son of former mayor James Pascoe, Ernie is also a Mason and a member of the Moose Jaw establishment, connections which do not make him popular with the NDP and union people. Fussy, nervous, anxious to please, Ernie Pascoe projects an image of timid dignity. "He wouldn't say shit if his mouth was full of it," snorts his archrival, ex-mayor L. H. "Scoop" Lewry, whom Pascoe defeated in 1970. Mayor Pascoe's brief term in office has not been a success. On a table in the corner of his office crowded with pen stands, souvenir ashtrays, and other civic memorabilia sits an air force pilot's helmet equipped with two large car headlights, blinking red taillights, and a flashing yellow light on top. A sign at the back of the helmet warns: "Caution — Student Walker." Mayor Pascoe was presented with the helmet when, at his very first council meeting, the Moose Jaw city council adopted a bylaw forcing pedestrians to walk on the right-hand side of the sidewalks. The city was convulsed in helpless laughter. Pedestrians walked around Indian file making elaborate arm signals, and some wag painted a dotted white line down the

middle of the sidewalk in front of city hall. "Is there a high
fatality rate in Moose Jaw as the result of pedestrian
collisions?" sneered one former resident in a letter to the
newspaper. "Often on a Saturday afternoon 20 or 30 people
would be milling around in the downtown area and the
chances of being injured in the rush is very great indeed."
When the city made *Time* magazine, a wave of Moose Jaw
jokes reverberated throughout North America, and Moose
Jaw didn't think it was so funny anymore. "It looks as if
the Friendly City is going to be the laughing stock of the
prairies," snapped one citizen. This is not the kind of
publicity the chamber of commerce had in mind. The incident became known as Pascoe's Fiasco.

Everybody laughs at Moose Jaw. The name is funny.
Moose Jaw is an irresistible joke, an automatic synonym for
everything that is square, cornball, backward. Moose Jaw
is Hicksville, the quintessence of the prairie boondocks.
The funniest thing about Moose Jaw is that all the jokes
are true. Moose Jaw's passion for publicity has created an
embarrassing credibility gap between its pretensions and its
achievements which widens as the city slips backward. The
harder Moose Jaw puffs out its chest, the more ridiculous
it looks. Moose Jaw is famous for its absurdities. In 1928
the city heralded the opening of its Wild Animal Park by
advertising "The Last Ride of the Indians," an extravaganza
in which 1,000 Indians on horseback were to chase a herd
of buffalo across the plains to where the Mounties would be
waiting in ambush. A huge crowd gathered to watch six
Rotarians in war paint gallop in hot pursuit of six sleepy
buffalo. The Wild Animal Park turned out to be a handful
of cages with a dozen scruffy bears, wolves, badgers, and
deodorized skunks; the moose all died off and moose
steaks have to be imported from Saskatoon for the Fish and
Game Association banquet.

Moose Jaw never acquired any sophistication. When
William Grayson died in 1926, he willed his art collection
to the city and it is now housed in a special gallery adjacent
to the public library — 130 unimportant paintings. All
Moose Jaw's urban aspirations couldn't conceal that it was
a jock town. "The city was always very big on baseball and
hockey," says a young man. "They had this insular little ball

league that took in Regina and Yorkton, a lot of big boys grown up, the beerbelly boys, who used to go out and flop around. The sporting life. The junior hockey team used to ball all the girls in town, knock up the fifteen- and sixteen-year-olds and everybody would get upset. They hung out in the Ambassador Cafe. Chips and gravy in the Ambassador — that was the 'in' thing in Moose Jaw in the Sixties. Moose Jaw was a car town. Main Street was a continual drag strip, from the station up to the top of the hill. Then there was the streetcar that ran out to 30th Avenue. There wasn't anything out there, but the streetcar went out there anyway, turned around and came back."

Moose Jaw's biggest joke was its mayor, Scoop Lewry, who for 20 years ran the city like a one-man sideshow. Another newspaperman (Moose Jaw has produced an incredible number of newspaper reporters and radio announcers. "It was," says one, "the only way to get out of town."), Lewry acquired his name and reputation when he hung from a transom to eavesdrop on a secret meeting of city council dealing with the presence of rats in the nurses' residence. His sensational scoop was front-page news the next day, and Scoop was subsequently catapulted into the mayor's chair. He beat out the mayor of Swift Current as pillow-fighting champion of Saskatchewan and sent crying-towels to all the sports teams about to meet Moose Jaw in competition. Round and red-haired with an irrepressible stream of salty chatter, Scoop turned up, invited or not, at every coffee party, beer bash, and wedding reception in the city. Dubbing Moose Jaw "the pearl of the western plains," he plugged the city mercilessly on weekly radio shows and personally typed out 100 letters a month asking companies to locate in Moose Jaw. As Moose Jaw reporter for the *Regina Leader-Post*, he covered his own council meetings and immortalized his feuds with Moose Jaw hardware merchant Ross Thatcher. Elected to the House of Commons in 1957 for the NDP, Scoop was beaten by Ernie Pascoe in the Diefenbaker sweep the following year and rocketed back as mayor on a "Clean Up River Street" campaign in 1964. "It wasn't safe to walk down River Street in broad daylight!" he exclaims. "The girls were operating right out in the open. There were three muggings in one week at high noon. They damn near killed a guy. I cleaned it up. People accused me of cleaning it up too well." Scoop Lewry was a barrel of laughs, and all the industry left Moose Jaw.

The more serious Moose Jaw's situation, the more trivial its politics. In 1961 the city council spent a lot of time hiding in the basement of city hall practicing in the event of nuclear attack; in 1971, with the taxes almost $1 million in arrears and the city too broke to shovel snow or mow boulevards, the city council declared a crackdown on litter. Citizens were harassed to tidy their yards, and students were fined for eating their lunches in parked cars and throwing the waxed paper on the grass; $3,500 was spent on anti-litter signs. The clean-up campaign did not, however, extend to the polluted creek for fear of angering the CPR. This milquetoast attitude has allowed Moose Jaw to be improverished by hordes of freeloaders attracted by taxes and land prices 30 per cent below Regina's. In 1972, 175 Moose Jaw properties owed $470,550 in back taxes, an increase of $100,000 over the previous year; all were more than three years in arrears yet council took no action against them. The largest debtors were businesses: a greenhouse owed $18,000, a laundry was in for $15,500, and three old River Street hotels owed a total of $77,800. The biggest offender was the Moose Jaw Country Club, a fancy golf course which had been floated on public debentures in 1967. Although the club owed $33,300 in back taxes, the city aldermen, most of whom owned debentures, refused to foreclose.

This loss of revenue has made it impossible for the city to maintain minimum public works. Streets near the heart of the city remain unpaved, water mains are falling apart, and the street lights are scattered and dim. Bus service has been cut back, creating a hardship for pensioners and harming business. Because of the ill-feeling between Scoop Lewry and Ross Thatcher, Moose Jaw was virtually cut off from provincial government investment during Thatcher's term of office from 1964 to 1971: no sooner was the NDP re-elected than Moose Jaw, with its traditional propensity for doom, elected a Conservative mayor. The city's most impressive public works, a downtown park and the Natatorium mineral baths, were both built with relief labor during the Depression. Because Moose Jaw's industrial base began to disintegrate as soon as the debenture debt was paid off in the Fifties, the city has never had any money for new construction. Three-quarters of Moose Jaw's homes were built before 1935, more than half are 50 years old. In 1964, before the current recession, half the homes were valued at less than $4,000 and 15 per cent were considered worthless. Moose Jaw's bones are sticking through, like an old scarecrow.

"Our image as a city has improved greatly," bubbles Bob Gaudry, Moose Jaw's hip young economic development commissioner, who has tried, unsuccessfully, to get a picture of Moose Jaw on Saskatchewan road maps. "I've watched people change the kind of tie they wear over the past two years," he says significantly. Gaudry himself is wearing a solid white tie and a purple shirt, an outfit that anywhere outside Moose Jaw stamps the wearer indelibly as a rube. "I tried to get the Mint for Moose Jaw," says Gaudry, shaking his head in bewilderment. The Mint didn't make it past Winnipeg. Moose Jaw has become almost entirely dependent on government largesse. Its major industries now are the Canadian Armed Forces air base south of town, a technical school, and the institution for the mentally retarded, which the city is too embarrassed to mention. The scramble for government handouts is humiliating. In the spring of 1972, Moose Jaw was engaged in a bitter fight with Saskatoon over a Romanian tractor factory. Nobody bothered to ask why Romania, which is even more impoverished than Saskatchewan, was building a tractor factory in Canada's leading socialist agricultural province; the tractor factory was economic salvation. Moose Jaw begged and pleaded and threatened. A week before the Saskatoon delegation was scheduled to visit Romania, Ernie Pascoe and a Moose Jaw delegation suddenly flew off to Romania armed with business cards, flip charts and Moose Jaw brochures all printed in Romanian. The whirlwind trip cost $10,000. "I like to do things big," said Gaudry, puffing out his chest. The tractor factory went to Saskatoon.

Chapter 12
Sid Cox

Sid Cox is an elderly, distinguished-looking man with white hair and a white military mustache. He retired from the farm in the mid-Sixties, moving into Miami, Manitoba, to care for his aged parents. He left the farm to his son. Using his father's land and good reputation as collateral, the son borrowed about $100,000 to buy new machinery and build a modern hog barn. He acquired the biggest, fanciest farm in the Miami area at the very time the farm economy slipped into a serious and prolonged depression. To pay the debts and save the farm, Sid Cox is out on the tractor every morning at six a.m. and stops at night only when he is too exhausted to walk or see. He rents and works his own land to support his wife and himself and spends all his spare hours helping out at his son's farm. After a lifetime of farming, Sid Cox has no land, no home (except a shabby cottage in Miami), and no money. He works harder now than he has in all his life. He might live long enough to see the family homestead sold to pay the bank; he will not live to see it free of debt.

Like most farmers of his generation, Sid Cox drifted into farming. "I was born on the farm," he says. "I never knew anything else. I never wanted anything else. There wasn't enough money to jaunt around and decide what you liked. My dad was a believer in hard work, so I stayed at home.

"We had herds of horses. They were hard work and expensive to keep. The farm lads took the place of a hired man. Even in those days a hired man was expensive. I can remember during World War One it cost ninety dollars a month to board a man in. My dad just couldn't afford it. So we did it ourselves, sloppin' hogs, milkin' cows. It was real grub work. We never got too far from home. But we made fairly good money. It was a heck of a better life than it is today." There was prestige to farming in the Twenties.

362

Farmers outnumbered everyone else on the prairies; they considered themselves to be men of prosperity which, although it wasn't evident at the time, was obviously just around the corner. They were free men, yeomen who took their duties as citizens very seriously. They scrimped and saved to pay off all the debts on their land so they could leave it unencumbered to their heirs; since there were always debts, they were always scrimping and saving. Land was gold; land was prestige. A man who owned his land clear was the epitome of hard work and frugality; he bequeathed to his sons not only wealth but honor. Many sons were willing to work for years without reward in the faith that when they took over they would reap their investment many times over. Instead, they were frozen into poverty by the Depression.

"We never knew there was a depression on," says Sid. "We were self-sufficient. The Depression didn't bother us. We could live off the land. What we had to buy didn't cost anything and we didn't have to buy very much. A barrel of gas would last all summer; we traded butter and eggs for groceries and binder twine. We had a lot of bush land and we peddled wood around town; everybody used wood for fuel. I remember it took sixty loads of wood to buy a coat for Dad. We didn't really mind because we wanted to clear the land anyway.

"We were happy.

"The mortgage companies took up the land, but they usually just renegotiated the mortgage. People got the money from somewhere. They ran into a relative or talked to their minister and got some more courage to carry on. It was pretty tough on the towns. There were bills owing here and bills owing there. The stores were owned by well-to-do men; they just wrote it off. In Darlingford just down the line they were canvassing for coal oil to burn the town up and get the insurance.

"Some people were on relief. They were people who were just making a go of it when times were good. It was more of a stigma then. If a person didn't have a strong back and a strong head, he was called shiftless. You don't call anyone shiftless today. The quarrels all get down to one thing — money. No matter where you go the dollar is there through the conversation. If you don't have money, you're *nothin'*.

"I've been desperate all my life to make a million dollars. Agriculture has slipped so badly that the good life has slipped away. So farmers buy skidoos to try to keep up. In the city you've always had a better life; you walk on concrete, we walk on a plank across a muddy yard. There just isn't the money.

"It would have been better if we had stayed with a few horses. Six a.m. to seven p.m. was the working day for a horse. It made for a far nicer life. It used to stop people working on Sunday. Now there's more work done on Sunday than any other day. Farmers have always been softies. We're just gasping for exotic machinery which will save us from drudgery. It started with the gas tractor. From that day we've never looked back. A farmer just imagines what he would like and lo!, there it is, and it's already been tested. But we're the slave now and the machine is the boss. It just steamrollered. Prices started going up in the Sixties and you just kept on buying. How do you stop? People are materialistic. How do you know when you've had enough?

"I'm scared about what's going on all over. The country life has gone. How do you return it? I don't like it at all. Maybe it's supposed to go. Everybody's got some place to go. They just drift away someplace. It's getting lonely out here. In some ways it's a better life. There's not the same jealousies today. It used to be you'd be quick to quarrel over the least little thing; now you're not too worried about what the other fellow is doing. The country was building then. You looked around to see who was fencing, breaking. It was a free society. The rules are all laid out now. Where in the H- - - would you see a barn being built today?

"Maybe it will come back again. I'm sure it will come back again. I can remember times when we had money hanging out of all four pockets. Twice we had it, in 1915-22 and 1939-45. I hope it comes back again before I'm too old."

Notes on Sources

Chapter 3: Breaking. This summary of the West's place in Confederation (pages 43-49) is based on information available in *Manitoba, A History* by W. L. Morton and *The National Policy and the Wheat Economy* by V. C. Fowke as well as documents about the colonization companies available in the National Archives, Ottawa. The quotation on page 51 and subsequent information about the Red River colony come from Alexander Ross's classic history, *The Red River Settlement,* an eye-witness account of the Selkirk settlement which was published in 1856. Homesteading and immigration documents are available in the National Archives and the first person accounts of homesteading life come from a collection of settlers' letters, manuscripts and interviews in the Saskatchewan Provincial Archives.

Chapter 4: Moose Jaw, 1882. The opening quote on page 62 is from Thorstein Veblen's essay, "The Country Town" in his *Absentee Ownership and Business Enterprise in Recent Times.* For information about the CPR and real estate speculation in Moose Jaw I relied on Pierre Berton's *The Last Spike, A History of Canadian Wealth* by Gustavus Myers and on unpublished research by Ray Davey, a graduate student in the department of sociology, University of Saskatchewan in Regina. The quotes from pioneers and early newspapers come from manuscripts, transcripts and documents available in the Saskatchewan Provincial Archives. A detailed account of Moose Jaw's history of vice is contained in James Gray's *Red Lights on the Prairies.* My account of Moose Jaw's bankruptcy (page 79 ff.) is based on unpublished research by Pam Smith, a graduate student in the department of sociology, University of Saskatchewan in Regina.

Chapter 5: Coalsamao. The best popular histories of the early farmers' movements are *Deep Furrows* by Hopkins Moorehouse and *New Breaking* by Hugh Boyd. An excellent account of political intrigues and the collapse of the Progressive Party is contained in W. L. Morton's *The Progressive Party*. Valentine Winkler's papers are in the Manitoba Archives. *The Politics of John W. Dafoe and the Free Press* by Ramsay Cook examines the extraordinary influence of the *Free Press* in the West.

Chapter 9: Bienfait. My account of the Estevan riot and subsequent events (pages 257-262) is based on reports carried in the Estevan *Mercury* and the Regina *Leader-Post*. For details of the living conditions at the mine and events leading up to the strike and riot (pages 252-257) I am indebted to Stanley Hanson's unpublished Masters thesis, "The Estevan Strike and Riot, 1931," Department of History, University of Saskatchewan in Regina, and to evidence given to a royal commission investigating the strike which is available in the Saskatchewan Archives. These sources were supplemented by my own interviews with people who had taken part in the strike.

Chapter 10: Biggar. My information about the early history of Biggar comes from personal interviews with pioneers and back issues of the Biggar *Independent* stored in the Biggar museum. For the quotes and interpretation of the temperance movement I relied on an unpublished Masters thesis, "Temperance and Prohibition in Saskatchewan" by Edward Pinno, Department of History, University of Saskatchewan in Regina. Quotes and details about the Ku Klux Klan come from personal interviews as well as two Masters theses, "The Rise and Fall of the Ku Klux Klan in Saskatchewan" by William Calderwood and "The Saskatchewan Provincial Election of 1929" by Patrick Kyba. All three theses are available in the Saskatchewan Archives. My interpretation of the early development of the CCF is based primarily on Seymour Martin Lipset's *Agrarian Socialism*. My account of the doctors' strike comes from personal interviews, reports in the Biggar *Independent* and *Doctors' Strike* by Robin Badgley and Samuel Wolfe.

Bibliography

This list of books and articles about western Canada does not include all the works available, or even all those I read, but those which I found most interesting and useful.

Badgley, Robin and Samuel Wolfe, *Doctors' Strike*. Toronto: Macmillan, 1967.

Barr, John and Owen Anderson (eds.). *The Unfinished Revolt*. Toronto: McClelland and Stewart, 1971.

Berton, Pierre. *The Last Spike*. Toronto: McClelland and Stewart, 1971.

　　The National Dream. Toronto: McClelland and Stewart, 1970.

Black, N. F. *History of Saskatchewan and the North-West Territories*. Regina: Saskatchewan Historical Co., 1913.

Boyd, Hugh. *New Breaking*. Toronto: Dent, 1938.

Burnet, Jean. *Next Year Country*. Toronto: University of Toronto Press, 1951.

Cook, Ramsay. *The Politics of John W. Dafoe and the Free Press*. Toronto: University of Toronto Press, 1963.

Fowke, V. C. *The National Policy and the Wheat Economy*. Toronto: University of Toronto Press, 1957.

Gray, James. *Booze*. Toronto: Macmillan, 1972.

　　Red Lights on the Prairies. Toronto: Macmillan, 1971.

　　The Winter Years. Toronto: Macmillan, 1966.

Hiebert, Paul. *Sarah Binks*. Toronto: Oxford University Press, 1947.

　　The Hills of Home. A History of the Municipality of Thompson. Altona: The History Committee, Miami, Man., 1967.

Innis, Harold. *A History of the Canadian Pacific Railway*. Toronto: University of Toronto Press, 1923.

Klippenstein, Laverna. "The Modern Mennonite Housewife," *The Mennonite Mirror*, Winnipeg, May 1972.

Laurence, Margaret. *The Stone Angel*. Toronto: McClelland and Stewart, 1964.

Leacock, Stephen. *My Discovery of the West*. Toronto: Thomas Allan, 1937.

Lipset, Seymour Martin. *Agrarian Socialism* (updated edition). New York: Anchor Books, 1968.

Moorehouse, Hopkins. *Deep Furrows*. Toronto: George McLeod Ltd., 1918.

Morton, W. L. *Manitoba, A History*. Toronto: University of Toronto Press, 1957.
    The Progressive Party. Toronto: University of Toronto Press, 1950.

Myers, Gustavus. *A History of Canadian Wealth*. Toronto: James Lewis and Samuel, 1972.

Newman, Peter C. *Renegade in Power: The Diefenbaker Years*. Toronto: McClelland and Stewart, 1963.

Partridge, E. A. *A War on Poverty*. Winnipeg: Wallingford Press, 1926.

Redekop, Calvin Wall. *The Old Colony Mennonites*. Baltimore: Johns Hopkins Press, 1969.

Ross, Alexander. *The Red River Settlement*. London: Smith, Elder & Co., 1856.

Ross, Sinclair. *As For Me and My House*. Toronto: McClelland and Stewart, 1941.

Swainson, Donald (ed.). *Historical Essays on the Prairie Provinces*. Toronto: McClelland and Stewart, 1970.

Veblen, Thorstein. *Absentee Ownership and Business Enterprise in Recent Times*. London: George Allen and Unwin, 1923.

Wright, James F. C. *Saskatchewan, History of a Province*. Toronto: McClelland and Stewart, 1955.

Unpublished Theses:

Calderwood, William. "The Rise and Fall of the Ku Klux Klan in Saskatchewan." Unpublished Masters thesis, Department of History, University of Saskatchewan, Regina, 1968.

Hanson, Stanley Duane. "The Estevan Strike and Riot, 1931." Unpublished Masters thesis, Department of History, University of Saskatchewan, Saskatoon, 1972.

Kyba, Patrick. "The Saskatchewan General Election of 1929."
    Unpublished Masters thesis, Department of History,
    University of Saskatchewan, Regina, 1964.
Pinno, Ernest. "Temperance and Prohibition in Saskat-
    chewan." Unpublished Masters thesis, Department of
    History, University of Saskatchewan, Regina, 1971.

Photographs